New Technologies
for the
Humanities

Also available in this series:

Information and Business Performance: A Study of Information Systems and Services in High Performing Companies
Ian Owens and Tom Wilson with Angela Abell
Electronic Publishing and Libraries. Planning for the Impact and Growth to 2003
edited by David J. Brown
Project ELVYN: an Experiment in Electronic Journal Delivery. Facts, Figures and Findings
edited by Fytton Rowland, Cliff McKnight and Jack Meadows
Networking in the Humanities
edited by Stephanie Kenna and Seamus Ross
The Value and Impact of Information
edited by Mary Feeney and Maureen Grieves
National Information Policies and Strategies: An Overview and Bibliographic Survey
Michael W. Hill
Changing Information Technologies: Research Challenges in the Economics of Information
edited by Mary Feeney and Maureen Grieves
Innovation in Information: Twenty Years of the British Library Research and Development Department
Jack Meadows
Teaching Information Skills: A Review of the Research and its Impact on Education
edited by Rick Rogers
Decision Support Systems and Performance Assessment in Academic Libraries
Roy Adams, Ian Bloor, Mel Collier, Marcus Meldrum and Suzanne Ward
Information Technology and the Research Process
edited by Mary Feeney and Karen Merry
Information UK 2000
edited by John Martyn, Peter Vickers and Mary Feeney
Scholarly Communication and Serials Prices
edited by Karen Brookfield
Scholarship and Technology in the Humanities
edited by May Katzen
Multimedia Information
edited by Mary Feeney and Shirley Day

New Technologies
for the
Humanities

Edited by Christine Mullings,
Marilyn Deegan, Seamus Ross
and Stephanie Kenna

BOWKER
SAUR

London • Melbourne • Munich • New Providence, NJ

British Library Cataloguing in Publication Data
A catalogue record for this book is available from the British Library.

Library of Congress Cataloging-in-Publication Data
A catalog record for this book is available from the Library of Congress.

Published by Bowker-Saur, a division of Reed Elsevier (UK) Limited
Maypole House, Maypole Road
East Grinstead, West Sussex RH19 1HU, UK
Tel: +44 (0) 1342 330100 Fax: +44 (0) 1342 330191
E-mail: lis@bowker-saur.co.uk
Internet Website: http://www.bowker-saur.co.uk/service/

Bowker-Saur is part of REED REFERENCE PUBLISHING

ISBN 1-85739-113-6 AZ 105 .N49 1996

New technologies for the
humanities

British Library Research and Innovation report 2

Cover design by John Cole
Desktop published by Mary Feeney, The Data Workshop, Bury St Edmunds
Index compiled by Elizabeth Moys
Printed on acid-free paper
Printed and bound in Great Britain by Antony Rowe Ltd, Chippenham, Wiltshire

Contents

Introduction

Contents of volume

Background

The 1990s are witnessing a growing interest in the application of information technology to research and teaching in the humanities. In 1990 the Humanities Information Review Panel (HIRP) was established by the British Library and the British Academy to review the current British scene and to highlight the opportunities offered to scholars by the new technologies together with the difficulties to be overcome before such applications can become the norm (BLR&DD 1993). The Panel's findings, published in 1993, have been widely disseminated in the UK and abroad, translated into Japanese and republished by the Zentrum für Historische Sozialforschung.[1] The work of HIRP has also been furthered by the resolutions and recommendations of two international conferences on Scholarship and Technology in the Humanities held at Elvetham Hall in 1990 and 1994 (Katzen 1991; Kenna and Ross 1995), and it is significant that humanities projects were among those funded in 1995 by the JISC Electronic Libraries Programme for UK Higher Education institutions. Parallel investigations have examined the situation in North America (ALCS 1992)and in Europe (Genet and Zampolli 1992).

New Technologies for the Humanities is a direct outcome of the work of HIRP. The project has been managed by the Office for Humanities Communication (OHC), a national centre funded by the British Library Research and Innovation Centre,[2] and concerned with disseminating information on scholarly activities involving the use of new technologies and promoting an awareness of current concerns among scholars, libraries, learned societies, and publishers. The editorial team, which includes representatives of the sponsors of HIRP, were also members of the organizing committee for the second Elvetham Hall conference.

Authors, selected from known experts in their field, have been invited to provide up-to-date surveys of the use and impact of information technology within their disciplines, to describe general methodologies and resources available to all scholars, and to examine the effects of the use of new technologies on research and teaching. As a parallel exercise, a questionnaire was distributed with the HIRP report and through other distribution lists to obtain information on current computer-based projects. Brief descriptions were sought on project aims, disciplines involved, hardware and software used, and whether the project was designed for use in research or teaching. Nearly 200 completed forms were received back. This combination of discipline-specific surveys, methodologies, and resources, with descriptions of individual projects is regarded as providing a timely successor to the excellent, but recently defunct, *Humanities Computing Yearbook*.

Audience

The volume seeks to offer both an overview for the non-specialist and a springboard for the specialist who has not yet felt either sufficiently confident or sufficiently inspired to explore the possibilities of the new technologies for teaching and research.

The specialist can go direct to his/her individual discipline; after considering general programs and resources, the non-specialist can move on to specific applications. This is not a how-to guide, but seeks to convince the reader that the new technologies have something to offer most humanities scholars and is part of an exciting new future for the humanities, and to encourage him/her to pursue the possibilities. It is hoped that it will serve as an encouragement to new use of information technology in the humanities, as a guide to specific applications, and as a research tool. While it is mainly research oriented, teaching examples are cited where appropriate and it could be used as a course book for general methodology training for humanities postgraduates and for undergraduates, either on a humanities-wide scale, or for those undertaking a liberal-arts programme.

What it contains

The first section looks at methodologies currently in use in the humanities in the 1990s, followed by studies of discipline-specific issues with an indication of how disciplines are being re-shaped by the use of new technologies. The final section looks at the wide range of information resources available to humanities scholars. Individual projects are used as illustrations, and further, regularly updated, information about these and many more can be found on the World Wide Web (WWW) via the

Oxford CTI Centre for Textual Studies Web page (URL http://www.ox. ac.uk/ctitext/survey/). Although most examples are British, US and European programs and projects are cited where appropriate.

The editorial team hope that there will be future updates of the book, and would consider publishing in digital form if this seemed appropriate. In this first edition the editors have recognized that they cannot hope to cover all possible disciplines and applications but plan to provide information on new topics or disciplines not included here in any future editions.

Humanities computing and humanistic scholarship

In the earliest days of the stored-program computer, new technology held out enormous promise for scholarly work. Potentially limitless amounts of data could be sifted, sorted, or interrogated. In the beginning, however, only a very few enthusiasts used the computer for anything at all, and many viewed with suspicion and fear the colleagues who made this technology central to their scholarship. Technology, for many, was antithetical to the humanistic tradition of investigation, debate, and delivery of materials. The computer revolutions of the 1980s and 1990s have changed that in many areas of work. First of all, the use of word processors was embraced eagerly, particularly when they became user-friendly and driven by graphical user interfaces. The idea of having a typescript which could be altered, scribbled on, then merely edited on-screen rather than completely retyped brought a freedom so seductive that almost none could resist. Then the advent of small, cheap personal computers which scholars could have initially on their desks, and now increasingly in their briefcases, meant that library work of transcribing, annotating, and keying in data could be done more easily and as part of the environments in which humanists traditionally work, rather than by going to a special place, such as a computing centre, which never felt natural to humanists. The greatest revolution of all in this for humanists, however, has been the more recent use of computers for communication, for rapid access to other scholars and to the source materials which are located all over the world and which are increasingly being made available in digital form. Scholars now exchange e-mail addresses or URLs as commonly as telephone numbers.

But these uses of computers by humanists, while exciting and revolutionary in the administration of their scholarship, do not change the nature of scholarship; they merely enable it to be carried out more efficiently or comfortably. They do, however, change the attitudes of scholars to technology, which then makes them much more amenable to, and much more competent to tackle, other applications which could radically change what they do. These applications are of two kinds. Some allow work to be done much faster, indeed on an almost unprecedented scale, but the work itself remains very much the same; for instance, concordances to the works of Shakespeare or to the Bible can be produced in twenty minutes instead of twenty years, but studies based on them might be substantially the same. Others, such as the program Collate developed for use in textual criticism, actually change the nature of scholarship itself, making possible investigations which were formerly inconceivable.

What is it about the process of humanistic scholarship which now makes the use of computers attractive where it was formerly felt to be the province of scientists? One important fact is that computers have changed a great deal in the last twenty years: they are smaller, faster, lighter, and easier to use. They also have a great deal more processing power and better screens, which enables them to process and display the kinds of information which humanists need. For example, one high quality uncompressed image of a medieval manuscript page can take around 80Mb to store. That, even two years ago, was the whole capacity of the hard drive of a personal computer, which even then would never have had the processing power or the screen quality to display this. The change in computers has brought their potential manipulations closer to the needs of humanists, and the development of exciting applications such as hypertext, multimedia, text and image databases, allows the integration of different kinds of media, a sophistication which humanists need and appreciate. In the past, humanists were regarded as the technological poor relations of scientists in universities, to the point that their pleas for equipment either went unheeded ('What do they want equipment for? They only use pencils, paper, and libraries' was the frequent refrain) or were answered by having passed down machines which science departments had outgrown. Of course, giving humanists equipment budgets is very frightening as universities are not given a larger grant to enable them to do this. It has to come from existing funds, funds which have to be diverted from elsewhere: the cake never gets larger, it is just divided into more pieces.

If we are to understand what humanists do, and therefore what they need to help them do it, we need to understand something about the nature of humanistic knowledge. Humanistic knowledge is of a different kind from scientific: in the sciences, new knowledge replaces old, and former theories and writings become of interest only to historians of science. When microbes were discovered, other theories about the transmission of infectious diseases were immediately untenable, and indeed it would be very dangerous to adhere to them. In the humanities, however, new knowledge supplements the old, and therefore knowledge is accretive. All the things which have been said or written at various moments in the past about a particular work of art underlie what may be said at the present moment. Some humanistic theories and ways of looking at the world become unfashionable and are supplanted by others, but the old becomes part of the new, it is not replaced by it, and there is no risk in adhering to old theories, other than perhaps to the scholarly reputation. The implications for the humanities of this accretive nature of information is that anything which has been written about a particular artefact at any time can be of interest. Given the complex matrix of interpretative material in which a work of art soon becomes embedded, one of the primary tasks of scholarship is to find and make sense of the mass of information about it which is available, possibly scattered in many libraries, art galleries, and museums throughout the world.

If, as the above suggests, the process of scholarship rests largely upon the discovery and interpretation of information among a large and scattered mass which has grown up around artefacts over many years, or even centuries, then technological aids in these tasks should be welcomed with open arms by scholars, as indeed they increasingly are. The present volume, in fact, shows just how diverse are the uses now being made by scholars of information technology.

A question which has been hotly debated in the world of computing humanists is: given that humanists are doing different and interesting things with computers, that this usage is growing rapidly, and that special training is needed to get the most from the technology, is there an emergent discipline which we could call 'humanities computing'? Centres for humanities computing and special courses are now common in universities, and some professionals working in humanities computing argue that it is indeed a discipline in its own right. Others look upon it as an aspect of computer science, still others as an aspect of computing service or support. It is also suggested as part of the humanistic disciplines themselves 'an inflection, an aspect of other disciplines', as Kathryn Sutherland argues. The diversity and richness of the collection offered here certainly bears witness to an active and vigorous area of intellectual activity, but it is perhaps too soon to suggest that the subject has the status of a separate discipline like literature, or history, or physics. This is a little problematic for academic practitioners and for professionals in the field, as academic and professional accreditation rests on the assumption that those offering assessments understand the nature of what they are assessing. It can sometimes be the case that a historian in a history department, say, who publishes on both history and historical computing, will get credit from within his or her department for the history but not for the computing. Collections like this should establish the subject as a worthwhile, rigorous, and exciting activity, which, whatever its status in relation to other disciplines, has great value in its own right.

Further information

Promotion and funding of teaching and research in the humanities

Funding of research in the humanities has been a matter of concern for some time. For example, at the European level, there is an almost complete absence of EC programmes devoted specifically to humanities research, though the EC libraries programme and access to information initiative are beginning to change this. In the UK, most of the research in the humanities is carried out at universities, and the system of dual funding (where money is obtained from the government recurrent grant and student fees to cover the cost of research facilities such as library facilities and staff time for research, while most of the direct costs (especially salaries and equipment) are obtained from the research councils in the sciences and social sciences) penalizes the humanities, which has no research council. Therefore researchers have to rely heavily on funds from the British Library Research and Innovation Centre, the British Academy, and the Leverhulme Trust.

In the USA the National Endowment for the Humanities (NEH) has an important funding role, as has the Andrew W Mellon Foundation. In Europe, funds are available from the European Union, but the submission process is rather onerous. Within individual European countries, some examples of funding agencies are: in France, the Centre National de la Recherche Scientifique (CNRS); in Germany, Max Planck Gesellschaft, and Deutsche Forschungsgemeinschaft (DFG); and in Italy, Consiglio Nazionale delle Richerche (CNR).

Computers in Teaching (CTI) Centres

In 1989, 21 subject-specific centres were established to promote and support the use of computers in teaching in UK universities, covering almost all academic disciplines. There are now 23 such centres, funded by the Higher Education Funding Councils (HEFCs) in England, Scotland, and Wales, and the Department of Education, Northern Ireland (DENI). They disseminate information to their discipline constituencies by means of newsletters, resources guides (for example, see the *Resources Guide* of the CTI Centre for Textual Studies (Hughes and Lee 1994)), visits to institutions, and networked delivery of information. There are four such centres serving the main core of humanities disciplines: Textual Studies at the University of Oxford covers literature, linguistics, theology, classics, philosophy, film studies, and theatre arts and drama; history with archaeology and art history is based at Glasgow University; music is at Lancaster; and modern languages is at Hull. Also possibly of interest to readers of this volume are the CTI Centres for geography at Leicester, library and information studies at the University of Loughborough, and sociology and the policy sciences at the University of Stirling. For further information on any of the CTI Centres, the aims of the Initiative, or its publications, contact CTISS, the Computers in Teaching Support Service, which is based at Oxford University Computing Services, 13 Banbury Road, Oxford OX2 6NN (URL: http://www.ox.ac.uk/cti/). CTISS produces a journal, originally titled *CTISS File*, and after issue 16 renamed *Active Learning*. As well as covering descriptions and evaluations of the use of computers across the range of disciplines covered by the CTI, some issues have been devoted to specialist topics. For example, issue 11 (*CTISS File*) dealt with networks and communications, issue 13 focused on authoring systems for courseware development, and issue 14 was devoted to multimedia. Issue 2 of *Active Learning* focused on using the Internet for teaching, while Issue 3 was devoted to teaching with multimedia.

Information Technology Training Initiative (ITTI)

Another initiative funded by the HEFCs in Britain, the ITTI, was set up to improve IT awareness and competence of staff in the university sector by means of providing training materials and courses. A considerable number of the projects funded were to develop software for use in the institutions, often using authoring packages based on multimedia principles. A number of projects funded by the ITTI are relevant to the humanities. Examples include: the Oxford Project, Hypermedia in Lit-

xiv Introduction

erature and Linguistic Studies; Multimedia Based IT Training for the
Humanities, based at Hull University; and the Emashe project at Glasgow University. For further information on the initiative generally, see
the URL: http://www.icbl.hw.ac.uk/itti.

Teaching and Learning Technology Programme (TLTP)
The latest initiative funded by the HEFCs was launched in 1992, and in
May 1993, 43 projects were funded, initially for a three-year period, to
enable universities to develop new methods of teaching and learning
through the use of technology. Two kinds of project were funded, single
institutions and multi-institutional consortia, aimed at producing courseware for the higher education market. Humanities subjects did not fare
particularly well. Some examples of consortia of relevance to humanists
are the TLTP Archaeology consortium, which has produced various
modules, such as ArchGIS and Human Remains (Web address, http://
www.gla.ac.uk/Acad/Archaeology/tltp/tltp.html). The project coordinator is Dr Ewan Campbell, Department of Archaeology, 10 The Square,
University of Glasgow, Glasgow G12 8QQ. The TLTP History consortium can be reached at e-mail address: tltphist@dish.gla.ac.uk. The
TELL (Technology Enhanced Language Learning) consortium has produced a leaflet giving a full description of all the TELL materials
(http://www.cti.hull.ac.uk/tell.htm). For more information on TLTP generally, see the URL: http://www.icbl.hw.ac.uk/tltp/.

Museums and library initiatives

The British Library Initiatives for Access Programme has been set up to
investigate the digitizing of different types of library materials and to
explore the opportunities offered by electronic networks to improve
access to the collections. Some examples are the Electronic *Beowulf*
project, Electronic Photo Viewing System, and Multimedia Document
delivery. Further information can be found at the URL http://portico.
bl.uk.

In 1995 a £15 million Electronic Libraries Programme (eLib) was
funded by the HEFCs and currently supports 30 projects to transform the
use and storage of knowledge in higher education institutions. This arose
from the Follett Review (Joint Funding Councils' Libraries Review
Group), and includes projects on on-demand publishing, new electronic
journals, and document delivery. Project ELSA at De Montfort University (e-journals and libraries) was funded through the European Com-

mission DG XIII and is investigating the delivery of documents to end-users in libraries. The project's Web address is http://www.elsa. dmu.ac.uk. Project ELINOR, the Electronic Library Project, is also at De Montfort University.

IVAIN, the International Visual Arts Network Ltd., which produces ITEM (Image Technology in Museums and Art Galleries database), is currently working on an ITEM WWW site. For details, e-mail ivainjr @gn.apc.org.

Some projects involve collaboration on a wide scale, such as RAMA (Remote Access to Museum Archives) in which museums throughout Europe have collaborated to make available images of museum artefacts through the networks.

Arts and Humanities Data Service (AHDS)

A new national Arts and Humanities Data Service (AHDS) has recently been set up, and is based at King's College London. It arose from a feasibility study commissioned by the Information Services Sub-committee of the Joint Information Systems Committee (JISC) of the Higher Education Funding Councils (Burnard and Short 1994). The Service will consist of a central executive and a number of distributed specialist data Service Providers, offering services of various kinds to the user community on a contractual basis. Some services will be provided centrally, such as the AHDS catalogue and Gateway.

The role of the AHDS is to promote effective low-cost access to the widest range of relevant digital resources by UK researchers and teachers from all arts and humanities disciplines. The functions to be performed will include: cataloguing and identification of resources; development and application of standards; documentation and training; archival preservation of existing resources; identification and creation of new resources; and protection of intellectual property rights.

International conferences

Major discipline-specific conferences are increasingly addressing the importance of using new technology in teaching and research within the discipline. Some examples of such conferences are the Association for History and Computing (AHC), CHaRT (Computers and the History of Art), CALL (Computer Assisted Language Learning) and EUROCALL. Here some pointers are given to some of the more generally applicable conferences in the humanities which are less discipline-specific, and tend to explore methodologies and resources.

- CATH—Computers and Teaching in the Humanities. There have been seven conferences in this series organized by the OHC between 1987 and 1995. The aim of the conference is to bring together people with an interest or expertise in computing in a humanities discipline, to demonstrate and discuss the latest computing/IT technologies, concentrating on practical experiences and approaches, describing problems as well as successes, and including examples of student feedback—all the conferences have included some element of practical demonstration, workshop, or software fair, as well as the more usual refereed paper sessions. Proceedings of some of these conferences have been reviewed in, for example, *Literary and Linguistic Computing*, the journal of the Association for Literary and Linguistic Computing (ALLC) and in *Computers and Texts*, the newsletter of the CTI Centre for Textual Studies. The proceedings have shown a progression over time from a basic, introductory approach aimed at those new to humanities computing, to a more advanced programme, including multimedia, markup, and networking skills. These conferences have been very influential to those involved in humanities research as well as teaching, judging by the numbers of new 'recruits' who enrol on each occasion and also the number of delegates who have returned time and time again—both groups have gained much satisfaction from the event, according to feedback received.

- The Elvetham Hall conference series on Scholarship and Technology in the Humanities. The first conference in this series was held in 1990 and addressed recent trends in humanities disciplines, the issues involved in creating and sustaining scholarship, and the implications of the conduct of research and education in an environment increasingly shaped and mediated by technology (Katzen 1991). The second conference was held in April 1994 to discuss Networking in the Humanities. An international audience of invited scholars, policy makers, funders, information providers, and information professionals took part in wide-ranging discussions on the opportunities offered to humanities scholars by networking, as well as the technical and intellectual challenges. A list of recommendations and resolutions were sent out to influential bodies following the conference and resulted in some actions being taken.

- ALLC/ACH (Association for Literary and Linguistic Computing and the Association for Computers and the Humanities). Joint annual conferences have been held every year since 1989, and are held one year in North America and the next year in Europe. Selected papers are published.

Centres for Humanities Computing

The Office for Humanities Communication is a national centre based at the University of Oxford until July 1996; it has been in existence since 1982. It has been instrumental in setting up innovative ways of disseminating information in the humanities such as HUMBUL, the Humanities Bulletin Board, the first of its kind in the world, now a homepage on the WWW. It has started a new publication series which as at May 1996 had produced nine titles, and organizes conferences and seminar series, 'The Humanities in the Electronic Age', as well as carrying out two major research surveys of computer use and awareness in higher education (Katzen 1985; Mullings 1992).

A number of institutions have recently established specialist Centres for Humanities Computing. Some are independent units within their institutions, while others are part of the computing centre, or part of another department, or maybe part of a humanities research unit or university library. A selection of those in existence for the longest time, and with the most experience are given here:

- The Humanities Computing Unit (HCU) in Oxford offers help and advice on all aspects of humanities computing, and provides resources, support, and courses for students and faculty at the University of Oxford. The Unit provides a worldwide information service by conventional and electronic means, runs a number of research projects, and houses the Oxford Text Archive (which is described in more detail in subsequent chapters).

- The Institute of Advanced Technology in the Humanities, University of Virginia, makes resources available over the Web, including the electronic journal, *Postmodern Culture*, co-edited by the Institute's director. Associated with this is the Electronic Text Center which has made available thousands of SGML-encoded electronic texts online. All the online texts are accessed through a single interface.

- The Center for Computing in the Humanities, University of Toronto, Canada, runs courses, sponsors a lecture series, and makes electronic (and other) resources available in its own library.

- The Norwegian Computing Centre for the Humanities, PO Box 53, Universitet, N-5027, Bergen, provides information and teaching services, develops programs, and has established an exchange with British researchers, largely through the journal, *Humanistiske Data*.

- The Center for Electronic Texts in the Humanities (CETH), Rutgers and Princeton Universities, USA, is developing a collection of good quality electronic texts, encoded in the Text Encoding Initiative's implementation of SGML. The texts will act as a testbed for research on the use of electronic texts. The URL for CETH is http://www.ceth.rutgers.edu.

- The Computing for the Humanities User Group (CHUG) at Brown University, USA, amongst other activities has special interest groups, e.g. Hypertext Working Group, Literary Tagging Working Group, Scholarly Technology Group.

Organizations and associations

There are several organizations which academics might consider joining. Many produce their own newsletters/journals, such as the MLA Newsletter, *Literary and Linguistic Computing*. A small sample includes the Association for Literary and Linguistic Computing, Association for Computers and the Humanities, Association for History and Computing, etc. A good start to finding such organizations would be the CTI Centre for Textual Studies *Resources Guide* (Hughes and Lee 1994). The URL is http://www.ox.ac.uk/ctitext/.

Networks, discussion lists, bulletin boards, electronic journals, etc. are all discussed where relevant and in detail in the chapters which follow, as are elementary textbooks, introductory books, and products from commercial publishers.

Notes

1. *Historische Sozialforschung,* 19 (1994) 1, 3-59.

2. Formerly the British Library Research and Development Department. In June 1996 (just as this volume was going to press) the Department changed its name to the British Library Research and Innovation Centre (RIC).

References

(ACLS), *Technology, scholarship and the humanities: the implications of electronic information. Summary of proceedings,* The American Council of Learned Societies and The J. Paul Getty Trust, Irvine, California, September 30-October 2, 1992.

(BLR&DD) British Library Research & Development Department, *Information technology in humanities scholarship: British achievements, prospects and barriers,* BLR&D Report 6097 (London: The British Library and The British Academy, 1993).

Burnard, L., and Short, H., *An Arts and Humanities Data Service: report of a feasibility study commissioned by the Information Services Sub-committee of the Joint Information Systems Committee of the Higher Education Funding Councils* (Oxford: Office for Humanities Communication, October 1994).

Genet, J.-P., and Zampolli, A. (eds.), *Computers and the humanities,* European Science Foundation (Aldershot: Dartmouth, 1992).

Hughes, L., and Lee, S. (eds.), *Resources guide 1994,* (Oxford: CTI Centre for Textual Studies, 1994).

Katzen, M., *Technology and communication in the humanities: training and services in universities and polytechnics in the UK,* Library and Information Research Report 32 (London: The British Library, 1985).

Katzen, M. (ed.), *Scholarship and technology in the humanities: proceedings of a conference held at Elvetham Hall, Hampshire, UK, 9-12 May 1990* (London: Bowker Saur, 1991)

Kenna, S., and Ross, S. (eds.), *Networking in the humanities: proceedings of the second conference on scholarship and technology in the humanities held at Elvetham Hall, Hampshire, UK, 13-16 April 1994,* (London: Bowker Saur, 1995).

Mullings, C., *Computers and communication in the humanities: a survey of use* (Oxford: Office for Humanities Communication Publications, number 1, November 1992).

Information on Authors

Peter Adman
Assistant Director, The University of Hull Computer Centre, Hull HU6 7RX.

Michael Allen
Centre for Creative and Performing Arts, School of English and American Studies, University of East Anglia, Norwich NR4 7TJ.

Professor Robin Alston
School of Library Archive and Information Studies, University College London, Gower Street, London WC1E 6BT.

Andrew Bennett
Faculty of Music, University of Cambridge, West Road, Cambridge CB3 9DP.

Professor Stephen R L Clark
Department of Philosophy, The University of Liverpool, 7 Abercromby Square, P O Box 147, Liverpool L69 3BX.

Dr Ian Cross
Faculty of Music, University of Cambridge, West Road, Cambridge CB3 9DP.

Dr Barry Dainton
Department of Philosophy, The University of Liverpool, 7 Abercromby Square, P O Box 147,Liverpool L69 3BX.

Professor Marilyn Deegan
International Institute for Electronic Library Research, De Montfort University, Hammerwood Gate, Kents Hill, Milton Keynes MK7 6HP.

Peter Doorn
Netherlands Historisch Data Archief, Rijks Universiteit Leiden, Doelensteeg 16, Postbus 9515, 2300 R A Leiden, The Netherlands.

Maria Economou
Linacre College, St Cross Street, University of Oxford, Oxford OX1 3JA.

Dr Michael Fraser
Research Officer, CTI Centre for Textual Studies, Oxford University Computing Services, 13 Banbury Road, Oxford OX2 6NN.

Dr Stuart Lee
Humanities IT Support Officer, Oxford University Computing Services, 13 Banbury Road, Oxford OX2 6NN.

Alan Marsden
School of Music, The Queen's University of Belfast, Belfast BT7 1NN.

David Meredith
Faculty of Music, University of Cambridge, West Road, Cambridge CB3 9DP.

Dr Jonathan Moffett
Department of Antiquities, Ashmolean Museum, Beaumont Street, Oxford OX1 2PH.

Michael Popham
Centre Manager, CTI Centre for Textual Studies, Oxford University Computing
Services, 13 Banbury Road, Oxford OX2 6NN.

Andrew Prescott
Initiatives for Access Programme, Manuscript Collections, The British Library, Gt
Russell Street, London WC1B 3DG.

Dr Peter Robinson
International Institute for Electronic Library Research, De Montfort University,
Hammerwood Gate, Kents Hill, Milton Keynes MK7 6HP.

Dr Seamus Ross
Assistant Secretary (Information Technology), The British Academy, 20-21 Cornwall
Terrace, London NW1 4QP.

Michael Rundell
252 Wincheap, Canterbury, Kent CT1 3TY.

Professor W H T Vaughan
Department of History of Art, Birkbeck College, University of London, 43 Gordon
Square, London WC1H 0PD.

Richard Wallace
Department of Classics, Keele University, Keele, Staffordshire ST5 5BG.

Dr Lorraine Warren
School of Systems and Information Sciences, University of Humberside, Cottingham
Road, Hull HU6 7RT.

Dr David Wheatley
Department of Archaeology, University of Southampton, Highfield, Southampton
SO17 1BJ.

SECTION 1
METHODOLOGIES

Text Encoding, Analysis, and Retrieval

Michael Popham

Introduction

The encoding, analysis and retrieval of electronic text plays a part in many areas of computer-assisted research across the range of humanities disciplines. This chapter is *not* intended to be a discussion of word processing software, or a comparison of various text analysis and retrieval packages, but instead offers an introduction to how the methodology of text encoding can affect the various ways in which an electronic text can be processed. The text encoding scheme used when creating an electronic text is probably *the* most crucial factor in determining such questions as the hardware and software required to process the text, the kinds of things that can be done with it, and the ease with which it can be adapted or reused by others.

Rather than attempt to describe any one particular text encoding scheme in detail, this chapter provides an overview of the process of creating and encoding an electronic text in order that readers will be able to judge for themselves the most appropriate kind of electronic texts for their needs. Whether your main concern is creating, finding, or using electronic texts—or a combination of all three—it is important to appreciate the benefits and problems, freedoms and limitations, possibilities and impossibilities that are dictated by text encoding decisions. It is also important to know *where* to look for electronic texts, and to have some idea of the range of tools that are available to help users find, analyse, and perform other kinds of computer-assisted processing of electronic texts. With that in mind, this chapter also provides details of the availability and types of text analysis and retrieval software, and directs readers towards several useful sources of further information.

Text encoding

Never forget that computers cannot read. It is very easy to credit them with more human-like intelligence than they actually possess, and this view is encouraged by the use of anthropomorphic terminology. We often talk about computers 'reading' and 'writing' files, 'searching' for particular words, and so on—but these actions are performed in a very different way from the methods a human being would use. To a computer, everything is represented and representable as a series of 1s and 0s; there are no fundamental differences between images and texts, audio and video, software applications and data, words and spaces, black and white—they are all made up of the same binary stuff.

In order to process words, a computer needs to load a succession of software (operating system, application program, and data) so that it can treat in a consistent manner the particular patterns of 1s and 0s that represent such things as a character of the English language, the whitespace between two words, the break at the end of a line of text, or information about the font which should be used to display a paragraph. The process is not so very different in principle from what a human reader must go through to learn a language, understand that certain kinds of marks made on paper (e.g. written or printed words) represent that language, appreciate that the organization of both the marks and pieces of paper conveys additional information about relatedness (e.g. a linear narrative), and so forth.

By the time most people come to use a computer they have forgotten just what a sophisticated act reading actually is—and the tendency to attribute human-like knowledge and intelligence to dumb boxes of electronic circuitry only makes it more frustrating when they will not do what is required.[1] In order to get a computer to do something useful with a text, it needs to be loaded into the computer in a format that can be understood and processed. In an ideal world, there would be a common format (i.e. internal encoding of a text) which every computer and every software application could understand and process in the same way. Unfortunately, we do not live in an ideal world—although, as we shall see, standards do exist for encoding texts independently of particular computers or applications.

Preparation

The assumption from this point on is that you have identified an existing text (i.e. a particular printed edition, a collection of manuscripts, etc.) which you wish to process with the aid of a computer. There are three common methods of getting text into a computer: scanning, keying, and reusing existing electronic text. Which of these you choose will depend on a combination of factors, such as the form in which the text currently exists (printed paper, manuscript, stone inscription, electronic file), the resources available to you (time, money, assistance, equipment), and your previous experience.

Scanning

Scanning is the generic term for the combined use of some kind of optical input device (a 'scanner') and the processing of that input by optical character recognition (OCR) software. In practice, scanning a text is little different from using a photocopier or a fax machine to create an electronic image of that text—with the vital distinction that the resultant image is subsequently turned into textual data that the computer can process.

For a human, looking at a photograph or a photocopy of a printed text does not interfere with the ability to process (i.e. read) that text; we perceive very little difference between the original and the representation. However, show a human a photograph of a three dimensional object like a vase, and there is a very perceptible difference between the original and the representation. To a computer, 'images' are one kind of data and 'text' is another, it cannot look *at* an image of a printed page and read the text thereon in the same way that you or I might be able to read from a photocopy or photograph of a text. Hence the need for OCR software which processes the image data and attempts to recognize patterns of text characters; the scanned image is translated into a file of text data which the computer and application software can process as normal. The fact that scanning involves two major transformations—the representation of the original document as an image, and the conversion of that image into a representation as electronic text—means that there are several opportunities for problems and errors to arise.

The main factor influencing the success or otherwise of scanning is the quality of the original source. The texts which scan best tend to be modern and well-printed, use Latinate characters, and are taken from clean, smooth paper. Even if the presentation is excellent, scanning text that is printed in multiple running columns, flowing round tables and figures, can be unsatisfactory—although success often depends upon the sophistication of the OCR software. It is probably not worth the effort to attempt to scan a sullied, crumpled manuscript, written in a highly-stylized hand and faded ink—unless your main concern is to capture an *image* of the original document.

The type of scanning hardware—and the software which controls it—is also important. Scanners come in a variety of shapes and sizes, but essentially there are 'hand-held' and 'flat-bed' types. Hand-held devices require the user physically to pass the head of the scanner over the text to be scanned—in a smooth, flowing, wobble-free manner. Flat-bed scanners are physically more akin to conventional desktop photocopiers, where the original document is placed face-down on a plate of glass, and a strong light is passed over its surface (the reflections being processed to create an electronic image). The quality of any single attempt at scanning a text can be improved by the resolution of the device being used (often expressed in dots per inch, cf. laser printer resolution), and the number of passes made by the scanning head over the source (successive scans can be compared by the controlling software, in an attempt to reduce anomalies). Robinson (1993) provides an excellent introduction to the process of scanning and digitization.

Once the scanned image has been generated, the quality of the translation from image to text data depends solely on the OCR software. The software may highlight character images that it is unsure about (e.g. a poorly printed character might be an 'a' or a 'u', an 'i' or an 'l', etc.), and/or it may include a spell-checker so that possible mis-scanned sequences of characters can be automatically corrected. Certain packages allow the user to 'train' them, for example to recognize the characters in a new font, to add words to the spell-checker's dictionary, and so forth. Even after the OCR software claims to have completed its task, the user should proof-read the electronic version of the text against the original source—indeed this will be a necessity if fidelity to the original source is of vital consideration to the entire project.

The rate of error correction frequently determines the wisdom of scanning a text. Quite apart from the cost of the scanning equipment and the time taken by the initial process, even if an average accuracy rate of 99 per cent is achieved, that would still mean that human editorial intervention would be required to correct an average of one in every hundred characters. For a short piece of text this may be worthwhile, but for large amounts it may be impractical.[2]

Keying

Another way to create electronic text is by 'keying' (sometimes called 'rekeying') in which the original text is simply copy-typed into an electronic file. The crucial decision is whether you should do it yourself, or pay someone else to do it. Factors which influence this decision might include your personal expertise and typing skill, the nature of the source text, and the financial resources available to you. Specialist bureaux exist to key information into a computer, and they can achieve very high levels of accuracy by keying the same text *twice* ('double-keying') then comparing the resulting files for any discrepancies. Major national libraries often adopt this approach when converting their holdings to electronic form—although they are particularly well-placed to take advantage of any economies of scale.

Keying can be much more efficient than scanning for certain types of original source document (e.g. when the text is difficult to read, or the printing is of poor quality), as it allows the early introduction of human intelligence into the production process, and errors in the data can be identified and corrected at the time of entry. However when misapplied, such human intelligence can create as many problems as it appears to solve. For example, a copy-typist might enter what s/he *thinks* is in the original (particularly true if s/he is a native speaker of the language of the text[3]), or subconsciously correct typographic/orthographic errors in the source document when those 'errors' should have been preserved.

Reusing electronic texts from archives

Archives are fast becoming an important source of electronic texts. They exist in two basic types: those distributed on portable media (e.g. CD-ROM or magnetic tape), and those accessible online (e.g. via the Internet). The first sort is frequently produced by commercial organizations in response to user demands for electronic texts which can be reused (that is, texts which are not inextricably tied to particular browsing and searching tools). The second type of archive is generally the result of efforts made by a university's library and/or computing service, or perhaps a group of dedicated individuals (not necessarily from the same institution). As the trend appears to be for archives to made accessible via online access, I shall concentrate on these.

At the time of writing, there are still only a handful of major electronic text archives available online, such as the Oxford Text Archive (URL: http://ota.ox.ac.uk/~archive/ota.html), and the Electronic Text Center at the University of Virginia (URL: http://www.lib.virginia.edu/etext/ETC. html). Many smaller, specialist archives exist on the Internet, and their numbers are growing extremely rapidly with the increasing popularity of the World Wide Web. A good place to start looking for both types of archive is via the HUMBUL Gateway (URL: http://www.ox.ac.uk/ departments/humanities/international.html). Compared to the holdings of conventional libraries and archives, those of the online electronic archives might seem disappointingly small. However, it is crucial to remember that the online archives have usually been created by and for academics, so it is *always* worthwhile checking that the text you want does not already exist before beginning to scan or key it yourself.

Online archives offer several immediate benefits. With luck, someone else will have undertaken the time consuming work of creating an electronic version of the text(s) you require. If the archive is well-run, the creator(s) of the electronic text will have provided extensive bibliographic information about the original text, along with details about the conversion process, and have produced files which can be easily reused by other scholars. Amongst librarians, archivists, researchers, editors, and authors there is presently a great deal of discussion about how to store, reference, and retrieve electronic texts, and ensure that quality standards are maintained, etc.

However, the nascent state of many current online archives has resulted in several teething problems. The quality of electronic texts can vary dramatically (not only between archives, but also within them)—depending on how the archive is maintained, who created and donated the texts, the purpose behind their creation, and so forth. The provenance of many electronic texts is difficult to establish, and their fidelity to the source documents (if known) may never have been properly checked. Even if an electronic text has been carefully created and documented, you may not want/need/agree with any descriptive markup it contains (discussed below)—although this should not be a problem if the text's creators have described their markup scheme, as you may be able to use, revise, or remove it without too much difficulty.

Encoding standards

All electronic text that is machine-readable has to be encoded in some way. The *de facto* standard for ordinary, Latinate characters is ASCII —which is often referred to as 'plain text' to distinguish a file of simple characters, punctuation, and line-breaks from one which contains formatting (e.g. text that is presented using different sizes or styles of font). Any attempt to represent additional textual features is usually specific to the person or software doing the encoding. For example, different software applications record presentational information (font size, font style, page breaks, page layout information, etc.) in different ways, whilst individuals may record logical information (i.e. about the role of an element of text—whether it is a title, sub-title, paragraph, verse, annotation, correction, etc.) using a variety of methods.

Markup

Markup is crucial to the processing of electronic texts; it is also a term and a concept that is used and abused in a multiplicity of ways. In one sense, every text (whether electronic or not) that contains inter-word spaces, line endings, capitalization, punctuation, extra space between paragraphs, left-to-right text flow, etc. makes use of markup. However, these conventions have come to be applied so consistently to written or printed texts that readers only tend to notice their absence (e.g. when a reader of English first encounters a text written in Japanese, or a typical example of ancient Greek).

When it comes to handling electronic texts, computers and the software they run care only about being able to interpret binary data. A computer has no real understanding of the difference between English and Japanese, or between codes to represent a text character, a single white space, the end of a line, a change of font, a page break, an instruction to centre the following text, and so on. The widespread adoption of ASCII means that almost all computers and software agree on the internal encoding of the standard Latinate characters ('a', 'A', 'b', 'B', ',', '1', etc.), but the same is not true when we consider less common characters (such as 'é', 'ü', 'ç', 'â', 'æ', '£', '#'), or information about typefaces (e.g. **bold**, *italic,* underline) or fonts (e.g. courier, helvetica, *zapf chancery*) let alone entire foreign language character sets (e.g. Hebrew, Greek, Cyrillic). Although efforts are being made to resolve these problems—for example by developing the Unicode Standard to facilitate processing different character sets—these problems will remain with us for many years to come (not least in all the millions of electronic texts that have been created in recent decades).

Markup generally falls into two distinct types: *specific* (sometimes called 'procedural' or 'presentational' markup) and *generic* (sometimes called 'descriptive' or, latterly, 'content' markup). Specific markup tells the processing software (and thus the computer) exactly what to do: print the following text in bold, centre the following text, change the current font to Helvetica, and so on. However, because software developers have never agreed on any standards for specific markup, electronic files created using one piece of software are often unreadable by other software packages—or worse still, the same markup codes are interpreted differently.

Generic markup is not inherently any more portable than specific markup, however it is used to identify (or 'describe') the semantic elements of a text (e.g. titles, paragraphs, lists, Act, Scene, verse, rhyming couplet, etc.). The significance of generic markup is normally user-definable, meaning that in some instances it may be converted by special processing software into presentational instructions (e.g. 'Print all text identified as a "title" in bold, 20point, Helvetica, centred'), and at other times it may be converted in different ways ('Display anything identified as "title" in red in the top right of a window', or 'Take anything identified as "title" and store it along with locational information in a database'). Indeed, the generic markup itself is also usually under the control of the user, so that s/he can decide whether the markup code for a title should be 'title', 'T', 'Heading', 'H1', 'chapter_title', or something else entirely.

For many years the only way to create electronic texts was by using a piece of software called a 'text editor' and inserting into the text particular markup codes chosen from a limited (software-specific) set. It was hard to tell the effects of the markup until the text was processed—for example, formatted and printed. The advent of WYSIWYG word processors meant that users were encouraged to focus on the *appearance* they wished the text to have, and they could let the software worry about inserting the correct markup codes. Also, as the software became more sophisticated users were encouraged to surrender control over tiresome decisions about line length, page breaks, etc. Nowadays, users often feel that they are taking a backward step when they start to use software based upon generic markup principles—particularly if their main objective is to produce conventional printed texts. The problem with this opinion is that it is based on the belief that printed texts are more accessible and reusable than their electronic counterparts—and whilst this may have been true in the past, it may not be so for much longer.

Prescriptive vs. descriptive
I have already stated that the assumption of this chapter is that, rather than creating electronic texts 'from scratch', users are working with texts that already exist in one form (e.g. manuscripts, printed editions, a

different electronic format), and are creating new electronic texts *with some specific purpose in mind*—such as computer-assisted text analysis, creating a concordance, preservation, or distribution on CD-ROM. If fidelity to the presentational information of the original source is all that concerns you, then you may well be satisfied with simply creating facsimile images using scanning technology. However, most other tasks will require you to have a machine-readable electronic text, and the markup scheme you choose (and how you apply it) will be crucial.

The well-worn arguments about descriptive and prescriptive approaches to the original materials will need to be considered, ideally prior to the actual electronic encoding of the text(s). For example, if you are using a system of descriptive markup to describe the features of a given text for later text analysis, you should document how you devised your categories of features and, where necessary, why you decided to mark up something as X rather than Y. It is all too easy to assume that you are describing some feature fairly and unambiguously, whereas a fellow scholar may see your decisions as unreasonably prescriptive. Ambiguity, uncertainty, and difficulty are not necessarily a problem when marking up an electronic text, provided that anyone else who comes to use your text is made aware of the markup decisions that have been taken. Similarly, a good descriptive markup system will be extensible in a controlled way—otherwise the person who is marking up an electronic text may be unable to mark up certain crucial features, or will be tempted to force them into categories to which they do not strictly belong.

Proprietary and non-proprietary
Proprietary markup and encoding schemes are those which are tied to a particular software product or developer, but it is not always an easy matter to judge whether or not something is proprietary. In recent years, developers have begun to realize that users do not like to feel that they are being *forced* into using a particular piece of software simply because their existing files are encoded/marked up using a scheme that is only supported by one product or family of products. Developers have made great claims about the 'openness' of their software, and/or its adoption as a particular 'industry standard'. Such claims should be treated with the utmost caution—especially if you will be investing large amounts of time and money in encoding your texts. For example, developers of word processing software often draw purchasers' attention to the fact that the latest version of their software can read files created by earlier versions, but why is this so noteworthy? On reflection, it is perhaps surprising that

developers were *ever* allowed to get away with producing incompatible versions of their software. What about the data that are trapped in these old files? Does this mean that you will have to convert *all* your existing files in order to ensure that they can still be used in the future? Will you have to do this each time the developers bring out a new version of their 'standard' encoding scheme?

Proprietary solutions are fine if you know exactly what software and hardware you want to work with. If you can be 100 per cent certain that you will never want to use your electronic text files with other software or hardware, and that no-one else will want to do this either, then you need have no concerns about using a proprietary encoding scheme. However, before you commit yourself irrevocably to your decision consider the fact that we can still use texts created hundreds of years ago (everything from early printed books, to medieval manuscripts, to ancient hieroglyphs carved on stone) whilst certain electronic files created within the last ten or twenty years—using particular combinations of proprietary hardware and software—are effectively now lost to us forever.

Ink on paper remains usable for as long as the ink does not fade or the paper does not decay because the access mechanisms used by humans to read have not altered fundamentally for thousands of years; the mechanisms that computers and software use to access electronic texts are changing frequently, and whilst the physical medium (disc, tape, or CD-ROM) may remain intact for many decades, the encoding scheme used to record information on that medium may be unreadable within a matter of years. A truly non-proprietary encoding scheme will not guarantee that your electronic files will be readable in a thousand years' time, but it will greatly improve the odds. Non-proprietary schemes are largely independent of commercial concerns, and so their development can be carefully controlled by the creators and archivists of electronic sources.

PostScript
Despite the remarks made above, a very few proprietary solutions do become adopted as *de facto* standards. Perhaps the best-known of these in existence today is the page description language PostScript. PostScript is an excellent way to tell a laser printer exactly where to put a dot of ink on a piece of paper, or, more recently, where to display a particular coloured dot on a screen. If your main concern is the appearance of an electronic text when printed or displayed, then PostScript may well be

the standard for you. On the other hand, in its present form PostScript is exceptionally difficult to edit—meaning that any text stored as a Post-Script file effectively becomes non-revisable (which may or may not be what you want). Similarly, you cannot load a PostScript file into a text analysis package and expect the software to build you a useful concordance of all the words in the text—as all the PostScript instructions will be included as well!

Portable electronic documents
Within the past two years, a number of tools, such as Acrobat (Adobe), Envoy (WordPerfect), Replica (Farallon) and Common Ground (No Hands Software), and proprietary standards[4] have emerged to meet the requirements of the electronic publishing market. Most of these attempt to guarantee that the visual appearance of an electronic document is retained, as far as possible, when it is moved between different hardware and software environments.

Most of these tools allow readers to annotate documents in a formal way, and then exchange both the document and annotations with other readers. The tools have usually been developed with a business scenario in mind, where an electronic document is circulated online for a group of readers to comment upon, then a final version of the document is distributed either in electronic form and/or printed exactly as it appears on screen. The tools to generate (or 'publish') the electronic document are usually expensive in comparison to the browsing (or 'reader') software, which is often readily distributable at no cost.

This approach to the distribution of electronic texts has proved very popular with publishers seeking to find a convenient method of electronic publication, particularly if it preserves the visual appearance of documents and does not allow consumers to access the raw data. However, all these tools tend to be proprietary—meaning that a document created by the publishing tools in one package are not usable by the reader software of another—and the emphasis on presentational information effectively stops users from doing anything more than reading an electronic text.

SGML
SGML is formally defined in the publication *ISO 8879:1986 Information Processing—Text and Office Systems—Standard Generalized Markup Language (SGML)*. However, it was never envisaged that users should have to read the publications of the International Organization for

Standards before they could start to take advantage of the benefits offered by SGML. Readers should consult other sources for a more complete introduction to SGML,[5] as in this short section I shall only attempt to highlight how SGML differs from the markup systems we have considered earlier.

SGML provides a standard grammar for defining markup languages. It is crucial to remember that SGML does *not* define what those markup languages are intended to do—only which markup codes are valid, and how those codes relate to one another in any one particular markup language. SGML encourages the use of descriptive/generic markup techniques, and gives the creator of an SGML conformant markup language complete freedom to decide which features should be described. SGML also enables the definition of a markup language to be expressed in a way that is independent of a particular hardware and/or software environment—meaning that any texts which are encoded using such a markup language are (potentially) much more portable and reusable than other types of electronic texts.

Using SGML encourages a conscious separation of the various aspects of a markup language. For example, information about which character sets can be used, the specification of a valid markup code, the 'depth' to which codes can be nested, etc. is kept separate from the process whereby the codes are defined, their relationships and permissible content types declared, and so on. Using SGML means that, as well as improving portability, the markup used to encode any one particular text can be checked against the formal declaration of the markup language to see if it conforms. For example, suppose you were working with a markup language which had markup codes (popularly referred to by SGML enthusiasts as 'tags'), which required that within everything tagged as a <CHAPTER> there must *always* be something tagged as a <TITLE> and *at least one or more* <P>aragraphs of text. This would make it difficult for anyone encoding a text using this markup language to forget to tag every chapter title—which would be crucial if they wanted to process a large collection of electronic texts to search for particular terms *only* when they occurred in chapter titles.

If there is a problem with using SGML, it tends to stem from the belief that it is difficult and expensive to implement. However, because it is a non-proprietary International Standard which has been adopted by several major industries for the long-term preservation of electronic information, the number of tools and experienced individuals is growing all the time. For more information contact the International SGML Users'

Group. Clearly it would be a false economy to begin a large-scale text encoding project using cheap, proprietary tools, if the long-term result was that the texts were severely restricted in their reusability.

The Text Encoding Initiative

The Text Encoding Initiative (TEI) is a major international academic endeavour, which has worked over a number of years to produce a set of *Guidelines for Electronic Text Encoding and Interchange* (otherwise known as TEI P3, or simply the *Guidelines*). The *Guidelines* represent one of the most significant applications of SGML yet developed, and readers are strongly recommended to consult one of the sources mentioned in the bibliography. The design goals of the TEI appear deceptively straightforward, namely:

- be sufficient to represent the textual features needed for research;
- be simple, clear, and concrete;
- be easy for researchers to use without special-purpose software;
- allow the rigorous definition and efficient processing of texts;
- provide for user-defined extensions;
- conform to existing and emergent standards

(Sperberg-McQueen 1995).

Only the last three of these goals relate directly to SGML (and when the *Guidelines* were first envisaged, it was not at all clear that SGML would play any part in meeting them). The advantage of using SGML is that it enabled the developers of the *Guidelines* to create a standards-based, non-proprietary, extensible markup scheme. The *Guidelines* support a modular approach to the marking up of text, allowing users to select and combine sets of tags appropriate to the textual features they wish to encode (e.g. for an electronic text of one of Shakespeare's plays, a user might combine the tag sets for drama and verse). Moreover, if the default set of tags does not include markup for a particular feature, users can add in their own tags in a TEI-conformant fashion. As long as tools exist which understand SGML-based encoding schemes, scholars will be able to create, exchange, and reuse TEI-conformant electronic texts.

Analysis

Computers have transformed certain aspects of textual analysis. They are ideal for performing highly repetitive tasks which humans find tedious and error-prone—such as searching though tens of thousands of words to find all the occurrences of a particular term. With appropriate software, a computer can create an index, build a concordance, or identify collocates in a text in a fraction of the time that it would take a human being.

A computer treats the words in a text as a sequence of *tokens*, and it is these that are counted by the word-count tool in a typical word processing package; no account is taken of the fact that a proportion of these tokens will probably be of the same *type*. For example, the word 'the' is a single type which may be represented by many identical tokens in a text. A text processing tool operates by identifying all the individual tokens in a text, storing information about where each occurs, and sorting the tokens by their type. If the processing tool also has knowledge of other features of the text—for example, it may have been specially prepared for a particular kind of analysis by having certain features identified by markup tags—then this makes additional kinds of processing much easier (e.g. performing context-based searches, or collocation).

Pros and cons of computer-aided text analysis

The promise of computer-aided text analysis has been widely touted for many years—but the potential benefits and problems have remained unchanged. Computerization offers clear advantages in terms of the sheer speed and accuracy with which electronic texts can be processed. It also means that from a numerical and statistical perspective, the results that one obtains should be reproducible by other scholars.

As more texts become available in electronic form, and as more scholars adopt standards-based techniques and tools for processing these texts (such as those recommended in the TEI's *Guidelines*), this will permit new kinds of research and text analysis. It will become both possible and practical to analyse, say, all the works of a particular author or school of writing—and, perhaps further in the future, all the works produced in a particular genre, period, or language.

Yet the preparation of the electronic text remains a crucial factor. The vast majority of texts existing in the world have not been created directly in electronic form, which means that they will have to undergo some sort of transformation before they can be subjected to computer-assisted text analysis (and this can be extremely expensive and time consuming). We have already seen that both scanning and rekeying are processes in which it is possible for the content of a text to be corrupted in some way. Similarly, marking up a text—for whatever purpose—introduces another stage where mistakes and invalid assumptions can have an effect on the results obtained by computer-aided text analysis. The results themselves may not be as accurate as the researcher may believe unless great care has been taken when constructing search terms, etc. and the raw data of the results are still likely to be subject to an element of interpretation. Until both researchers and tools start to use the available standards, most electronic texts will continue to be prepared with a specific task (and a specific tool) in mind—which will limit the texts' usefulness to other scholars, and may make it difficult or impossible to check an electronic text against its original source.

A short overview of text analysis software

There is a growing range of text analysis software available for most types of computer—from basic desktop machines to powerful mainframes. At present this software can only use texts which have been specially prepared according to their own specific requirements, meaning that users may have to define tokenization rules (e.g. whether hyphenated words should be treated as a single token) and/or be constrained by the sophistication and extensibility of the markup scheme supported by the tool.

Text analysis software such as TACT and WordCruncher designed to run on personal, desktop computers is becoming increasingly sophisticated. For example, with a minimal amount of preparation TACT can be used to index all the words in a text, present several different kinds of display (e.g. KWIC (Key Word In Context) and distribution), present all the collocates and Z-scores relating to a particular word, search the text for user-defined words or patterns, and so forth.

When working with very large electronic texts, or if there is a need to perform particularly complex kinds of processing, most users will need to work in a mainframe environment. For example, to perform a sophisticated search of the entire 100 million words of the British National Corpus (BNC) described elsewhere in this volume, the text and searching software need to reside on a mainframe computer (which acts as the server), whilst the user initiates processing using a dedicated client application (called SARA) from a terminal connected to the mainframe. Of course as the power of desktop computers continues to grow, such distinctions will become less crucial.

Commercial texts supplied on CD-ROM are usually intended for use on personal computers. The large capacity of CD-ROMs, combined with the fact that storing electronic text is very efficient (compared to graphics, sound, and video), means that the source text usually only takes up a fraction of the space available. For example, on the CD-ROM of the *Oxford English Dictionary (OED) (Second Edition)*, the marked up dictionary text takes up about one third of the storage space on the CD-ROM—the rest is filled with various kinds of index which enable the searching software to produce results much more rapidly than would otherwise be the case. However, it should be noted that most of the electronic texts published on CD-ROM are usable only with the specialist searching and analysis software supplied as part of the whole 'package' (which means that you cannot normally take the electronic text of something like the *OED* and load it into your personal copy of, say, TACT).

A number of specialist text analysis and processing tools also exist. For example, if you wanted to produce a critical edition of a text from many different manuscripts, Collate is a program which can assist this process by automatically collating the variants in up to one hundred texts simultaneously. Similarly, if you wanted to build a bilingual concordance of two aligned texts in different languages ('aligned' means that each sentence in one text is matched by a translated sentence in the other text), then you might turn to a tool like ParaConc. New tools such as these are appearing all the time—from both academic and commercial sources—so readers should be prepared to consult the available resources (e.g. printed sources, specialist discussion lists, Web sites) in order to find out which tools are available (see the section on further information at the end of this chapter).

Retrieval

Creating electronic texts is one thing—retrieving them is quite another. Until recently, the majority of electronic texts were probably created solely for the purposes of a particular research project; the sharing of the *results* was more important than the sharing of the electronic *texts* themselves. Although this situation has begun to change, this in turn brings a whole new set of complications. There are no agreed standards on how to store electronic texts, how to classify them, or what 'meta' information should be attached and included (e.g. bibliographic information, or transcription documentation). This makes it all the more difficult to find and reuse any of the growing number of electronic texts being made available.

Finding information online (Internet/WWW)

Many university staff and students around the world have ready access to the Internet, and find it an efficient way to disseminate publications, pre-prints of articles, source files, etc. amongst colleagues in the academic community and beyond. Some of the electronic texts on the Internet are only accessible locally (e.g. within a particular university)—perhaps because of copyright or privacy restrictions—whilst others are made publicly accessible, and may be retrieved by anyone who has a connection to the Internet. As an end-user, it is often impossible to tell if a text has been distributed in breach of local, national, or international restrictions. Indeed, the current situation makes it extremely difficult to verify accurately the provenance of an electronic text, and many users of texts obtained via the Internet seem prepared to place a surprising amount of trust in the integrity of text providers (for example with regard to the authorship, ownership, completeness, and accuracy of texts). In the absence of any strict controls over the provision and dissemination of electronic texts, certain Internet sites (such as the Oxford Text Archive, or the Electronic Text Center at the University of Virginia) have tended to emerge as reliable sources of particular kinds of texts.

A number of tools have been developed to make it easier to search the Internet 'as a whole', and new ones are appearing all the time. The most common—such as Archie, Veronica, JugHead, InfoSeek, Lycos, Yahoo, and Harvest—have tended to appear in tandem with key developments in document and information delivery over the Internet (e.g. ftp, Gopher, WAIS, and now the World Wide Web). The tools work by creating a database of sites and files on the Internet, which is then used to provide file location information in response to users' queries. The latest tools use specially developed programs—automated 'software agents' which go under such exotic names as Knowbots, Spiders, and WebWanderers—to scour sites on the Internet and report back their findings to a central program. The central program then creates a unified database which is used to provide answers to users' enquiries.

There are two obvious limitations to the approach outlined above. First, users must remember that the unified database only represents a 'snapshot' of the files available on the Internet at the time the information was retrieved by the software agent (so there is no guarantee that a particular machine and the files it holds will still be accessible and unchanged). Second, it would be far too time consuming for the searching and cataloguing tools to identify multiple 'hits' automatically on the same information—for example, a text file which has been copied onto several different machines—and/or cases where files may have slightly different names but the same contents (or perhaps worse still, the same name but *different* contents). This situation should change as agreed standards emerge to uniquely identify texts, handle version control, location information, etc. There may also be performance issues to consider; for example, users in the UK will find that if they send a query to a popular search tool in the US during the afternoon (UK time), they are likely to experience very poor response times due to heavy morning use (US time) of the North American network.

Considering the sheer volume of electronic texts and other information available on the Internet, modern search and retrieval tools do a surprisingly good job. As long as users remember that the tools have certain inherent limitations, they offer an excellent way to start searching for an electronic text on the Internet. Some of the tools are very sophisticated and enable users to construct advanced search queries such as using Boolean logic and weighted search terms. For example, see the Open Text Web Index (URL: http://www.opentext.com:8080/). However, they may not be particularly helpful when seeking a very common electronic text (such as a play by Shakespeare), when a large number of 'hits' are likely to be returned as a result of the search; in such cases, it is usually better to try to seek out a reputable electronic text centre or consider purchasing a good electronic edition of the text. In the near future, it may be possible for users to launch their *own* intelligent software agents onto the Internet, which will report back the location of any piece of information which meets certain criteria (e.g. 'Tell me whenever you encounter a text by or about Joseph Conrad')—but there are several practical and technical questions that will need to be resolved before this is likely to become common practice.

Several groups and organizations, reflecting the range of interested parties—Internet developers and users, librarians, publishers, etc.—have been investigating the problems and solutions of finding materials on the Internet. The Center for Electronic Texts in the Humanities (CETH), sponsored by Princeton and Rutgers Universities, working in consultation with academics, publishers, and librarians, has produced some formal guidelines for the documenting and cataloguing of electronic texts. The Online Computer Library Center (OCLC), which is also based in the US, has been attempting to coordinate efforts amongst libraries and institutions of higher education to create, implement, test, and evaluate a searchable database of USMARC-format bibliographic records, complete with electronic location and access information for Internet-accessible materials.

Similarly, volunteers of the Internet Engineering Task Force (IETF), have been investigating ways in which the location and addressing mechanisms used by Web software can be adapted and extended to facilitate the search and retrieval of particular pieces of information accessible via the Web. The Internet changes continually, with sites, hosts, and files all liable to become temporarily or permanently unreachable; they may change names, be deleted, altered, copied, and so on. Electronic files and the information they contain, differ in fundamental ways from (relatively) static and durable physical objects such as particular manuscripts or books, and it is likely to be some time yet before all the search and retrieval implications of storing information in an electronic rather than a print-based medium have been satisfactorily identified and addressed.

Finding information in databases

A great deal of the electronic text currently available is stored in databases, either on CD-ROMs or on the hard discs of machines—which may or may not be publicly accessible over the Internet. Commercial databases of electronic texts, such as Chadwyck-Healey's English Poetry Full Text Database, exhibit the same degree of academic rigour and have the same guarantees of content quality that scholars have come to expect from traditional printed works produced by reputable publishers. Similarly, many of the serious academic electronic text centres are moving their collections into searchable databases—as opposed to the more traditional organized hierarchy of directories, sub-directories, and files. The searching of each of these databases normally requires the use of specific tools, but most of them work on the same basic principles of assisting the user to construct certain types of search query. However, although the principles are the same, users often find it time consuming and frustrating to learn the idiosyncrasies of different tools and interfaces—and usually it is not possible to search across several databases of electronic texts simultaneously (unless, perhaps, they have been created by a single provider).

It is one thing to search a database of texts on the basis of a limited set of known information (e.g. simple bibliographic records about author, title, date of publication, etc.), but quite another to search the *content* of the texts themselves. Amongst information retrieval experts there is regular debate over the best way to represent the content of texts, and this may be influenced by the choice of underlying database technology (for example, relational vs. object-oriented database management systems—an argument which will not be discussed here). However, amongst those who study the texts themselves there is a strong (and perhaps growing) school of thought that texts are representable as an ordered hierarchy of content objects (OHCO) (DeRose *et al.* 1990)—whereby a text consists of a number of containing elements, each of which may contain either content (e.g. text) or certain sub-elements, and this descriptive process can be repeated recursively until the content and structure of the whole text has been captured.

From the point of view of someone defining a database to store a text, it seems quite natural to simply translate the OHCO description of the text into the terms of the database management system. However, this raises practical issues about the 'granularity' of the best size of searchable units of a text. For example, from an informational retrieval standpoint it may make sense to give more weight to search terms that are found in the titles, rather than the body, of a text—but this can only be done if the contents of title and body elements of a text have been identified (using some sort of markup), and stored appropriately in the database. Yet whilst this approach might be appropriate for users who typically wish to retrieve certain texts (or parts of texts) on the basis of titles, it might not be the best approach for users who are interested in different kinds of analysis. For example, in an electronic text of an anthology of poetry, users may want to search for, say, all the rhyming couplets which contain a certain phrase or metrical pattern—which would mean that the database management system would also need to have access to such kinds of information. Similarly, in a very large collection of prose texts, if every single paragraph was stored as a separate database entry (to increase the efficiency of searching at the paragraph level and below), there might be a considerable delay if a user wanted to retrieve several complete works (because the software would need to reconstruct each work by combining the relevant paragraphs).

Although database technology is developing rapidly, there is always likely to be a trade-off between the speed of searching and retrieval, and the smallest identifiable/searchable unit of an electronic text.

Networked electronic versions of library catalogues (OPACs, etc.), are now very familiar to most scholars—but it is important to realize that most of these only enable users to search bibliographic records *about* texts, rather than the contents of the texts themselves. The international library community has yet to agree on a single standard representation of bibliographic information in electronic form, and until they do it will remain a time consuming process to search across multiple library catalogues. For an overview of the library perspective on the relevant emerging standards such as Z39.50 see Dempsey (1994). However, as more texts become available in electronic form, it would seem likely that the functions of libraries and electronic text centres will merge.

The combined Higher Education Funding Councils in the UK have recently agreed to fund the Arts and Humanities Data Service (AHDS), 'to promote effective, low-cost access to the widest range of relevant digital resources by UK researchers and teachers from all Arts and Humanities disciplines' (Burnard and Short 1994). The AHDS, and the growing number of archives and electronic text centres around the world, show the increasing concern to preserve electronic texts for use by other, future scholars. The absence of accepted standards makes this a difficult process, but the rapid growth in the volume of electronic text and other digital materials makes it a necessity. Many of those concerned are now starting to agree on standards for basic text (e.g. using the SGML-based approach suggested by the TEI's *Guidelines*) but it is still not clear how best to preserve non-text elements such as the graphic, audio, and video files which now so often form part of many electronic texts. In addition to the questions of preservation and access, including these other types of content in electronic texts will further complicate the process of providing thorough bibliographic information, making the texts searchable and usable over the Internet, and so on.

Most current commercial CD-ROMs use a proprietary presentation system and set of search tools—which reflects the eagerness of publishers to protect their considerable investment—and this has a number of implications. It is rarely possible to search across several CD-ROMs simultaneously (unless, perhaps, they have come from the same publisher) and many CD-ROM publishers limit the amount of text and other types of content which can be retrieved from their discs and reused in other applications (e.g. such as a word processor); this is in notable contrast to much of the electronic text available on the Internet which, apart from an occasional copyright notice, is often freely reusable in its entirety. The commercial manufacturers' use of proprietary markup systems in the production of their CD-ROMs also tends to restrict the usefulness of any extracted text; for example, users are normally only granted permission to extract limited amounts of ASCII text—without any formatting or structural markup. However, it is possible—perhaps even probable—that this situation will change as standards are agreed and adopted (particularly with regard to the notion of exporting structural markup) in response to users' demands.

Copyright

No discussion of electronic text and text retrieval would be complete without mentioning the problems of copyright. The proliferation of electronic text available over the Internet, and the difficulty of restricting access and/or controlling reuse implies to many people that existing copyright legislation will need to be substantially revised. Many authors and copyright holders welcome greater public access to their materials but still wish to assert their traditional rights, yet it is not clear if (or indeed how) these rights can be enforced in a networked global electronic context. Similarly, it is rarely possible for those who obtain electronic texts via the Internet to establish whether or not a text is under copyright, the identity of the copyright holder, what payment or acknowledgements should be made, and so forth.

In spite of these complex technical and legal problems surrounding the assertion of the rights of copyright holders, there are also many potential benefits to be gained. For example, providing text as online electronic files opens up numerous possibilities for publishers to charge users according to new models, e.g. pay-per-view, payment per page, or number of words, etc. Authors and publishers are no longer constrained by the delays and expense of traditional print production—meaning that books could be electronically published chapter by chapter, texts could update themselves with the latest factual information (e.g. taken from elsewhere on the Internet). Depending on one's opinion of the purpose and merits of existing copyright legislation, it is conceivable that new forms of control and reward may be available to the copyright holders of electronic texts, and that these may more than compensate for the loss of traditional benefits. However, until the situation is resolved, users should treat the copyrights relating to electronic texts with at least the same amount of consideration and respect that they accord to conventional printed sources.

Future trends

The next few years are likely to see five key developments in the area of electronic text:

- *More and more texts will become available in electronic form.* In the short-term the majority of commercial electronic texts will be delivered via CD-ROM, but the long-term trend will be for them to be delivered online over a network (probably the Internet or a derivative). Also, the volume of non-commercial electronic texts will continue to grow dramatically, particularly on the Internet.

- *Proprietary solutions will gradually be replaced by standards-based approaches.* It is possible that different sectors of electronic publishing, and/or different types of electronic texts will conform to different *de jure* and *de facto* standards. For example, commercial electronic publishers, libraries, and electronic text centres may adopt SGML-based approaches, whilst individuals and small groups doing self-publishing on the Internet may favour something like Hypertext Markup Language (HTML) with the proprietary extensions developed by Netscape.

- *The growth of standards-based texts will be matched by a growth in the number of related tools for searching, retrieving, and analysing such texts.* In the short-term users may need to know what standards have been used to create an electronic text (for example, to tell a text analysis package that a text includes markup conforming to a TEI-based Document Type Definition (DTD)), but this requirement will disappear as tools become more aware of the available standards.

- *Tools for processing electronic texts will continue to become easier to use, and simultaneously more powerful.* As computer and software interfaces become more sophisticated, they will be better able to interpret requests and give the user what s/he requires.

- *New electronic texts will include more multimedia content.* As well as scanning-in existing printed sources, publishers (both private individuals and commercial concerns) will increasingly provide access to facsimile page-images where this is felt to be appropriate. Commercial electronic texts will include more images, audio, and video content. Both of these developments are likely to increase the demand for new types of searching tools and techniques to retrieve information stored in different kinds of media.

It is perhaps all too easy to imagine that electronic texts offer a panacea for many of the problems of conventional texts; and whilst this may indeed be true in many crucial respects, this remedy does not come without a price. Creating a good, well marked up electronic edition of a text may take just as long as producing a good non-electronic edition of the same work—not least because it is arguably much easier to spot the *flaws* in an electronic text (with the aid of appropriate tools, such as a simple spell-check program) than it is to identify the same errors in a conventional work (via proof-reading). The essential difference is that users of an electronic edition expect it to be quickly corrected, whilst they are prepared to accept that a non-electronic edition will remain erroneous until a subsequent revised printing.[6] Copies of the flawed paper edition may sit on bookshelves around the world for many years, but the providers of electronic texts are increasingly being expected to provide corrected editions as soon as they can (perhaps in the form of updated files of electronic text which can be downloaded from an Internet site).

Yet with good cataloguing and/or full-text indexing of electronic texts, scholars can identify, search, and retrieve texts far quicker than they could ever have done by conventional, non-electronic means. Moreover, once a text has been obtained it can be processed using computer-assisted techniques to establish in seconds results which might have taken months of work by traditional methods. In other words, all the time invested in the creation (and updating) of an electronic text can almost certainly be recouped many times over once it is made available for study—provided that sufficient thought and care have been given to its production and intended purpose.

Notes

1. This statement is left intentionally ambiguous as its interpretation depends upon the reader's perception of who is the master in the human-machine relationship!

2. For example, in this short paragraph there are 379 characters—so an accuracy rate of 99 per cent would suggest that there might be three characters requiring identification and correction.

3. Absolute fidelity to the original source should be the aim of any keying exercise, which is why some of the specialist keying bureaux make a point of using non-native speakers to process certain texts.

4. The best known of these is probably Adobe's Portable Document Format (PDF), which is supported by the Acrobat suite of products.

5. For a gentle introduction, see Burnard (1995). For a more comprehensive picture of SGML, consult Herwijnen (1990) or Travis and Waldt (1995). But for the final word on SGML, see Goldfarb (1990).

6. The adoption of electronic text is encouraging people to think of it as something that is (or should be) regularly maintained and updated—in the same way as computer software—whereas similar demands are not made of the publishers of 'static', conventional printed texts.

References and bibliography

Burnard, L., 'What is SGML and how does it help?', *Computers and the Humanities*, 29.1 (1995), 41-50.

Burnard, L., and Short, H., *An Arts And Humanities Data Service: report of a feasibility study commissioned by the Information Services Sub-committee of the Joint Information Systems Committee of the Higher Education Funding Councils* (Oxford: Office for Humanities Communication, October, 1994).

Butler, Christopher S. (ed.), *Computers and written texts*, (Oxford: Basil Blackwell Ltd., 1992).

Dempsey, L., 'Network resource discovery: a European library perspective', in Smith, N. (ed.), *Libraries, networks and Europe: a European networking study*, (London: British Library Research & Development Department, 1994).

DeRose, S. J., Durand, D. G., Mylonas, E., and Renear, A. H., 'What is text, really?' *Journal of Computing in Higher Education*, 1.2 (1990), 3-26.

Flynn, P., *The World Wide Web handbook*, (London: International Thomson Computer Press, 1995).

Goldfarb, C.F., *The SGML handbook*, (Oxford: Oxford University Press, 1990).

Herwijnen, E. van, *Practical SGML*, (Dordrecht: Kluwer Academic Publishers, 1990).

Robinson, P., *The digitization of primary textual sources* (Oxford: Office for Humanities Communication Publications, 1993).

Sperberg-McQueen, C.M., 'The design of the TEI Encoding Scheme', *Computers and the Humanities*, 29.1 (1995), 17-39.

Sperberg-McQueen, C.M., and Burnard, L. (eds.), *Guidelines for electronic text encoding and interchange* (Chicago and Oxford: April 8, 1994).

Travis, B., and Waldt, D., *The SGML implementation guide* (Berlin: Springer-Verlag, 1995).

Further information

The fields of electronic text, text analysis, and text retrieval are developing rapidly and continuously. Many journals in the humanities now include information about the use of computers for processing texts in specific disciplines. For general information, readers should consult a journal such as *Computers and the Humanities* (published by Kluwer Academic Publishers). For information specifically about using computers in text analysis, see *Literary & Linguistic Computing* (the Journal of the Association for Literary and Linguistic Computing, published by Oxford University Press). For information about the Text Encoding Initiative, readers should contact:

(In Europe) Lou Burnard, Oxford University Computing Services, 13 Banbury Road, Oxford OX2 6NN, UK.

(In East Asia) Prof. Syun Tutiya, Department of Philosophy, Chiba University, 1-33 Yayoi-cho Inage-ku, Chiba 263, Japan.

(In US/Rest of World) C.M. Sperberg-McQueen, University of Illinois at Chicago, Academic Computing Centre (M/C 135), 1940 W. Taylor, Rm. 124, Chicago IL 60612-7352, USA.

The TEI also runs an electronic discussion list; to join send an email message containing the text 'JOIN TEI-L Firstname Lastname' to: LISTSERV@UICVM.UIC.EDU

For general information about SGML and national user groups, contact the International SGML User's Group, c/o Database Publishing Systems Ltd. 608 Delta Business Park, Great Western Way, Swindon, Wiltshire SN5 7XF, UK. There is also an excellent SGML Web page maintained by Robin Cover at URL: http://www.sil.org/sgml/sgml.html

There are several good sources of online information about electronic texts and tools. A good place to start looking for texts is via the Humanities Bulletin Board (HUMBUL) at the URL:
http://www.ox.ac.uk/departments/humanities/international.html

For information about tools, readers should consult the online version of the Computers in Teaching Initiative (CTI) Centre for Textual Studies at the URL:
http://www.ox.ac.uk/ctitext/resguide/index.html

To join a general discussion about the use and implications of computers in Humanities research, readers should subscribe to the HUMANIST discussion list by sending an email message containing the text 'JOIN HUMANIST Firstname Lastname' to: LISTPROC@LISTS.PRINCETON.EDU

Databases in the Humanities

Jonathan Moffett

Corporate and humanities databases

'So what exactly is a database system?' This is a question asked by C.J. Date in his *An Introduction to Database Systems (Third Edition)*. His answer: 'basically, it is nothing more than a computer-based record-keeping system: that is, a system whose overall purpose is to record and maintain information' (Date 1983, 3). The examples he uses in the rest of the volume are taken from the corporate world of business and administration. James Martin, in his *Principles of Database Management*, begins by looking back at a time before the advent of computer databases: 'In those days data processing was done by a clerk with a quill pen who was perched on a high stool and perhaps wearing a top hat. In front of him he had a set of thick and well-bound ledgers' (Martin 1976, 2). Again, Martin then proceeds to describe databases where accounts and stock-control are the primary functions.

Although both of these volumes are over ten years old, it is generally the case that most database textbooks cover much of the same ground. This is unfortunate because humanities databases are generally unlike the corporate databases described in such volumes. Commercial databases primarily administer and manage; they are designed to operate throughout a single organization, centralizing common datasets, pooling resources, and generally making the operation of the enterprise more efficient. These databases are there to answer many different types of question, storing a wide range of data, while ensuring that common data in the database only needs to be updated once. The overriding concern is one of cost-benefit to the organization; the database system must help to provide a competitive advantage over rival companies. Date lists seven characteristics of such a database system: redundancy is reduced, inconsistency is avoided, data are shared, standards are enforced, security restrictions are applied, integrity is maintained, and conflicting requirements are balanced.

To take one of these concepts; a database system has the role of reducing the amount of redundant information. This came about because some types of data are common to a variety of tasks performed in various departments in an enterprise. An obvious example would be names and addresses. When departments retained their own records, any change in such information would need to be made several times, once in each set of records. However, in a database it is possible to store such information 'centrally' so that any changes that need to be made to this core data are only made once. The changes would then be reflected automatically in the records of other departments.

In contrast, although administration and management are a factor, humanities databases generally fall into two categories: research or resource. Research databases answer very specific questions and so tend to be very limited in scope and accessibility. Resource databases provide a service for humanities researchers, particularly access to information which often encompasses a very limited range of data. Thus a research database, for instance the Ingres database used by the British Academy funded Lexicon of Greek Personal Names (LGPN), has the primary function of producing files of sorted and formatted information which can be used to produce camera ready copy for publication. On the other hand, a resource database such as a bibliographic database as found in most libraries, has a limited range, although potentially large number, of fields, the vast majority of which will be required by all the users of such a database. Since references may be books, papers, monographs, offprints, or a host of other forms, the information is still of use to the researcher whatever its format. It is the content of the data that determines which fields are used, rather than the user.

Although it would be hard to question the efficacy of the seven characteristics when applied to humanities research and resource databases, the priorities are different. Thus the issues which are important in the development and use of a humanities database are likely to differ from those of a commercial database. Cost-benefit is not a priority and this paper seeks to highlight some of the issues that are of importance for databases in the humanities. The aim is to enlighten the reader, giving an overview of the questions that may need to be addressed and the answers that may be found, rather than attempting a detailed technical introduction which is better suited to a textbook.

Concepts and *caveats*

Before venturing further into this subject, it is necessary to establish some basic concepts and highlight a number of *caveats* which should be taken into account when using databases. The term 'database' is a much abused word and is often used as shorthand for referring to the whole variety of tasks encompassed by the phrase 'database management system'. A formal definition of a database is as follows (after Martin):

> A collection of interrelated data stored together with a controlled redundancy to serve one or more applications in an optimal fashion; the data are stored so that they are independent of the programs which use the data; a common and controlled approach is used in adding new data and modifying and retrieving existing data within the database.

A more succinct definition that is more relevant to the humanities is:

> A database is an organized collection of useful and related facts and figures, stored in such a way as to make that data easily and efficiently retrievable and updatable.

A database management system (DBMS) is the software used to handle the database. This can be something as complex as packages like IDMS or Ingres, where the software is a set of building blocks that need to be carefully designed and put together, or something as simple as dBase III+, which lacks the sophistication of the larger packages, but has immediate functionality. In this chapter the phrase 'database system' will be used to encompass both the database and the DBMS.

There are eight keywords in the shorter definition which deserve further elaboration: *stored*, *useful*, *organized*, *related*, *retrieved*, *updatable*, *easily*, and *efficiently* (see Table 1 for a summary).

A database comprises *useful*, *stored* data. This implies that a database should not store data that will not be used. However, there is a reverse implication. If the required data are not in the database they cannot be used. As a consequence it is possible to suggest that if there is any doubt about whether to include or exclude some facts or figures then they should be included. It is easier to discard irrelevant data than it is to have to go back and enter a completely new set of information. With most humanities research, even if some significant fact or figure has been

Table 1: A humanities database is ... Therefore ...

A database is:	Therefore:
stored and useful data	do not store data that will not be used, but if in doubt include them
data that are organized and related	know the data and know the question, but be prepared to change both
data that are retrievable and updatable	make sure the data are not lost in a black hole
more efficient and makes work easier than a manual system	is it really better than a manual system?
only as good as the data it contains	the answers will only be as good as the data from which they are derived

missed, there *may* be an opportunity to go back and acquire it, but it will always be at an extra cost.

A database comprises data that are *organized* and *related*; it is not a jumbled mass of information. The design of a database requires much forethought about what is wanted from the data before they are used. Although the purpose may be known, there is a good chance that the initial vision was limited. Consequently, any project should anticipate modifying a database structure more than once as the research progresses. A greater understanding of the data involved in the research will inevitably lead to things becoming clearer or new facets being revealed, and, the more a database system is used, the more other possible functions will present themselves. This applies to both research and resource databases. With the British Academy funded Prosopography of the Byzantine Empire it was discovered that, '... the enquiries made possible by the database have surprised even its creators' (BLR&DD 1993, 10). It became possible to answer questions regarding documented people of the Byzantine Empire which had been impossible to ask previously, or, at the very least, so time consuming that they were to all intents and purposes unanswerable.

A database comprises data that can be *retrieved* and *modified*, and it would be a waste of resources if the information it contains cannot be changed when found to be wrong, or more significantly, cannot be extracted. There is a tendency for database textbooks to concentrate on the internal design of a database system rather than what can be called the 'front-end' or 'user interface'. However, this aspect is as important and leads on to the two final keywords, *easily* and *efficiently*. If a computer database is more difficult to handle than a manual system, then the use of a computer as a tool for that project should be re-evaluated. The computer is a tool to deal with the inadequacies of the human mind, notably in speed and retention of detail. A database is a tool for coping with the inadequacies of a computer system, allowing it to extract information effectively from the data it retains. If the human mind with pen, paper, and filing cabinet are more efficient than both of these then there is no place for a database system.

A final *caveat* in the context of databases, and one which is generally ignored in textbooks, is that a database is only as good as the data it contains. If the data are not of a good quality, for instance poorly recorded context information from an archaeological site, then the conclusions that can be drawn from using those data will be poor as well, no matter how sophisticated the retrieval mechanism. Also, if data are changing or being re-interpreted over a period of time, and if the database is not kept up-to-date, the conclusions drawn from it will also be poor. Such a warning applies to resource databases too; a bibliographic database is only as good as the number of references it contains.

The database life-cycle

The issues that are of relevance to the humanities can be grouped into five separate ages in the lifetime of a database (Figure 1):

- Conception—determining a database system's *raison d'être*.
- Birth—selecting fields, organizing, and structuring a database system.
- Formative phase—implementing and testing a database system.
- Working life—using and monitoring the effectiveness of a database system.

- Retirement—the long-term issue of eventual replacement or shelving of a database system.

Figure 1: A database system life-cycle

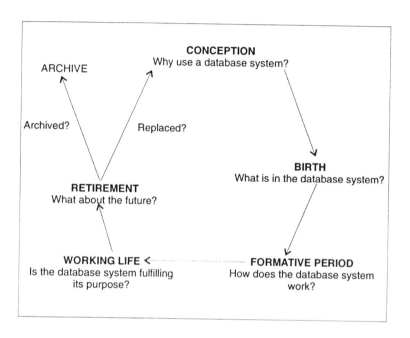

An important fact to recognize is that once a database project has begun there is generally no going back, especially if it is to be a resource database. To parody a television information service announcement, 'a database is for life', especially if manual records are no longer maintained. Of course, it is possible to abandon a database project and return to non-computer based records, but the transition may be more painful than the initial conversion from a manual system.

Conception

For a database project to succeed it must have a well-defined purpose, or a specific set of questions to be answered. Projects which fail are generally those where this was not the case. For instance, the LGPN has the basic task of collecting and publishing all known Greek personal names from earliest historical times to the mid-seventh century AD (prior to the Islamic conquest). Material is gathered from literary sources, inscriptions, papyri, coins, vases, lead pipes, and other artefacts. The published volumes have a specific format and order, and the database is used as an intermediary, allowing the data to be collated and organized and eventually extracted in a form suitable for eventual publication (Moffett n.d.). The role of the database system can be stated simply: to accept data in one format, sort them, and then reproduce them in a different format.

The Beazley Archive, based in the Ashmolean Museum, also has a well-defined database project. The purpose of the Archive is to create a resource based on figure-decorated Greek vases made in the Athens region between the sixth and fourth centuries BC. It is a resource which is used by scholars as diverse as classical archaeologists, social historians, dramatists, linguists, and economists. The Archive comprises notes, drawings, and photographs, and the database is used to assemble the material relating to each vase and make it accessible to researchers (Moffett 1992). Again, the role of the database system is to accept data in a specific format and to make them accessible to researchers in another format, so that retrieval is more efficient and easier than a manual search. The availability of the database across the Internet makes this especially true for scholars who are based in countries outside the UK.

On the other hand, a project which is too general, for instance documenting a museum's collections, is very likely to fail. Indeed, when the scope and extent of such a database project is large the available financial and human resources need to be assessed. One of the reasons for the Ashmolean Museum's Department of Antiquities' ARIADNE (Ashmolean Retrieval Index and Data Network) project failing was that, '... neither the Museum nor OUCS (Oxford University Computing Services) had the resources to ensure that it could be completed' (Moffett 1994, 163).

The ARIADNE project was intended to form a knowledge base, so that information was available about objects not only in terms of form, function, and provenance, but also who attributed that form, function, or provenance, and why. This information did not exist in any coherent form but had to be compiled prior to entry into the database. Also, the task of data entry was given to one part-time research assistant; consequently the project never got beyond the formative phase.

Projects should be limited to the available resources, but an important factor in the development of humanities databases is who actually develops them. There are generally two alternatives: the first is to produce a system 'in-house'; the second is to use consultants, but here there is always the possibility that they will abandon the project. As Mary Beal records, when describing the development of the British Government Art Collection's computer system, '... while the consultancy doubtless had its own good reasons for withdrawing its support, the news was about as welcome as a head crash' (Beal 1989, 150). Furthermore, employing outsiders is always a hazard as there are likely to be communication problems. Is knowledge of the raw material more important than a knowledge of the technology? Misunderstanding is an easily identifiable problem, but failure can also result from over-enthusiasm. With the Department of Antiquities' ARIADNE project, despite many meetings between the Museum curators and the computing professionals, the practical help a database could provide to the functioning of the department seemed to be lost in discussing the sophisticated potentials the computer could offer. Knowledge was placed on a pedestal so that the focus moved away from the actual problems of the data that formed the basis of that knowledge. This is not an attempt to allocate blame, but solely to highlight a lesson that has been learnt, and with the ever growing sophistication of IT, it is an even more relevant lesson today.

Finally, it should be noted that there is always one alternative open at this stage of the life-cycle, and that is not to use a database system at all. A database system may be inappropriate for the project, or even beyond the available resources. If a manual system is demonstrably better, then it should be the preferred option.

Birth

Once the question(s) to be addressed is(are) known, along with an evaluation of available resources, the database can be born. There are four aspects which need to be considered: what attributes need to be recorded to answer the question; what database structure will relate them together in an efficient way; how will the data be captured; and which software should be used.

By asking the question—how many gold artefacts does a museum collection have from a particular geographical region?—it becomes clear that it is necessary to know what type of objects the museum has, what they are made of, and where they come from. The process of selecting attributes is one of honing such questions until there is sufficient detail to move on and decide what sort of database structure will produce the desired answers.

A crucial element in the design process is to determine exactly what the users of the database want. In the case of a research database this will probably be easy to determine because the number of users will be few, but a resource database requires careful attention to such detail. Unfortunately, users do not necessarily know what they want and may even change their minds several times during the design process. Flexibility is the key. Michael has pointed out that, '... if the person creating the database has not produced a hand drawn exemplar from which to work, building charts from the database may prove frustrating and the exercise almost useless' (Michael 1989, 205).

The subjects of attribute selection, and database and user interface design could easily encompass papers of their own. Rather than detailing them here, it is suggested that reference be made to database textbooks such as Korth and Silberschatz (1991) and Beynon-Davies (1991), or papers such as Burnard (1987) and Hubbard (1981), which discuss the principles of database design in more detail. This chapter will look at two issues that are as important but are less frequently covered.

Data entry considerations

The first issue relates to the question of how the data are to be captured. Are the data to be compiled as they are fed into the computer, or will the details be entered from already existing material? Are the data to be put into data files to be reformatted and then loaded into a database, or is data capture to feed the database directly?

For instance, with the Beazley Archive, the information to be fed into the database is initially written on to record cards, as original source material is examined for new vase publications. This information is then fed directly into the database via specially written data-entry screens. This may seem time consuming, but the keyboard work is carried out by students, while data compilation is done by specialists. With the LGPN, the raw data were originally typed from record cards into computer-stored data files. As each volume is prepared these data files are edited on the computer using a text-editor and then specially written data file conversion programs are used to reformat the data into a form which can be loaded into the database. In the case of the Ashmolean Museum's Department of Western Art, data are compiled as the database is being fed with the information. A hard and fast rule is that the more compilation required, the longer it will take to add a single entry.

Choice of software
Although data and software are supposed to be independent this position is rarely achieved in the real world of database applications. However, no matter what the choice of database system, whether the package be off-the-shelf or a do-it-yourself system, even commercially available packages need some work to make them function as desired. The paramount factor in any choice should be how the original questions are to be answered, but cost is almost as important. This is particularly the case in the museum world, where collections documentation and management systems are available. However, they are almost without exception very expensive to purchase and costly to maintain. Furthermore, they tend to be proprietary; museum staff are constrained in the changes they can make, and fundamental changes may well have to be carried out by the software suppliers.

By contrast, such is the simplicity of setting up personal computer-based databases, together with their low cost, the power to tailor a database system to individual needs is becoming ever greater. Oxford University's Department of the History of Art chose Business Simulations' Cardbox Plus as the most appropriate for their library cataloguing system, for the reason that it was a cheap and flexible package which met their requirements. The Ashmolean Museum's Department of Eastern Art, having used dBase III+ for a number of years, also converted its databases to Cardbox. The searching abilities combined with the simplicity of the concept of a card proved an overriding attraction. The Ashmolean's Department of Western Art rejected the use of Vernon Systems' collection management system, Collection, because it was too sophisticated for their needs, as well as too expensive. An in-house system has been developed instead.

The formative phase

This phase involves putting into practice the decisions already made. It involves implementing the database structure, developing the user interface and testing both to determine whether they meet the requirements. Original designs will probably need fine-tuning and it will undoubtedly be the case that users will change their minds about the 'look and feel' of a system. Again, these are issues which are easily anticipated. However, others are not always considered.

More data entry considerations
During the implementation and testing phase it will become apparent how much time it will take to enter the necessary data into a database. Mary Beal has pointed out that, '... data input is a long, tiring, and very time consuming process, which depends entirely on the dedication of each member of staff to this end' (Beal 1989, 146). In the case of the British Government Art Collection, she recorded that 12,000 records had been entered in nearly seven years. With the Beazley Archive there are anticipated to be around 200,000 records, of which only about a quarter have been entered in some ten years. It may be possible to speed up the data entry process; for instance, it may become apparent that the software originally chosen is too slow. Ian Morrison (1989) reported that in the Moray District, Scotland, experiments comparing the entry rate between the Museum Documentation Association's MODES system and a dBase III+ database, found that the former took twice as long as the latter to enter a single record. Even with a simple index such as that of the Witt Library, John Sunderland pointed out that compiling an index of just five basic items of information (name, title, medium, size, and location), '... in terms of the 1.5 million illustrations in the Witt this would still have meant, even with a staff of, say, ten, a timescale to completion of about twenty years or more' (Sunderland 1989, 131). As he states later, '... it takes time to create a large database and especially if the archive or collection has its information in a form which needs considerable change in order to be entered into a computer' (*ibid.* 131).

That a database is going to take so long to create may warrant a rethink. With developing technology, timescale is an important issue if the database is to include an image base. This is not something to be undertaken lightly. If a 10 by 8 inch colour photograph takes four minutes to scan at a high resolution, three minutes to enhance or edit on screen, and another three minutes to store on a disc in a compressed form, then six photographs can be captured in an hour, 25 to 30 in a day, up to 150 in a week. In a year, it is possible for around 8,000 scanned images to be captured by a computer system. This assumes that the equipment and the personnel function correctly and without a break throughout that year. This is a very optimistic estimate.

Another factor has been pointed out by Mary Beal: '... since all records cannot be computerized overnight, we still have to keep up-to-date tedious and cumbersome manual records for all those items which have not been computerized' (Beal 1989, 146). For a resource database a manual system will have to be maintained, a problem well known to libraries. Creating a computer-based catalogue of hundreds of thousands of books is 'long, tiring, and very time consuming'. In the case of libraries it is possible for data to be shared, as many publications are held in common. This is not necessarily the case with archaeological, art historical, or historical museums where individual objects, although similar, will have different contexts and significance.

Documentation and training
Another important aspect of the formative phase is the writing of documentation to go with the system. This extends beyond documenting the database structure and a statement of purpose. User guides need to be written, and they are all too easy to overlook. Furthermore, they need to be written by the users of the database rather than the developers. The author of such documentation needs to be one step away from the design of the system. Even so, development and documentation must go hand-in-hand, as Beal comments: '... thinking that there will be time to "pick up" documentation in retrospect is almost cloud-cuckoo land' (Beal 1989, 150).

Training of users is a related factor which needs to be taken into account. Although the general level of understanding of how a computer works has grown over the years, the increasing complexity of some systems can still baffle many serious users. There will always be a period of hand-holding as a new database system is introduced and this must be anticipated from the start.

The working life of a database

The working life of a database falls neatly into three areas. The first is the constant addition of new information and correction of errors; the second is providing the answers to the original questions; the third is the possibility that new questions will arise as more information is added.

Changes of direction
There is often a hidden assumption in database textbooks that once a database has been designed, implemented, tested, and accepted as up-and-running the project is completed. To suggest that the range of data types and characteristics are fully known from the initial phases of a

database project is to overlook the developing nature of our understanding and advances in technology. As Lutz Heusinger has noted, '... to date no databank or retrieval system is known to this author that can cope with the complexity of art historical data' (Heusinger 1989, 17). This is likely to be true throughout the humanities.

For instance, the Beazley Archive has undergone a change in direction recently. As a photographic archive, it has always been obvious that pictures are worth at least a thousand words, but because database systems have not been able to cope with the former, long text descriptions have had to suffice. However, in recent years, technology has changed, images within databases are a feasible proposition, and once the decision was made that images were to be included a whole new set of questions had to be asked, taking the project almost back to the beginning of the development cycle. The old database system needed to be replaced.

The Department of Western Art is currently re-evaluating its current database needs. The existing database system was set up in such a way that data entry was given priority; retrieval did not need to be very fast, although it was certainly required. However, with the growing quantities of information stored, some 12,000 records, the need for speedy retrieval is becoming increasingly important, and a new system will be needed to reflect the different emphasis.

Accessibility, security, and currency
During the working life of a database system another important issue is likely to be access to the information, which must be weighed against security, particularly protection from hardware failure. However, with the growth in computer networks, the possibility of databases being corrupted, maliciously or even accidentally, is increasing (although this must not be exaggerated). There are ways and means of protecting information from unauthorized access, but no system will ever be completely 'hacker-proof'. The safest form of protection is not to be online, which negates the idea of accessibility. Alternatively, multiple copies of the entire database system, stored in different locations is a more practical solution.

This raises a final issue, which also extends to resource databases published in computer-readable form, namely, keeping track of which is the most up-to-date version of a database system. It is a similar problem to traditional paper publication where different editions mark the progress of knowledge and correction of mistakes. The LGPN has so far published two of the planned six volumes, and already it would be possible to publish addenda to the first volume. If the LGPN were published in CD-ROM form it is conceivable that a second edition of Volume One could be produced relatively quickly. However, the frequency and quantity of changes would have to be assessed. Angela Blackburn, in discussing the dissemination of scholarly knowledge, has pointed out that with a '... number of alternative versions of [a] database, it may not be easy to tell which is the "canonical" version, on which we should rely' (Blackburn 1991, 152). If multiple copies of a database system exist, then changes should only be made to a master version and then copied. The Beazley Archive plans to have two internationally accessible copies of its database, each using different software, but a third will be retained as the updatable version, separate from the others. The online versions will then be updated periodically.

Retirement

Research databases are generally only used over the time of the project; little thought is given to what happens to the database once the project is complete, although with very long-term projects this is not surprising. The choice is to send it to an archive (the equivalent of a database museum, or sometimes graveyard) or to create a resource database. The latter involves the cost of maintenance and probable upgrading. Although the LGPN project has some way to go before all the volumes are published, the time will come when a decision is needed as to whether the database is 'packed up' and stored away, or whether it continues as an accessible resource, either online over the Internet or published as a CD-ROM.

With resource databases, retirement comes when the existing hardware fails or the software becomes so obsolete that it no longer meets the needs it is meant to fulfil. At this point the question of moving the database system becomes important. However, this is not always an easy matter.

First, the technology is likely to have advanced considerably and the software available may no longer be compatible with the original system. Although the data contained in a database are by far the most important element of a database system, the interface used to get to the data is also significant, but is less likely to be directly transferable. Both the LGPN and the Beazley Archive have gone through this process. A change from the networking database IDMS to the relational database Ingres meant a complete redesign of database structure and a complete rewriting of the interfaces for getting data into and out of the database. These tasks take time and it is essential to have two systems running in parallel for a while to ensure that the new system can deliver at least the same answers as the original.

However, such is the nature of progress, that any new system is likely to provide more facilities, so it may be appropriate to start the whole database life-cycle again. May Katzen once wrote, '... above all, the switch from traditional to technologically based methods of creating, retrieving, organizing, and analysing information not only entails the additional costs of hardware and software, but always involves the looming threat of technological obsolescence—the inevitable consequence of rapid technological development and change' (Katzen 1991, xi). Switching from one database system to another also carries additional costs and the threat of obsolescence. The death of one database system may result in the birth of another, but the process may be painful.

With the Beazley Archive, the advances in technology which have brought about the capability of image handling have meant that a further development is taking place. This requires completely new interfaces, as well as the creation of an image base that runs along side the original database. Fortunately, the Archive has been able to take part in the European Commission (EC) funded project Remote Access to Museum Archives (RAMA), and this has helped to alleviate the cost, in terms of both financial and human resources. However, collaboration has pitfalls of its own, not least the hidden agendas of every institution and what they expect to get out of such ventures.

Conclusion

Table 2 summarizes the questions to be asked during the lifetime of a database system. It is by no means a comprehensive list, but these are issues which are often ignored or passed over until it is too late. It is in the hope that others will be spared such grief that these questions are documented.

Finally, to some extent the era of the database is passing. The traditional database as a species may soon be extinct and will have evolved into something even more powerful. In recent years IT has developed dramatically. There has been a slow but steady convergence of applications packages, such that not only are word processors taking on more of the attributes of desktop publishing, but also spreadsheets are acquiring traditional database capabilities, and text retrieval and document

Table 2: Some questions to be asked during a database life-cycle

Conception	Why use a database system? What is the purpose of the database? What are the available financial and human resources? Who designs and implements the system? Is a manual system more appropriate?
Birth	What attributes should be used? How do they relate to each other? What is involved in capturing the data? Are data to be compiled from original material? Are data to be fed directly into a database or some intermediary form? What software package should be used? Does it meet the requirements? Is it too expensive?
Formative phase	Does the structure function as required? Does the interface function as required? What are the anticipated costs of data entry? Has suitable documentation been written? Is there a training plan?
Working life	Have any new questions arisen as a result of using the database system? Are there suitable backing-up procedures to make copies of the database system? Is there protection against accidental or malicious damage? Are there multiple copies of a database system? Are changes only made to one version?
Retirement	Has the database system accomplished its task? Has the hardware failed or become obsolete? Is it to be archived or to become/continue as a resource system? Is it necessary to restart the life-cycle from the beginning?

management systems are becoming more alike. Existing database software is encroaching on the abilities of other packages such as text retrieval systems, while advances in hardware make it possible to incorporate new types of data, namely images and sound, within a database system. Given the greater intercommunication between these packages encouraged by such environments as Windows, the database will be seen as just one part of a more flexible and powerful 'information-base'. Nonetheless, the issues addressed in this paper will undoubtedly remain valid as considerations when developing these 'info-bases', perhaps even more so.

References and bibliography

Beal, M., 'The British Government Art Collection computer system: the user's view', in Hamber, A., Miles, J., and Vaughan, W. (eds.), *Computers and the history of art* (London: Mansell, 1989), 144-53.

Beynon-Davies, P., *Relational database systems: a pragmatic approach* (Oxford: Blackwell Scientific Publications, 1991).

Blackburn, A., 'The dissemination of scholarly knowledge', in Katzen, M. (ed.), *Scholarship and technology in the humanities* (London: Bowker Saur, 1991), 147-56.

(BLR&DD) British Library Research & Development Department, *Information technology in humanities scholarship: British achievements, prospects and barriers*, BLR&D Report 6097 (London: The British Library and The British Academy, 1993).

Burnard, L., 'Principles of database design', in Rahtz, S. (ed.), *Information technology in the humanities* (Chichester: Ellis Horwood, 1987), 54-68.

Date, C.J., An introduction to database systems, third edition (London: Addison-Wesley, 1983).

Heusinger, L., 'Computers in the history of art', in Hamber, A., Miles, J., and Vaughan, W. (eds.), *Computers and the history of art* (London: Mansell, 1989), 1-22.

Hubbard, G.U., *Computer-assisted data base design* (New York: Van Nostrand Reinhold, 1981).

Katzen, M., 'Introduction', in Katzen, M. (ed.), *Scholarship and technology in the humanities* (London: Bowker Saur, 1991), ix-xii.

Korth, H. F., and Silberschatz, A., *Database system concepts, second edition* (New York: McGraw Hill, 1991).

Martin, J., *Principles of database management* (Englewood Cliffs, New Jersey: Prentice-Hall Inc., 1976).

Michael, M., 'Computers and manuscript illumination', in Hamber, A., Miles, J., and Vaughan, W. (eds.), *Computers and the history of art* (London: Mansell, 1989), 200-6.

Moffett, J., 'The Lexicon of Greek Personal Names: a case of data metamorphosis', (unpublished report on this British Academy project (n.d.)).

Moffett, J., 'The Beazley Archive: making a humanities database accessible to the world', *Bulletin of the John Rylands Library*, 74.3 (1992), 39-52.

Moffett, J., 'Archaeological information and computers: changing needs, changing technology and changing priorities in a museum environment', *Archaeologia e Calcolatori*, 5 (1994), 159-174.

Morrison, I., 'Computer-aided cataloguing in Moray district', in Hamber, A., Miles, J., and Vaughan, W. (eds.), *Computers and the history of art* (London: Mansell, 1989), 164-173.

Sunderland, J., 'The catalogue as database: the indexing of information in visual archives', in Hamber, A., Miles, J., and Vaughan, W. (eds.), *Computers and the history of art* (London: Mansell, 1989), 130-143.

Further information

Lexicon of Greek Personal Names
Mrs Elaine Matthews, Editor, Lexicon of Greek Personal Names, Clarendon Building, University of Oxford, Oxford

Prosopography of the Byzantine Empire
J.R. Martindale, Department of Classics, King's College London, The Strand, London WC2R 2LS

Beazley Archive
Donna Kurtz, Beazley Archivist, Ashmolean Museum, Beaumont Street, Oxford

Remote Access to Museum Archives (RAMA)
Matilda Dijk, Museon, Stadhouderslaan 41, 2517 Hv, The Hague, Netherlands

British Government Art Collection (BGAC)
St Christopher House Annexe, Sumner Street, London SE1 9LA

Image Capture and Analysis

Peter M. W. Robinson

In the last few years, the possibilities of image digitization have captured the imagination of humanities scholars, to the extent that no electronic publication project seems complete unless it plans to include images. This can be seen in the descriptions of the Hartlib, Wittgenstein, *Canterbury Tales*, and Corpus of Romanesque Sculpture projects given elsewhere in this volume. Several factors have combined to provoke this interest. One, of course, has been the advancing power of personal computers, which now brings to the desktop a capacity to make, manipulate, and display digital images previously found (if at all) only in very large and expensive mainframe computers. But more significant than this is the realization that scholars have been very poorly served by traditional print and microfilm images. Particularly in the area of manuscript images, scholars have had to make do with black-and-white microfilms, always inconvenient and awkward to handle, and often not showing just what the scholar wants to see. Where there are better high-quality printed facsimiles, these are expensive and frequently inaccessible. Image digitization offers in the short term a chance to remove the inconvenience of microfilm, and in the medium to long term the possibility of far better images of far more objects.

In theory, digital images are both easier to handle and offer better quality than their traditional equivalents. In terms of ease of handling: the digital format guarantees that computer images will never fade or distort; they will not decay in copying or be damaged in use; they may be located and transmitted in seconds across a network; they may be enlarged or compared with one another with ease on a suitably powerful computer. In terms of quality: where colour photography and processing is prohibitively expensive for many materials, it costs little or no more to make and distribute colour computer images than it does monochrome images. In the last few years, advancing computer power and falling prices have begun to convert these possibilities to actualities. But there is still much to do: to make and view a photograph of a manuscript page you need only a camera, and your local pharmacy. To do the same with a digital image you will need the right software, a computer monitor and the computer, and probably a high-speed network and a digital camera. In traditional photography, there are many different films, many different cameras, many different developing and printing processes. Even at this early stage in computer image capture, there are many different methods of making digital images, with many choices to be made: the desired resolution, level of colour, systems of storage and distribution, etc. This chapter will survey these methods, and aims to offer a starting point to projects considering digitization.

What is image digitization?

A digitized image is a computer representation of an object. This digitized image can be stored, viewed, copied, or otherwise manipulated on the computer. All systems of image digitization work by dividing the image into dots, giving each dot a value, and then storing all the dot values in sequence in the computer. The computer can reconstruct the digital image just by reading all the dot values and displaying them on the screen, with the dots in the same order and with the same value as they had in the original. For example: take a page where the top half is black, the bottom half white. The computer image of this page will divide the page into dots, and all the dots for the top half will have the value 'black' and all those for the bottom half will have the value 'white'.

In image digitization, each dot is called a 'pixel', or picture element. The range of values each dot (or pixel) can have is called the pixel depth, or the image depth. Accordingly, a computer image can be varied in two ways:

- you can increase or decrease the number of dots, or pixels, in the image;
- you can increase or decrease the pixel depth, that is the range of values each pixel can have.

In the simplest kind of digitization, the dot or pixel values are just black or white. This is a binary image: binary, because each pixel may have just two values, either black ('0', for absence of light) or white ('1', for presence of light). These images are sometimes called one-bit images, as only one '0' or '1' (a single bit) is needed for each pixel on the image.

They have a pixel depth of two. Binary images are (by definition) satisfactory when the original object is plain black or white, either printed text or line art. In these cases, a page can indeed be divided into black or white dots and represented in the computer as just that. Thus, the great majority of commercial digital imaging applications record business documents (printed letters, reports) as binary digital images. The Cornell 'brittle books' project has shown that binary images are also suitable for archiving printed books (Kenney and Personius 1992). Binary images may also be satisfactory for distribution of images derived from microfilm, as the *Canterbury Tales* project has found.

Many objects are not just black and white, but contain greys. Even when computers record only black and white, as in binary images, they can create the illusion of grey by grouping black and white pixels into cells (a process called 'dithering') so that the eye thinks it sees one grey and not some black and some white. A better solution is to let the pixels have not just two values but many values. Thus, instead of plain black or white the pixel values could be different levels of grey. For example, each pixel could have four values: in binary arithmetic, pure white ('11'), light grey ('10'), dark grey ('01'), and pure black ('00'). This is a greyscale image. Notice that in this example we need two 0s or 1s, or two bits, for each pixel on the image. This is a four greylevel, two-bit image. It has a pixel depth of four. Because we need two bits for each pixel for a four greylevel image, as opposed to just one bit for each pixel for a binary image, a two-bit image file will be twice the size of its one-bit counterpart.

We can increase the number of greylevels just by increasing the number of bits used for each pixel. Typically, a greyscale image might use up to 8 bits (e.g. '00000000') for each dot. In binary arithmetic, 8 bits is 256, or 2 to the power of eight, and so an eight-bit greylevel image might contain 256 levels of grey. It has a pixel depth of 256. An eight-bit image will be eight times the size of its one-bit counterpart, four times the size of its two-bit counterpart. Studies of human perception suggest that the eye can discriminate around thirty levels of grey. Capturing 256 levels provides sufficient over-sampling to reconstruct 32 discrete greylevels (Willis 1992, 37). Eight-bit greylevel images are suitable for monochrome material containing greys: the Creswell and Tchalenko Archive projects in Oxford have found greylevel images excellent for capture of low-contrast monochrome prints, with widely varying tonal ranges.

Beside greys, the world has colour. Instead of using the extra values for each pixel to represent levels of grey, one could use them to represent colours. Thus as the computer divides the image into pixels it measures the colour of each dot and assigns that colour a value. Again, the number of different colour values available to the computer is determined by the number of bits used for each pixel. Each pixel in an eight-bit colour image, for example, would have one of 256 possible colour values. In fact, for colour images it is increasingly common to use not eight bits for each pixel, and 256 possible colours, but 24 bits for 16.7 million colours (2 to the power of 24, actually 16,777,216). These images have a pixel depth of 16.7 million. In 24-bit images, the colour of each pixel is made up of three eight-bit values: in the common 'RGB' format one value represents the 'redness' of the image on a 256 level scale, another value its 'greenness', another its 'blueness'. In 24-bit images, the computer reconstructs the colour of each pixel by giving it so much red, green, and blue as each of the three eight-bit values specify.

The range of 16.7 million colours given by 24-bit images is quite enough usually to satisfy the human eye, and so 24-bit images are sometimes referred to as 'real colour'. Eight-bit colour images, with only 256 possible colours, can be satisfactory for many uses. However, the palette of the 256 colours must be carefully chosen: the outstanding success of the National Gallery's Micro Gallery CD-ROM shows how a skilfully selected 256 colours may convey the varied rich colours of paintings. In general, however, the more colours the better: 36-bit colour (12 bits per channel) is already standard in some high-quality printing standards, and may well yet emerge as standard for all types of colour digital image capture.

The movement to 24-bit colour, and then to 36-bit colour, reminds us that apparently reasonable decisions about levels of digitization may be rendered absurd by the increasing power of computers. Already, flatbed scanners capable of 1200 dots per inch (dpi) resolution are appearing; already some colour-capture devices work with 48-bit colour. We cannot guess where this march of technology might end, and what finally might be deemed an 'archival' level of digitization. However, there appears general agreement that 300 dpi digitization of printed and handwritten materials, with pixel depths ranging from 2 for black and white materials to 24-bit for colour, gives very usable images. One measure of the quality of these images is to relate them to traditional printed images. For example, a 300 dpi image with 24-bit colour is equivalent to a printed screen ruling of 200 lines per inch: considerably better than magazine quality printing (around 130 lines per inch) or artbook quality (160 lines per inch). By this measure, we already have the means to make images of the highest quality and there is no need to wait for devices which offer yet more dots per inch, yet more colour per dot.

General rules for image capture and analysis

The previous section outlined two rules for digitization: the more dots per inch the better the image; the more colours the better the image. To these we may add two further rules:

- there is no point trying to capture resolution and colours which are not there to be captured;
- there should be as few links as possible in the chain between the original object and the computer image.

On the first point: if one is digitizing a printed book there is no point in making anything other than a binary image. Less obviously, if one is digitizing from a reproduction and not from the original object, there is no point digitizing at higher resolution than is available in the reproduction. This brings us to the second general rule, that one should digitize from the original where possible, or from the best possible reproduction of it. For various reasons (convenience, the unavailability of the original) it is common practice to digitize from some sort of reproduction. This can give perfectly usable results, but projects should be aware of the dangers of this process. For example, while digitization of microfilms can be quite satisfactory for printed materials it can lead to critical loss of information (hairline marks just visible in microfilm of manuscripts may disappear in the digitized image). Also, as discussed in the next section, certain widely-used methods of digitization (video cameras and Kodak's Photo CD) may introduce serious distortions.

In general: for the best results, go from the original material to the digitized image by the shortest route possible, preferably by digital camera, or by other direct digitizing device. Where direct digitization is not possible, inform yourself of all the steps in the chain and of the possible consequences of each step. In particular, be wary of the potential distortions which might be introduced by some methods.

Image capture: how it works; some dangers

The basis of all systems of digitization is a device for measuring light energy at a particular point: a picture element on a 'charge-coupled device' or CCD. In the simplest case, a single picture element on a CCD measures the amount of light reflected from a single point on the original. It then converts the light energy value it receives into an electrical energy value. This electrical energy value may be extracted from the picture element and further converted to a digital value (e.g., either 0 or 1 for binary plain black and white systems, or on a scale of 0 to 255 for eight-bit systems). This digital value is stored in the computer and used to make the image reproduction. By accumulating the readings of many picture elements on a CCD, each measuring the light at part of the object, a reproduction of the whole object is built up. By using different filters (typically, red, green, and blue), one can measure the different colour values at each point and so create a full-colour image of the object.

The most familiar means of digitization is the flatbed scanner. In these, the CCD is arranged as a strip, so measuring the light values of a whole line at a time. First, the original must be placed flush against a glass. A light source then passes over the original, usually as a strip advancing down the original. The reflected light value is then picked up by the CCD. The CCD moves down the original with the light source, so building up the digital image line by line. Flatbed scanners are comparatively inexpensive and are very well integrated into common personal computer systems. One can choose from a wide variety of machines, and have one running with one's own computer with just a few minutes' work. There is much easy-to-use software, allowing ready capture of images and export of the images to other programs, for example graphics, word processing, or OCR (optical character recognition) packages. Flatbed scanners are also capable of very high resolutions, with 600 dpi now quite common, and some may also give 24-bit colour output.

However, there are many problems with the use of flatbed scanners. The object to be scanned must be flat against the glass, exactly as if it were being photocopied. This severely limits the range of primary materials with which flatbed scanners can cope. They cannot cope with any three-dimensional object (sculpture, even coins and seals) and with any manuscript that will not lie flat. Less obviously, the intense light passed over the object may damage delicate pigments. Furthermore, there is no facility to vary the light passed over the object: compare the experience of the VASARI (Visual Arts System for Archiving and

Retrieving of Images) project, where the light is carefully adjusted for each scan. The colour sensitivity of flatbed scanners may also be uneven and poorly calibrated. For these reasons, while flatbed scanners will certainly be adequate for capture of monochrome printed materials they are unlikely to be adequate for capture of coloured materials, and especially manuscripts. However, they are very efficient with dealing with printed materials, or with monochrome photographs.

An important variant of the flatbed scanner is the transparency scanner (for example, those made by Mekel and Sunrise). In essence, these too are 'line scanners', but with the CCD capturing the light value in a projection from a microfilm or similar. These are specialized and expensive devices, capable of exceptional speed: digitization of 20 frames per minute is possible. They are well suited to digitization of large batches of microfilm; indeed they were designed for this, and are being used in several such large projects (for example, the digitization of microfilms of some 40,000 printed volumes for the Bibliothèque de France contracted to Headway Technology of England). For such large runs, the costs may work out very cheaply. However, for smaller runs they are less likely to be economic.

A transparency scanner is also at the heart of Kodak's Photo CD process: in this case, a full-colour scanner. Here, a transparency is made from the film by the standard photographic process, the transparency then scanned, the resulting computer file manipulated into Kodak's Photo CD format and then written to a CD-ROM. This system is extremely convenient; there is a built-in security in having the images in both film and computer form; the provision of the images on CD-ROM solves the problem of storage; it is cheap, at around 50 pence an image. For certain types of material—artistic materials, as paintings, sculpture, etc., especially where there are already existing transparencies—Photo CD gives very usable results. Accordingly, many projects are making use of Photo CD: examples in the UK include the Elise and Corpus of Romanesque Sculpture projects. However, there are inherent problems with the Photo CD technique. Firstly, in its standard format it relies on 35 mm (millimetre) colour transparency film for primary image capture. If the 35 mm film is not capable of good reproduction of the object, then the digitized image will be poor. This is particularly true for manuscript materials: in even the best printing from an expertly-photographed manuscript taken with 35 mm colour film the manuscript is barely readable. Photographers, publishers, scholars, and archivists have known for decades of the inadequacy of 35 mm film, and used larger format transparencies (as 60 mm, 5 x 4, or 10 x 8, etc.) for the best quality images. Secondly, the scanning process itself gives cause for concern. During scanning, image capture is adjusted automatically, according to 'exposure variations, lighting conditions, and the make and type of film' (Kodak 1992, 7). From experience, it appears that this automatic adjustment may not be satisfactory with manuscript materials, with their characteristically low contrast and narrow colour range. Images may appear flat, or glary, with colours dulled or over-bright. Many projects (for example, the Wittgenstein and Toyota projects) have found it necessary either to go to a specialist Photo CD bureau, to optimize the scanning process, or to carry out considerable adjustment to the images after capture. Both are expensive, with bureaux charging around three or four times the standard High Street cost. Adjustment of the images after capture is especially unsatisfactory, as it is likely to be very time consuming and also may lose information in the pursuit of a good visual impression. The lesson is that no project should expect to achieve satisfactory digitization just by taking bundles of transparencies to a High Street shop.

A third reason for caution concerning Photo CD is to do with the proprietary 'YCC' file format Kodak uses, and the processes of translation into and out of this file format. As explained above, digital colour images are commonly made by recording the red, green, and blue values of each pixel. One might expect that the YCC file format would give access to the exact red, green, and blue information for each pixel as it was scanned. This is precisely what the Kodak YCC file format does not do. Instead of recording the red, green, and blue of each pixel, Kodak uses rather complex mathematical equations to convert these three colour values into three different values, one for luminance ('Y') and two for chrominance ('C'). The advantage of this conversion is that the images can then be converted from YCC format to analogue video, for display on a domestic or high-definition television set, with great efficiency and speed. But the disadvantage is that the mathematics of the conversion are not exactly reversible: for each pixel one can only recover the approximate colour values of the original scan. In addition, the YCC scheme incorporates a scheme of compression which loses information: in effect, most of the red and blue information for every second pixel in both horizontal and vertical directions (three-quarters of the red and blue information) is discarded. Effectively, around three-quarters of the red and blue information is lost. Kodak justify this by stating that there is no 'significant loss in perceived visual quality' (1992, 28), and there is no doubt that the images are adequate for many purposes. But these purposes do not appear to include reproduction of printed or manuscript materials. Users have found difficulty with adequate reproduction of printed text in Photo CD, with edges of letters not being sharply defined. With manuscript images, this is compounded by poor contrast and brightness, and uncertainties about colour response.

Another common and convenient method for digital image capture is using a video camera. Video cameras are widely available and inexpensive, and images taken by video cameras can be readily brought into a computer system. Furthermore, they do not suffer some of the disadvantages of a flatbed scanner system, with their inability to vary the lighting or to handle anything but a flat object. You can use a video camera to make an image of an object of any shape, and light the object with any lighting you wish. However, video cameras were not designed specifically for the making of digital computer images. They were designed instead for the making of images to appear on television screens. As a result, they do not produce data in digital form, suitable for computer processing. Rather, they produce signals suitable for television display. These signals are 'analogue' signals: that is, they are continuously varying, with their relative strength or weakness conveying the characteristics of the image. Further, the signals produced by a video camera are not dot-by-dot representations of the image. They are actually line-by-line representations. For each line of the object, the camera produces a continuous signal in the form of an electric wave. In standard television applications, this signal is then used to control the video guns which paint the image, line by line, onto the television screen.

The resolution of the video camera image, then, is first limited by the number of lines into which the image is divided. Video camera documentation usually quotes this in terms of 'horizontal resolution of 600 lines', or similar. Over an A4 page, if we use a 600-line video camera to capture it along its 8.67 inch breadth, we get a possible dpi of 600 / 8.67 dpi, or around 70 dpi. If we use the camera to capture it along its 11.25 inch length, the possible dpi drops to below 60 dpi. This is a far lower resolution than is available from flatbed scanners, for example.

There are other factors at work which suggest that digitization via video cameras makes images of even lower quality than this dpi figure suggests. It is noted above that video cameras produce for each line of the image an analogue signal in the form of an electric wave. This analogue signal has to be converted into digital form for computer processing. This is commonly done by an image capture board, a piece of computer hardware that accepts the analogue signal representing the lines of the video image. The image capture board converts this analogue signal into a sequence of pixels. It then gives each pixel a value based on the analogue signal corresponding to that part of the image. There are various weaknesses in this. The first is the analogue signal itself. Where digital information is by its nature secure, analogue signals are liable to degradation. Noise at any point along the device can distort the signal. Observe too that the analogue signal will effectively smooth the image. Accumulation of the charges from individual cells into a single electric wave will mean that abrupt transitions from cell to cell are represented by a graduation of the wave curve, and so are somewhat averaged out. In summary: standard video cameras produce low resolution digital images, and the information is likely to be distorted even at these low resolutions.

Still rare, though becoming increasingly common, are 'true' digital cameras. These are designed specifically for the making of computer images, not for the making of images for broadcasting. As a result, digital cameras retain the strengths of video cameras, and can work with different lights and make images of objects of any shape and size. They can also use the superb range of lenses and filters developed for traditional photographic purposes in the last century.

Because digital cameras have been developed specifically for the making of computer images, they have been able to avoid many of the problems noted above with video cameras. Thus, digital cameras differ in two fundamental respects from video cameras. First, they may use many more picture elements to capture an image than do video cameras, with resolutions up to 700 dpi for an A4 page possible through the Primagraphics digital camera. Secondly, digital cameras read the light value direct from each picture element and then convert this into digital form. This means, firstly, that the digital value is a direct measurement of the light value at that particular picture element. It is not an indirect measurement, derived from the arbitrary segmentation of the video signal and subject to the smoothing implicit in the signal. Accordingly, digital cameras are capable of far better results than other methods discussed in this survey. They can digitize direct from the original, unlike the film-based methods of microfilm scanning or Photo CD. They can work with objects of any size or shape, under many different lights, unlike flatbed scanners. They can make images of very high resolution, unlike video cameras. Experiments with digital cameras have fully confirmed this promise. The work of Kevin Kiernan and Andrew

Prescott with the Kontron ProgRes camera and the *Beowulf* manuscript has shown that images of remarkable quality, at least as good as those of the best printed facsimile, may be made by digital cameras. At present, they have the disadvantage of being expensive, and the more powerful varieties usually require physical attachment to a bulky computer. However, this is changing rapidly.

Making the images available: file types, sizes, CD-ROMs, and networks

The world of computing is cursed by invention, such that it appears that every hardware and software developer has to devise their own way of storing digital image files: see the survey in Carpenter and Mumford (1992, 26-36). However, in the last few years one image file format has achieved, by its wide acceptance, the status of a *de facto* standard. This is the TIFF format, for 'Tagged Image File Format'. TIFF is the most widely supported image file format in the microcomputer world, with Microsoft, Aldus, and Adobe all having applications which read and write TIFF files. TIFF files are also designed to be hardware independent (though expecting the host computer to support eight-bit bytes), and one can take a TIFF file written on a PC and read it on a Macintosh, or *vice versa*.

Because a computer image file of even a small image may record information about each one of tens of thousands, or millions, of pixels (a one inch square image recorded at 100 dpi contains 10,000), they can be very large indeed. An A4 page captured at 100 dpi in black and white only will be around 100 kilobytes in size, so that one can fit around 5,000 images on a CD-ROM. The same page captured at 300 dpi in plain black and white will be 900 kilobytes (600 images on a CD-ROM); at 24-bit colour it will grow to 22 megabytes (25 images on a CD-ROM). Because of these huge file sizes for colour images in particular, many systems of image compression have been developed. Two are worth special mention as they have achieved widespread use: these are CCITT (Comité Consultatif Télégraphique et Téléphonique) (groups 4 and 5) methods for black-and-white images and JPEG (Joint Photographic Experts Group) for colour images. The CCITT methods are 'lossless', permitting exact recreation of the original from the compressed form, and achieve typical 15-fold compression rates: thus a 900 kilobyte image file of an A4 page at 300 dpi in black-and-white can be reduced to around 70 kilobytes, enabling some 8,000 images to fit onto a single CD-ROM. JPEG compression, for colour and greyscale images, is 'lossy', and works by discarding information to which the eye is not sensitive. It is remarkably effective and typical compression rates of twenty to one for full colour, somewhat less for greyscale, are possible with no perceivable loss of information. Accordingly, a 22 megabyte image file of an A4 page at 300 dpi in 24-bit colour can be reduced to around one megabyte, enabling some 500 images to fit onto a single CD-ROM.

Once images are made and stored, they may need to be distributed. As the references to CD-ROM distribution in the preceding paragraphs suggest, this medium is very well suited to distribution of large numbers of images. As suggested above, with compression images of some 8,000 printed A4 pages, or 500 full-colour manuscript pages, can fit on a single CD-ROM. CD-ROMs are cheap to produce, with a run of 500 copies costing around £3 a disc to master and press; CD-ROM drives are becoming increasingly common and indeed are often sold as standard equipment with new computers. Publishers feel comfortable with them, as physical and saleable objects not too dissimilar from books. Copyright holders also feel more at ease with distribution of images on CD-ROMs than over networks, with their clear potential for loss of control of the images.

From the recent intense interest in the 'Information Superhighway', and the astonishing success of World Wide Web, one might conclude that high-speed networks will be the way of the future for distribution of image materials. But this future is still some way hence. Many problems will have to be solved before a scholar in America can routinely summon up images of manuscript pages from a computer server based in the British Library. First, the current generation of computer networks are simply not capable of moving many 20 megabyte image files (and the files may be far larger than this) at once. The advent of SuperJANET (Mumford 1992, Appendix A) and its successors may change this, but it will be years rather than months before all the links are in place to allow files of this size to travel around the world in seconds. Second, the networks must be made secure. Many of these images are under copyright, and the holders are understandably eager to know who has access to the images, where. Systems of controlled access, with encryption and 'pay-per-use'—as pioneered by the European Union-funded CITED (Copyright in Transmitted Electronic Documents) project (Cornish 1993)—must be put in place to enforce this security. Until these requirements are met, we can expect that most distribution of large bodies of valuable image material will be by CD-ROM rather than by network.

Image capture strategies for different materials: case studies

In the preceding sections, I describe some of the different methods of digitization available, and suggest how different methods might suit different needs. In this section, I will take three examples of projects which have found various solutions to their particular digitization problems.

The Beowulf *manuscript: digital camera*

The *Beowulf* manuscript is one of the most important of the holdings of the British Library, with many scholars wishing to consult it every year. It was damaged in the 1731 Cotton fire; many pages are difficult to read and the whole is very fragile. In particular, the state of the manuscript means that many words or letters can only be read with ultraviolet or other special light. Accordingly, following experiments by Kevin Kiernan (Kiernan 1991) it was decided to make the best possible digital record of the whole manuscript. After various trials, the Kontron ProgRes 3012 camera was chosen for this work. Many pages have been photographed at different resolutions under different lights. In general, the project has found 300 dpi resolution at 24-bit colour entirely adequate: or, to put it another way, increasing the resolution has not shown anything which could not be seen at 300 dpi. The images they have made give a startling sense of closeness to the manuscript, in part because of their extraordinary sharpness, in part because they are typically seen at magnifications of two or four times the manuscript size.

The project plans to complete photography of the *Beowulf* manuscript, to make it all available to scholars working at the British Library, and also to publish some of these images on CD-ROM with network publication also possible later. Other manuscripts in the British Library may also be captured in the same manner. The project has established that digital photography is capable of manuscript images of the highest quality, and opened up the possibility of a new age of manuscript photography.

The Canterbury Tales *project: microfilm by flatbed scanner*

This project proposes to make available digital images of every page of every manuscript of Chaucer's *Canterbury Tales*, together with transcriptions of every page. Initial publication will be on CD-ROM and there are around 24,000 manuscript pages altogether. It is intended to reproduce the most important manuscripts in 24-bit colour at 300 dpi resolution, using the same techniques and (probably) the same Kontron camera as the *Beowulf* project described above. With JPEG compression, as described earlier, some 500 such images may be fitted onto a single CD-ROM: enough for a whole manuscript. The most important manuscripts (perhaps, six to ten of the 88 pre-1500 witnesses) will certainly warrant this treatment.

However, the cost of digital photography and the practical difficulty of persuading libraries to permit new photography mean that it will not be possible, in the short term at least, to photograph all the manuscripts with a digital camera. Accordingly, digital images of most manuscripts will be made from existing microfilms. These images could have been made by a bureau using a microfilm scanner, but the project has chosen not to do this. Instead, each manuscript page image is printed from the microfilm onto A4 paper; the image so produced is usually about 25 per cent larger than the original manuscript page. The printed page is then placed on a flatbed scanner and scanned at resolutions of between 170 and 220 dpi. Taking into account the 25 per cent enlargement, this produces an image of between 210 and 275 dpi. While this may be somewhat more expensive than bureau scanning, it has the great advantage of giving far more control over the final image. The print to paper from the microfilm can be optimized, and then the scanned image itself adjusted to the best possible effect. The cost of this whole process is around 20 pence a manuscript page for the scanning; this does not include the cost of printing from or purchase of the microfilms. The images, though manifestly microfilm based, are sharp and usable, especially when viewed beside the transcriptions. File sizes after capture average 250 kilobytes without compression: a single CD-ROM could accommodate around 2,500 such images. With lossless compression (CCITT groups 3 or 4) file sizes could be reduced to around 80Kb, making it possible to fit around 7,000 manuscript pages on a single CD-ROM, or all the manuscript pages on four CD-ROMs.

The Corpus of Romanesque Sculpture: Photo CD

This project aims to photograph and catalogue the surviving heritage of sculpture produced in Britain and Ireland between c.1066 and 1200 (Ross 1994). It will provide a computerized archive containing an estimated

60,000 images and approximately 15,000 pages of text. As images are widely dispersed and need to be photographed *in situ*, image capture will be by the Photo CD process from 35 mm transparencies of photographs taken by project workers. The images will be scanned as eight-bit greyscale. As commonly happens with Photo CD, it was found necessary to use a specialist scanning service to give the desired results. This done, the project has found Photo CD very satisfactory for its images. In practical terms, the use of Photo CD has allowed the capture of many images in many places by many people at reasonable cost.

Distribution of the images will be incremental: as sections of the database become complete they may be made available by network access, or on CD-ROM. A particular problem this project has had to address is that of scholarly recognition. At first, the uncertain status of electronic publication and the collaborative nature of the project was seen as inhibiting individual contributions. However, the incorporation of a comprehensive acknowledgement system at every point of the project has eased this.

Image analysis

Anyone who has seen the standard image-processing demonstrations, for example that in which a fully formed foetus suddenly appears from the grey wash of an X-ray image of a womb, will have been struck by the potential for image enhancement techniques. In fact, experiments so far have not confirmed this potential. Image enhancement has not produced new crops of readings. The reason for this is that at its best, digital photography (the raw material from which image enhancement must begin) will produce an image similar to the manuscript viewed under good light. If there is anything to be read in the manuscript then it can be (and probably will have been) read with close scrutiny of the manuscript itself, at least as well as it might be read from the computer image with or without enhancement. Accordingly, one will do better not to see image enhancement as a magic means of recovering the otherwise irrecoverable, but rather as a means of making difficult-to-read manuscript images easier to read. In part, this might be no more than compensating for failings in the original photograph. Indeed, if the object is photographed digitally to the highest possible standard there is likely to be no need for any further enhancement, beyond simple magnification. That said, in certain special cases (smoke damaged manuscripts, or extreme 'bleed-through'), even the best manuscripts may be made more readable by the straightforward tools now common in computer imaging programs (e.g. Aldus Photoshop), notably contrast and brightness controls.

The justification of digital image capture, then, should not be that it might permit the recovery of a very few readings but that it may make available far better images far more conveniently and cheaply than can print or microfilm. The greatest potential for computer manipulation of these digital images may not lie in the area of enhancement at all, but in the development of systems of automated analysis of these images. Andrea Bozzi and his colleagues at the Institute for Computational Linguistics in Pisa have created methods for automatic linking of words in a transcription of a manuscript page to their images in a computer graphics file. From this, one could develop a system of identifying all the digital images of particular letters, thence loading them into a database and using advanced pattern matching techniques to explore scribal hands. But first, we need the best possible digital images of the largest possible range of materials.

References and bibliography

Avedon, D. M., *Introduction to electronic imaging* (Silver Spring, MD: AIIM, 1992).

Bozzi, A., 'Towards a philological workstation', *RISSH*, 29 (1993), 33-49 (with A. Sapuppo).

Carpenter, L. A., and Mumford, A. M., *File formats for computer graphics* (Advisory Group on Computer Graphics Technical Report Series no. 10, 1992).

Cornish, G., 'Copyright management of document supply in an electronic age: the CITED solution', *Interlending and Document Supply*, 21.2 (1993), 13-20.

Elkington, N. E. (ed.), *RLG preservation microfilming handbook* (Research Libraries Group, 1992).

Hamber, A., 'Conventional photography vs. analogue and digital electronic imaging', in Hamber, A., Miles, J., and Vaughan, W. (eds.), *Computers and the history of art* (London: Mansell, 1989).

Hamber, A., 'High resolution images', in Thaller, M. (ed.), *Images and manuscripts in historical computing* (Göttingen: Max-Planck-Institut für Geschichte, 1992).

Kenney, A. R., and Personius, L. K., *Digital capture, paper facsimiles and network access*. Joint Study in Digital Preservation. Report: Phase I. (Cornell University, Xerox Corporation, and the Commission on Preservation and Access, 1992).

Kiernan, K., 'Digital image processing and the *Beowulf* manuscript', *Literary and Linguistic Computing*, 6 (1991), 20-7.

Kiernan, K., 'Digital preservation, restoration, and dissemination of medieval manuscripts', World Wide Web URL http://www.uky.edu/~ dhart/dhart.html

Kodak Limited, 'Photo CD products: a planning guide for developers'. Eastman (Rochester, NY: Kodak, 1992).

Martinez, K., and Hamber, A., 'Towards a colorimetric digital image archive for the visual arts', *Electronic Imaging Applications in the Graphic Arts.* SPIE Vol. 1073, (1989), 114-21.

Mumford, A. M., *From graphics to multimedia workshop report* (Advisory Group on Computer Graphics, 1992).

Robinson, P. M.W., *The digitization of primary textual sources* (Oxford: Office for Humanities Communication, 1993).

Ross, S., 1994, 'Designing a tool for research in disciplines using multimedia data: the Romanesque Sculpture Processor', in Bocchi, F., and Denley, P. (eds.), *Storia & Multimedia*, Proceedings of the Seventh International Congress of the Association for History and Computing, Bologna 29.8–2.9., 1992, 629–35.

Saffady, W., *Electronic document imaging systems: design, evaluation and implementation* (Westport, London, and Melbourne: Meckler, 1993).

Shiel, A., *Document imaging: a guide and directory* (Cimtech Limited and UKAIIM: University of Hertfordshire, 1992).

Thaller, M. (ed.), *Images and manuscripts in historical computing* (Göttingen: Max-Planck-Institut für Geschichte, 1992).

Wallace, G. K., 'The JPEG still picture compression standard', *Communications of the ACM*, 34.4 (1991), 31-44.

Willis, D., *A hybrid systems approach to preservation of printed materials* (Washington, DC: The Commission on Preservation and Access, 1992).

Further reading

Most of the accessible literature which deals with image capture is heavily commercial in emphasis: this technology has been largely driven by the dream of the 'paperless office'. William Saffady's 1993 *Electronic document imaging systems: design, evaluation and implementation* is a good introduction to office imaging systems, and accordingly very useful on capture of printed text. The publications of Cimtech Ltd., based in the University of Hertfordshire, are also aimed at the commercial world. Cimtech's American counterpart AIIM (the Association for Information and Image Management) and the attractively-produced journals *Advanced Imaging* and *Image Processing*, while fundamentally commercial in orientation also carry considerable material relating to the archive world, and especially reports on colour digitization systems. The leading technical journal in the field is *SPIE* (The International Society for Optical Engineering): most of its material is uncompromisingly specialist. The numbers of *SPIE* are worth browsing for a feel of the complexities behind the apparently simple. The articles by Anthony Hamber listed in the Bibliography are an excellent introduction to the technical issues, with particularly telling comparisons between film and digital photography.

There are few specialist studies in this area for the humanities scholar or archivist. Don Willis' 1992 *A hybrid systems approach to preservation of printed materials* is a lucid account of the issues as seen by an American archivist. Manfred Thaller's 1992 collection, *Images and manuscripts in historical computing*, offers some fascinating accounts of European initiatives in the field. My 1993 *The digitization of primary textual sources* is intended as an introduction for the humanities scholar, especially those actively considering the possibilities of large-scale image capture in the near future.

Multimedia in the Humanities

Maria Economou

Introduction to multimedia

Some terms and definitions

The term 'multimedia' is used very frequently nowadays in connection with various kinds of computer-based systems for education, museums and public presentations, professional training, entertainment, and information management. It is often used interchangeably with 'hypermedia' or in conjunction with 'hypertext'. There are many different definitions which appear in the relevant literature (Conclin 1987; Hoffos 1992; Nielsen 1993; *Multimedia and Related Technologies: a Glossary of Terms*) and the products which are considered to belong under this umbrella vary quite considerably. Multimedia systems are a recent and continuously evolving phenomenon and this is also reflected in the lack of standardization in terminology. Therefore, the following definitions are not of universal acceptance but tend to be the ones more frequently used. Although all three concepts share common characteristics, there is a distinction among them.

'Hypertext', the oldest of the three terms, is used to describe a body of textual documents joined together with automated conceptual links, or the computer system used to create and read these types of documents. It allows the users to browse freely through related themes, words, ideas, following various paths, and comparing different pieces of information. The first part of the word 'hypertext', the Greek preposition *hyper*, means over, above, beyond and is indicative of the vision which its first creators had about hypertext, that of crossing boundaries and of freer association of information and concepts. The individual units which form hypertext, known as 'nodes', can be textual data of variable size and type, from one word to a whole book. Large hypertext systems consist of very complex sets of links and nodes and the navigation through them can be quite confusing. The choice of the most appropriate links is one of the most difficult areas of hypertext research and requires a deep understanding of the information included in the program.

The term 'hypermedia' describes a hypertext system enhanced by audiovisual capabilities, with links between various media besides text. Images, graphics, texts, video sequences, and sounds which refer to a certain subject, or share common distinctive features can be put together in a way which allows a non-linear exploration according to the choices of the user. The basic principle behind hypermedia, as with hypertext, is that it does not impose a unique, pre-designed path through the data, but rather tries—to a different extent among various systems—to allow the user to decide upon the way of traversing the available information. Control over the flow of the program is given to the user, not the programmer. The additional advantage of combining different forms of information makes hypermedia an extremely powerful tool for a variety of applications, from research and education to industry and leisure.

'Multimedia' refers generally to the combination of various forms of information—text, images, graphics, sound, video—in a single medium, in most cases a computer enhanced by audiovisual resources. Multimedia is actually not a specific technology, nor a product, but rather a communication system which employs various technologies in order to integrate and deliver in a multi-sensory way information in disparate forms.

Although hypermedia and multimedia share the particular feature of combining multiple media types, multimedia systems do not necessarily have the non-sequential, user-controlled structure which is characteristic of hypermedia and hypertext programs, and can sometimes be designed in a very linear way. However, these distinctions are becoming blurred and the majority of multimedia programs today have at least a basic hypertext structure. Most people use the terms interchangeably, with a recent preference for the use of the term 'multimedia'. This more general term will also be used in this chapter to refer to programs which integrate various media and are organized in a non-linear, interactive fashion.

Basic characteristics

Multimedia and interactivity
A basic characteristic of modern multimedia systems is their interactivity, which supports two-way transfer of information between the user and

the system. The user is in control of the flow of the program, asking questions, making choices, selecting paths through the available information.

At a higher level some interactive systems require the viewer to add her own information and create her own links. For example, in Discovering French Interactive, an award-winning multimedia program, French is taught using recorded native speakers, authentic video scenes, and related exercises, while the students' oral and typed responses can be saved and assessed. Typical multimedia systems are modular, organizing data in small groups without a pre-set beginning, middle, or end. The selections of every user establish a route along these modules and bring together information from many different parts of the system.

Well-designed multimedia systems offer information at various levels, give the opportunity for comparisons and combined examinations of different materials, features and ideas, and are still easy to use and navigate. Being also able to incorporate different instructional methods and ways of presenting information, they can address very wide audiences with different backgrounds, interests, and needs.

Another characteristic of multimedia, closely related to interactivity, is transparency. The users should be able to interact easily with the system, visit different parts and get responses to their requests, without seeing the way it works or being distracted by the mechanics of interaction.

The idea of free interaction between a user and a responsive machine offering information, promoting, and testing skills at an individual pace has a considerable impact on modern learning methods. Multimedia's appeal rises as self-paced instruction and learner-centred education become increasingly popular in schools and universities. The interactive and entertaining character of multimedia systems also offers great potential for informal learning environments such as museums, cultural centres, and libraries.

Branching and navigation
Multimedia systems can support multiple links between their various components. The structure of the different parts can be hierarchical or very open and free. In the case of complex systems with numerous cross-references and connections, the user can easily get disorientated and lost. This phenomenon is often described as 'being lost in hyperspace' (Edwards and Hardman 1989) and there are a number of mechanisms that can prevent it from happening, such as maps of the program's

Figure 1: A concept map used in the hypermedia program, Isaac Rosenberg's 'Break of Day in the Trenches'

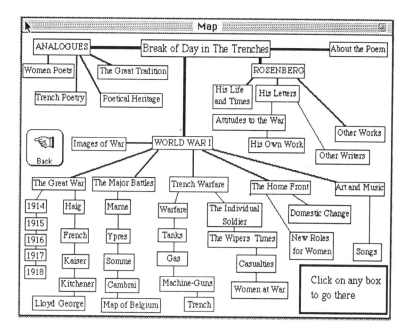

content, indexes, list of contents, and thumbnail pictures of the screens already viewed (see Figure 1).

Designers of multimedia applications should remember that, irrespective of the amount of data contained in their systems, the users should feel comfortable exploring them and free to move easily to the parts which interest them most.

A short history of hypertext and hypermedia

Vannevar Bush

The basic idea behind hypertext, the non-sequential linking of information according to conceptual associations, was first developed in the 1940s by Vannevar Bush (1890-1974), President Roosevelt's Senior Science Adviser. He was interested in the ways of organizing and retrieving information on scientific literature and believed that the effort to record the increasing amount of knowledge was hindered by inflexible indexing mechanisms which allowed only one way of approaching a piece of information. In the frequently-cited article, titled 'As we may think', which appeared in *Atlantic Monthly* of 1945 Bush wrote:

> Our ineptitude in getting at the record is largely caused by the artificiality of systems of indexing. When data of any sort are placed in storage, they are filed alphabetically or numerically, and information is found (when it is) by tracing it down from subclass to subclass. It can be only in one place, unless duplicates are used; one has to have rules as to which path will locate it, and the rules are cumbersome. Having found one item, moreover, one has to emerge from the system and re-enter on a new path. The human mind does not work that way. It operates by association. With one item in its grasp, it snaps instantly to the next that is suggested by the association of thoughts in accordance with some intricate web of trails carried by the cells of the brain.

Bush tried to address the problem of associative indexing by designing a device which he called 'Memex' (Memory Extender). This would store a very large library in microfilm. Although Memex was never actually constructed, the ideas behind it were quite revolutionary for the time because it allowed any two items to be linked automatically together and also let the users leave a mark of the path they had followed. Users could also interact with the system, adding information or comments of their own.

Doug Engelbart and the Augment project
The next important initiative in this field was taken by Doug Engelbart at Stanford Research Institute in the 1960s, who applied Bush's ideas in practice, introducing many computer hardware and software innovations. He designed the first hypertext system to be run at a computer, as part of his Augment project (implemented as oN Line System, NLS), whose main purpose was to improve productivity and thinking by the use of technology (Engelbart *et al.* 1973). This included innovative applications like a mouse, a five-key keyboard, multiple windows, automatic outline structuring of text, and videoconferencing; also novel concepts, such as the idea that the user should be treated as an 'informa-

tion pilot', that all information should be explicitly structured, and that there should be specific tools to provide multiple views of the structure.

Ted Nelson and Xanadu

In 1965 Ted Nelson, another hypertext visionary, started his ambitious Xanadu project which planned to link together all the world's literature and make it available through computers. 'The basic Xanadu idea is that it is a repository for everything that everybody has ever written and thereby of a truly universal hypertext' (Nielsen 1993, 35). Despite the enormous practical difficulties, this imaginative idea is still being developed and is indicative of the often exaggerated enthusiasm of the first days of hypertext. It currently supports not only textual, but also graphical information, storing all forms of digital information. If it ever becomes commercially available, it will allow concurrent use of information pools of documents of unlimited size with very flexible linking which could support citations to references, annotations to drawings, or comments from multiple editions of particular documents. According to Nelson's idea, this dynamic corpus can be enriched by users without defacing the original documents, thus diminishing the difference between authors and users (Autodesk 1991).

Nelson is also responsible for the term 'hypertext', which he devised to describe a system of shared information which would follow more closely than printed books the non-sequential way the human mind functions (Nelson 1987).

Brown University's Intermedia

Another significant contribution to hypertext systems came in the 1960s and 70s from the Institute for Research in Information and Scholarship (IRIS) of Brown University in the United States which created and experimented on several hypertext systems as part of the Intermedia project. Intermedia is not so much a single hypertext program, as it is a framework for using and creating hypertext documents. It offers an integrated environment consisting of several specialized programs and features, such as animations, timelines, and e-mail. Linking protocols define the way existing hypertext applications can be integrated with Intermedia documents. The system offers great flexibility in creating links between documents and incorporates several kinds of overview diagrams (Haan *et al.* 1992). Today they are still researching hypertext at Brown and using it as an interactive medium for teaching and providing study materials for students.

Developments since the 1980s

Many other interesting projects and applications have followed during the last decade. Among the most prominent ones are Xerox PARC's NoteCards, Shneiderman's Hyperties, Tektronix Neptune, Carnegie-Mellon University's ZOG. (See Conclin 1987 for further details on these). It seems that, although the basic concepts and advantages of hypertext were obvious from its early history, more widespread interest and use were delayed by technological and financial constraints. Another important factor impeding hypertext's expansion is that only recently has it been accepted and understood that computers can also be tools for interhuman communication and processing of ideas and symbols, in addition to data and numbers.

Apple computers played a role in this direction with their friendly graphical user interfaces. These used a real world metaphor, that of a desktop, and a number of icons to communicate with the user, in contrast to command line systems, and are now being applied to most types of computers. In general, the whole philosophy which Apple projected of computers as useful and liberating tools for all subjects, had an impact on humanists and contributed to the rejection of the sterile dichotomy which associated computers only with the sciences.

The 1980s also saw the development of Compact Discs (CD) which expanded the power of computers, allowing better manipulation and storage of sound and image. The different types of compact discs can store large amounts of text, animation, images, sounds, graphics, but do not yet support full-screen, full-motion video. The various products under this category—Compact Disc–Digital Audio (CD–DA), Compact Disc–Interactive (CD–I), Compact Disc–Read Only Memory (CD–ROM), CD–ROM Extended Architecture(CD–XA)—are described in the following section.

Furthermore, the great technological advancements in digital sound- and image-processing, compression techniques, and video-digitizing have made possible the integration of all necessary information in one format at relatively low prices, thus increasing the popularity of multimedia and providing tools for almost limitless combinations and applications with hypertext principles.

Today there are many commercial products available which allow not only the use, but also the creation of hypertext and multimedia documents by non-computer specialists. The authoring tools, the special programs which allow the creation of multimedia packages, will be discussed further in a separate section. It is worth mentioning here that another important development in the evolution of multimedia was the launch of HyperCard from Apple in 1987. The way it was marketed encouraged many people to experiment with the idea of hypertext: until recently it was offered free with every Macintosh computer sold and even now its price is kept relatively low. This led to the creation of a worldwide community of HyperCard enthusiasts as many Macintosh owners, who would not have otherwise thought of working with multimedia, started exploring the possibilities offered by the program. Unfortunately, the vast number of amateur programmers who seized eagerly on HyperCard has also resulted in some very poor products being developed.

What started as special research projects, became available in the late eighties as reasonably priced products for use with microcomputers. The authoring systems currently on offer are being continuously improved and developed. They do not require very advanced programming skills and are fairly easy to master. They have given the opportunity to educators, researchers, information managers, and artists with basic computer skills to create their own applications for their special needs. The technology develops rapidly in this field and although multimedia has a short history, its future looks long and promising.

Multimedia design and production

Well-designed and sophisticated multimedia programs require a wide range of skills and specialities: graphic design, educational psychology, computer programming, user interface design, content expertise, artistic talent. However, few multimedia productions can afford such large teams, and people working in smaller groups are expected to catch up with many different areas and abilities and become multi-talented Leonardos! In any case, the good management of such projects, the clear definition of roles and responsibilities, as well as the ability to work in a team are vital for the success of multimedia ventures.

After the roles and objectives have been defined, the content of the application has been researched, and the basic design elements have been decided, the production of the program can begin. Three design documents are often prepared during this process: a flowchart, a storyboard, and a scenario. The *flowchart* illustrates the general structure of the multimedia application and the main branching alternatives in the form of a diagram where concepts are represented as boxes linked by lines. The *storyboard* is a graphical representation of the way the user will perceive the content (e.g. a sequence of screen designs). The *scenario* offers the detail about each component of the storyboard, relating these with the user-interface guidelines and the general philosophy of the application.

Once the flowchart, storyboard, and scenario have been prepared, the actual design and production of the multimedia application are carried out using specialized software packages, the authoring tools, as they are known. Using an authoring tool, multimedia designers combine and integrate the multiple media segments which constitute the program, the text, graphics, video, and sound.

Technical characteristics (hardware and software)

Authoring programs
Several authoring tools are available today which vary considerably in terms of characteristics and cost. Choosing the most appropriate program involves a consideration of the particular features of the task at hand, the quality and quantity of audiovisual information needed, and the overall scope and approach of the project.

Although a degree of computer competence is necessary to use them, simple applications can be created without advanced programming knowledge. As the compatibility between different hardware platforms increases, and authoring tools become more flexible and efficient, these programs allow educators, researchers, and artists with basic computer skills to focus on their craft and create interesting applications which meet their special needs. It should be mentioned though, that the design of successful and attractive multimedia applications is a demanding task, requiring a wide range of skills, and is often more labour intensive and time consuming than most manufacturers advertise.

Most tools integrate text and graphics editors (some also video and sound) and allow the design of 'hot-spots' or buttons which link different parts of the program. The programming scripts control navigation, coordinate the position of pictures on the screen, and synchronize the playing of video and sounds. Few packages today are truly cross-platform, but many offer run-time players for multiple platforms, which run the completed application without allowing major alterations.

The most popular and affordable packages are mentioned here briefly, while detailed reviews can be found in the Further Reading section (e.g. Deegan *et al.* 1992, Riley 1994) and in current computer magazines. The first four—Guide, HyperCard, Multimedia Toolbook, and Super-

Card—bear many similarities and are the most widely used low-end packages.

- Guide of OWL International was the first hypermedia system released commercially for personal computers. The most recent commercial version operates in a Windows environment, while there are previous versions for Macintosh and Unix machines. Guide documents can easily handle large amounts of text in scrolling windows and can include graphics anywhere within the text. Any piece of text or graphic can have an active link to another part of the program; these links are called *reference buttons*. *Expansion buttons* hide information behind a word, icon, or title which appears in full when these are selected. *Note buttons* operate rather like on-screen equivalents to footnotes in printed text; when selected they activate a pop-up window to annotate text, sound, and graphics with details such as definitions, illustrations, and notes. *Command buttons* use scripts written with LOGiiX, Guide's programming language; these can expand beyond the Guide document, opening other applications, and controlling external devices, such as videodisc players and modems. Each of these button-links can be identified by the form the cursor takes when it moves over their active area.

  The Anglo-Saxons Interactive CD–ROM, based on the collections of the British Museum, is one of the products designed by Research Machines using Guide (see Figure 2).

- HyperCard for Apple computers, launched in 1987, remains probably one of the most widely used multimedia authoring systems. It has a large network of users, as well as a very good support system with special interest lists, publications, and re-sources.

  HyperCard organizes information in cards, the computer equivalent to a piece of paper, which is usually the size of the screen. A group of cards forms a stack, the basic HyperCard application. Cards and stacks can be linked together with buttons and commands, creating a network of information. The programming language of HyperCard is HyperTalk, which is—at a basic level—relatively easy to master, as it follows the grammar of spoken English. HyperTalk allows the customization of cards

Figure 2: Screenshot of The Anglo-Saxons Interactive CD-ROM which was produced with Guide.

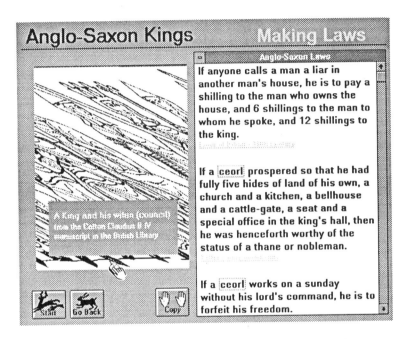

and the introduction of numerous effects and searching facilities. One of the main drawbacks of HyperCard is its idiosyncratic support of colour, which remains cumbersome and less integrated than in other packages, even after the release of version 2.2 with Colouring Tools.

Perseus, the multimedia resource on Ancient Greece, was developed using HyperCard (Crane and Mylonas 1991) (see Figure 3). Numerous other stacks are available as shareware or freeware from ftp sites. Several authoring tools were developed based on HyperCard's structure, such as Toolbook and SuperCard.

Figure 3: Perseus, the interactive resource on Archaic and Classical Greece, was developed with HyperCard

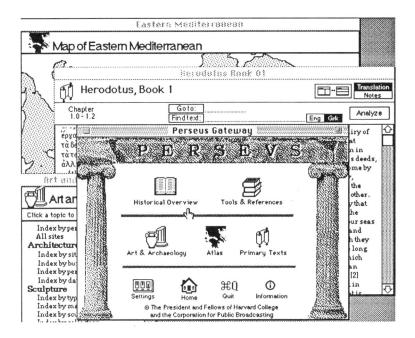

- Multimedia Toolbook for Windows comprises Toolbook and Asymetrix Multimedia Resource Kit. It is possible to use specific software (e.g. Convert-It) to transform HyperCard stacks into Toolbook applications. The basic metaphor used for every screen of information is that of a page, while each application is called a book. As it is able to use Windows features, Toolbook offers a wide range of fonts, graphics, and colours. Its programming language, OpenScript, allows the execution of more complex scripts and the incorporation of video and sound.

The Dream of the Rood of Oxford's Humanities Computing Unit is a multimedia teaching resource based on the Old English poem, which was designed with Multimedia Toolbook (see Figure 4).

Figure 4: The Dream of the Rood is a multimedia teaching tool designed with Toolbook

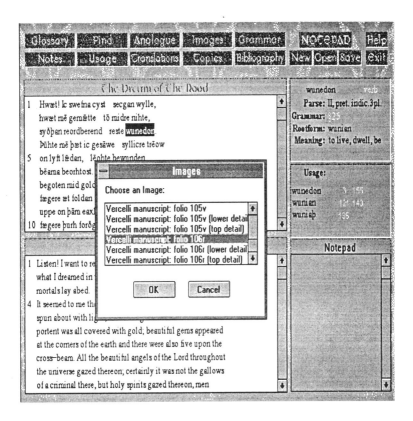

- Allegiant Technologies' SuperCard for Macintosh was also designed along the lines of HyperCard. It is possible, as with Toolbook, to transfer HyperCard stacks into SuperCard projects, as the applications created with this program are called. SuperCard offered from its first release better support of colour, while there are also animation facilities. Each project can display a number of windows concurrently on the screen and it is possible for SuperCard to control the whole Macintosh interface.

The following authoring programs have a slightly different scope and are intended for larger projects:

- Authorware Professional, available for both Windows and Macintosh platforms, is suitable for highly interactive applications. It uses the structural metaphor of a flowchart, where the designer can program actions like *display, decision, wait,* and *calculation,* in the form of icons. This graphical interface makes Authorware's programming language less intimidating to novice designers. However, as with most of these programs, the learning curve remains steep if one wants to produce advanced and sophisticated applications. The main weak point of the package is in the support of hypertext, as the non-linear linking of text and other media is rather poor. Its student tracking and record keeping features make it very suitable for education and training. Authorware is being used by the TLTP (Teaching and Learning Technology Programme) to develop a range of multimedia resources for undergraduate teaching.

- Microcosm was developed by a team at the University of Southampton; it is an open multimedia system for DOS and Windows, which allows the linking and browsing of several applications and documents prepared with other software (including Toolbook, Macromedia Director, and Authorware). Versions for Macintosh computers and for Unix machines running X-Windows are also under development. Microcosm operates as an 'umbrella' environment allowing the user to make links from documents in one application to documents in another. These links are held separately from data and can also be generic (for example, to link automatically every use of a single word with its definition in a separate glossary). It is being used, among others, by various humanities disciplines at the University of Southampton to create courseware which connects text, graphics, still and moving video.

Towards the more sophisticated and costly end of the market the following two authoring packages are the most popular:

- Macromedia Director, with Macintosh and Windows versions, is often used for high-end presentations and commercial titles. It incorporates animation, paint, media integration, and interactivity using the metaphor of a movie. The Cast Window serves as a multimedia database, providing easy access to text, graphics, animation, video, and sound. The Score Window is used for creating, editing, and synchronizing media elements, controlling transitions, colour palettes, sounds, etc. For those interested in building advanced interactive applications, Director has a rather steep learning curve, as it requires use of Lingo, its complex programming language.

The National Museums of Scotland are creating Macromedia Director applications to interpret the collections in the museums, and also to reach remote sites, initially in Scotland, but eventually further afield.

- Apple Media Kit consists of Apple Media Tool (an authoring application) and Apple Media Tool Programming Environment. Authoring can only be performed on Macintosh machines, but completed applications can also be played in a Windows environment. A novice or somebody uncomfortable with complex programming languages can use this system to create sophisticated interactive pieces using the user-friendly interface of Media Tool. It seems ideally suited to a team where the tasks are split between artists, or content specialists, and programmers. In this case, the package is very appropriate for storyboarding and prototyping, allowing the creative producers to communicate quickly and flexibly their ideas to the programmers.

  Apple Multimedia Kit was used by the Center for Educational Computing Initiatives (CECI) of Massachusetts Institute of Technology (MIT) and the MIT museum to develop a gallery application based on Harold Edgerton's work (a well-known MIT professor, famous for his stop-action photographs).

World Wide Web (WWW)

Apart from off-the-shelf authoring packages for creating multimedia applications, it is worth mentioning here the multimedia documents available on the World Wide Web. Developed at CERN (Centre Européen de Recherche Nucléaire), this is a system which organizes documents available on the Internet in a hypertext manner. Anybody with access to electronic networks can view WWW documents with various shareware programs, called browsers, such as Mosaic, Lynx, or Netscape.

The developments in telecommunications, standards, and exchange mechanisms have made possible the circulation not only of textual files and e-mail messages on the network, but also the delivery of multimedia information. Universities, libraries, institutions, museums, and individuals can now create documents using HTML, the HyperText Markup Language, which allows them to be platform-independent. Data can thus be linked following a hypertext structure and include pictures, sounds, and video—although, at the moment, these can take some time to appear on the screen, depending on their size.

With the rapid expansion of the Internet, the WWW is becoming a powerful communication tool, providing free access of information (ranging from the Vatican's collection to Dante Gabriel Rossetti's original manuscripts) to an international audience.

Major multimedia platforms

Once the production has been completed, a variety of devices and discs are available for delivering multimedia programs. These are usually described collectively as platforms. The rapid developments of the last years have resulted in a wide range of products which make the choice of the most suitable platform a difficult task. What follows is a brief description of the main multimedia platforms and their basic characteristics.

Interactive videodisc

Since the 1970s the technology of audiovisual systems started being developed as a way of effectively exploiting the ease with which the computer can handle digital resources. The interactive videodisc is an analogue medium which offers the ability to combine full-screen moving colour images and sound from a videodisc or tape with the text, graphics, and processing power of computers. Videodiscs or laserdiscs, are 30 cm/12inch optical discs, (i.e. the information they hold is written on their surface using a laser and is read by a lower intensity laser beam), which can store 54,000 or 108,000 frames (on two sides) of analogue still images, or 30 minutes' to one hour's video. After the creation of a master disc, further copies can be produced at low cost. In interactive video programs, a computer is connected with the videodisc player to structure the program, control text and graphics, and issue appropriate commands for the retrieval of specific images or videoclips from the disc.

Although videodiscs were popular until recently among schools and museums due to their dependability and durability, the degree of interaction they can offer is limited. Lately the technology is shifting towards digital systems, which offer greater storage capacity, speed, and fidelity, and open up a wider range of processing opportunities with more data types than analogue systems can offer (such as television, radio, audiotape). However, because of the video quality and the wide availability of analogue systems, the transfer to digital ones will likely take some time to occur.

A videodisc covering the World of the Vikings was developed jointly by the York Archaeological Trust in collaboration with the National Museum of Denmark (Maytom and Torevell 1993). Among the first uses of this platform in education was the Palenque prototype, which presented aspects of Mayan civilization and was developed in the USA for use in schools (Wilson 1988).

Compact Disc–Read Only Memory (CD–ROM) and its various types
CD–ROM was first introduced in 1985, the result of a joint agreement between Philips and Sony. It is also based on optical disc technologies. Smaller in size than the videodisc (12 cm/4.75inch), it looks similar to the audio CD. CD–ROM can store significant amounts of digital information (usually 650 megabytes, which is more than 450 times the capacity of conventional floppy discs) together with search and retrieval software. The whole *Oxford English Dictionary*, which runs to twenty volumes in conventional print and includes definitions for more than half a million words, has been stored on a single disc. This technology has opened up numerous possibilities for encyclopaedias, and Microsoft's Encarta is a good example of one which takes advantage of multimedia technologies, using the storage capacity of CD–ROM to enrich its presentation. CD–ROM has also proved very popular with libraries which use it to store bibliographic databases, dissertation abstracts, etc. CD–ROM players can be connected externally to computers, while many computers are now manufactured with internal CD–ROM drives.

There are various sub-products under this category which apart from enriching the jargon, try to address many different needs and audiences.

Initially, CD–ROMs stored only textual information, but as the need to include multimedia formats increased, a new type of disc was created in the late 1980s, CD–ROM eXtended Architecture (CD–XA). This is a multimedia platform supporting digital audio, graphics, and images.

A further development of CD–ROM and CD–XA is the Compact Disc–Interactive (CD–I) whose main target audience is the consumer market for home education and entertainment. CD–I players look very much like CD–Audio ones, have their computing power hidden in a simple, compact box, and can be connected to all types of televisions or computers. CD–I can be computer system independent, is compatible with existing electronic products, like CD–ROMs, and is easy to operate.

The ability of CD–I to display concurrently video, sound, graphics, and support windowed or overlaid information, was explored in a proto-type archaeological application; the EC-funded Sacred Way Project attempted to provide a tutorial training in archaeological method and theory, a multimedia resource on Classical Greek society, and a computer simulation of the site of Eleusis, near Athens (Lock and Dallas 1990).

Another type of compact disc released a few years ago by Kodak, is the Photo CD, which is a medium for storing digital photographs at different resolutions (Ross 1993). This holds up to 100 images from 35 mm film at very good quality, for display on an ordinary television, or for use with a computer-based system. At the Victoria and Albert Museum Photo CD is being used to create a database of high quality images of the collection (Seal 1994).

Multimedia applications in the humanities

Advantages and strengths

Although multimedia was from its early history connected with human-istic topics, and particularly with literature, it started having a noticeable impact on humanities in general only in the late 1980s. The initial interest and excitement about hypertext which had developed among linguists, philologists, and writers, spread later into other humanities disciplines, such as education (Ambron and Hooper 1990), biblical studies (DeRose 1991), music (Peterson 1991; Drone 1988), art history (Bearman 1989; Krämer 1994), museums and libraries (Besser 1987; Bearman 1991; Hoffos 1992, Lees 1993), and philosophy (Burkholder 1992).

Because visual information is of primary importance to many humani-ties disciplines, like archaeology and art, while sound is the essence of music, the ability of multimedia to integrate text, images, graphics, and sound offers immense potential for applications in these areas. Pictures have the power to offer visual descriptions or summaries of particularly complex phenomena, and can thus assist communication with peers, as well as the general public. Multimedia's ability for data visualization, and also for supporting limitless links between different images and data of various formats, provides humanists with a versatile tool for the construction of interpretation models, teaching, and public presentation.

The simulation of physical environments and processes on screen in a system which allows self-paced learning and free interaction can have useful applications in education and training. For example, multimedia tools have been used for teaching excavation principles and methods to archaeology students. Through a computer-based simulation of excavation environments students are prepared for real field work and excavation management.

Another positive effect of multimedia applications is that they can increase the access to specialized databases by making them more attractive and comprehensible to a wider audience. Since research databases are very demanding on time and resources to create and update, it would be reasonable and desirable to look into ways of making them appropriate for more generalized use. In the case of a research project in France presenting mosaics in the ancient Greek world (*Mosaïque dans le monde grec*), simply adding images from a videodisc to a documentary database made it interesting and useful, firstly, to a wider range of specialists and researchers, and, secondly, to the general audience which was initially attracted by the images (Guimier-Sorbets 1992).

Museums and libraries have been particularly interested in multimedia systems because of their potential to open entire collections to the public with minimal risks for conservation and security; the range of possibilities they offer for encouraging research; their ability to support education activities, assist exhibition planning, and enrich the interpretation of artefacts. For example, the Smithsonian Institution was one of the first museums to produce a CD–I titled 'The Treasures of the Smithsonian'. This was a 'take away' product for the general public, illustrating the highlights of the collections. The National Gallery in London has designed the Micro Gallery, a special area separated by the display galleries; there, the Micro Gallery multimedia program is available at several computer terminals offering information about the collection, the painters, artistic movements, and the geographical and historical background, using text, pictures, and maps. The National Gallery in Washington, DC, followed the British example and designed a similar educational application. Completed in 1995, this addresses the general public and utilizes text, images, animations, and diagrams. The British Library in London has developed several multimedia projects (for more information, see their WWW service at http://portico.bl.uk). 'The Image of the World: an interactive exploration of ten historic world maps' is a CD–ROM presenting ten world maps dating from 1250 to 1994 in full colour with audio commentary and on-screen text. Another initiative of the British Library is the Electronic *Beowulf* Project which created an extensive multimedia database of digital images of the famous eleventh-century manuscript (see Figure 5). These include important information for researchers, such as fibre-optic readings of hidden letters and ultra-violet readings of erased text (Kiernan 1995).

Another area where multimedia is being actively explored is electronic publishing. Reference tools like encyclopaedias are being produced in a cost-effective way, including images, video, and sound which make them more accessible and easier to understand. Using one of the electronic encyclopaedias available, for example Microsoft's Encarta, to look up Beethoven, you find the traditional text entry, but can also listen to a 30-second part from the Ninth Symphony; clicking again, you can hear the results of Beethoven's influence on Wagner. Similarly, in another example, the entry on Edvard Munch allows you to view a high-resolution image of *The Scream*.

In another field of electronic publishing, specialized publications such as excavation reports or historical monographs, can be produced, including all primary data and images of original documents which would not have been possible in traditionally printed books (Smith 1992). Academic publishing in electronic form, particularly in the humanities, is an area still in its infancy, but with great potential for further development in the future.

In the areas where multimedia has been applied and experimental projects tried out, the results indicate that it encourages interdisciplinary collaboration and research and the integration of various techniques. Additionally, evidence so far shows that, in contrast with printed publications where readers do not usually question the selection of the author or editor, in the case of multimedia documents users are more demanding and intellectually aggressive, challenging the authority of the proposed interpretation of culture against the wealth of primary evidence (Crane 1991).

Figure 5: *The Electronic Beowulf is one of the multimedia projects developed by the British Library*
The Netscape presentation was prepared by Professor Kevin S.. Kiernan, University of Kentucky, and is reproduced by permission of the British Library Board.

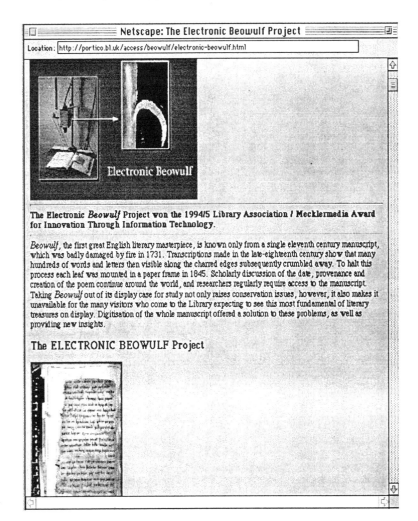

Limitations and weaknesses

Utopian enthusiasm about the effect of multimedia should be controlled, though, as it is still a technology under development with many areas that need to be further researched and developed.

The lack of standardization in software and hardware and the speed at which multimedia systems become obsolete constitute a serious problem. Despite the rapid growth of the last few years, the general maturing of software, and the emergence of certain platforms, we are still some way from standardized, compatible systems.

Another factor which impedes the widespread use of multimedia is the initial high costs involved in acquiring delivery systems and powerful computers. These programs are also memory-hungry and very demanding in disc space.

Copyright and intellectual property is also a problematic area affecting multimedia production, distribution, and use. These issues become even more complex when different institutions, languages, cultural backgrounds, and legislation systems are involved. It is very difficult to set rules for the use of these products by others and draw clear limits, especially since visual, textual, and auditory information can be manipulated and changed drastically in an integrated multimedia product which cannot be easily placed under one particular copyright category.

Although electronic publishing is developing rapidly, complete publication of research results over a network or on a CD–ROM does not yet seem a valid and respected form of professional communication, capable of earning researchers the same credit as a printed monograph. The same could be claimed about the development of multimedia applications for teaching (Martlew 1990).

Another problem related to multimedia applications in the humanities is that the main developments in this area are in most cases market-driven. Considerable sums are being invested in this industry and mass markets have been predicted—although these have not materialized yet. One gets the impression that often it is a case of the technology looking for an application, rather than the other way round.

Conclusion

Although it is still too early to predict the exact use and influence of multimedia interactives, they are already proving a powerful and revolutionary tool in the hands of researchers, educators, and artists. Their optimal use can lead to the empowerment of the user and the establishment of new trends in research. They are offering to the whole community of academics and researchers the opportunity to use an innovative teaching tool, a means to follow transdisciplinary paths in research, a way to display different—and often contradictory—views of cultural phenomena. As the novelty of these programs is wearing off and the technology is being further developed, humanists learn from past mistakes and experiences and start taking advantage of multimedia's potential and appeal.

Acknowledgements

I would like to thank Dr Seamus Ross, Dr Nikos Dessipris, Thaddeus Lipinski, and Dr Marilyn Deegan for useful suggestions on earlier versions of the manuscript.

References

Ambron, S., and Hooper, K. (eds.), *Learning with interactive multimedia: developing and using multimedia tools in education* (Redmond, WA: Microsoft Press, 1990).

Autodesk, *Xanadu documentation for Spire (Tm)* (Palo Alto, CA: Autodesk, Inc., 1991).

Bearman, D., 'Implications of interactive digital media for visual collections', *Visual Resources,* 5 (1989), 311-23.

Bearman, D. (ed.), *Proceedings of the first international conference on hypermedia and interactivity in museums,* Archives and Museum Informatics Technical Report No. 14, (Pittsburgh, PA: Archives and Museum Informatics, 1991).

Besser, H., 'The changing museum', in C. Ching-Chih (ed.) *Proceedings of the fiftieth ASIS Annual Meeting* (Medford, NJ: Learned Information Inc, 1987), 14-18.

Burkholder, L. (ed.), *Philosophy and the computer* (Boulder, CO: West View, 1992).

Bush, V., 'As we may think', *Atlantic Monthly,* 176 (July 1 1945), 101-08.

Conclin, J., 'Hypertext: an introduction and survey', *IEEE Computer,* 20.9 (1987), 17-42.

Crane, G., 'Composing culture—the authority of an electronic text', *Current Anthropology,* 32.3 (1991), 293-311.

Crane, G., and Mylonas, E., 'Ancient materials, modern media: shaping the study of classics with hypermedia', in Delany, P., and Landow, G. P. (eds.), *Hypermedia and literary studies* (Cambridge, MA: MIT Press, 1991), 205-20.

DeRose, S., 'Biblical studies and hypertext', in Delany, P., and Landow, G. P. (eds.), *Hypermedia and literary studies* (Cambridge, MA: MIT Press, 1991), 185-204.

Drone, J. M., 'HyperBach: a prototype, hypermedia music reference system', *OCLC Newsletter*, 173 (May-June 1988), 11-12.

Edwards, D. M., and Hardman, L., '"Lost in hyperspace": cognitive mapping and navigation in a hypertext environment', in McAleese, R. (ed.), *Hypertext: theory into practice* (Oxford: Blackwell Scientific Publishing, 1989), 105-25.

Engelbart, D. C., Watson, R. W., and Norton, J. C., 'The augmented knowledge workshop', *Proceedings of the American Federation of Information Processing Societies Conference and Exposition*, New York, 4-8 June (Montvale, NJ: AFIPS Press, 1973), 9-21.

Guimier-Sorbets, A.-M., 'Ouvrir à un large public l'access à une information specialisée', in Boardman, J., and Kurtz, D. (eds), *Proceedings of an international conference on data and image processing in classical archaeology*, Ravello, 1992 (European University Centre for the Cultural Heritage, 1992), 67-72.

Haan, B. J., Kahn, P., Riley, V.A., Coombs, J.H., and Meyrowitz, N.K., 'IRIS hypermedia services', *Communications of the ACM*, 35.1 (1992), 36–51.

Hoffos, S., *Multimedia and the interactive display in museums, exhibitions and libraries* (London: The British Library, 1992).

Kiernan, K. S., 'The Electronic Beowulf', *Computers in Libraries* (February 1995), 14–15.

Krämer, H., 'Believe your eyes and get the picture. Artworks and museums in the age of electronic communication', in Bruederlin, M., and Rothauer, D. (eds.), *Aura. The reality of the artwork between autonomy, reproduction and context* (Vienna: Wiener Secession, 1994), 93-100.

Lees, D. (ed.), *ICHIM 1993. Museums and interactive multimedia —Proceedings of the sixth international conference of the MDA and the second international conference on hypermedia and interactivity in museums* (Cambridge: The Museum Documentation Association, 1993).

Lock, G. R., and Dallas, C. J., 'Compact Disc-Interactive: a new technology for archaeology?', *Science and Archaeology*, 32 (1990), 5-14.

Martlew, R., 'Videodiscs and the politics of knowledge', in Miall, D. S. (ed.), *Humanities and the computer: new directions* (Oxford: Clarendon Press, 1990), 39-47.

Maytom, J., and Torevell, K., 'The world of the Vikings: an interactive video project', in Andressen, J., Madsen, T., and Scollar, I. (eds.), *Computing the past* (Aarhus: Aarhus University Press, 1993), 449-56.

Multimedia and related technologies: a glossary of terms, (Falls Church, VA: Monitor Information Services, 1991).

Nelson, T. H., 'The report on, and of, Project Xanadu concerning wordprocessing', *Literary Machines*, 87.1 (1987).

Nielsen, J., *Hypertext and hypermedia* (London: Academic Press, 1993).

Peterson, L. W., 'Music and multimedia: a progress report', *Institute for Advanced Technology Briefings* (1991), 12-13.

Ross, S., 'From conventional photographs to digital resources', *Archaeological Computing Newsletter*, 35 (1993), 14-21.

Seal, A., 'The creation of an electronic image bank: Photo-CD at the V&A', *ASLIB Managing Information*, 94.1 (1994), 42-4.

Smith, N., 'An experiment in electronic exchange and publication of archaeological field data', in Lock, G., and Moffett, J. (eds.), *Computer applications and quantitative methods in archaeology* 1991 (Oxford: Tempus Reparatum, 1992), 49-57.

Wilson, K. S., 'Palenque: an interactive multimedia digital video interactive prototype for children', *CHI '88* (conf. proceedings) Washington, DC, 15-19 May 1988 (New York: ACM, 1988), 275-9.

Further reading

General bibliography on multimedia technologies

Berk, E., and Devlin, J. (eds.), *The hypertext/hypermedia handbook* (New York: McGraw-Hill, 1991).

Feldman, T., *Multimedia in the 1990's* (London: The British Library, 1991).

Riley, F., *Understanding IT: a review of hypermedia authoring packages* (Hull: CVCP/USDU, 1994).

Shneiderman, B., and Kearsley, G., *Hypertext hands-on! An introduction to a new way of organizing and accessing information* (Reading, MA: Addison-Wesley Publishing Company, 1989).

Woodhead, N., *Hypertext & hypermedia—theory and applications* (Wilmslow: Sigma Press, 1990).

Yildiz, R., and Atkins, M., 'Evaluating multimedia applications', *Computer Assisted Education*, 21.1-2 (1993), 133-39.

Multimedia in the humanities

Barrett, E. (ed.), *Sociomedia—multimedia, hypermedia, and the social construction of knowledge* (Cambridge, MA: The MIT Press, 1992).

British Library Research & Development Department (BLR&DD), *Information technology in humanities scholarship: British achievements, prospects, and barriers*, BLR&D Report 6097 (London: The British Library and The British Academy, 1993).

Delany, P., and Landow, G. P. (eds.), *Hypermedia and literary studies* (Cambridge, MA: MIT Press, 1991).

Deegan, M., Timbrell, N., and Warren, L., *Hypermedia in the humanities* (Oxford/Hull Universities: ITTI, 1992).

Welsch, E. K., 'Hypertext, hypermedia, and the humanities', *Library Trends*, 40.4 (1992), 614-46.

Designing multimedia

Apple Computer, *Human interface guidelines: the Apple desktop interface* (Wokingham: Addison Wesley, 1987).

Blattner, M. M., and Dannenberg, R. B. (eds.), *Multimedia interface design* (Reading, MA: Addison-Wesley Publishing Company, 1992).

Edwards, A. D. N., and Holland, S. (eds.), *Multimedia interface design in education* (Berlin: Springer-Verlag, 1992).

Hoffos, S., with Sharpless, G., Smith, P., and Lewis, N., *The CD–I designer's guide* (London: McGraw-Hill Book Company, 1992).

Laurel, B. (ed.), *The art of human-computer interface design* (Reading, MA: Addison-Wesley, 1990).

Further information

Conferences

Hypertext
International meeting held annually since 1987 by the Association for Computing Machinery (ACM). In 1991, ACM decided to hold its annual meeting in Europe every second year under the name *ECHT'xx* (European Conference on Hypertext) and in North America in odd years under the name *Hypertext'xx*. ACM Headquarters, 1515 Broadway, New York, NY 10036. e-mail: acmhelp@acmvm.bitnet

CATH conferences (see also Introduction for further details)
Multimedia applications for teaching are often presented at these conferences.

ICHIM (International Conference on Hypermedia and Interactivity in Museums)
The first one was organized in Pittsburgh in 1991 and the second in Cambridge in 1993. Both have published proceedings which give a wealth of information on different projects and issues that relate to museums and public displays, but are also relevant to other disciplines. The last one was held in San Diego in October 1995, together with the annual conference of the Museum Computers Network.

Journals

Hypermedia
The first scientific journal dedicated to hypertext, it started in 1989. For subscription information or a free sample copy, contact: Taylor Graham Publishing, 500 Chesham House, 150 Regent Street, London W1R 5FA.

Journal of Educational Multimedia and Hypermedia (USA, vol.1-1992).

Many *electronic discussion lists* deal with technical matters for each authoring tool, (e.g. HYPERCRD@MSU.EDU for HyperCard), while theoretical issues are dealt with in lists of the various disciplines (e.g. MUSEUM-L for museums issues, ARCH-L for archaeology, etc.).

Geographic Information Systems in Humanities Research

David Wheatley

Introduction

It is often true of 'emergent' information technologies that you can tell when they have finally become mainstream when someone writes of their demise. This is now the case with GIS, with Allinson's (1994) claim that: 'Geographic Information Systems have nothing to offer. Their time is past and the "Third Wave" of computing has broken ...'. In disputing the premature obituary of GIS, it is possible to observe that Geographic Information Systems (GIS) are no longer the preserve of physical geographers, geologists, and hydrologists. At the same time that local government and commercial organizations were investing heavily in GIS to store and retrieve data about the built and natural environments, the potential of dedicated GIS for humanities research was also becoming apparent to researchers in disciplines such as socio-economic geography and archaeology. It now seems likely that the GIS will become a part of the standard 'research toolkit' of the humanities alongside text processing, networked communications, and database management systems.

This chapter aims to provide a general overview of what constitutes a GIS, and how the technology has already found applications and might find future applications within humanities research. The first section gives a general introduction to GIS, with particular emphasis on what distinguishes GIS from other forms of information technology. The informed reader may wish to skip this overview and move swiftly to the section which discusses some of the spatial analysis techniques which may be applied and/or improved on with the use of GIS. The final section of the chapter discusses some of the newer ways in which GIS is finding application in the humanities, such as predictive modelling, cost surface analysis, and landscape visibility analyses. Some illustrative examples are scattered throughout, and although these are mostly from archae-ological applications, this is a reflection of the author's particular research area and should not be taken to imply any 'special relationship' between GIS applications and archaeological research.

What is a Geographic Information System?

Geographic Information Systems (GIS) have proved surprisingly difficult to define comprehensively and exclusively, by which is meant that it has proved impossible to create a definition which both includes all commonly accepted examples of GIS, and excludes all other related forms of information technology. According to Burrough (1986) a GIS can be defined as:

> ... a powerful set of tools for collecting, storing, retrieving at will, transforming, and displaying spatial data from the real world for a particular set of purposes.

Alternatively it is possible to define GIS in terms of components. According to Marble (1987), for example, a system is a GIS if it contains each of four component subsystems for entry, storage, manipulation, and visualization of spatial (geographic) data. Each of the possible definitions has merit, although characteristically the definition by Burrough is both comprehensive and to the point. GIS, in reality, comprise a wide variety of hardware and software systems which are not particularly susceptible to precise definition. Sometimes examples of software which all claim to be GIS are connected only because their main purpose is the manipulation of data which are referenced by geographic position.

The spatial database

The basic component of a GIS is the spatial database, which consists of a digital record of the geographic entities in the area of interest. The representation of these components can be achieved in two fundamentally different ways: either through a raster approach, similar to that used in digital image processing (see Robinson in this volume), or through a vector approach comparable with that used by computer-aided design and drawing systems. In a vector system the locations, courses, or boundaries of geographic features are stored as a series of coordinate pairs which are used to describe fundamental mappable objects. In a raster system, the study area is divided into a finite number of (usually square) cells in which are placed the recorded attributes of the corresponding geographical location.

As in all areas of computer graphical representation, each approach has particular strengths and weaknesses: raster systems are simple to comprehend and good at representing variables which exhibit continuous variation over space, while vector systems are more complex but allow the user to undertake network analyses and provide more efficient storage of most types of geographic data. Raster systems, like image processing systems, are frequently data-intensive unless storage is at a low resolution, although this can be mitigated through the use of data compression. Vector systems, while generally more complex in their database model, are more suitable for the storage and analysis of discrete topological geographical systems such as river networks or pipelines.

Many systems now allow the use of a mixture of both types of representation with utilities to translate data from raster to vector and from vector to raster. This is becoming increasingly common because it offers a flexible way of manipulating spatial data. In fact most GIS systems incorporate elements of both vector and raster representation of data: although the GIS systems IDRISI (Clark University) and GRASS (US Corps of Engineers) are both generally regarded as 'raster' systems because they both perform the majority of their analysis on raster data, each has the capability to read and write vector data files. Similarly ARC/INFO (ESRI), and GeoNavigator (PAX technology), which are regarded as essentially 'vector' GIS systems, now contain modules for manipulating and displaying data in a raster form.

Layers and themes

Regardless of whether a raster or vector representation is selected, the data within the database are generally organized into layers which represent themes. A spatial database can be considered to be similar to a collection of thematic maps, each representing a different aspect of the same area. Each thematic map is contained in one section of the database. Raster systems usually refer to these separate thematic sections of the database as 'layers' while vector systems generally use the term 'coverages'. To avoid confusion, the term 'layer' will be used here to indicate both.

Layers differ from maps in that they generally contain only one type of geographic entity which refers to one specific geographic theme. For example, where a map may show roads, rivers, and contours all on the same sheet, this is rarely the case in a GIS. In the spatial database such a map would be split into separate layers with one layer for the elevation model or contour map, one layer for the river network, and one for the roads.

Layers also differ from a collection of maps in that the layers all share a common georeferencing system. A group of maps may differ fundamentally in both scale and projection, while the equivalent data within a spatial database are usually stored in a common projection, and usually (but not always) to a common resolution.

Georeferencing

The term 'georeferenced' refers to data which may be referenced according to their location in geographic space, and defined by a specified coordinate system. With raster images a simple form of georeferencing is to indicate the reference system (e.g. latitude/longitude or plane), the reference units (e.g. degrees or metres), and the coordinate locations of the corners of the raster image. In a vector system, a similar 'bounding rectangle' will usually be present so that the vector entities can be tied to a fixed standard. Georeferencing is a vital part of any GIS, because it is through georeferencing that data on separate layers can be analysed together and spatial analyses undertaken on them. The georeferencing mechanisms of a comprehensive GIS usually include the ability to set up appropriate coordinate transformations between a digitizing tablet and computer for accurate digitizing of map data, and routines to undertake cartographic projection from, for example, latitude/longitude into a common reference system such as the National Grid Reference system.

Locations, attributes, and topology

A spatial database must store three separate components of geographical entities: a *locational component* which defines the position of the entity in two-dimensional space; an *attribute component* which defines the non-spatial characteristics of the entities; and also a *topological component* which represents the logical relationships between the entities on a particular theme. Traditional (non-spatial) databases are explicitly concerned only with the attribute data of objects, although traditional database management systems, such as relational or network systems, can certainly be used to create and manipulate spatial databases suitable for GIS.

The four main types of mappable object are usually said to be points, lines, areas, and surfaces (see, for example, Berry 1987). The difference between area data and surface data can essentially be regarded as similar to the difference between nominal or ordinal level data. Area data (also called choropleth data) refer to geographic variables which are constant within a discrete area and have an abrupt boundary with other values. Surface data exhibit no such abrupt boundaries, and vary continuously over space. These basic entities can be used to represent objects from the real world such as sites, findspots, or sample locations (points); rivers, roads, or trade routes (lines); World Heritage Sites, geological substrates, soil type, or counties (area or choropleth data); or topographic elevation, slope, or distance from something (surfaces).

As well as this locational component, the spatial database must also store the non-spatial data which describe the properties of the spatial objects: the attribute component of the entities. In many cases a single spatial entity will have a number of attributes associated with it. Thus a point entity which is used to store a house may have attributes to record its length, width, height, colour, orientation, owner, and name.

Topological (logical) relationships between data entities occur in vector representations of line and area entities. Consider a simple road network, for example: the locational component of this can be represented as a series of lines, and attributes (for example, the name) can be recorded for each of the roads. This is shown in Figure 1 (left). However, this in itself is insufficient to fully record the road network. If we are interested in the possibilities of transport within this system, we need to know whether we can drive from the A31 onto the M4, and this is unclear. To understand this, we need to record not only where the roads are, but also where the roads meet and where they cross each other with bridges. This sort of information about the relationships between objects is referred to as the *topological* component of the spatial model.

In the case of the road network this means that it is necessary to introduce another spatial object into the model, referred to as a *node*, to record the way in which the roads relate to one another. In Figure 1 (right) the nodes have been included—only at the nodes are there road junctions—and we can now observe that to get from the A31 to the M4 we must use the A35.

In the case of choropleth data, such as County or Parish maps, it is usual to divide the data model into arcs, nodes, and areas, and then explicitly code the topology between these entities. Arcs are chains of lines which are used to represent the shared boundaries between the area

Figure 1: Left, roads represented as line entities with attributes. Right, introducing nodes (the black dots) into the model makes the relationship between the roads clear.

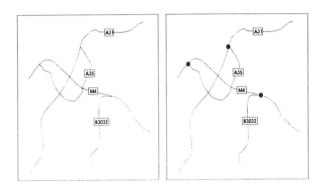

entities; nodes are the points at which the boundaries meet. Areas are then provided as a 'point of attachment' for the attribute data relating to each of the entities in which we are interested. This arc-node topological data structure is characteristic of vector GIS (such as ARC/INFO and MapInfo), and ensures two things. First, it ensures that the system stores the data efficiently because it prevents repetition of the boundaries which may be shared by several areas. Second, it ensures that the relationships between the spatial areas, such as which areas are adjacent to which others and which are wholly enclosed by others, are embedded within the data structure and, consequently, can be taken for granted by the analytical modules of the system.

Spatial analysis with GIS

One of the most important characteristics of GIS for the researcher is the ease with which quantification and statistical analysis of spatial patterns can be undertaken. Spatial analysis in the humanities, particularly within geography and archaeology, encompasses a wide range of analytical techniques and has a reasonably long history: spatial statistics were central to the 'new geography' and 'new archaeology' of the 1960s and 1970s. There is no inherent link, therefore, between spatial analysis and GIS: it is not necessary to work with a GIS in order to undertake spatial analysis, and statistical spatial analyses are not the only tasks for which GIS are useful. However, without wishing to re-invent the new geography, it is useful to reflect on the ways in which GIS can be used to apply and extend spatial analysis techniques within the humanities.

To that end, a very small number of spatial statistical methods will be covered here, and in very little detail. More detail on spatial analysis can be found in Hodder and Orton (1976), and on general statistical techniques appropriate to the humanities in Shennan (1988). Both of these are written by archaeologists (although with a wider audience in mind), but similar material can be found in a number of 'new geography' texts such as Haggett (1965).

The following briefly discusses some approaches to the spatial analysis which are commonly implemented in GIS. The reason for the inclusion of this section is not to encourage the reader to undertake such analyses with paper, pen, and calculator, but so that a researcher new to the field might have a better, and more critical, understanding of what the GIS is doing with the data. The reader should also be aware that this section contains only a tiny fraction of the variety of spatial analysis techniques which are implemented with GIS and consequently should be regarded simply as an illustration of the *kinds* of analyses which it is possible to undertake.

Analysis of point patterns

Point entities are a convenient shorthand representation for real-world objects which can be considered to have no spatial extent at the scale at which a researcher is interested. Thus point entities are used to represent, for example, archaeological artefact findspots within a region, towns or cities within a continent, or augered sample locations within a field. In analysing point patterns for spatial variation, the first requirement is generally to establish that there is a non-random spatial pattern of the points. Put simply, the first question in a spatial analysis of points must be *'is it likely that this pattern occurred through random processes?'*. If the answer to this question is no, then there is probably a pattern which requires explanation. Deviation from randomness can be either in the form of clustering, or in the form of regular spacing (see Figure 2).

Figure 2: *Types of point distributions: totally ordered (left), randomly ordered (middle) and clustered (right).*

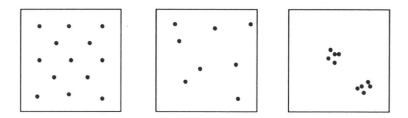

Quadrat methods
One approach to the measurement of randomness within point distributions is called *quadrat analysis*. This involves placing a regularly spaced grid over the distribution and comparing the contents of each grid cell. In a random population of points, the resulting frequency distribution of the number of points in each grid cell should be a Poisson distribution. One property of the distribution of quadrat counts which can be exploited is the *Variance* to *Mean* ratio $(V \, / \, m)$ of the distribution. In a Poisson distribution (random) this will be approximately one (the mean number of points per quadrat will be the same as the variance). In a clustered distribution this will be greater than one (the variance will tend to be greater than the mean, due to high numbers in single quadrats), while for a dispersed distribution it will be less than one, because there will be little deviation from the mean. An index of dispersion can be calculated from:

$$(V \, / \, m) \times (n - 1) \quad \text{(where } n \text{ is the number of points)}$$

and this can be compared with the χ^2 statistic for $(n - 1)$ degrees of freedom to form a significance test at a chosen significance level.

Quadrat analysis is implemented in many GIS, most commonly within raster systems where rasterized occurrence data can be regarded to be in the form of quadrats already. Typical output (in this case from the IDRISI GIS) is shown in Figure 3, which shows a variance to mean ratio of 0.14, indicating a more dispersed pattern than might be expected. The GIS has

Figure 3: Typical output from a GIS quadrat analysis of a 10×10 region with 100 points. This result shows a very low variance to mean ratio, suggesting unusually dispersed points. The system has also conducted a Student's t-test which shows that this result is significant at the 0.001 level.

```
  IDRISI   : Quadrat Analysis                                v.4.03


 n                          :                    100
 mean (density)             :               1.000000
 variance                   :               0.141414

 Variance/Mean Ratio        :               0.141414
 t                          :              -6.040687
 df                         :                     99

 Significance Level         :                <0.001

 Values significantly smaller than 1 suggest a regular pattern

 Quadrat area is from 1.00 to 2.00 times estimates of "ideal" quadrat area
```

also conducted a Student's t-test which shows that this deviation from a random result is significant at the 0.001 level.

Although quadrat methods are easy to apply, and convenient in a number of situations such as the analysis of archaeological fieldwalking data, there are a number of disadvantages of using an approach based on quadrats. Quadrat studies can be badly affected by the size of quadrat selected for the study: if the quadrat unit size selected is too small or too large, then the variations between the numbers of points within each unit will be dramatically changed, and the result will suggest randomness where a clustered pattern is present. Quadrat studies can also be adversely affected by the regular shape of the units (almost always squares) and by the starting point of the quadrat grid. To reduce these effects, it is possible to perform several quadrat analyses with differing sizes of quadrat, or to repeat several analyses with offset grid origins. However, these mitigation strategies do not overcome the inherent weaknesses of quadrat methods.

Nearest-neighbour distances

Because of such limitations, alternative approaches based on nearest-neighbour statistics can be used. These rely on the distance of each point to the nearest other point (usually called *r*). In a region of area *A*, with *n* points, which has ρ points per unit area, then the mean nearest-neighbour distance of the points in a random point pattern will depend only on the density of points. The 'randomness' or otherwise of the distribution can then be assessed by comparing the expected $\bar{r}$ (if the distribution were random), with the observed $\bar{r}$ in the actual distribution. This can be expressed as a ratio *R* where:

$$R = \left(\bar{r}_{observed}\right) / \left(\bar{r}_{expected}\right)$$

In a random distribution of points *R* will be approximately 1, while in a clustered distribution it will be between 1 and zero, and in a dispersed pattern it will tend towards a maximum of 2.1491 (which occurs in a 'perfect' dispersal pattern of a triangular lattice).

As with quadrat techniques, it is possible to construct a significance test for randomness using the standard error of the expected $\bar{r}$ calculated from:

$$\sigma\left(\bar{r}_{expected}\right) = 0.26136 / \sqrt{(n\rho)}$$

which can be used to generate a test statistic as follows:

$$C = \left(\bar{r}_{observed} - \bar{r}_{expected}\right) / \sigma\left(\bar{r}_{expected}\right)$$

If the number of points is greater than about 100, then this can be compared with the normal distribution so that *C* = 1.96 is a significant result at the 0.05 significance level, and *C* = 2.58 is significant at the 0.01 level.

Although not entirely without problems, particularly with respect to the imposition of boundaries on a point pattern, nearest-neighbour analyses generally produce a more robust assessment of randomness in a point pattern.

Spatial autocorrelation

The amount of spatial autocorrelation in a variable is a description of the extent to which the value of a spatial variable in one location makes a similar value in a neighbouring location more or less likely. If the presence of a high value makes it more likely that a neighbouring location will also have a high value, then the spatial variable is said to exhibit positive spatial autocorrelation, while if the presence of a high value makes it more likely that a neighbouring location will have a *low* value, then the variable is said to exhibit negative spatial autocorrelation. Spatial autocorrelation can be present in any kind of data, from categorical data, such as geological maps, through to continuous data, such as artefact measurements. It is an equally valid concept with point data, as with choropleth maps.

Identifying spatial autocorrelation is often the first step in an analysis of some spatial variable, because if data can be shown to be spatially autocorrelated, then there is usually some geographical or cultural process which needs to be explained.

One of the most widely applied measures of spatial autocorrelation is the Moran's *I* statistic which has been widely discussed in relation to archaeological applications (see, for example, Cliff and Ord 1973 for the most widely cited discussion, or Kvamme 1993 for a more recent one). Moran's *I* is defined as:

$$I = \left[\frac{n}{\sum_i \sum_j W_{ij}} \right] \left[\frac{\sum_i \sum_j (x_i - \bar{x})(x_j - \bar{x})}{\sum_i (x_i - \bar{x})^2} \right]$$

where $\bar{x}$ is the mean value of the spatial variable. Each observation x_i, is compared with each other observation x_j with consideration of the spatial relationship between them contained in the term W_{ij} which is a weighting. In practice this weight is usually $1/d_{ij}$ the inverse of the distance between the locations being compared. Alternatively, in situations where 'county' data are being used W_{ij} can be set to 1 for the case where x_i and x_j share a border, and 0 for the case where they do not (sometimes the proportion of the border which x_i shares with x_j is used to modify this crude weighting).

However the weighting is calculated, Moran's *I* theoretically varies from −1 (for negative spatial autocorrelation) to +1 (for positive autocorrelation) although in practice it is rarely found to exceed +0.8 or −0.8 in 'perfect' cases. Moran's *I* can be used to construct a significance test either by assuming that the x_i observations are drawn from a normally distributed population (normality assumption) or by considering the calculated value of *I* relative to the set of all possible permutations of *I*

Figure 4: *Extreme cases of positive (left) and negative (right) spatial autocorrelation*

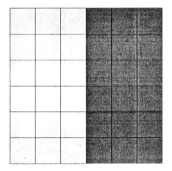 

with the n observations (randomization assumption). The randomization assumption is generally more useful in situations where the characteristics of the population cannot usually be ascertained.

Spatial association

All of the analyses described above provide indications of the spatial characteristics of some phenomenon. However, neither the non-random arrangement of the observations, nor the amount of autocorrelation within a spatial variable can be said to provide any explanation of these things. To look for explanations, it is necessary to try and associate the pattern in which we are interested with other, possibly explanatory, variables. One of the most useful products of the GIS is that the system is capable of producing all the information needed to undertake analyses of the associations between spatial phenomena in which we have an interest, with other spatial variables which might be supposed to have an effect on them. This is because GIS is not only capable of producing all the data necessary for a traditional two-sample significance test, but also the sample and population statistics necessary to construct a more powerful one-sample test (Kvamme 1990b).

Two-sample significance tests

Given a set of interesting locations (such as archaeological monuments, shops, or murders), and the desire to know whether or not they are randomly distributed with respect to some other spatial phenomenon (for example roads, soil productivity, economic status) traditionally requires the construction of a two-sample significance test. For this, the characteristics of the locations are tabulated, a random sample of locations from the same region is generated, and the appropriate characteristic recorded for these locations as for the locations of interest.

A pair of hypotheses are then constructed to test the idea that the locations are non-randomly distributed with respect to the overall distribution of the supposed explanatory variable, and the two samples (the interesting one and the random one) are compared in order to ascertain how likely it is that they were drawn from the same statistical population. If they seem to have been drawn from the same population, then H_0 (the hypothesis of no difference) holds, and the interesting locations cannot be held to be non-randomly distributed with respect to the variable of interest. If it is likely that they are drawn from different populations then H_0 is rejected and it can be said that the sites are non-randomly distributed with respect to the characteristic. Examples of this might include a test to find if a particular type of decorated pottery was non-randomly distributed with respect to supposed distribution centres, or whether the distribution of football fields in the UK is associated with the incomes of the local inhabitants (I have no idea whether either of these are true).

GIS can produce all the information necessary to conduct a two-sample test by generating random point locations from the same geographical region as the archaeological locations and then rapidly assigning the spatial variables to both the interesting locations and to the random sample. A test appropriate to the nature of the data can then be undertaken, for example a χ^2 test may be appropriate for nominal scale data, a Kolmogorov-Smirnov test for ordinal or higher level data (see Shennan 1988 for further details of these procedures). An example of a two-sample test using the Mann-Whitney U statistic (from Wheatley 1995a) is given below in relation to an analysis of visibility.

One-sample significance tests

Two-sample approaches such as these are hampered by the fact that the characteristics of the population from which the samples are drawn are not directly observed. Instead they are inferred from the characteristics of the random sample, allowing for the possible sampling error. Obviously, the larger the random sample, the more accurate the estimate of the population characteristics will be, but a more powerful one-sample approach is made possible by GIS. Because a GIS can produce statistics which summarize the values of a spatial variable for an entire geographic region, it can effectively produce the statistics which are needed to characterize the population from which the archaeological locations are drawn. Under these circumstances, it is possible to compare the characteristics of the archaeological locations directly with the characteristics of the population and perform a one-sample significance test.

For example, if the spatial variable in which we are interested is mapped for the entire region, then it is possible to generate a histogram of all occurrences of that variable—in other words, it is possible directly to observe the characteristics of the population from which the interesting locations are drawn. With this information, it is then possible to compare the characteristics of the interesting things directly with the population from which they are drawn, and therefore make more secure inferences about how likely it is to be non-randomly selected. The ability to perform a one-sample test, as opposed to a two-sample test, is of some importance because the one-sample approach makes use of all the available information, and as Kvamme (1990b) has pointed out: 'one-sample statistical tests which compare a site sample against a background standard are conceptually and statistically superior'. An example of a one-sample Kolmogorov-Smirnov test (also from Wheatley 1995a) is given below in the section relating to visibility and intervisibility.

New directions with GIS

Predictive modelling

One of the most common applications of GIS has been the construction of what have come to be known as predictive models, particularly of archaeological resources. In archaeological contexts, this means that the aim is to construct an hypothesis about the location of archaeological remains which can be used to predict the locations of sites which have not yet been observed. Kvamme (1990a) puts it as follows:

> ... a predictive archaeological locational model may sim-
> ply be regarded as an assignment procedure, or rule, that
> correctly indicates an archaeological event outcome at a

land parcel location with greater probability than that attributable to chance.

Most of the work on the development of archaeological predictive models has been undertaken in the United States, by governmental organizations such as the National Parks Service. Since the late 1970s, such agencies have been interested in the prediction of the locations of archaeological sites within fairly large regions from information based on surveys of far smaller areas. The main impetus for the development of predictive methods was therefore practical and economic: it was believed that such methods could reduce the effort required to create a justified land-management strategy for a large region by reducing the area which needed to be surveyed, and hence reducing the expenditure. Again, Kvamme (1990a) describes well the motivation for the development of the techniques:

> If powerful resource location models can be developed then cultural resource managers could use them as planning tools to guide development and land disturbing activities around predicted archaeologically sensitive regions. This planning potential of predictive models can itself represent significant cost savings for governmental agencies.

Predictive modelling is not a single method, but essentially describes a wide range of approaches to one specific problem. Predictive models can be based on two different sources of information:

- theories about the spatial distribution of archaeological material;
- empirical observations of the archaeological record.

When a model is based entirely on theory then the model is referred to as a deductive or theory-driven model. If the model is based entirely on observations it is referred to as an inductive or data-driven model. Conceptually, it should be possible to create a model based either on pure induction, or on pure deduction: for example we may theorize a relationship between site location and environmental resources and then implement this relationship as a predictor in a GIS without any recourse to the actual locations of the sites. Alternatively it may be possible to derive a mechanical method for using the environmental characteristics of a group of known sites to deriving such a relationship without recourse to a hypothesis about the function or meaning of the sites.

It should be recognized, however, that such a distinction between data and theory is not universally recognized, and most theorists now accept that the two are not independent—data are collected within a theoretical context, and so may be regarded as theory-laden, while theories are generally based to some extent on empirical observations. However, although it is not practically possible to devise a predictive modelling method which is based entirely on either of these tactics, it is useful to maintain the distinction between the two approaches at a methodological level.

Inputs and outputs

The inputs to predictive models are usually in the form of information about the landscape which is likely to have an effect on the presence or absence of whatever we are interested in. Various inputs may be used, including the physical and environmental characteristics of the region, which are the most easily obtained inputs in GIS contexts, and therefore the most widely used inputs to models. Which variables are selected should be determined by knowledge that they are related to the location of the sites in question, which may be determined either by the experience of a particular archaeologist or more formally by a statistical analysis of existing sites. A huge variety of characteristics may be used as predictors, and those which have been employed include elevation, landform derivatives such as slope, aspect, indices of ridge/drainage, local relief, geological and soil data, nominal classifications of land class (such as 'canyon', 'plain', 'rim', etc.), and distances to resources such as water (rivers), or raw material sources (flint). In cases where the vegetation is considered not to have changed significantly, vegetation classes may also be used. Spatial parameters can sometimes be used in cases where sites are known to have spatial relationships—in other words, they tend to cluster or to be noticeably dispersed; this information can then be used as a predictor in the model. For example, if it is assumed that a particular type of site is likely to form a clustered distribution, then the likelihood of an undiscovered site occurring in any given location will decrease with distance from known sites. Cultural features can also be used: in many cases the cultural features of a landscape can be of use in predicting the presence/absence of something—for example, it may be that sites occur in close proximity to road networks or to related central places.

The output from the model may be very simple or fairly complex, and may take a variety of specific forms, such as presence/absence of site. Presence/absence models usually represent one specific site type with general characteristics which can be reliably claimed, but these site classes may be defined by function or by chronology. Output in this case is binary, or at best it varies between zero and the number of predictors (as in, for example, van-Leusen 1993).

The main alternative to simple presence/absence models are probability models which produce an indication of the probability of a site occurring at each location in the landscape. The most widely used and advocated method of probability modelling is logistic regression analysis (discussed in, for example, Warren 1990a). This is a multivariate probability model in which a series of known cases with two possible states are used to predict the probability of unknown cases having each of these states. The inputs are therefore scores for known cases on supposed predictors, and the output is a regression equation which describes the probability of an unknown case with known scores being one of the states. Logistic regression has a number of advantages as for predictive modelling, notably that it allows the use of predictor variables measured at a nominal, ordinal, or ratio level. For example, Warren (1990b) uses logistic regression to predict the presence or absence of prehistoric Shawnee sites in a 91 square kilometre region of the Ozark hills in Southern Illinois from a wide variety of environmental characteristics such as elevation, soil type, local relief, and land productivity. Probability models have also begun to find some use in British archaeology, although a recent attempt to use logistic regression to predict the densities of prehistoric lithic scatters on Salisbury Plain (Wheatley forthcoming) showed that there are problems associated with the methodology.

Distance and cost surface analyses

Buffers, corridors, and proximity surfaces
One of the most useful features of GIS is the generation of distance maps, either in the form of distance surfaces or as distance buffers. Distance surfaces are maps of continuous variation in which the magnitude at any point of the map is the proximity to a particular geographic entity. Distance buffers and corridors are simply discrete versions of distance

surfaces in the form of choropleth maps where the classes represent a range of distances from the entity.

It is also possible to extend the calculation of distances to include measures of 'friction' or the cost of traversing the landscape. In this way GIS distance calculations can be extended into a form of model, the output of which is generally interpreted as a representation of the time taken to reach any given location from a place of interest. The products of these types of analysis have been applied to the identification of site territories or regions of control (e.g. Gaffney and Stancic 1991, and Hunt 1992) as an improvement on the use of Thiessen's polygons.

Cost surface analyses have also found considerable use in the application of optimization theories, where the locations of a particular site or group of sites are interpreted in terms of the maximization of the resources available to them. Obviously the resources available to a particular site depend not only on distance, but also on the effort expended on reaching the resources. One example of the application of cost surfaces in this respect is the use by Gaffney and Stancic (1991) of cost surfaces to modify Site Catchment Analysis, in order to better understand the location of Iron Age Hillforts on the Island of Hvar, Croatia.

The basic tenet of site catchment analysis is that the farther from a base site resources are, the greater the economic cost of exploiting them. Eventually there is a point at which the cost of exploitation outstrips the return and an economic boundary can be defined at this point to define the exploitation territory of a site. The exploitation territory or catchment of any given site can then be approximated as a circular area centred on the site in question—the proportions of given resources within this area can then be analysed and compared with the resources within similar territories from other sites. Having obtained the characteristics of each of the catchments to be compared, the different character of the sites should then become apparent. For example, if some sites are settlements used for cereal growing, while others are bases for hunting activities, then the catchments of the settlements associated with agriculture might be expected to exhibit higher proportions of lighter, fertile soils.

Gaffney and Stancic's (1991) study suggested that the incorporation of cost estimates into site catchment analyses can have a significant effect on the characterization of the sites. In the case of Hvar, this not only affected calculations of available resources for the sites, but also revealed that catchments which overlapped when circular estimates were used could be seen to be mutually exclusive when cost of movement was incorporated (Gaffney and Stancic 1991).

Visibility and intervisibility studies with GIS

In a GIS which has elevation as one of the layers, lines of sight can be extrapolated between any two points in the landscape. A large number of such observations can then be combined to provide new data themes which represent a landscape classified according to whether or not a particular place or series of places is visible. Such images are commonly referred to as 'visibility maps' or 'viewshed maps' and have already found some application within the humanities: Gaffney and Stancic, for example, generated a viewshed map for the watchtower at Maslinovik, Hvar, which demonstrated that a similar watchtower at Tor would have been visible from Maslinovik, which would in turn have been able to pass warnings to the town of Pharos. Their result supported the assumption that such towers formed 'an integral system connected to the town and Pharos whereby watch was kept for any approaching danger' (Gaffney and Stancic 1991, p.78). Viewshed maps were also used by Ruggles *et al.* (1993) as part of a method for investigating the locations of the short standing stone rows of the island of Mull. This method suggested that viewshed maps for each of the standing stone row sites should be combined to create a binary *multiple viewshed map* consisting of the logical union of the individual maps. From this, prominent landscape features on which the stones may have been aligned could be identified, and viewshed maps generated from these locations. Finally a count could be made of the number of stone row sites falling within these landscape features, and 'the landscape features which best explain the observed placing of the stone rows are those for which this number is greatest' (Gaffney and Stancic 1991).

Another approach to analysing this information is to concentrate on the *area* of terrain which is visible from the locations of interest. Wheatley (1995a, 1995b) analysed the locations of Neolithic funerary mounds (long barrows) in Southern England in this way, first by generating individual visibility maps from each monument, then by calculating the areas which these maps represent. A random sample of locations within the same region was then generated, and treated in the same way. Of the two regions analysed, one provided a significant result which suggested preferential siting of one group of funerary monuments in areas of high visibility.

Intervisibility within samples of sites

In situations where the intervisibility within a group of sites is of interest, it is possible to obtain a viewshed map for each site location. These individual maps can then be summed, using simple map algebra techniques, to create one surface. This surface then represents, for each cell within the landscape, the number of sites with a line of sight from that cell. For a sample of n sites, the value of this surface will obviously consist of integers which are constrained to vary between 0 and n. Such a map may be referred to as a *cumulative viewshed map* for the sample of sites within the particular region of interest.

Having generated a cumulative viewshed surface from a sample of sites, it is then possible to perform a point-select operation on this surface based on the site locations, and thus to obtain, for each site, the number of other sites which are visible from it. This can then be regarded as a statistical population while the new attribute values of the sites can be regarded as a sample from that population. Given these, it is straightforward to construct a pair of testable hypotheses as follows:

- H_0—That the sites are distributed irrespective of the number of other sites which are visible;

- H_1—That the sites are not distributed irrespective of the number of other sites which are visible.

Using the GIS capability to summarize the characteristics of the cumulative viewshed map (population) and the site attributes (sample), it is then possible to construct a one-sample hypothesis test, at an appropriate confidence interval, to accept or reject this hypothesis.

As for the two-sample analysis, the study from which this was drawn (Wheatley 1995a) found significant results in one series but not the other, suggesting monuments in at least one of the areas may have been deliberately sited not only for maximum visibility within the landscape, but also with some regard to the number of other barrows which would have been visible.

Conclusions

This chapter started with the suggestion that a technology can genuinely be thought of as 'mainstream' only when researchers begin to write about it in the past tense. It is possible, I think, to recognize Allinson's unduly pessimistic conclusion (referred to in the introduction) for the sensationalism that it is. However, at the same time it should also be recognized that GIS do not represent a panacea for the humanities any more than Internetworking or database management systems do. Instead, their ability to manipulate large quantities of data about the landscape rapidly will ensure that they form part of the humanities research toolkit for some time.

GIS, far from representing anything particularly new, merely represents something liberating: a technology which allows the researcher to concentrate on doing better research, rather than on counting points or measuring areas. For this reason, GIS has now progressed from an 'emergent' phase, in which commentators heralded its merits with little or no evidence that it could or would be used in the humanities, to a 'mature' phase in which genuinely useful applications of GIS in archaeology, geography, and the social sciences are appearing. Analytical and research methods, such as catchment analyses, and the various approaches to spatial statistics are all being applied in a more comprehensive and sophisticated way than ever before with GIS, while new techniques and methods such as visibility analyses, network analysis, and cost-surface approaches are being developed and discussed.

I have no idea whether the 'third wave' referred to by Allinson has broken or not, but whatever the state of the tidal race we can be reasonably sure that humanities research has its surfboard ready.

References and bibliography

Allen, K.M.S., Green, S., and Zubrow, B.W., *Interpreting space: GIS and archaeology* (London: Taylor and Francis, 1990).

Allinson, J., *The breaking of the third wave: the demise of GIS.* AGI '94 conference proceedings. (London: Association for Geographic Information, 1994).

Berry, J.K., 'Fundamental operations in computer aided map analysis', *International Journal of Geographic Information Systems,* 1 (1987), 119-136.

Burrough, P.A., *Principles of Geographic Information Systems for land resources management* (Oxford: Clarendon Press, 1986).

Cliff, A.D., and Ord, J.K., *Spatial autocorrelation.* Monographs in spatial and environmental analysis (London: Pion, 1973).

Downie, N.M., and Heath, R.W., *Basic statistical methods* (London: Harper and Row, 1965).

Gaffney, V., and Stancic, Z., *GIS approaches to regional analysis: a case study of the Island of Hvar.* (Ljubljana: Filozofska fakulteta, 1991).

Haggett, P., *Locational analysis in human geography* (London: Edward Arnold, 1965).

Hodder, I., and Orton, C., *Spatial analysis in archaeology* (Cambridge: Cambridge University Press, 1976).

Hunt, E.D., 'Upgrading site catchment analysis with GIS', *World Archaeology*, 24.2 (1992), 104–112.

Kvamme, K.L., 'The fundamental principles and practice of predictive archaeological modelling', in Voorips, A. (ed), *Mathematics and information science in archaeology: a flexible framework*. Studies in Modern Archaeology Volume 3, 257-295 (Bonn: Holos-Verlag, 1990a).

Kvamme, K.L., 'One-sample tests in regional archaeological analysis: new possibilities through computer technology', *American Antiquity*, 55.2 (1990b), 367-81.

Kvamme, K.L., 'Spatial statistics and GIS: an integrated approach', in Andresen, J., Madsen, T., and Scollar, I., *Computing the past—CAA92*, (Aarhus: Aarhus University Press, 1993).

Lock, G., and Stancic, Z., *Archaeology and GIS: a European perspective* (London: Taylor and Francis, 1995).

Marble, D.F., 'The computer and cartography', *The American Cartographer*, 14 (1987), 101-103.

Martin, D., *Geographic Information Systems and their socioeconomic applications* (London: Routledge, 1991).

Ruggles, C.L.N., Medyckyj-Scott, D.J., and Gruffydd, A., 'Multiple viewshed analysis using GIS and its archaeological application: a case study in northern Mull', in Andresen, J., Madsen, T., and Scollar, I., *Computing the past—CAA92*, (Aarhus: Aarhus University Press, 1993).

Shennan, S.J., *Quantifying archaeology* (Edinburgh: Edinburgh University Press, 1988).

Star, J., and Estes, J., *Geographic Information Systems: an introduction* (London: Prentice Hall, 1990).

Tomlin, C.D., *Geographic Information Systems and cartographic modeling*. (Prentice Hall Publishers, 1990).

van-Leusen, P.M., 'Cartographic modelling in a cell-based GIS', in Andresen, J., Madsen, T., and Scollar, I., *Computing the past—CAA92*, (Aarhus: Aarhus University Press, 1993).

Vita-Finzi, C., and Higgs, E.S., *Prehistoric economy in the Mount Carmel area of Palestine. Site Catchment Analysis*. PPS 36 (1970), 1-37.

Warren, R.E., 'Predictive modelling of archaeological site location: a case study in the Midwest, in Allen, K.M.S., Green, S.W., and Zubrow, E.B.W., *Interpreting space: GIS and archaeology* (London: Taylor and Francis, 1990a).

Warren, R.E., 'Predictive modelling of archaeological site location: a primer', in Allen, K.M.S., Green, S.W., and Zubrow, E.B.W., *Interpreting space: GIS and archaeology* (London: Taylor and Francis, 1990b).

Wheatley, D.W., 'Cumulative viewshed analysis: a GIS-based method for investigating intervisibility, and its archaeological application', in Lock, G., and Stancic, Z., *Archaeology and GIS: a European perspective* (London: Taylor and Francis, 1995a).

Wheatley, D.W., *The application of GIS to archaeology with case studies from Neolithic Wessex*. PhD Thesis, University of Southampton, 1995b.

Wheatley, D.W., *The use of GIS in the interpretation of extensive survey data*. Paper given at CAA1995, Leiden, Netherlands. Forthcoming.

Worboys, M.F., *GIS: a computing perspective* (London: Taylor and Francis, 1995).

Further information

Further information on GIS can be obtained from a variety of textbooks. A widely used text in teaching which provides a general introduction is Burrough (1986), although alternatives might be Star and Estes (1990), Tomlin (1990), or Worboys (1995). The socio-economic applications of GIS are discussed by Martin (1991). Archaeological applications can be found in Allen *et al.* (1990), and in Lock and Stancic (1995).

A variety of electronic sources may be of interest, including comp.infosystems.gis (Usenet newsgroup) which is identical in content to the GIS-L mailing list. To subscribe send an e-mail message to: listserver@urisa.org
including in the body of the text the following command:
SUScribe GIS-L firstname lastname

The Association for Geographic Information (AGI) holds annual conferences on GIS and publishes the proceedings of these. The AGI can be contacted at: Association for Geographic Information, 12 Great George Street, Parliament Square, London, SW1P 3AD. United Kingdom. The AGI also has a WWW site: http://www.geo.ed.ac.uk/root/agidict/html/agi.html

Other WWW sites of value might include Edinburgh University's GIS home page http://www.geo.ed.ac.uk/home/gishome.html which has introductory material about GIS as well as information about current research in Edinburgh. Alternatively, the United States Geological Survey provides a great deal of information about GIS:
http://www.geo.ed.ac.uk/research/gis/title.html

An online tutorial for ARC/INFO is available from:
http://boris.qub.ac.uk/shane/arc/ARChome.html

Symbolic Representations for Music

Alan Marsden

The application of computers in musical research has by now a twenty-five year long history, but the plea for a generally accepted common computer-readable representation for musical information (see, for example, Lincoln 1974) remains unanswered. In contrast to some other areas of computer application, it is still uncommon for a musicologist to use software written by another musicologist, or even to use another musicologist's data. The most common pattern remains the apparently least efficient one of each musicologist designing her or his own tools and encoding her or his own data. There are, however, notable exceptions of increasing importance, and there are representations (e.g. MIDI, Musical Instrument Digital Interface) which have received wide acceptance in certain areas of music. Furthermore, the literature discussing general issues in the representation of music (e.g. Roads 1984; Pope 1986; Hewlett and Selfridge-Field 1987, 1-22; Carter *et al.* 1988; Garnet 1991; Huron 1992; Marsden 1993; Wiggins *et al.* 1993) is disproportionate to the quantity describing actual representations. Together these facts suggest that a more realistic outcome in the medium term is not the attainment of a single generally accepted common representation, but a number of more specialized representations accepted within the appropriate communities. The intention of this paper is not to survey these representations comprehensively, but rather to uncover, through examination of selected examples, the principles which underlie symbolic representations of music in order to guide the development of new representations and of mechanisms to facilitate their coexistence.

Theory of representation

The basis of representation is the well-known relationship of signifier and signified: an entity in the representation—the 'signifier', refers to or stands for something in the world represented—the 'signified'. A representation consists of 'signifiers' corresponding to 'signifieds' in the world represented. The term 'representation scheme' will be used to mean a particular relation of signifiers and signifieds.

Requirements of a representation scheme

There are two essential requirements of a representation scheme. First, different situations in the world represented must correspond to different representations. However, a representation cannot but be *selective* with respect to the aspects of the world which are represented (otherwise the representation must *be* the world). It is common in music, for example, to ignore the spatial aspects of a musical performance, i.e. where the performers sit or stand. Therefore the first requirement more properly requires that situations in the world which differ *with respect to the aspects represented* correspond to different representations. (The element of circularity in this requirement is unavoidable.) Note that the mapping of situations (or, more properly, equivalence classes of situations defined by equivalence with respect to the aspects represented) to representations can be one-to-many, so that different representations can correspond to the same situation. This can be undesirable, and has led, in the case of the commonly used DARMS (Digital Alternate Representation for Music Scores) representation for music, to attempts to define a *canonical* manner of representation (McLean 1988).

The purpose of a representation is to allow one to perform manipulations on the representation by which one may make predictions about, or effect changes in, the world represented. Generally speaking, these manipulations correspond to some action in the world represented. The result of performing a manipulation on a representation is another representation, not necessarily within the same representation scheme. It is required that the resultant representation correspond to the world as it is or would be, following the corresponding action in the world as first represented. This second requirement, therefore, strictly concerns not only the representation but also what one does with it.

In designing a representation scheme which is intended for general use, therefore, one needs to make predictions both about the aspects of the world researchers will want to represent and about the manipulations to be performed on representations. One can be precise about the former—embodied in the representation scheme is a definition of the aspects of the world it is capable of representing: if a difference in the world is not reflected in a difference in a representation, that aspect of the world is not represented—but one cannot be precise about the latter since, unless the number of different possible representations is finite, the number of manipulations which may be performed on a representation is infinite. It therefore becomes the responsibility of the *user* of the representation scheme to honour the requirement that manipulations of a representation correspond with actions in the world. However, the task of designing such manipulations can be helped. (Examples will be given below.)

Symbolic representation

To describe a representation as 'symbolic' will be taken to indicate that the representation will consist of distinct items (symbols) as signifiers, relating to at least notionally distinct items (let them be called 'entities') as signifieds in the world represented. Distributed representations, in which the relationship of signification is between *patterns* within the representation and things in the world represented, and continuous representations, in which there are no distinct symbols, are therefore excluded.

***Figure 1**: Three-way relation of signification in representations for computer use*

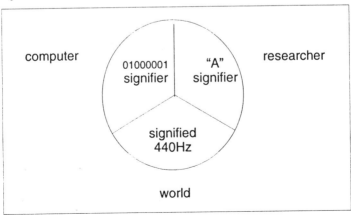

Since our concern is with the use of computers in research and not, for example, with the use of computers embedded within a larger machine, a representation must be meaningful (i.e. a relationship of signifiers to signifieds must exist) for human researchers as well as for computers. There is thus a three-way relationship between human, computer, and world (Figure 1). The symbol 'A', for example, can relate to a particular concept for a researcher, a particular bit-pattern for a computer, and a particular pitch in the musical world. There are frequently many intervening layers of representation which complicate this picture. For example, a researcher wishing to communicate the pitch associated with fundamental frequency 440Hz to a computer will first translate this concept to the concept of the character 'A'. Then a pattern of ink is found on the top of a key which conforms to the researcher's expectations of the manifestation of this character in the real world. By virtue of the physical arrangement of this pattern of ink on top of a key mounted above an electrical switch, when the researcher presses the key, an electrical signal identifying the key pressed is generated in the wire connecting the keyboard to the computer. The computer associates this signal with a particular bit-pattern and modifies its 'working memory' accordingly. To confirm to the researcher that the message has been received, the computer uses a channel of communication in the opposite direction. The bit-pattern in 'working memory' is associated, probably with a number of intervening steps, with a bit-pattern in the computer's 'screen memory', which in turn causes a particular signal to be sent in the wire to the computer's screen, which causes a particular pattern of glow (or opacity in the case of LCD (Liquid Crystal Display)screens) on the screen. This pattern again conforms to the researcher's expectations of the real-world manifestation of 'A', and so the communication of the pitch and its confirmation are complete. Note that the symbol 'A' cannot be simply identified with the pattern on the key or screen: first, the patterns can vary widely in a physical sense; second, the pattern only becomes a symbol by virtue of its role in the communication process. Notice also that in this process there are stages involving distributed representation (e.g. the patterns of ink and glowing pixels) and continuous representation (e.g. the signal between computer and screen). The idea that one can type *an 'A'* to a computer and receive *an 'A'* back via the screen is thus a sort of fiction. Furthermore, it is possible for the same concept to be communicated via a different channel with no pretence at using a symbol. If the computer is equipped with a MIDI interface and music keyboard, and a sound generator and speakers, the researcher can press a particular key on the keyboard and, via a number of steps, the computer's 'working memory' can be modified in exactly the same way as before, and confirmatory output can be provided via the sound generator and speakers so that the researcher hears a sound with fundamental frequency 440Hz.

Further complications arise from the fact that the world represented is not the real world but an artificial musical world. Music does have manifestations in the real world—sound, printed scores, recordings, etc.—but it is not embodied in any of these. To determine precisely what the entities are in the musical world which are to be represented, and what the relationships are between them, is no small matter (Marsden 1991, 1993). This is an issue in many areas of representation, of course. As soon as one gets away from handling real objects one is dealing with an artificial world. Indeed, the real value of symbolic representations is that they aid the resolution of this issue by *defining* entities and relations. In designing a symbolic representation scheme, therefore, consideration must be given not only to the aspects of the world to be represented and the manipulations to be performed, but also to the definition of entities within the world represented.

In summary, there are three questions to be asked of any representation scheme:

1. What aspects of the world does it represent and how are entities in the world defined?

2. What kinds of manipulation does it facilitate (i.e. what kinds of computer use does it facilitate)?

3. Is it readable (i.e. does it facilitate human use)?

(The first two of these correspond in part to the dimensions of 'expressive completeness' and 'structural generality' in Wiggins *et al.* (1993) but these are better thought of not as linear dimensions in a plane but as multi-dimensional spaces in their own right. These can be taken to be legitimately collapsed to linear dimensions in the paper of Wiggins *et al.* since they confine themselves to completeness with respect to manifestation in sound and to hierarchical structure.)

Music representation

Music representation is particularly problematic for three reasons:

1. Music is multi-faceted. It has many different physical manifestations, as already noted, and various different kinds of conceptual existences. There is not necessarily a simple correspondence of entities on one facet with entities on another. It is difficult to arrive at a definition of the entities a researcher is concerned with without knowledge of the researcher's task, so designing a general-purpose representation scheme is difficult.

2. Music is variable. The musical world is an artistic one in which creativity is a virtue. Composers create new kinds of entity and new kinds of relations between them. Music from different cultures and periods therefore often demands different representation schemes. Representation schemes cannot be adequate for future music unless their designers predict how music will change, which is likely to be impossible.

3. Music is multi-dimensional. Although music always has a linear aspect of time, it also has other dimensions. Until recently most channels of communication with computers have been linear (principally through character streams), and many useful channels continue to be linear. Designers of representation schemes have to resolve issues of mapping the various dimensions of music to a linear stream of symbols. (In fact representations need not be linear at all, as shown below when discussing Charm, but it will generally be possible for them to be manifested in a sequence of characters, or at least in some linear form suitable for writing to a file.)

Six representation schemes for music will now be discussed, according to the facets of music represented. Representations for the three common real-world manifestations of music will be discussed first: digital audio for sound, MIDI for performance activity, and DARMS for scores. Then representations which aim at a more conceptual level will be discussed, using ESAC (Essen Associative Code) as an example. Finally, two representation schemes which are multi-faceted or potentially multi-faceted, Humdrum and Charm (Common Hierarchical Abstract Representation for Music), will be discussed also. For comparison, the manner of representing pitch and time, commonly the most significant aspects of music, will be described briefly for each example representation scheme.

Representations of sound

Representations of sound are not strictly symbolic as defined above, since sound in the real world is understood as continuous but mapped to discrete symbols via a process of *sampling*. In the most common representation schemes for sound, which can be grouped under the heading 'digital audio', the amplitude of a sound signal over a particular short time period (often c. twenty microseconds) is mapped to a number, the amplitude over the next time period to another number, and so on, resulting in a representation consisting of a sequence of numbers (Figure 2). Formats for digital audio vary with respect to the manner of representation of numbers and to associated information in the header, but there are a number of accepted standards (see Pope and van Rossum 1995). Each is capable of representing any sound signal subject to limitations of frequency governed by the sampling rate and limitations of fidelity governed by the accuracy of the number representation used. Note, however, that this is not to say that any real *sound* may be represented and reproduced with a certain degree of accuracy. There is nothing in the representation, for example, to indicate the absolute amplitude of the sound (this will of course vary according to distance

Figure 2: Digital representation of sound, showing sampling of sound wave (left) and resultant sequence of numbers (right)

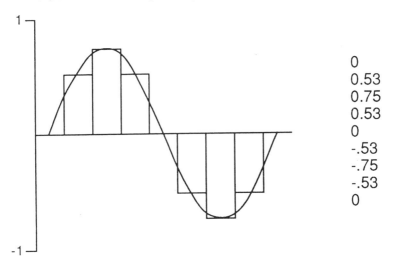

from the sound source) or the position in space of the various sources contributing to the sound (this is partly answered by representation in two or more channels). Even at this level *aspects* of the real sound are selected for representation.

Certain manipulations, such as cutting, pasting, scaling, and mixing, are easily performed on such a representation. Others require complex mathematics, but this has been an area of considerable research, and much has been achieved, particularly in the field of composition. (See Strawn 1985, for examples). Digital audio is not readable at all, in the sense of a musician gaining any musical knowledge from looking at the numbers, and is not intended to be.

Time is represented implicitly in digital audio in the sequence of 'samples'. (The sampling rate is generally represented explicitly in a header.) Pitch information, on the other hand, is distributed among the samples. Other representation schemes for sound (e.g. 'phase vocoding' (Gordon and Strawn 1985; Dolson 1986)) represent frequency information explicitly. (This is not exactly pitch information, since a pitch can be manifested in a sound with a number of frequencies in a harmonic series, but related to it.) Frequencies are generally represented by real numbers. Such representations facilitate manipulations such as lengthening or shortening a sound without affecting its pitch, but the representations are generally even less arguably symbolic than digital audio.

Representations of performance activity

Some argue that music is better defined as an activity than an object (Baily 1985; Lischka 1991). It is therefore logical to consider a representation of the manipulations of an instrument made by a musician in the course of performing a piece of music. This is essentially what is done, with respect to keyboard instruments, by the most widely used representation scheme for music after digital audio: MIDI (Musical Instrument Digital Interface). (The many published explanations of MIDI include Rothstein 1992. The MIDI standard includes a hardware level which is of no concern here.) MIDI represents, in a sequence of bytes, 'messages' to indicate particular actions such as the depression of a key, the release of a key, the status of a controller such as the foot pedal, etc. It also includes 'messages' to represent other information associated with the control of synthesisers such as a change of synthesis parameters. The representation scheme was originally intended as a means of allowing one electronic instrument to control another, and in this it serves its purpose well. It has also been used successfully as a means of capturing performance data for analysis. An example of MIDI representation is given in Figure 4.

Figure 3:. *Music for use in examples of representation schemes*

Figure 4: *MIDI representation of Figure 3—key velocities could vary from the numbers given here*

note on	pitch	key velocity		note off		
144 65 100 (F4 on)	144 60 75 (C4 on)	144 67 50 (G4 on)	128 65 64 (F4 off)	128 60 64 (C4 off)	144 53 60 (F3 on)
144 69 75 (A4 on)	128 67 64 (G4 off)	128 69 64 (A4 off)	128 53 64 (F3 off)	144 69 110 (A4 on)	144 48 85 (C3 on)
144 67 75 (G4 on)	128 69 64 (A4 off)	128 67 64 (G4 off)	128 48 64 (C3 off)		

Pitch is not represented as such in MIDI, but integers in the range 0-127 are used to identify the key pressed or released. The number 60 represents the key normally associated with the pitch middle C, but a synthesiser is free to associate this key and number with a different pitch. In the standard interpretation, MIDI is therefore confined to representing pitch in the twelve-tone scale, without regard to spelling (e.g. C sharp and D flat above middle C are both represented as 61). Since MIDI was originally intended for real-time control, time is represented implicitly in the actual time intervals between MIDI messages. Standard MIDI file formats generally 'time-stamp' messages with numbers to represent their position on a single time line.

Manipulation of representations in MIDI is not as simple as one might hope, since 'note-on' information is separated from 'note-off' information. Performers generally consider a key press (on *and* off) as a single action, of which several may occur in parallel. However, MIDI is confined to a single byte stream, so key presses and releases must be separated and interleaved into the single stream. This results in a poor match of entities as represented and entities as significant in manipulations. Thus, for example, shortening each note to transform a legato performance into a staccato one could involve not only a change in timing of note-off messages to bring them closer to their associated note-on messages, but also a change in the order of messages so that some note-off messages now come before some note-on messages. Reuniting note-on and note-off information is generally straightforward, however, and much software operating with MIDI does this so that a 'quasi-MIDI' representation is used in practice.

MIDI is hardly readable in its raw form, and is not intended to be. However, musicians operating software to manipulate MIDI data do need to be able to read the data somehow. Generally the numbers are translated to a more meaningful form (e.g. NOTEON instead of 144), but the data are still difficult to read because of the separation of note-on and note-off data.

The ubiquity of MIDI and software for its manipulation has led to an attitude in some quarters that it constitutes a suitable general standard for the representation of music. Unfortunately this is far from the case. Its representations of both pitch and time are severely impoverished and there is much else, conceptual and concrete, which is ignored. Even in its original intended realm of instrument control, it cannot be regarded as the final word. (The recently proposed ZIPI representation scheme, for example, is intended to overcome some of MIDI's limitations in this area (McMillen *et al.* 1994).)

Representations of scores

Software for preparing, editing, and printing musical scores is now widely used, though a steep trade-off between quality of output and ease of use prevents such software being as much a standard tool of the trade for musicians as word processors are for writers. User input to most such software is via a graphic interface, and information concerning representation schemes, such as must be used in storing files and could be used for the input of information into other software, is often not made public. This seriously compromises the usefulness of such software for research. A notable exception is Leland Smith's SCORE (1972) which employs a well defined input representation. Furthermore, a consortium of bodies who market, develop, or are otherwise interested in music-printing software have recently announced their intention to promulgate a standard file format for the exchange of music-notation information (NIF for Notation Interchange Format), (Music-Research Digest vol. 9 no. 36 (27 Jan. 1995), available by ftp from ftp.comlab.ox.ac.uk in directory Music-Research).

One of the earliest symbolic representations for music was DARMS, Digital Alternate Representation of Music Scores (Erickson 1975; Brinkman 1990, 137-154) (Figure 5). The philosophy of DARMS is to represent each symbol on a score by a character or characters in a sequence, with a minimum of interpretation. Thus, for example, curved lines in a musical score can variously represent slurs (an indication to play legato), phrase marks (indicating the beginnings and ends of phrases), or bowing (an instruction to string players to play all the notes in a single stroke of the bow), according to context, but these are all represented in the same way by DARMS.

Figure 5: Two DARMS representations of Figure 3: full representation (top) and abbreviated representation (bottom) relying on default values

```
!& 23!G !K1- !M3:4 22Q.UL1 23EU 24QUL2 / 24QUL1 23QUL2 RQ /
& 27!F !K1- !M3:4 RQ 31QD 27QD / 24HU RQ /

!& !G !K1- !M3:4 2Q.L1 3E 4QL2 / 4L 3 R /
& !F !K1- !M3:4 RQ 31 7 / 4H RQ /
```

Pitch, therefore, is not represented directly in DARMS but rather it is a note's position on the stave which is represented. Thus the number 19 is used to indicate a note on the first ledger line below the stave. The interpretation of this is context-dependent with respect to the latest clef occurring on the same stave. If this clef is a treble clef, then the note represented has the pitch middle C. If the latest clef is an alto clef, a note of pitch middle C would be represented by the number 25.

However, this is not to say that DARMS represents the arrangement of symbols on a page regardless of their musical meaning. Two different kinds of dots, for example, *are* distinguished in the representation since the context-dependency is simple and generally unambiguous: if the dot is to the right of a note head, it indicates a lengthening of the note; if it is above or below the note, it indicates a shortening of the note.

The time of occurrence of a note in DARMS is generally represented implicitly by the corresponding character's position in the character sequence. However, there are special symbols which indicate simultaneity for chords or return to a previously marked point in time for concurrent streams of music. A consequence of these is that there are different ways of representing the same score. The duration of a note is represented by a character mnemonic for the name of the note symbol (in American nomenclature: quarter note, half note, etc.).

DARMS is nearly comprehensive in its power to represent music notation, which would seem to make it well-suited to its original intended purpose of an input system for music-printing software. However, it has been remarkably little used for this and is used more frequently as a representation scheme for music analysis. This means, however, that manipulations can rarely be performed on the DARMS representation directly. More frequently it must first be interpreted, in a process analogous to a musician reading a score, and manipulations must be performed on the resultant interpreted representation (see Brinkman 1990, 752-9 and 825-56 for an example).

A representation in full in DARMS is difficult to read because of the large quantity of information interleaved into the single sequence of characters. However, many abbreviations may be made, and data may be left out, resulting in a more concise representation which is not difficult to read once one has become familiar with the common mappings of numerical codes to pitches and with the mnemonics for durations.

Conceptual representations

The use of score representations in musicological research is often legitimate and even appropriate, since the score is often the raw datum in such research. Furthermore, a musical score is often itself a graphical representation of the music at some conceptual level. In contrast to, for example, tablature notations, a score is not a set of instructions telling a performer how to manipulate his or her instrument (though such instructions are included) but rather a representation at a conceptual level of the music to produce. Thus many representation schemes occupy a middle ground between representations of a score as symbols on a page and representations of music at a conceptual level. Since there are many different kinds of musicological research, each involving different sets of concepts, it is not surprising that there should be a large number of representation schemes, some entirely *ad hoc* for a particular project, in this category.

The representation scheme to be discussed here, ESAC (Essen Associative Code, Schaffrath 1992) (see Figure 6), has no relation to common musical notation, though it is rather close to numeric representations used in Chinese notation of music. It is also extremely simple, though well suited to its purpose of representing folk song melodies. Pitch in ESAC is pitch relative to a particular key or scale, with 1 always representing the first note of the scale, 2 the second, etc. The symbols + and - indicate the upper and lower octaves, and their absence indicates the middle octave. (Three octaves are sufficient for folk song melodies.) The symbols # and b, similar to the common music notation symbols for sharp and flat, are used to indicate alterations from the notes of the scale. Time of occurrence is again represented by position in the character sequence. Notes which have no symbols to indicate duration are taken to be of unit duration. Longer durations are represented by the addition of underscores (_) and dots. Each underscore indicates a 100 per cent increase in duration and a dot an increase of 50 per cent. A tune's phrase structure is represented by splitting the representation into separate lines.

Figure 6: *ESAC representation of Figure 3 (top line only)—time signature and key information would be recorded elsewhere in the database*

1_.23_ 3_2_0_

ESAC's representation of both pitch and duration is thus in relative terms—pitch relative to a scale, and duration relative to a notional unit. Many types of musicological research are concerned mostly with the internal relations of a piece of music, and these are often best captured in a relational representation such as this. Certain kinds of manipulation, such as recognizing recurrent patterns with significance in a folk-song repertoire, are therefore very easily performed with an ESAC representation. The manner of pitch representation would create problems in music which either did not use a seven- (or fewer) note scale, or used more than one scale in the course of a piece (i.e. if the piece modulated), but this does not occur in the intended area of application. The representation is also extremely easy for musicians to read—it is quite possible to sing a tune directly from its ESAC notation. The representation of time also follows this pattern of ease of reading, but it is not quite so easily manipulated. A similar but more easily manipulated representation gives every symbol unit duration and employs a special symbol to indicate continuation of the previous note. (For a development of this kind of representation, see Bel 1990.) Thus a note whose duration is N units is represented by the symbol(s) for the note followed by N-1 continuation symbols. N can be any whole number greater than zero. Compare this with the incapacity of ESAC, as described, to represent durations of, e.g., five units. (By incorporating a means of altering the unit in the course of representation, Bel's scheme is able to represent, while retaining easy manipulation, not just any whole number multiple of the unit duration, but any duration pattern whose durations stand in rational ratios to each other.)

Multi-faceted representations

In 1991 SMDL (Standard Music Description Language) (ISO 1991; Sloan 1993) was proposed for adoption by the International Organization for Standards (ISO), but it was turned down, largely because many details of its definition were not complete. The proposed standard was based on Standard Generalized Markup Language (SGML) and HyTime (Hypermedia/Time-based Structuring Language, itself based on SGML and proposed at the same time as SMDL, but accepted). The relevant committees still exist, and, while doubts have been expressed that SMDL will ever be completed, a new draft has recently been made available which is considerably improved (ISO 1995). One interesting aspect of the proposed standard, is that it includes four different 'domains' (facets):

logical, gestural (performance activity), visual (score), and analytical (conceptual). Every representation must include data in the logical domain, but a representation can also include data in one or more of the other domains. A weakness of the proposal is that the logical domain is not actually a necessary layer in every representation, but rather a conceptual domain which has been given privileged status by the designers of SMDL. Whether this privilege is justified or not depends on the use to which SMDL is put.

A recent representation scheme, and one which might become increasingly important among musicologists because of the availability and quality of its associated software, is David Huron's Humdrum (available by FTP from archive.uwaterloo.ca in directory uw-data/humdrum, or from the Centre for Computer-Assisted Research in the Humanities (CCARH), 525 Middlefield Road, Suite 120, Menlo Park, CA 94025, USA) (Figure 7). The philosophy of Humdrum is to define a standard syntax for the representation of streams of data, allowing the coordination of streams which can represent concurrent data or different representations of the same data. There are also well-defined syntaxes for comments, heading information, etc. A Humdrum representation consists of a number of 'spines', represented in columns separated by tab characters. Each spine (column, except in special cases) represents a

*Figure 7: A Humdrum representation of Figure 3 using the '**kern' interpretation for each line and also giving a '**mint' (melodic interval)*

**kern	**kern	**mint
*M3/4	*M3/4	*
*F:	*F:	*
=1	=1	=1
(4.f	4r	[f]
.	4c	.
8g	.	+M2
4a)	4F	+M2
=2	=2	=2
(4a	4C	P1
4g)	.	-M2
4r	4r	r

concurrent stream of data. Different streams may use different representation schemes (in Humdrum terminology 'interpretations'). Each line represents coincident data. Thus the arrangement, rotated through 90 degrees, is not unlike that of a musical score, where staves, each carrying a line of music, are arranged horizontally and coincident notes are aligned vertically.

Certain interpretations are defined for common tasks. For example, the '**freq' interpretation encodes frequency information in numbers representing Hertz, the '**MIDI' interpretation encodes aspects of MIDI data using numbers to match MIDI pitch codes, and the '**kern' interpretation encodes aspects of music notation, somewhat along the lines of DARMS but using letter names for pitches. The associated software includes tools to translate from one interpretation to another. There are well defined means for users to add their own interpretations, and in simple cases the tools make this very easy to do. More complex additions require the use of AWK (Aho *et al.* 1988) and KornShell (ksh) (Bolsky and Korn 1989) (or possibly another shell), but these are common components of most UNIX systems.

While the representations of pitch in Humdrum are intentionally multifarious, there are certain common characteristics to the representation of time. As with many representation schemes, the time of occurrence of a note is represented implicitly by its position, but this time it is position in a column rather than in a stream. The duration of a note can, as in DARMS, be represented by a symbol or by a number, or it can, as in Bel's scheme, be represented by continuation symbols.

Humdrum representations can be easy to read. The separation into columns with different meanings allows a signifier in one column to be reused to mean something different in another column. For example, the letter 'E' might represent the pitch E in one column, and an eighth note in another. This facilitates the creation of mnemonic representation schemes. Furthermore, the separation into columns also allows a column to contain only the data of interest so that this may be read more easily without the clutter of other data such as exists, for example, in DARMS.

Essentially, then, Humdrum allows the representation of a sequence of 'events', each of which is represented by a set of 'parameters'. The meaning of each parameter, in the sense of interrelations between parameters, the results of manipulations, and the relation between the world and the representation, is defined by the user through the header which identifies the interpretation used, the software which manipulates the representation, and the description the user gives of the mapping of signifieds to signifiers. It is possible for parameters to indicate separate (sub)events occurring concurrently as part of a composite event. Furthermore there is a standard means of indicating null data for a parameter, which can be taken to indicate the continuation of data for that parameter from the previous event. An event is represented by a separate line in a Humdrum file, with parameters separated by tabs. Events occur in sequence, represented by the sequence of lines in the file. Except in special cases, parameters are identified by position, so parameters with the same meaning in successive events form the columns which make up Humdrum 'spines'. A weakness of the design is that duration information can occur anywhere within the parameters and so the duration of an event, in the sense of the time between its beginning and the beginning of the next event, can be difficult to derive.

To represent a piece of music as a set of events whose properties are described in a list of parameters is also the approach taken in Charm (Harris *et al.* 1991, Smaill *et al.* 1994) (see Figure 8). (The approach is also taken in the LISP Kernel (Rahn *et al.* 1989), which was explicitly intended as a means of connecting diverse types of musical information.) However, in contrast to all other representation schemes discussed here, both the time of occurrence of an event and its duration are represented explicitly in the parameters. The order of signifiers in the representation (above the level of the order of parameters) is therefore insignificant. On the one hand, this overcomes the problem identified above of representing music which is multi-dimensional in a uni-dimensional linear fashion, so there is no need for the splitting of events into start and finish (such as occurs in MIDI) or start and continuation (such as occurs in Humdrum). On the other hand, manipulation of data can be less efficient since, except on a parallel computer, it must be done in a linear fashion and the opportunity for coordinating this linear processing with linear temporal representation is lost.

Charm represents an event (such as a note) as a combination of a unique identifier, a pitch, a time, a duration, and other parameters. The representation of pitch, time and duration is not fixed. One of the important characteristics of Charm is that it uses the concept of 'abstract data type', common in programming language theory. It is required that there be certain operations on the representations of each of pitch, time, and duration which follow certain properties, but the details of representation are otherwise free. (Thus the representations of pitch and time may vary from those used in Figure 8.) Essentially, any representation which allows pitches (or times) to be ordered and allows the proper

computation of pitch intervals (or time intervals and durations) is acceptable. Thus, like Humdrum, multifarious representations are possible for
pitch and time (and presumably other parameters also). Actual alternative representation schemes are not (yet) specified in Charm, in contrast
to Humdrum, but, again in contrast to Humdrum, meaningful constraints
are defined on the nature of representation which can be incorporated.
While the constraints can be useful—allowing, for example, manipulation of the temporal aspects of Charm data without knowing the details
of the representation scheme used, in contrast to Humdrum—they could
also be unduly restrictive. Circularity of pitch, for example, which is
required for common manipulations of pitch in atonal music (see Forte
1973, for example), is forbidden. (It might be argued that in this case one
is representing pitch class rather than pitch, but then one might need to
be able to represent events which have pitch class but do not have pitch.)

*Figure 8: A Charm representation of Figure 3 including one 'constitu-
ent' representation to identify the 'events' which constitute the theme*

ε(e0, ‹f,♮,4›, 0/1, 3/2, ...)
ε(e1, ‹c,♮,4›, 1/1, 1/1, ...)
ε(e2, ‹g,♮,4›, 3/2, 1/2, ...)
ε(e3, ‹a,♮,4›, 2/1, 1/1, ...)
ε(e4, ‹f,♮,3›, 2/1, 1/1, ...)
ε(e5, ‹a,♮,4›, 3/1, 1/1, ...)
ε(e6, ‹c,♮,3›, 3/1, 2/1, ...)
ε(e7, ‹g,♮,4›, 4/1, 1/1, ...)

κ(c1, ‹series,{}›, theme, { e0 e2 e3 e5 e7}, _)

The other important characteristic of Charm is that it allows representation of the grouping of events into, in Charm terminology, 'constituents'. This is a very powerful feature, allowing the representation of

aspects of the *structure* of a piece of music which are either absent or difficult to derive from other representations. (MIDI, for example, has insignificant means for representing structure. In DARMS structural information must be extracted by 'reading' the represented notation. ESAC includes phrase structure, as noted, which would appear to be adequate for its folk song repertoire. Humdrum can include structure in the arrangement of 'spines' and through certain symbols incorporated into various interpretations, but this lacks the generality and clarity of Charm.)

While Charm is very powerful and has admirable design, it is not easy to read. The main reason for this is one of its strengths in other respects: the abandonment of the use of a linear sequence in representation. Human readers seem to rely heavily on recognizing patterns, but sequential pattern is obscured in Charm. Charm is also verbose, requiring many separators such as brackets and commas, and this does not aid reading.

A more serious drawback with Charm, and most other representation schemes (including Humdrum and most others) is that the representation of *properties* of data items is given a privileged status over the representation of *relations* between data items. (In fact relations can be represented in Charm using the mechanism for constituents, but this would be cumbersome.) Yet, as mentioned above, it is frequently relations which are of most interest in musicological research. One might want, for example, to represent a musical motive which is defined by the relations of pitch and time between its notes, but in which the actual pitches and times are irrelevant. ESAC, as noted above, represents pitch and time in relative terms, but the relations represented are confined to those between consecutive events. Humdrum can similarly represent relations between consecutive events, and interpretations could be defined which represented relations between non-consecutive events (e.g. between an event and the event two before), but these are represented as if they were properties of an event. This makes manipulation of relations difficult. Deleting an event, for example, might require the data for other events to be changed. Mechanisms for the representation and manipulation of relational data do exist, of course, in relational database management systems, but these have rarely been used for music (but see Eaglestone 1992). However, it is difficult to see how a relational representation could be symbolic in the sense defined above. When communicating relational data, musicologists frequently resort to diagrams which use a distributed representation, e.g. the 'shape' of a motive (its pattern of upwards and downwards intervals) might be represented by a line with analogous shape.

Conclusion

It is now clear that the diversity of musical information, and of the manipulations scholars wish to perform on it, makes impractical the single generally accepted representation scheme Lincoln foresaw in 1974. Such a single representation scheme is not impossible, but it would be far too complex to be usable. A standard framework to accommodate multiple representation schemes is a more realistic goal. The frameworks discussed here are too recent for adoption as standards, and are likely to require further development or replacement. An acceptable standard would combine the thoroughness of Humdrum with the logical design of Charm.

It is likely that digital audio, MIDI, and possibly NIF will become or continue to be the standard representation schemes used for the facets of sound, performance activity, and scores respectively. For each of these there is a moderately fixed domain so that a degree of completeness in representation can be achieved. More conceptual facets are subject to greater variability, and it is likely that scholars will continue to need to design their own representation schemes from time to time. A standard framework for multiple representations, such as envisaged above, should include mechanisms to facilitate this. The following principles should apply:

1. The representation scheme should be logical—i.e., there should be a small number of underlying principles consistently applied;

2. The representation scheme should result in (humanly) readable representations;

3. There should be an explicit statement of the aspects of the world represented by the representation scheme;

4. The abstract properties of the representation scheme should be made explicit.

Those designing representation schemes are advised to consult Huron (1992), who makes a number of detailed recommendations expanding the first three principles above. The fourth principle is intended to facilitate the combination of representation schemes. Humdrum, for example, is able to accommodate different schemes because of the well defined properties of the general Humdrum syntax. Charm is able to do so because of the use of abstract data types.

Any framework imposes constraints; a common standard could not be monolithic because different projects will require different constraints. More feasible would be a standard composed of different levels. Any acceptable standard should also incorporate existing standards such as MIDI. Incorporation of relational data is more problematic and, as suggested above, is perhaps best considered in a form of representation that is not wholly symbolic.

References and bibliography

Aho, A., Kernighan, B., and Weinberger, P., *The AWK programming language* (Reading, Mass: Addison-Wesley, 1988).

Baily, J., 'Music structure and human movement', in Howell, P., Cross, I., and West R., (eds.) *Musical structure and cognition* (London: Academic Press, 1985), 237-58.

Bel, B., 'Time and musical structures', *Interface*, 19 (1990), 107-35.

Bolsky, M. I., and Korn, D. G., *The KornShell command and programming language* (Englewood Cliffs: Prentice Hall, 1989).

Brinkman, A. R., *Pascal programming for music research* (Chicago: University of Chicago Press, 1990).

Carter, N. P., Bacon, R. A., and Messenger, T., 'The acquisition, representation and reconstruction of printed music by computer: a review', *Computers and the Humanities*, 22 (1988), 117-36.

Dolson, M., 'The phase vocoder: a tutorial', *Computer Music Journal*, 10.4 (1986), 14-27.

Eaglestone, B. M., 'Extending the relational database model for computer music research', in Marsden, A., and Pople A. (eds.), *Computer representations and models in music* (London: Academic Press, 1992), 41-66.

Erickson, R., 'The DARMS project: a status report', *Computers and the Humanities*, 9 (1975), 291-8.

Forte, A., *The structure of atonal music* (New Haven: Yale University Press, 1973).

Garnet, G. E., 'Music, signals, and representations: a survey', in De Poli, G., Piccialli, A., and Roads, C. (eds.), *Representations of musical signals* (Cambridge, Mass.: MIT Press, 1991), 325-69.

Gordon, J. W., and Strawn, J., 'An introduction to the phase vocoder', in Strawn, J. (ed.), *Digital audio signal processing, an anthology* (Maddison, Wis.: A-R Editions, 1985), 221-65.

Harris, M., Smaill, A., and Wiggins, G., 'Representing music symbolically', in proceedings of *IX Colloquio di Informatica Musicale* (Genoa, 13-16 November 1991), 55-69.

Hewlett, W. B., and Selfridge-Field, E. (eds.), *Directory of computer assisted research in musicology* (Menlo Park, Ca.: Centre for Computer Assisted Research in the Humanities, 1987).

Huron, D., 'Design principles in computer-based music representation', in Marsden, A., and Pople, A. (eds.), *Computer representations and models in music* (London: Academic Press, 1992), 5-39.

ISO (International Organization for Standards) Committee Draft International Standard 'Information Technology—Standard Music Description Language' (ISO/IEC CD 10743, 1991).

ISO (International Organization for Standards), 'Standard Music Description Language' (ISO/IEC DIS 10743,1995).

Lincoln, H. B., 'Use of the computer in music research: a short report on accomplishments, limitations, and future needs', *Computers and the Humanities*, 8 (1974), 285-9.

Lischka, C., 'On music making', in proceedings of *IX Colloquio di Informatica Musicale* (Genoa, 13-16 November 1991), 80-4.

Marsden, A., 'Musical abstractions and composers' practice', in proceedings of *IX Colloquio di Informatica Musicale*, (Genoa, 13-16 November 1991), 40-54.

Marsden, A., 'Musical informatics: an emerging discipline?', *Revue. Informatique et Statistique dans les Sciences Humaines*, 29 (1993), 77-90.

McLean, B. A., 'The representation of musical scores as data for applications in musical computing', Ph.D. thesis (State Univ. of New York, Binghampton, 1988).

McMillen, K., Wessel, D., and Wright, M., 'The ZIPI music parameter description language', *Computer Music Journal*, 18.4 (1994), 52-73.

Pope, S. T., 'Music notations and the representation of musical structure and knowledge', *Perspectives of New Music*, 24 (1986) 156-89.

Pope, S. T., and van Rossum, G., 'Machine tongues XVIII: a child's garden of sound file formats', *Computer Music Journal*, 19.1 (1995) 25–63.

Rahn, J., Karpen, R., Weston, C., and Hiestand, C., 'Using the "LISP Kernel" musical environment', *Musicus*, 1 (1989), 144-63.

Roads, C., 'An overview of music representations', in Baroni, M., and Callegari, L. (eds.), *Musical grammars and computer analysis* (Florence: Olschki, 1984), 7-37.

Rothstein, J., *MIDI, a comprehensive introduction* (Oxford: Oxford University Press, 1992).

Schaffrath, H., 'The retrieval of monophonic melodies and their variants: concepts and strategies for computer-aided analysis', in Marsden, A., and Pople, A. (eds.), *Computer representations and models in music* (London: Academic Press, 1992), 95-109.

Sloan, D., 'Aspects of music representation in HyTime/SMDL', *Computer Music Journal*, 17.4 (1993) 51-9.

Smaill, A., Wiggins, G. A., and Miranda, E., 'Music representation—between the musician and the computer', in Smith, M., Smaill, A., and Wiggins, G. A. (eds.), *Music education: an artificial intelligence approach* (London: Springer-Verlag, 1994), 108-19.

Smith, L., 'SCORE—a musician's approach to computer music', *Journal of the Audio Engineering Society*, 20 (1972), 7-14.

Strawn, J. (ed.), *Digital audio signal processing, an anthology* (Maddison, Wis: A-R Editions, 1985).

Wiggins, G., Miranda, E., Smaill, A., and Harris, M., 'A framework for the evaluation of music representation systems', *Computer Music Journal*, 17.3 (1993), 31-42.

Computer Usage and the Law

Lorraine Warren and Peter Adman

Introduction

Over the last fifty years, society has become increasingly dependent on the use of computer technology. Computer usage is now an integral part of almost every professional, commercial, industrial, and leisure activity. Inevitably, a wide variety of criminal offences can be committed either as a result of, or by means of computer technology.

The extensive permeation of society by a rapidly evolving, immature technology has posed novel problems for the legal system. Law tends to develop in a reactive manner: statute law is usually the result of lengthy campaigns mounted by pressure groups; case law results from the resolution of specific disputes. In computing, the pace of technological change has, not surprisingly, often outstripped the development of the legal system. However, there are three main areas where legislation specific to computer usage has recently been introduced:

- system security (the Computer Misuse Act, 1990);
- copyright (the Copyright, Designs and Patents Act, 1988);
- data protection (the Data Protection Act, 1988).

Notwithstanding the inevitable uncertainties, it is of key importance that those responsible for managing institutional computing services have full knowledge of these laws. Until the 1980s, most academics in the humanities were largely insulated from such concerns. Humanities computing was limited to a relatively small number of groups and individuals mostly concerned with computationally intensive tasks such as the quantitative analysis of textual information. Such tasks were confined to large, centrally maintained mainframe computers running dedicated software written in-house. In such situations, legal requirements could largely be dealt with unseen at institutional level.[1,2]

However, recent technological developments have necessitated a shift in emphasis away from institutional responsibility towards individual responsibility. This shift is the result of the trend away from centralized systems towards distributed systems based on desktop microcomputers. Local area networks (LANs) of microcomputers, usually PCs, are becoming increasingly commonplace, not only in established computing centres, but in academic departments and in other access areas such as libraries and halls of residence.

The advent of the desktop microcomputer, combined with access to national and international communications networks, has dramatically extended both the scope and the sophistication of potential activity in teaching and research in all disciplines. Some representative examples of activity include:

- use as a clerical tool (e.g. for word processing);
- use as a functional tool (e.g. the use of database management systems in the study of history);
- contact with special interest groups and bulletin boards;
- access to remote online databases;
- access to banks of teaching resources;
- computer-supported collaborative working;
- support of distance learning.

The growing integration of computers into the mainstream of humanities teaching and research has brought increasing numbers of humanities academics into closer contact with the legal issues surrounding computer usage. The reasons for this are threefold:

- There are managerial and administrative issues to be resolved. Responsibility for monitoring and maintaining the legal status of distributed LANs must be clearly allocated.

- The ease of unauthorized copying of electronic material poses a threat to academics as owners of rights in intellectual works.

- Academics are now becoming actively involved in the production of software, either as individuals, or through the establishment of the Higher Education Funding Councils' £25 million Teaching and Learning Technology Programme (TLTP) in 1992.

The first three sections of this chapter are intended to raise awareness of the implications of recent legislation for those involved in humanities computing. As effective management of computing activity depends heavily on the establishment of secure systems, this subject is discussed first. Then we proceed to cover the subjects of intellectual property and copyright, and data protection respectively. The last section highlights key areas of contract law which need to be considered by those becoming involved in software production.

It is emphasized that a full discussion of computer law would demand complexity far beyond the scope of this book. Those requiring more information in any area are referred either to their institutional computing service, or to the more detailed texts listed in the bibliography.

System security

The need for an IT security policy

The need for an IT security policy has always been taken very seriously by the corporate sector. Despite this, a recent survey by the Department of Trade and Industry, ICL, and the National Computing Centre (Woollacott 1994) reported that IT security breaches cost UK businesses £1.2 billion a year. Because the greater part of this sum can be attributed to fraud and theft from financial systems, it might be assumed that the issue of security has less relevance to the academic world. However, this is not the case: all computer systems are vulnerable to abuse.

Criminal damage may be committed against the computer system itself, or the data, or software stored within. Such damage can be caused inadvertently by inexperienced users, or there can be malicious intent on the part of both authorized and unauthorized users. This latter category includes the dissemination of computer viruses: self-replicating programs which can be designed to carry out destructive activity. Inadequate security can also lead to breaches of the Data Protection Act. Another area of concern is the use of the computer to commit other crimes, for example theft, or illegal copying of software.

Fortunately, the legal system does afford protection against the abuse of computer systems. The Computer Misuse Act was passed in 1990 to combat the problems outlined above. The Act created three new categories of criminal offence: unauthorized access to computer material, unauthorized access with intent to commit or facilitate commission of further offences, and the unauthorized modification of computer material (Austen 1993).

The first of these offences is aimed at 'hackers', those who break into, or 'hack' computer systems merely for the sense of achievement in overcoming the host security systems. A conviction renders the hacker liable to a jail term of up to six months, or a fine of £2,000, or both. To secure a conviction, it must be proved that the perpetrators knew they were unauthorized at the time of access. The second category of offence is designed to deter those who penetrate systems with the intent of committing further crimes. This offence is punishable with an unlimited fine, or a prison term of up to five years. The third offence is aimed primarily at those who write or disseminate viruses. Again, the offence is punishable with an unlimited fine, or a prison term of up to five years.

However, whilst legal redress is available, this is one area where prevention is certainly better than cure. One virus attack on a network file server, for example, can render every linked workstation useless for substantial periods of time, and cause irreversible damage to software and data. In education, the costs in terms of disruption, loss of reputation and wasted effort often far outweigh the financial costs. Where using computers to commit crimes is concerned, although an institution may be an unwitting and innocent host to such activities, clearly, the resultant bad publicity is best avoided.

Unauthorized access on a local scale, whether to a central mainframe, or a PC cluster, has always presented a threat. However, nowadays, the computer communications revolution has brought not only benefits, but also dangers. The uncontrolled interlinking of academic, government, corporate, and individual users by means of the Internet has created a situation where illegal activity can easily be carried out by remote access. There have been allegations that use of the Internet has turned to abuse, with software piracy becoming more blatant, and sinister material becoming widely available.

In theory, any network host computer has the potential to be accessed and misused, whether remotely or locally. In practice, it is often open-access bulletin boards which have been used for highly public, inappropriate activities. The threat to educational establishments is certainly very real, as the ongoing cases outlined below prove.

- A student at the Massachusetts Institute of Technology was charged with illegally conspiring to supply major software packages globally free of charge on an Internet-connected bulletin board (Stavrinou 1994). It is alleged that he did not copy the software himself, but sent electronic messages under two aliases asking if anyone owned a range of packages including Microsoft Excel 5.0 and WordPerfect 6.0. Once the packages had been copied onto the Institute's free bulletin board, it was estimated that users copied over $1million worth of the unlicensed software.

- A research associate at Birmingham University was allegedly acting as librarian for those interested in pornographic material (Ohajah 1994). Whilst, technically, it is not illegal to possess digitally stored obscene pictures, showing them to someone is an offence, which can be more difficult to prove.
- Canadian academic, Dr Laurence Godfry, (Braithwaite 1994) has issued a libel writ in London against another academic based in Geneva, claiming he was defamed by a bulletin board message posted on the Usenet system. Although this is a test case, most experts now agree that, if defamatory, even transitory computer screen messages are sufficiently permanent, once stored in memory, to be held libellous; that being so, messages on bulletin boards are likely to be considered even more damaging.

In an imperfect world, it is impossible to prevent misuse of computers completely. However, it is possible to develop effective strategies to limit such activities. Some suggestions are outlined below.

Minimizing criminal activity

The majority of computer crimes occur because of lax security. Operating an effective security system requires, above all, the clear allocation of responsibility; *ad hoc* interventions are unlikely to be successful. This is particularly important in education, where departmental LAN management is often carried out by several hard-pressed academics, rather than by computing professionals. The expertise in the institutional computing service is a valuable resource in these circumstances. The needs of those using the system must always be borne in mind, alongside the safety of the installation; security must result in usable, as well as manageable systems. This is particularly true in the education environment, where a high proportion of users are likely to be inexperienced and thus easily thwarted by complex security procedures. A full description of measures to ensure computer system security is far beyond the scope of this chapter. What follows is intended merely to highlight some fundamental procedures, the absence of which would be seen as negligence.

Security procedures can be electronic or manual. One of the more primitive, though highly effective, manual security systems is the insistence that machines are only available when an attendant is present. However, this has considerable resource implications, particularly when many institutions are looking to implement round-the-clock access to computers. If necessary, this problem can be overcome by technological methods, such as the use of electronically controlled access systems.

The most widely used electronic security measure is the establishment of a hierarchical password system. Those using a computer system should only be able to access those parts of the system which they are entitled to use. For example, in a database system, some users (e.g. students) will only need to inspect data; others will be allowed to add to the data; some will be allowed to edit or delete data (e.g. research students). The most privileged users will be allowed access to the database software itself and will be able to alter the database structure (experienced staff). For a password system to work effectively, users must be aware of the need to change passwords frequently, and to avoid the use of easily guessed passwords. The system must log user access, noting user identification and times of entry and exit; if possible, these should be periodically checked with the user. Checks should also be made on any account which shows sudden activity after being dormant for a long time. The location of passwords is important; they must be encoded so that they are not easily obtainable by anyone accessing the computer operating system.

The importance of keeping backup copies of important programs and data cannot be overemphasized. In a corporate environment, this process is often carried out automatically on a daily basis; this is unlikely to take place in education, where activity takes place on a more individual basis. Backup copies should be kept in a secure place, preferably in a separate building from the computer.

Virus protection software should always be present, although none can ever be 100 per cent effective. As a result, software of unknown or dubious origin may contain unknown viruses and should never be installed on systems, no matter how useful it might seem to be. Indeed, the benefits of using genuine software should always be emphasized: these include documentation, support, and the availability of updates, for example. Moreover, illegal copying may lead the licensor of the software to revoke the licence and claim damages, which is clearly counterproductive.

In conclusion, when defining operational procedures, it is almost always necessary to compromise security to achieve greater access, or better performance, or rapidity of control. Economizing on costs will also be a factor. Against this background, risk can only be minimized, never eliminated.

Intellectual property and copyright

Copyright basics

The principle that a work of the intellect is the *property* of its creator is known as copyright. Holders of copyright in materials are able to control the use made of them, and, by implication, make a charge for such usage. Therefore rigorous copyright law encourages intellectual output, to the benefit of society.

Copyright provision in the UK is determined by the Copyright, Designs and Patents Act, 1988 which came into force in August, 1989. The Act was introduced to replace the Copyright Act of 1956, and was intended to reflect the changes brought about by the spread of devices which facilitate the copying and recording of a wide range of source material (NCET 1993). Copyright was declared to exist in the following categories of works: original literary, dramatic, musical, or artistic works; sound recordings, films, broadcasts, or cable programmes; the typographical arrangement of published editions (Bainbridge 1990, 12).

Copyright is a property right and is therefore 'owned'—hence the term 'intellectual property'. Copyright protection is automatic from the moment of creation or production; there are no formal procedures to be undertaken to establish ownership.[3]

Owners of a copyright are granted exclusive rights to certain acts, including, amongst others, making copies, giving public performances, and adapting the work. Copyright is infringed if any person other than the copyright owner carries out or authorizes any of these acts, without the copyright owner's permission. If such permission is not obtained, the owner may sue for recompense. Those seeking to use works may not have to contact the owner on an individual basis. Permission may often be obtained through organizations which exist to administrate copyright and rights in performances, for example, the Performing Rights Society. A full list of this kind of organization may be obtained from the British Copyright Council.[4]

The term 'copying' refers to the creation of any material form; copyright resides in the content, not the medium. In law, there is no difference between photocopying a document, taping a compact disc, or recording a broadcast onto videotape. This includes the conversion and storage of works by electronic means, which has particular implications for the creation of databases, and the creation of electronic copies—even backups—of works.

In addition to intellectual property rights, the 1988 Act introduces the principle of 'moral rights'. This principle gives an author of a literary, dramatic, musical, or artistic work the right first, to be identified whenever their work is used, and second, to object to derogatory treatment and false attribution of authorship. Unlike copyright ownership, moral rights cannot be transferred, and remain with the author, even when the copyright of the material itself is in other hands.

Despite its rigour, and fortunately for education, the Act contains a number of exceptions; copyright is not infringed by 'fair dealing' with a work for the purposes of research or private study, or for criticism, or review. Academics in the humanities are used to working within copyright restrictions where use of printed source materials is concerned. However, there are additional implications where electronic materials are concerned. For the first time, protection is extended to the authors of, first, computer software (that is, programs), and second, works which have been created with the aid of computer software (for example, word processed documents). The scope of this protection is outlined in the remainder of this section; and in the section below, the implications for the humanities are discussed.

- *Computer software.* The Act places computer software, including programs and associated documentation, such as manuals, in the category of literary works. This legislation is intended to cover not only individual efforts, but also 'off-the-shelf' software: mass-produced word processors, databases, and spreadsheets. Purchasers of such software do not buy the software, or the copyright in the software, but merely obtain a licence to use the package. The Act itself contains no provision for copying such software, even for backup copies: such permissions may only be granted within the terms of the licence. A licence may specify that a set number of copies may be produced, or alternatively, a site licence may be granted where an indeterminate number of copies may be made within the confines of an organizational structure.

- *Works created using a computer.* The Act stipulates that whoever provides the expertise to produce a work by means of a standard computer package is the author of that work for copyright purposes. For example, rights in a document produced using a word processor belong to the author, not to the software company, or to the person entering the text.

Implications for the humanities

The 1988 Act has implications for the humanities in two main areas: first, unauthorized copying; second, the production and use of courseware.

Unauthorized copying

The ease of unauthorized copying and transmission of digital materials through national and international networks such as JANET, Super-JANET, and the Internet poses a considerable threat to academics as (a) owners of intellectual works and (b) holders of licences in commercial software packages. These situations are discussed in turn below.

- *Owners of works.* Although rights in works are indisputably protected by the Act, the ease of copying materials presents a major problem. Once a work is in electronic form, an unlimited number of high quality copies can be made and distributed almost instantaneously on a global scale. Unlike traditional reprographic technologies, a tenth-generation electronic copy is indistinguishable from the original.

  Another difficulty can arise even when permission to alter electronic material has been granted. The final product of alteration may be copyright-protected itself, provided that enough originality has been incorporated. This implies that financial gain can be made from such derived works. However, it may be difficult to determine what constitutes a new product: the Act specifies that an infringement has only occurred if a 'substantial part' of the original has been used. There is no legal definition of the term, in order that individual courts may decide that certain parts of the content are by their nature more important than the physical proportion of the product volume which they occupy. This is a very grey area with little established case law: for example, consider the situation where digitized photographic images may be altered at pixel level. At what point is the altered version deemed to be a new image?

There is no doubt that, in spite of the law, current conditions favour unauthorized copying and use of materials which can be difficult to control. Some authors may feel reluctant, for these reasons, to make their materials available in digital form. However, intellectual property has to be made available to the public so that it can be used; mechanisms which prevent this defeat the purpose of publishing at all.

The issues outlined above have resulted in concern at international level. The advent of 'digital superhighways' has focused most discussion on the financial concerns of multinational corporations, particularly in the media industry, rather than on the needs of the academic community. However, there is a European initiative, the Copyright in Transmitted Electronic Documents (CITED) project,[5] which is designed to address academic concerns more directly. Rather than trying to prevent access and use of intellectual property, the aim of the CITED project is to develop a computerized system to link monitoring, control of type of use, and financial compensation. An ideal system would capture 'events' (actions which users wish to undertake) and match them with 'rights' (of owners, distributors, and the end-users themselves). The CITED consortium has produced a conceptual model for such a system, and is currently testing a number of demonstrator document delivery systems. Whilst such a system would undoubtedly solve the very real problems encountered by authors, it should be remembered that the rate of change in the computer industry has made international standardization extremely difficult to impose. In volatile markets, equilibrium is usually reached in advance of legislation, by means of market dominance.

• *Owners of commercial software packages.* It is estimated that unauthorized copying of commercial packages costs the software industry billions of pounds every year. In response, leading software manufacturers have established FAST, the Federation Against Software Theft to combat the problem. FAST has extensive powers of entry and cooperates with the police and Trading Standards departments to effect prosecutions. In one recent case, a Humberside computer dealer was sentenced to 120 hours community service after being convicted of a third offence.

Licences for centrally purchased software are usually effectively policed by the institutional computing services. However, as autonomous PC networks become more widely distributed in educational establishments, it is imperative that responsibility for monitoring the installation of software on networks is clearly allocated.

Production and use of courseware
The shortage of discipline-specific courseware has spurred a number of humanities academics to become involved in software production projects, some as authors in their own right. The current TLTP initiative is an attempt to support and coordinate their endeavours on a multi-institution scale. While there is a considerable breadth of activity, the majority of humanities courseware production projects will use authoring tools: proprietary systems suitable for producing computer-based learning (CBL) materials without the requirement for extensive computer programming (Deegan *et al.* 1993, 19-42). Authors must consider three situations: copyright ownership of the authoring software itself, the rights of owners of 'third party' works, and copyright ownership of the finished courseware. Each situation is considered separately below.

- *Copyright ownership for authoring software.* Courseware materials created within authoring systems cannot generally be displayed in isolation from the authoring package used in their production; clearly, mass distribution would be too expensive within the constraints of the majority of software licences (unless a receptor institution possessed a site licence for the authoring package). Fortunately, many software companies supply 'run-time' versions of the authoring systems. These are cut-down versions of the full system which allow the courseware to be read but not significantly altered. Again, however, run-time versions of software are subject to licence agreements: some software companies charge royalties for this facility; others charge royalties only if the courseware is actually sold for a profit, rather than freely distributed; some make no charge at all. Clearly, such costs must be determined at the outset of any project. It is useful to bear in mind that software companies can be very flexible, particularly where large-scale, or high profile distribution is envisaged; in these circumstances, direct negotiations may sometimes yield favourable results.

• *The rights of the authors of 'third party works'.* Many courseware products are heterogeneous in nature, containing text, graphics, photographic images, sound, and video from a wide range of authors who may not be members of the production team. The term 'third party works' is often used to refer to source material from external authors. In compiling courseware, copyright clearance must be obtained from all owners of rights, before inclusion of the material takes place. Clearance usually takes the form of a licence of rights to use the work in the product, including the right to amend, adapt, or edit the work as necessary. The issue of moral rights is also of importance here: where possible, it is advisable to obtain a waiver of such rights, if only as a protective measure.

If the proportion of third party works in courseware is high, the process of clearance is likely to be both lengthy and costly and should be borne in mind at the design phase of projects. This is a potential problem for the current TLTP initiative which has raised concerns amongst copyright organizations. This concern was highlighted by the British Universities Film and Video Council (BUFVC) (Weston 1994), an organization with long experience of dealing with copyright-related issues. In a recent conference,[6] a number of copyright clearance organizations made it clear that, although it would be highly desirable for a blanket licensing scheme to be established quickly to meet the needs of the TLTP, such a scheme is unlikely to be forthcoming within an appropriate timescale. The legal obligations must therefore be dealt with by the individual projects themselves.

For text and graphical material, clearance usually presents no more of a problem than if printed material were the outcome. However, the inclusion of musical or film/TV/video material is more complex. For musical compositions, separate rights of copyright exist both in the musical composition itself and in any particular recording of that composition. Moreover, royalties may be due every time the musical sequence is accessed, thus causing a requirement for usage to be effectively monitored. In film clips, every actor's performance creates performing rights. A written agreement must be obtained from every actor on screen before the sequence can be used in a courseware product. Clearly, it is inadvisable to include crowd scenes without good reason!

- *Copyright ownership of the finished courseware.* A courseware product is created using a computer; the content results from the skill and expertise of the author(s), and copyright belongs to the author(s). However, this does not apply if the product is considered to be created in the course of the author's employment. Then, unless there is prior agreement to the contrary, the employer institution is regarded as the owner of the work. In the past, employers' rights over the exploitation of teaching materials have often been waived, particularly as the employment contracts of university academic staff are often vague. It is difficult to ascertain precise hours of work, and, as a result, to determine whether a work has been produced within the course of employment or otherwise. Where multi-site collaboration has taken place, for example in the TLTP initiative, the ownership of rights in courseware is more difficult to ascertain, particularly where there is an absence of formal agreement between sites. Clearly, it is important to resolve any potential conflicts before work commences.

One of the main attractions of courseware is that it may be adapted and customized by the end-user to meet the needs of a particular situation. Indeed, such flexibility was demanded by the terms of the recent Funding Council initiatives. The ultimate product of the user's activity may be copyright-protected itself, provided that enough originality has been incorporated. However, without the consent of the owners of copyright in the underlying materials, including both the producers and any third-party rights holders, the new product will be in infringement of copyright. In addition, as previously described, it may be difficult to determine what constitutes a new product.

Data protection

The key legislation in this area is the Data Protection Act, 1984. The purpose of this Act, according to the preamble, is to 'regulate the use of automatically processed information relating to individuals and the provision of services in respect of such information'. The Act places obligations on those who collect, record, and use personal data ('data users') and gives rights to individuals who have information about themselves stored on computer. Contravention of the Act is a criminal offence; there is also provision for civil remedies such as compensation.

As both teaching and research activities can involve the collection of data, it is important to be aware of the constraints of the Act. It is not intended to supply a comprehensive description of the Act; instead, a broad outline of its structure is provided, and key exemptions relevant to higher education are identified.

Whilst the Act is commonly believed to refer only to data stored on a computer, the actual definition is much wider, covering data on disc, punched tape, punched cards, and bar codes. Any automatic data processing equipment is allowed for, ranging from computers to mechanical punched card readers. The principle is of automation, not of the technology used. Personal data is defined as that consisting of information relating to a *living* individual who can be identified from that information. Therefore a seventeenth-century historical database is not personal data; nor is a collection of information about companies or organizations. The Act also takes into account the manual storing of complementary information; it would not be possible to avoid the Act by keeping, for example, a separate card index which allowed the identification of individuals by a simple cross-referencing process. The data user is defined as the person who holds the data. This can include not only living persons, but companies, organizations, and statutory authorities. Unless exempt, all data users must register with the Data Protection Registrar. In higher education institutions, this is usually done on behalf of the academic staff by a senior administrative officer.

The Act defines eight main principles covering the following five main points:

- Data about individuals which are held for processing must have been obtained for a specific lawful purpose;

- The data must only be used for the specific purpose and may only be disclosed in accordance with the specific purpose;

- Data must not be excessive for the purpose but merely adequate and relevant;

- Data must be accurate, up-to-date and kept no longer than necessary;

- The data must be protected and held securely against unauthorized access or loss but must be accessible to data subjects on request.

Failure to comply with the principles of the Act can result in the data user being liable to prosecution for a series of defined criminal offences, provided that the offence was carried out either knowingly or recklessly. The failure to establish effective security procedures on a computer system is likely to be classed as reckless behaviour.

There are a number of exemptions from the subject access provision referred to above; of most relevance to education is section 33(6) of the Act. This permits personal data to be held for the purpose of either preparing statistics or carrying out research, on condition that they are not used or disclosed for any other purpose and the ensuing statistics or results are not made available in a form identifying any of the data subjects. Section 35 of the Act also makes provision for delaying disclosure of exam marks to data subjects, that is, candidates. Normally, a data user must comply with a subject request within forty days, but in respect of examination marks, this is extended until either five months after the request, or forty days after the day the results are announced, whichever is earlier.

It should also be noted that there are exemptions to the principle of non-disclosure; these include circumstances where disclosure is for the purpose of safeguarding national security, for other legal purposes, or relates to an emergency situation.

Contract law, electronic publishing, and software production

Introduction

Where computers are concerned, contract law has major implications in three main areas: contracts with software companies for the creation of new software, licence agreements for 'off-the-shelf' software, and contracts between software authors and publishers. In higher education, experienced personnel in the institutional computing services are usually responsible for the writing or commissioning of new software. Licence agreements for 'off-the-shelf' software are handled in a similar way. It is not usual for academics within the humanities to be involved with these activities, except as an end-user. However, the advent of the electronic publishing era, and the growth of courseware production will undoubtedly lead many in the humanities to consider becoming authors of software in their own right. Those who do so may consider marketing that software through a software publishing company. While expert advice should always be sought by those in this position, this section highlights some of the legal aspects which must be considered prior to embarking on new ventures of this kind. It should be noted that the term 'electronic publishing' refers not only to the production of software, but also to the distribution of works by electronic mail, either to bulletin boards, or to publications listed in the *Directory of Electronic Journals and Newsletters.*[7] This section does not apply to this area of activity.

Broadly speaking, computer software products fall into two main categories: those which combine a databank with software which allow the end-user to manipulate the information in various ways; and traditional computer programs designed to manipulate the user's own data. It is products in the first category which have excited most interest in the humanities, particularly with the growing availability of multimedia technologies which allow the construction of databases which combine text, graphics, sound, photographic stills, animation, and motion video clips. Of such systems, some perform an archival, or reference function, combining a database with software which enables the user to search for information as required. Examples include the *Guardian* newspaper and the *International-Herald Tribune* newspaper. Others perform a more instructional function, where the database is supplied with software which supports a broader range of user interaction, including testing, assessment, and feedback—traditional courseware. Such information-based products will require a large amount of storage and are often, though not always, supplied on CD-ROM.

The majority of academics are familiar with conventional publishing procedures which are based on mass distribution; books are handled by large companies who sell to unknown purchasers. The publication of electronic material is, alas, more complex, due to the varying nature of potential products, the possible requirement for finance during the development phase, and the immature state of the market. In spite of this complexity, certain key factors which must be taken into account can be identified. These factors are highlighted in the following section.

Publishing software

The possibility of increasing the scope and sophistication of publication by means of multimedia and the CD-ROM has been the springboard for the launch of what is now referred to as the electronic publishing industry. These technological advances have inevitably led to competition between two established industries looking for a market share in this potentially lucrative field. The publishing industry sees electronic publishing as a natural progression from its traditional paper-based activities; the computer software industry sees digital technology as its home territory. As yet, the market is still in an immature state; there is no real harmonization of standards, nor any established large-scale consumer base. As a result, there is little mass distribution of multimedia products in the UK; parties from different sectors of both industries act as financiers, producers, and distributors. There is no set pattern, or established practice; therefore, a cautious approach must be taken throughout the negotiation process, as the legal and business problems which may be encountered are unpredictable (Dickens and Derbyshire 1992).

Any software, particularly multimedia software, is time consuming and expensive to produce, in comparison with a traditional book. It may therefore be necessary to find commercial partners to finance production. Whilst this has obvious advantages in terms of risk-sharing and resource provision, it will undoubtedly be necessary to relinquish a degree of control over the eventual product and its exploitation. This can have unfortunate consequences, if clear price structures have not been agreed from the outset. For example, hardware companies are often willing to invest in software production, with the proviso that the developer is bound to a specific hardware platform. There is also the potential for a conflict of objectives: the hardware manufacturer may insist that the software is sold at minimum cost, to encourage hardware sales, rather than maximize revenue on the software itself.

More typically, however, software authors will not be subject to such restrictions. They will be at liberty to choose a software publishing company with a good reputation and a high volume of sales. Usually, the author will grant an exclusive licence to the publishing company allocating the sole rights to deal with the software: that is, to market the product on the basis of agreed royalty payments. Under copyright law, the publishing company will have the same rights as if it owned the copyright itself and would be able to take legal action if infringements occurred.

Payment terms must be agreed and understood at an early stage, to avoid disappointment or disagreement later on. This process is not always straightforward, as royalties can be calculated in different ways. For example, there might be a fixed sum payable for every unit sold;

alternatively, the percentage of the price charged for the software might be used. In the latter case, does the price refer to the retail price, or the payment the publisher receives from the dealer? When are royalties due? Even when terms have been agreed, it is still necessary to build in as many fail-safe procedures for future contingencies as possible. Some useful guidelines are provided below (Bainbridge 1990, chapter 16); however, this is not intended as a comprehensive checklist:

- What does the author have to provide, in terms of electronic material and supporting documentation, and when must it be provided?
- How will the software be marketed and distributed, and what happens if this does not occur?
- What happens if the publisher decides to distribute the software at cut price?
- How does the author know that sales figures are correct—is there the right of access to the publisher's sales accounts?
- What if the publisher is late in making royalty payments?
- If the publisher decides to stop marketing the software, does this terminate the agreement?
- Can the author terminate the agreement, and under what circumstances?
- Who corrects defects in the software?
- Will the publisher, within the terms of the licences granted to the ultimate customer, ensure that the author is protected against any claims for losses to those customers caused by defects in the software?

Whilst it is clearly of vital importance to establish rights and responsibilities from the beginning, it should always be borne in mind that the market is changing rapidly. Therefore, short term commitments have advantages, building in flexibility and allowing the possibility of renegotiation in response to changing circumstances.

Conclusion

The law is breached daily by millions of computer users around the world; their numbers will no doubt include some academic staff. In many cases, it is ignorance of the law which causes infringement. However, no-one is exempt from the law, and ignorance of the law does not constitute a defence. Although institutions have a duty to ensure that their staff are able to acquaint themselves with the law, the advent of desktop computing has caused a shift towards individual responsibility. Clearly, avoiding painful legal disputes will require a cautious approach combined with increased personal awareness.

Notes

1. To some extent, this distinction still applies. One recent example of institutional direction would be the drawing up of codes of practice relating to the implementation of the European Health and Safety Commission's 1993 Directive on health and safety requirements for employees who 'habitually work with display screen equipment'.

2. Of course, individual academics have always been personally responsible for the consequences of misusing their own data.

3. This presumes that certain requirements for qualification are met, for example, that the author of an original literary work is a British citizen, or has certain residential qualifications, or that the work was first produced in the UK.

4. British Copyright Council (BCC), Copyright House, 29-33 Berners Street, London W1P 4AA.

5. The Copyright in Transmitted Electronic Documents (CITED) project coordinator is Mr J-F Boisson, Bull SA, + 33 1 3902 4293; fax +33 1 3902 4197. See also: *XIII Magazine*, October 1992, published by DGXIII of the Commission of the European Communities (CEC).

6. The re-use of copyright materials in computer courseware development, held in London, March 1993; organized by the British Universities Film and Video Council (BUFVC) in association with the Computers in Teaching Initiative Support Service (CTISS).

7. Obtainable through the Internet by means of the following command: LIST-SERV@ACADVM1.UOTAWA.CA, GET EJOURNL1 DIRECTORY GET EJOURNL2 DIRECTORY.

References and bibliography

Austen, J., 'Computer crime: ignorance or apathy?', *The Computer Bulletin 4th ser.* 5 (October 1993), 23–4.

Bainbridge, D. I., *Computers and the law* (London: Pitman Publishing, 1990).

Braithwaite, N., 'Why bulletin boards are a libel minefield', *Computer Weekly* (May 12 1994), 28.

The Copyright, Designs and Patents Act (London: Her Majesty's Stationery Office, 1988).

Deegan, M., Timbrell, N., and Warren, L., *Hypermedia in the humanities* (Oxford/Hull Universities: ITTI, 1992).

Dickens, J., and Derbyshire, J., 'Legal and commercial?', *The European multimedia yearbook* (1992).

Flint, M. F., *Know your rights! A user's guide to copyright* (London: Butterworth, 1993).

Klinger, P., and Burnett, R., *Drafting and negotiating computer contracts* (London: Butterworth, 1994).

National Council for Educational Technology (NCET), 'Copyright—the Act of 1988', *Information Sheet, IDcopy 6.1*, (1993).

Ohajah, E., 'Highway patrol', *Computer Weekly* (June 16 1994), 50.

Stavrinou, M., 'Student charged in Internet conspiracy', *Computer Weekly* (April 14 1994), 2.

Weston, M., 'Rights and wrongs', *The Times Higher, Synthesis supplement,* (May 13, 1994), vii.

Woollacott, E., 'Keeping trespassers at bay', *Computer Weekly* (May 5 1994), 30–31.

SECTION 2
DISCIPLINES

Archaeology

Seamus Ross

Introduction

During the last forty years the process of archaeological research from data collection to information creation to knowledge distribution has been influenced by advances in computer technology. From the 1950s through the 1970s quantitative methods formed the main focus of archaeological computing and these analyses were mainly done during the post-excavation phase. There were three primary reasons for this: quantification was seen as objective and therefore more science-like; early computers were viewed as number-crunchers; and the difficulties of access to and lack of portability of computers made it impossible for researchers to use them outside large institutions. Quantification continues to play an important, but more balanced, role as one of a range of tools information technology (IT) can provide. Over forty years the power, storage capacity, and portability of machines have increased dramatically. Technological improvements and the results of experimentation have shown the diverse opportunities computers offer archaeologists, from electronic distance measurement (EDM) equipment to geographic information systems (GIS) and databases.

The 1980s and early 1990s were characterized by a greater breadth of computational techniques and an increase in the use of computers for onsite recording. There were more extensive uses of databases, experimentation with geographic information systems, investigations of the opportunities image capture and manipulation might provide, an increase in the use of computer-aided design (CAD) tools, and attempts to understand better how using computers could aid more conventional research. The barriers to use also dropped as hardware became cheaper and faster, and software more user-friendly and versatile. Researchers discovered that not only could traditional tasks be undertaken more efficiently, but also that it was possible to manipulate and analyse data in ways otherwise impossible. With visualization tools archaeologists can examine landscapes and reconstruct buildings (Reilly 1988; 1991), and study such topics as change over time in landscape usage and the relationship between space and power. Simulation and modelling have made it possible to demonstrate the viability (or lack thereof) of certain hypotheses and explanations (Aldenderfer 1987; Gilbert and Doran 1994). Numerous activities, such as onsite data collection, solid modelling, computer-aided design and GIS, which began as investigations of possibilities have become mainstream tools for archaeological research. Some techniques, such as knowledge representation, have not been widely exploited within archaeology, but in areas such as classification they show much promise (Gardin 1991, 1990a, 1990b; Gardin *et al.* 1988; Ross 1991). Electronic dissemination of results opens new avenues because it offers ways to present data, information, and ideas about the past impossible in conventional publications: multiple views of objects, online databases, reconstructions, simulations, and walk-arounds. In the area of access and usage, the growth of the Internet in the 1990s has had an influence on archaeology as more information is available on demand (e.g. images, data, textbases, and electronic journals) and archaeologists can communicate with both local and distant colleagues more easily (Heyworth *et al.* 1996). Networked services should increase the diversity of the audience and continue to improve how they access archaeological information.

There are two main approaches to discussions about the use of computers in archaeology. The first depends upon the description of the tasks that archaeologists carry out and the detailing of how these can be aided by computers. The second involves the examination of the tools and methods that computers make available and the explanation of how these might be used in archaeology. This chapter combines both approaches. Three critical questions need consideration:

- Do computers change how archaeologists work? And, if so, what do these new practices look like, in what areas have results been demonstrated, and how was that work done?
- What are the trends in archaeological computing, and which are helping archaeologists better to understand the past and present that knowledge?
- What are the resource and support implications if archaeologists are to have suitable facilities and training to use IT to maximum advantage?

Field archaeology consumes scarce financial, intellectual, and labour resources and involves the destruction of the very material it is recording. For these reasons the primary and secondary datasets created during these processes must be preserved for future archaeologists if they are to be in a position to replicate the results of earlier research and perform new analyses on historic data.

Data handling

Archaeological research accumulates vast amounts of data, whether the focus of investigation is a survey, an excavation, a study of a material culture group (such as La Tene or Anasazi pottery), or an examination of a complex of ecofacts (e.g. pollen, or animal bones). Archaeologists have developed a variety of methods for handling data—these range from old fashioned and discredited approaches, such as selective recording and only saving 'significant finds', to the application of advanced technologies. There are a number of problems inherent in archaeological data handling and these are especially apparent in the use of databases and statistics. In the latter case a vast amount of number crunching can provide a myriad of output, which often represents the results of poorly framed questions or the application of inappropriate techniques. Occasionally, even the results of well-used techniques are misinterpreted. With statistics, as with most tools, it is fundamental to understand the concepts underlying the methods selected, the types of data required for a given kind of analysis or result, and how to interpret meaningfully and accurately the output of analyses (Fletcher and Lock 1991; Shennan 1988). Likewise, database development needs careful planning. It requires an understanding of the data to be modelled, the purpose of the modelling activity, and the conceptual process of data modelling (Moffett, this volume). Indeed, the poorly-planned use of computers will, in all likelihood, result in unsuitable solutions being supplied and inaccurate conclusions being drawn. The ability of computers to process tens of thousands of data points or thousands of context records rapidly can be seductive. The temptation to run a variety of analyses should be resisted until the nature and structure of the data have been defined, the questions which their analysis might plausibly be used to answer formulated, and in light of the data and the question, the best statistical technique for answering the question selected. Pam Crabtree's study of the vertebrate faunal assemblages from the early Anglo-Saxon settlement of West Stow provides a clear and accessible example of just how statistical analysis of large amounts of data provides an essential foundation for its interpretation (1989). Classification is an example of a task that can be made more rigorous when statistical analyses are used to identify and verify patterns in the dataset.

Researchers have employed quantitative methods to investigate archaeological data for decades (Taylor 1948; Thomas 1978; Clark 1982). Such analyses, as Crabtree's case study makes evident, have become a mainstream activity and quantitative studies have now acquired a central position in most efforts to interpret the past (Aldenderfer 1987). Nearly two decades have passed since D.H. Thomas, in a perceptive and witty essay, called our attention to 'the awful truth about statistics in archaeology' (1978). He recounted the dangerous repercussions caused by the indiscriminate and imprecise application of statistical procedures and he lamented the frequent misinterpretations and misrepresentations of the results of such analyses. Thomas had hoped that a change in the formal training of archaeologists might promote the more appropriate and successful application of these methods. Hole (1980), Scheps (1982), and Fletcher and Lock (1991), have noted a continuing problem; archaeological studies are still rife with statistical errors. During the last decade newer and easier to use software and more efficient hardware have made statistical methods effortless to apply and this has only exacerbated the problem. As Lyman explained, in a discussion of *Quantitative units and terminology in zooarchaeology*, 'both how quantitative units are defined and how they are operationalized must be explicit in order to ensure concordance between counting units used and the research question addressed with those units' (1994, 63).

As with most methods, a crucial preliminary stage is understanding the reasons why the techniques are being employed and how the results of analyses reflect the data being examined and the techniques applied. Clark and Stafford (1982, 99) have succinctly described why archaeologists undertake statistical analyses: first, 'the summarizing or reduction of information in such a way that certain facts which data patterns suggest become apparent'; and, second, 'inferring properties of a population on the basis of known sample results or formulating general laws on the basis of repeated observations'. The approaches range from simple statistics to complex techniques, such as principal components analysis, factor analysis, or discriminant analysis. Often, as Whallon (1987) has argued, simple statistical procedures provide vast amounts of data about the material under investigation and if this level of analysis does not prove sufficient these efforts still represent a fundamental initial step.

The availability of software packages which incorporate a full range of statistical processes has changed the profile of those undertaking statistical investigations of their data. As Clive Orton (1993) has shown, archaeology makes special demands on statistical tools and Pie-Slice is an example of a tool designed to fill one such specialized need; in this case for assisting with work with ceramic assemblages.

Fundamental to any project can be the use of database technology. The proliferation of the database has been facilitated by an improved conceptual understanding of how data should be structured and by the proliferation of Windows-based database packages which provide versatile and user-friendly development and delivery environments. The conceptual modelling of data is a critical precursor to actually processing those data. A finds database can assist in post-excavation analysis and where this is linked to contextual details it forms an essential tool in site recording and analysis.

Onsite data collection systems are based around databases. Andresen and Madsen have described opportunities (1992) and Powlesland has demonstrated over a fifteen year period how the process of archaeological excavation (1991, 1996) can be greatly assisted by onsite recording systems. During the excavations at West Heslerton (Yorkshire), staff working in the field used small computers to record information about contexts, finds, and spatial data. Excavations were often plagued by variation in the way various supervisors recorded data in site notebooks. The electronic recording tools helped to make certain that a more comprehensive, consistent, and easier to use record was created. The software managed data entry so that staff recorded sufficient information to guarantee that complete records were created. What was a rare practice has now become common as most major excavations rely on computers for information capture.

Databases not only assist during onsite data collection. In studying Teotihuacan, George Cowgill has made use of databases of thousands of finds since the late 1960s (1974; 1996). As he points out, he as been able to examine the interrelationship of finds within the context of some 500 variables, something which would never have been possible manually. His work has very much depended on the continued access to the original data and this has led to conclusions about the use of the site, spatial differentiation, and change over time. These datasets become increasingly important as sources of material for other researchers who may wish to evaluate the conclusions which have been reached, and sometimes the databases become almost publications in their own right—a development which can prove problematic for archaeologists. Statistical usage has been subject to years of debate; the methods are well understood, and a certain critical outlook is reserved for the use of statistical techniques. The same, unfortunately, cannot be said for databases. Too often projects embark on the development of database systems without preparing for the development with careful planning. This is to be avoided. The Arretine Pottery project based at the Institute of Archaeology at Oxford is an excellent example of a project which benefited from a detailed analysis of the variety and quality of information that it would collect and how it would need to be structured if conclusions were to be drawn about the distribution of pottery finds and their manufacture (Kenrick, 1994). Indeed, Kenrick's *Potters' stamps on Italian Terra Sigillata: towards a new catalogue* is a excellent case study of the issues involved in database development and use for artefact studies (1993).

The use of electronic data acquisition equipment both in the field and laboratory has improved the process of data collection dramatically. As Raab has noted, 'inadequate data acquisition techniques limit the potential variety, quantity, and accuracy of data available to researchers' (1993, 219). Digital callipers and precision balances are two examples of laboratory devices that can aid data laboratory recording. In a study of the material from San Clemente Island the use of these tools increased recording accuracy and productivity by between seven and twelve times. The use of electronic distance-measuring equipment and total stations has transformed both excavation and survey work. Where data are collected in this way it is possible to transfer them directly to systems to produce site plans and distribution maps.

Computer imaging and graphics

Computer graphics provide archaeologists with a powerful tool to present and manipulate image data. Graphs, site plans, artefact illustrations, building elevations, reconstructions, and distribution maps are all features of most excavation reports. The great majority of illustrations are still produced manually. This state of affairs reflects the general situation in computing; graphics (used here in its broadest sense) require special hardware for display and printing, powerful processors, and extensive memory and disc storage capabilities. These are now widely available. In 1991, in *Computing for Archaeologists*, the claim was made that:

> If our earlier experience of statistics and databases holds
> true for graphics (and there is nothing to suggest it will
> not) we can safely predict that computer graphics will
> acquire a major role in archaeology. Graphical systems
> may yet redefine the processes of collecting, representing,
> and interpreting archaeological evidence.
> (Ross 1991, 127)

This hypothesis has been borne out and increasingly excavations rely on computer-aided design (CAD) tools to produce site plans, elevations, and distribution plots. The use of CAD tools and rendering software ease the transition from data points to hypothetical reconstructions.

Unlike many computing techniques, where the distinction between representational and interpretive activities is clear-cut, graphics cross both boundaries. Colley *et al.* (1988) argued that graphics provide a framework for data exploration and that this data exploration modifies how we look at archaeological evidence. They were, for example, able to demonstrate that by using graphical representations it was possible to explore a range of different configurations and interpretations of the evidence—it was possible to re-excavate the site virtually, or at least to re-excavate the recorded material. Archaeologists can test a variety of interpretations of the recovered data, and then modify the presentation and explanations to account for factors which had initially been missed. The interpretation of the process of deposition of the late Bronze Age midden in the village of Potterne, Wiltshire was made possible by the use of a system to produce three-dimensional plots showing the position of objects in the midden and their interrelationship.

The ability to store and manipulate graphical representations offers archaeologists what Paul Reilly has referred to as a 'second look'; now it is possible to generate, view, and reconsider hypotheses dynamically (1991). Such re-examinations extend beyond testing various posthole configurations or artefact (and/or ecofact) deposition patterns to re-studying landscapes in a post-excavation context under varying light and weather conditions. These kinds of representations compensate for some of the destructive effects of excavations. Some representations of archaeological data, in the form of malleable reconstructions, will make it possible to search for meaning and function in aspects of archaeological data which had previously been difficult to study from this point of view. From reconstructions of the Temple Precinct at Roman Bath, it proved possible to draw some conclusions about building design and layout and about Roman attitudes towards power.

There is no established method for defining the parameters of archaeological reconstruction, and interpreting these reconstructed images beyond the restrictions imposed by computers themselves, common sense, and learned rules (i.e., acquired archaeological rules of analysis). Such a methodology will be vital if graphics are to take on a larger role in archaeological interpretation. Quite probably some of the approaches employed by ethnohistorians or visual anthropologists (e.g. Collier and Collier 1986, esp. 29-42) will provide the vital background to investigating reconstructions.

Computerized data capture and processing also resolve the problem of verbal description; in the past this has created a range of unnecessary biases, such as terminological ambiguities. Automatic recording of artefact shapes removes numerous human and archaeological biases. These seemingly objective processes of recording, for example, remove the limitations generated by pre-recording interpretative subjectivity (i.e. attribute selection) but, as Ackerly has demonstrated in his re-examination of the American Pipeline Project, vision systems introduce their own biases: for example, under some conditions their system recorded the shadow of the object as if it were a part of the object itself (Ackerly 1996). They do create a host of other difficulties, because even 'vision systems' are subject to preferential recording of certain features as opposed to others.

Presentation of graphical images will increase and change the archaeological audience. The generation of pictorial representations and complex video images shifts the process by which archaeological data can be presented to the public at large. It also changes how outsiders can understand the past. Quite clearly, graphic modelling yields new information and ways of presenting archaeological evidence. The pictorial representation of data in maps, artefact drawings and graphs has long been known to clarify and enhance data presentations. The functional characteristics of the computer support the redrawing and representing of information in a variety of formats and permit archaeologists to test a range of configurations of the data and hypotheses which in the past they could not.

A visual record of archaeological evidence, whether contexts or small finds, is essential and digital images provide an economical way to capture and store this record (Ross 1993). The advances in software and hardware have made it possible to generate large-scale pictorial databases of objects, site plans, and other records of archaeological evidence. Where currently these image banks must be indexed using verbal descriptions, research in content-based image retrieval systems is changing this (Flickner *et al.* 1995). There are two main areas in which image processing is used: to manipulate and enhance image quality; and to perform tasks of image recognition. First, image enhancement makes it possible to identify the grey-scale tones of stored images and, using histogram equalization, to change the spectral character of the image and thereby make it clearer and bring lost shapes into the foreground. This process would be extremely useful in enhancing, for example, x-ray images of silver-inlaid iron. Microcomputer-based image manipulation packages have become quite common and they will become more so. In addition, it is possible to perform various types of artefact recognition using computer-based image analysis techniques. There are, for instance, various edge-recognition paradigms to support the identification of objects. Gero and Mazzullo (1984), and Main (1986; 1988) have suggested how the use of graphical outline shapes can assist in the automatic classification of some artefacts.

Remote sensing offers many opportunities. The term has many broad definitions, but Kruckham's states that it refers to the use of 'cameras, thermal infrared scanners, side-looking radar, and multi-spectral systems' to 'record and analyse man-made features' (1987, 343). Kruckham drew attention to numerous research projects which took advantage of remote sensing data in order to improve understanding of specific cultures. Although archaeologists have used aerial photography for nearly seventy years, this kind of remote sensing data remains underexploited. It is, however, now possible to access large amounts of these data using microcomputers. The images collected by the American Space missions and satellites are the best known, but the French (i.e. Spot) and the Soviets (i.e. Sojuzkarta) also make available the images they have collected.

Large-scale images of areas of the earth are available on disc or over the Internet and make it possible to set a site within its ecological, environmental, and geological contexts (Custer *et al.* 1983; 1986). The difficulties of handling these images have been greatly eased by the appearance of geographic information systems (GIS) (Burrough 1986). Sever and Sheets' (1988) description of their Costa Rica project has given dramatic proof to the claims about the untapped potential of remote sensing images. Lyons and Avery (1977) and Sever and Wiseman (1985) are two valuable introductions to the applications and techniques of remote sensing.

Spatial analysis assists in the process of interpreting site contexts and structures. Enloe and David (1994) have demonstrated that the same data, in this case a combination of faunal and other artefactual evidence, can be used to support a variety of conclusions about spatial distribution and site usage. The role of spatial analysis is also seen in the use of geographic information systems (GIS) as David Wheatley has shown (this volume). Now the plotting of survey data, the examination of the relationship between sites and landscape, and the impact of environmental factors can all be included in the questions archaeologists can ask of their data (Allen *et al.*, 1990; Kvamme 1989; Lock and Harris 1992). GIS facilitates the testing of a range of hypotheses dependent upon the spatial distribution of data as well as the relationships between such distributions and environmental and geological features. Hinshelwood and Bona's study of a highway corridor west of Thunder Bay Ontario illustrates the use of GIS systems (1994, 12-20). The study of the settlements of the island of Hvar is another, but more ambitious case study (Gaffney and Stancic 1991; 1992).

Knowledge-based systems and archaeological simulation

Expert systems get little coverage in discussions of humanities computing, but they could be of immense benefit. Sadly, though, in the forty years since Gardin first drew attention to them few archaeologists have taken advantage of the opportunities and there are hardly any systems in use. This is changing. Recent work by the French (e.g. Francfort 1987; Guenoche and Hesnard 1983) and in particular by Gardin (Gardin *et al.* 1988) and the team of Lagrange and Renaud (1984; 1985), work being undertaken in England (Kippen 1988; Doran 1977; Doran and Corcoran 1985; Palmer and Doran 1993; Ross 1992), and in the Netherlands (van den Dries 1994), demonstrate the potential benefits of these methodologies to archaeology.

What has become apparent is that research in artificial intelligence, and, in particular, advances in expert systems theory and knowledge representation, will radically alter how archaeologists organize information, investigate material culture, build models, and interpret the past. In the process, these developments will change what information archaeologists present, how we present it and lead us to understand better how we represent knowledge (e.g. Gardin 1987). Many of these changes will occur whether or not expert systems applications become widely available in archaeology. They will arrive as a result of the more rigorous order of logical thinking and argumentation which expert system development forces. While it is likely that expert systems will bring their first major benefits to areas such as systems to assist in the identification and classification of artefacts (Ross *et al.* 1991) a team lead by Juan Barceló has shown the possibilities of using such systems to study social organization (Barceló *et al.* 1994, 165-172).

Computers have a wide role to play in archaeological simulation (Gilbert and Doran 1994; Doran 1987; Doran and Corcoran 1985), reconstruction modelling (see above) and GIS modelling of spatial interrelationships (Wheatley, this volume). Whether you are developing a database, a knowledge base, or a reconstruction drawing, you are drawing conclusions about how you interpret the recovered archaeological deposits. Moreover, computers support the modelling of systems and testing of their behaviour under varying conditions. Belovsky (1987; 1988), for instance, used a very simple model developed in a Lotus spreadsheet to examine hunter-gatherer behaviour in an effort to understand how they optimized behaviour strategies.

Computers in teaching

Computers hold out many opportunities for those who wish to learn about archaeology, as part of museum displays or in the classroom for computer-aided learning. The Pompeii exhibition in 1990 was an excellent case study in how effectively computers could help visitors to a museum to contextualize the material culture and the world of its use and creation (AA.VV, 1990). The Teaching and Learning Technology Programme (TLTP) in the UK has developed a substantial system for teaching students about archaeology and the process of managing an excavation (Campbell 1994). But even beyond these pre-packaged systems computers have teaching and learning value, for they have a great deal of potential to help students learn the skills of analysis and synthesis. In particular database development offers some of the greatest educational benefits. For instance, the process of designing a database to hold information about axes from neolithic contexts forces the researcher to study individual axes carefully and to consider properties of axes in general. The process of conceptual modelling is an essential requirement before one can implement a computer-based model, whether it be a representational or interpretative one.

Dissemination of information

Data presentation

Despite prognostications about the 'paperless office' and the opportunities of data transfer and presentation in electronic form, researchers still produce vast quantities of paper output; indeed, rather than declining, this seems to be increasing. Scholars and archaeological units quickly discovered the many benefits of word processing. In general, word processors perform very simple tasks of text management and low quality document production. For a relatively modest outlay, a unit, department, or museum could procure the equipment and software (e.g., a microcomputer, scanner, laser printer, mouse and desktop publishing (DTP) application software) which will enable the production of first-rate publications. This effectively means DTP capabilities, including the ability to perform functions such as page layout, displaying portions of text in different typefaces and font sizes, and the placing of photographs and illustrations directly into the text. Like many other areas of computing DTP has become a specialist subject and has acquired its own vocabulary. Essentially, DTP makes it possible for an individual or small group to generate documents effectively to meet specific requirements and to look as professional as those produced by most publishers. The layout and presentation are critical to the production of print or electronic documents—the design of presentations must be left to professionals with experience in how look and feel influence the accessibility of information, and this is especially true for electronic publications (cf: Banning, 1993, 441-7).

Three important print sources for archaeological computing are: the annual publication of the *Computer Applications in Archaeology* (CAA), *Archeologia e Calcolatori* and *Archaeological Computing Newsletter*. Print publications are in many ways being supplanted by the increasing use of networks, such as the Internet which has opened new opportunities for the dissemination of information. The Council for British Archaeology has, for instance, launched an information service (URL: http://britac3.britac.ac.uk:80/cba/). Many archaeological units, such as the Birmingham University Field Archaeological Unit (URL: http://www.birmingham.ac.uk/BUFAU), have established their own presence on the

Internet to ease the dissemination of information about their work. One of the best ways to obtain information about the archaeological information services is through ArchNet (based at the University of Connecticut which maintains up-to-date links to a wide range of archaeological information services (URL: http://spirit.lib.uconn.edu/ArchNet/Arch Net.html). But these information services are only a part of the dissemination opportunities made possible by networks. Access to online databases is now feasible, such as the National Archaeological Database (NADB), which is a bibliography of some 120,000 American archaeological reports that are rarely available in libraries (URL: http://www.cast.uark.edu/products/NADB/). There are an increasing number of national sites and monuments records. In England the National Sites and Monuments Record of the Royal Commission on Historical Monuments has created a database containing nearly 300,000 records about the terrestrial and maritime archaeological sites and buildings.

Network-based electronic publications make it possible to produce articles which incorporate a great diversity of data types in developing arguments. This new electronic environment should result in a radical rethink of scholarship and how it is presented. Networked journals make it possible to present material in support of hypotheses that could not be distributed before. Archaeological evidence and its analysis are currently straight-jacketed by conventional printing. With electronic media archaeologists will be able to distribute full excavation data, in addition to their interpretations, allowing other researchers to re-analyse the material to confirm conclusions or to draw new ones. It will also be possible to distribute photographs, drawings, data, images of data visualization, and dynamic reconstruction images. Archaeologists can also incorporate the computer programs they have used to analyse their data so that their colleagues can assess whether the analytic programs hide hypotheses that may have influenced the analysis of the data. Of course, there are problems such as credibility, copyright, access, and preservation which must be addressed as this technology is developed. Electronic publication will require a culture change, but it will enable authors to use the medium most appropriate to their topic or argument and it will enable readers to interact with the original data or sources. *Internet Archaeology* is one such journal (Heyworth *et al.* 1995; http://britac3.britac.ac.uk/cba/projects/ejournal.html; URL http://intarch.york.ac.uk).

Conclusion

The process of using computers brings to the foreground the fact that much of archaeological research and interpretation is founded on learned behaviour. The kinds of interpretations which we make and why we make them reflect both our background and our training. In this there should be nothing surprising. The process of using computers and seeking objectivity only makes more apparent the significant role that learned behaviour plays in archaeological investigation and interpretation. Computers do not necessarily create more objective archaeologists, but then again objectivity is not necessarily the single most important criterion for a science. Certainly, the use of computers must not be viewed as a method of becoming objective; a method of becoming rigorous, vigilant and exhaustive, absolutely; but a method of becoming objective, absolutely not. Computers do nothing to relieve the critical importance of interpretation and the role of learned behaviour in archaeology. Conceptualization of data and knowledge is essential to understand the data, whether they are artefacts, archaeological sites, or cultures.

There is a final problem which faces archaeologists creating or using this electronic material and that is that it must be preserved for the longer term. Excavation results in the destruction of the object of study. As the recording of information in electronic form during excavations and the generation of digital reconstructions from the data become more and more widespread the preservation of this material will become more and more critical. These reconstructions, the associated data, and the images taken on site need to be preserved if future scholars are to have access both to the evidence of our past and to evidence of how we interpreted it (Ross 1995). As technology comes to play an increasing role in understanding our cultural heritage, that very technology will be essential to future generations who may want to understand why we held the views we did (Ross 1996).

References and bibliography

AA.VV., *Rediscovering Pompei. Exhibition by IBM Italia, New York City, IBM Gallery of Science and Art, 12 July-15 September 1990*, (Roma: L'Erma di Bretschneider, 1990).

Aberg, F.A., and Leech, R.H., 'The national archaeological record for England. Past present and future', in Larsen, C. U. (ed.), *Sites and monuments: national archaeological records*, (Copenhagen: The National Museum of Denmark, 1992), 157-69.

Ackerly, N.W., 'On the lessons of computers in archaeology: Lessons from the all-American Pipeline Project', in Ross, S. (ed.), *Electronic information in archaeology: opportunities and obstacles* (Oxford: Oxbow Books, 1996).

Aldenderfer, M.S., 'Assessing the impact of quantitative thinking on archaeological research: historical and evolutionary insights', in Aldenderfer, M.S. (ed.), *Quantitative research in archaeology: progress and prospects*, (London: Sage Publications, 1987), 9-29.

Allen, K.M.S., Green, S.W., and Zubrow, E.B.W. (eds.), *Interpreting space: GIS and archaeology* (London-New York-Philadelphia: Taylor and Francis, 1990).

Andresen, J., and Madsen, T., 'Data structures for excavation recording. a case of complex information management', in Larsen C. U. (ed.), *Sites and monuments: national archaeological records*, (Copenhagen: The National Museum of Denmark, 1992) 49-67.

Banning, E.B., 'Hypermedia and archaeological publication: the Wadi Ziqlab Project', in Andresen, J., Madsen, T., and Scollar, I. (eds.), *Computing the past, CAA92: computer applications and quantitative methods in archaeology*, (Aarhus: University Press, 1993), 441-7.

Barceló, J.A., Vila, A. and Argeles, T., 'KIPA—a computer program to analyse the social position of women in huntergather societies', in Johnson, I. (ed.), *Methods in the mountains*, (UISPP Commission Conference IV), Sydney, 1994, 165-172.

Belovsky, G., 'Hunter-gather foraging: a linear programming approach', *Journal of Anthropological Archaeology*, 6.1 (1987), 29-76.

Belovsky, G., 'An optimal foraging-based model of hunter-gatherer population dynamics', *Journal of Anthropological Archaeology*, 7 (1988), 329-372.

Booth, B.K.W., Grant, S.A.V., and Richards, J.D. (eds.), *Computer usage in British archaeology*, Second Edition 1989, (Birmingham: The Institute of Field Archaeologists, 1989).

Burnard, L., and Short, H., *An Arts And Humanities Data Service* (Oxford: Office for Humanities Communication for Joint Information Systems Committee of the Higher Education Funding Councils, 1995).

Burrough, P.A., *Principles of geographical information systems for land resources assessment* (Oxford: Clarendon Press, 1986).

Campbell, E., *TLTP Archaeology Consortium Newsletter*, 1 (1994).

Chartrand, J., and Miller, P., 'Concordance in rural and urban database structure: the York experience', in Moscati, P. (ed.), Choice, representation and structuring of archaeological information, *Archeologia e Calcolatori* 5 (1994), 203-218.

Clark, G., 'Quantifying archaeological research', *Advances in Archaeological Method and Theory*, 5 (1982), 217-273.

Clark, G., and Stafford, C.R., 'Quantification in American archaeology: historical perspective', *World Archaeology*, 14.1 (1982), 98-119.

Clubb, N., 'Computer mapping and the scheduled ancient monument record', in Rahtz, S.P.Q. (ed.), *Computer and quantitative methods in archaeology*, BAR International Series, 446, (Oxford: British Archaeological Reports,) (ii).

Colley, S.M., Todd, S.J.P., and Campling, N.R., 'Three-dimensional computer graphics for archaeological data exploration: an example from Saxon Southampton', *Journal of Archaeological Science*, 15 (1988), 99-106.

Collier, J., and Collier, M., *Visual anthropology: photography as a research method* (Albuquerque: University of New Mexico Press, 1986).

Cowgill, G. L., 'Computers and prehistoric archaeology', in Bowles, E. (ed), *Computers in humanistic research*, (Englewood Cliffs, New Jersey: Prentice-Hall, 1967), 46-56.

Cowgill, G.L., 'Quantitative studies of urbanization at Teotihuacan', in Hammond, N. (ed.), *Mesoamerican archaeology: new approaches*, (London: Duckworth, 1974), 363-396.

Cowgill, G.L., 'The Teotihuacan mapping project data files', in Ross S. (ed.), *Electronic information in archaeology: opportunities and obstacles* (Oxford: Oxbow Books, 1996).

Crabtree, P., 'Sheep, horses, swine, and kine: a zooarchaeological perspective on the Anglo-Saxon settlement of England', *Journal of Field Archaeology*, 16.2 (1989), 205-213.

Custer, J. F., Eveleigh, T., and Klemos, V., 'A Landsat-generated predictive model for prehistoric archaeological sites in Delaware's coastal plain', *Bulletin of the Archaeological Society of Delaware*, (1983), 14.

Custer, J. F., Eveleigh, T., Klemos, V., and Wells, I., 'Application of Landsat data and synoptic remote sensing to predictive models for prehistoric archaeological sites: an example from the Delaware coastal plain', *American Antiquity*, 51.3 (1986), 572-588.

Dallas, C. J., 'Information systems and cultural knowledge: the Benaki Museum case', *Computers and the History of Art Journal*, 3.1 (1992), 7-15.

Delooze, K., and Wood, J., 'Furness Abbey survey project', in Lockyear, K., and Rahtz, S. (eds.), *Computer applications and quantitative methods in archaeology 1990*, BAR International Series, 565, (Oxford: British Archaeological Reports, 1991), 141-8.

Doran, J., 'Knowledge representation for archaeological inference', in Elcock, E.W., and Michie, D. (eds.), *Machine intelligence 8*, (Chichester: John Wiley and Sons, 1977), 433-454.

Doran, J., 'Formal methods and archaeological theory: a perspective', *World Archaeology*, 18.1 (1986), 21-37.

Doran, J., 'Anthropological archaeology, computational modelling, and expert systems', in Aldenderfer, M.S. (ed.), *Quantitative research in archaeology: progress and prospects*, (London: Sage Publications, 1987), 73–88.

Doran, J., and Corcoran, G., 'A computational model of production exchange and trade' in Voorrips, A., and Loving, S.H. (eds.), *To pattern the past*, PACT, 11 (1985), 349-359.

Doran, J., and Hodson, F.R., *Mathematics and computers in archaeology* (Edinburgh: Edinburgh University Press, 1975).

van den Dries, M. H., 'WAVES: an expert system for the analysis of use-ware on flint artefacts', in Johnson, I. (ed), *Methods in the mountains*, (UISPP Commission Conference IV), Sydney, 1994, 173-182.

Enloe, J. G., and David, F., 'Patterns of faunal processing at section 27 of Pincevent: the use of spatial analysis and ethnoarchaeological data in the interpretation of archaeological site structures', *Journal of Anthropological Archaeology*, 13.2 (1994), 105-124.

Fletcher, M., and Lock, G., Digging numbers. elementary statistics for archaeologists, (Oxford: Oxford University Committee for Archaeology Monograph 33, 1991).

Flickner, M., Sawhney, H., Black, W.N., Ashley, J., Huang, Q., Dom, B., Gorkani, M., Hafner, J., Lee, D., Petkovic, D., Steele, D., Yanker, P., 'Query by image and video content: the QBIC system', *Computer*, (September 1995), 23-32.

Francfort, H.-P., 'Un système expert pour l'analyse archéologique de sociétés protour-baines. Première étape: le cas de Shortughaï', *Informatique et Sciences Humaines*, 74 (1987), 73-91.

Fraser, D., 'The British archaeological database', in Hunter, J., and Ralston, I. (eds.), *Archaeological resource management in the UK: an introduction*, (Alan Sutton Publishing Ltd, 1993), 19-29.

Gaffney, V., and Stancic, Z., *GIS approaches to regional analysis: a case study of the island of Hvar.* (Ljubljana: Filozofska fakulteta, 1991).

Gaffney, V., and Stancic, Z., 'Diodorus Siculus and the Island of Hvar, Dalmatia: testing the text with GIS', in Lock, G., and Moffett, J. (eds.), *Computer applications and quantitative methods in archaeology 1991*, BAR International Series, S577, (Oxford: British Archaeological Reports, 1992), 113-125.

Gaines, S., 'Computerized data banks in archaeology: the European situation', *Computers in the Humanities*, 15.4 (1981), 223-226.

Gardin, J-C., *Expert systems and scholarly publications*, The Fifth British Library Annual Research Lecture, (London: The British Library, 1987).

Gardin, J.-C., 'The structure of archaeological theories', in Voorrips, A. (ed.), *Mathematics and information science in archaeology: a flexible framework. Studies in modern archaeology 3*, (Bonn: Holos Verlag, 1990a), 7-28.

Gardin, J-C., 'Interpretation in the humanities: some thoughts on the third way', in Ennals, R., and Gardin, J-C. (eds.), *Interpretation in the humanities: perspectives from artificial intelligence*, (London: The British Library, 1990b), 22-59.

Gardin, J-C., 'The impact of computer-based techniques on research in archaeology', in Katzen, M. (ed.), *Scholarship and technology in the humanities*, (London: Bowker-Saur, 1991), 95-110.

Gardin, J-C., and Peebles, C. (eds.), *Representations in archaeology* (Bloomington: Indiana University Press, 1992).

Gardin, J.-C., Guillaume, O., Herman, P., Hesnard, A., Lagrange, M.-S., Renaud, M., and Zadora-Rio, E., *Artificial intelligence and expert systems: case studies in the knowledge domain of archaeology* (Chichester: Ellis Horwood, 1988).

Gero, J., and Mazzullo, J. 'Analysis of artifact shape using fourier series in closed form', *Journal of Field Archaeology*, 11 (1984), 315-322.

Gilbert, N., and Doran, J., *Simulating societies: the computer simulation of social phenomena* (London: UCL, 1994).

Guenoche, A., and Hesnard, A., 'Typologie d'amphores romaines par une methode logique de classification', *Computers in the Humanities*, 17.4 (1983), 185-198.

Haigh, J.G.B., 'Rectification of aerial photographs by means of desk-top systems', in Rahtz, S., and Richards, J. (eds.), *Computer applications and quantitative methods in archaeology 1989*, BAR International Series, 548, (Oxford: British Archaeological Reports, 1989), 111-19.

Harris, T.M., and Lock, G.R., 'Toward a regional GIS site information retrieval system: the Oxfordshire Sites and Monuments (SMR) prototype', in Larson, C.U. (ed.), *Sites and monuments: national archaeological records*, (Copenhagen: The National Museum of Denmark, 1992), 185-99.

Heyworth, M.P., Ross, S., and Richards, J., 'Internet archaeology: an international electronic journal for archaeology', in Kamermanns, H. (ed.), *CAA95: Computer applications and quantitative methods in archaeology, 1996.*

Hinshelwood, A., and Bona, L.D., 'GIS and intrasite analysis: an example from Northwestern Ontario, Canada', *Archaeological Computing Newsletter*, 40 (1994), 12-20.

Hole, B.L. 'Sampling in archaeology: a critique', *Annual Review of Anthropology*, 9 (1980), 217-234.

Kenrick, P., 'Potters' stamps on Italian Terra Sigillata: towards a new catalogue', *Journal of Roman Pottery Studies*, 6 (1993), 27-35.

Kenrick, P., 'Hommage au Professeur H. Comfort: La Suite du Corpvs Vasorum Arretinorum.' S.F.E.C.A.G., Actes du Congrès de Millau, 1994, 175-182.

Kippen, J., 'On the uses of computers in anthropological research', *Current Anthropology*, 29.2 (1988), 317-320.

Kruckham, L., 'The role of remote sensing in ethnohistorical research', *Journal of Field Archaeology*, 14.3 (1987), 343-351.

Kvamme, K.L., 'Geographic information systems in regional research and data management', in Schiffer, M.B. (ed.), *Archaeological method and theory 1*: (Tucson: University of Arizona Press, 1989) 139-203.

Lagrange, M.-S., and Renaud, M., 'Deux expériences de simulation des raisonnements en archéologie au moyen d'un système expert: le système SNARK', *Informatique et sciences humaines*, 59-60 (1984), 161-188.

Lagrange, M.-S., and Renaud, M., 'Intelligent knowledge-based systems in archaeology: a computerized simulation of reasoning by means of an expert system', *Computers in the Humanities*, 19.1 (1985), 37-52.

Lock, G., and Harris, T., 'Visualizing spatial data: the importance of geographic information systems', in Reilly, P., and Rahtz, S. (eds.), *Archaeology and the information age. A global perspective* (London: Routledge, 1992).

Lyman, R. L., 'Quantitative units and terminology in zooarchaeology,' *American Antiquity*, 59.1 (1994), 36-71.

Lyons, T. R., and Avery T.E., *Remote sensing: a handbook for archaeological and cultural resource managers* (Washington D.C.: National Park Service, 1977).

Main, P., 'Accessing outline shape information efficiently within a large database', in *Computer Applications in Archaeology*, (1986), 73-82.

Main, P., 'Assessing outline shape information efficiently', in Ruggles, C.L.N., and Rahtz, S.P.Q. (eds.), *Computers and quantitative methods in archaeology 1988*, BAR International Series, 393, (Oxford: British Archaeological Reports, 1988), 243-251.

Moreno, G. M., Orton, C., and Rackham, J., 'A new statistical tool for comparing animal bone assemblages', *Journal of Archaeological Science*, (Forthcoming).

Murray, D.M., 'Towards harmony: a view of the Scottish Archaeological Database', in Larsen, C.U. (ed.), *Sites and monuments: national archaeological records*, (Copenhagen: The National Museum of Denmark, 1992), 209-216.

Orton, C., *Mathematics in archaeology* (London: Collins, 1980).

Orton, C., 'Quantitative methods in the 1990s', in Lock, G., and Moffett, J. (eds.), *Computer applications and quantitative methods in archaeology 1991*, BAR International Series, S577, (Oxford: British Archaeological Reports, 1992) 137-140.

Orton, C., 'How many pots make five? An historical view of pottery quantification', *Archaeometry*, 35.2 (1993), 169-84.

Palmer, M., and Doran, J., 'Contrasting models of Upper Palaeolithic dynamics: a distributed artificial intelligence approach', in Andresen, J., Madsen, T., and Scollar, I. (eds.), *Computing the past, CAA92: computer applications and quantitative methods in archaeology*, (Aarhus: Aarhus University Press, 1993), 251-262.

Powlesland, D., 'From the trench to the bookshelf: computer use at the Heslerton Paris Project', in Ross, S., Moffett, J., and Henderson, J. (eds.), *Computing for Archaeologists*, Oxford University Committee for Archaeology, Monograph No. 18, (Oxford: Oxbow Books, 1991), 155-169.

Powlesland, D., 'Computer applications at the Heslerton Parish Project', in Ross, S. (ed.), *Electronic information in archaeology: opportunities and obstacles*, (Oxford: Oxbow Books, 1996)

Raab, L.M., 'Laboratory automation: computer-linked measurement devices and videomicroscopy', *Journal of Field Archaeology*, 20.2 (1993), 219-224.

Reilly, P., *Data visualisation: recent advances in the application of graphic systems to archaeology*, (Winchester: IBM UK Scientific Centre Report 185, 1988).

Reilly, P., 'Visualising the problem: advancing graphic systems in archaeological analysis', in Ross, S., Moffett, J., and Henderson, J. (eds.), *Computing for archaeologists*, Oxford University Committee for Archaeology, Monograph No. 18, (Oxford: Oxbow Books, 1991).

Reilly, P., and Rahtz, S. (eds.), *Archaeology and the information age* (London: Routledge, 1992).

Richards, J.D. (ed.), *Computer usage in British archaeology* (Birmingham: Institute of Field Archaeologists, 1986).

Ross, S., 'Viewing data and representing the past', in Ross, S., Moffett, J., and Henderson, J. (eds.), *Computing for archaeologists*, Oxford University Committee for Archaeology, Monograph No. 18, (Oxford: Oxbow Books 1991), 127-129.

Ross, S., *Dress pins from Anglo-Saxon England: their production and typo-chronological development* (unpublished D.Phil. thesis), Oxford, 1992.

Ross, S., 'From conventional photographs to digital resources', *Archaeological Computing Newsletter*, 35 (1993), 14-21.

Ross, S., 'Preserving and maintaining electronic resources in the visual arts for the next century?', *Information Services and Use*, 15 (1995), 373-384.

Ross, S. (ed.), *Electronic information in archaeology: opportunities and obstacles* (Oxford: Oxbow Books, 1996).

Ross, S., Moffett, J., and Henderson, J., *Computing for archaeologists*, Oxford University Committee for Archaeology, Monograph No. 18, (Oxford: Oxbow Books 1991).

Scheps, S., 'Statistical blight', *American Antiquity*, 47.4 (1982), 836-851.

Scollar, I., 'The Bonn Archaeological Database', in Larsen, C.U. (ed.), *Sites and monuments: national archaeological records*, (Copenhagen: The National Museum of Denmark, 1992), 97-114.

Semeraro, G., 'The excavation archive: an integrated system for the management of cartographic and alphanumeric data', in Andresen, J., Madsen, T., and Scollar, I., (eds.), *Computing the past, CAA92: computer applications and quantitative methods in archaeology*, (Aarhus: Aarhus University Press, 1993), 205-211.

Sever, T., and Sheets, P., 'High-tech wizardry', *Archaeology*, 41.6 (1988), 28- 35.

Sever, T., and Wiseman, J., *Remote sensing and archaeology: potential for the future*, (Gulfport: Earth Resources Laboratory, NASA, 1985).

Shennan, S., *Quantifying archaeology* (Edinburgh: Edinburgh University Press, 1988).

Spaulding, A.C., 'Statistical techniques for the discovery of artifact types', *American Antiquity*, 18.3 (1953), 305-313.

Startin, B., 'The monuments protection programme: archaeological records', in Larson, C.U. (ed.), *Sites and monuments: national archaeological records*, (Copenhagen: The National Museum of Denmark, 1992), 201-6.

Stutt, A., and Shennan, S., 'The nature of archaeological arguments', *Antiquity*, 64 (1990), 766-777.

Taylor, W.W., 'A study of archaeology', *American Anthropologist 50 (3.2) Memoir No. 69*, (Washington D.C.: American Anthropological Association, 1948).

Thomas, D.H., 'The awful truth about statistics in archaeology', *American Antiquity*, 43.2 (1978), 231-244.

Voorrips, A., 'Expert systems and archaeologists', in Voorrips, A., and Ottaway, B.S., *New tools from mathematical archaeology*. (Warsaw: Scientific Information Center of the Polish Academy of Science, 1990a).

Voorrips, A. (ed.), 'Mathematics and information science', in *Archaeology: a flexible framework*. Studies in Modern Archaeology 3. (Bonn: Holos, 1990b).

Whallon, R., 'The computer in archaeology: a critical survey', *Computer and the Humanities*, 7.1 (1972), 29-45.

Whallon, R., 'Simple statistics', in Aldenderfer, M.S. (ed.), *Quantitative research in archaeology: progress and prospects*, (London: Sage Publications, 1987), 135-150.

Classics

Richard Wallace

Introduction

It seems strange to recall that thirty years ago, in the days when computers were mysterious and enormous machines tended by white-coated
experts in special buildings to which the uninitiated were denied access,
when texts could be processed only by laboriously entering them in
arcane codes word by word onto punched cards, and when it could take
days to complete even the simplest process, fears were being expressed
that the computer threatened to make the literary scholar redundant, or,
at best, that it would force the scholar into alien modes of thought about
her subject. Today, at any rate in classics, when a computer is almost a
normal part of the scholar's equipment, and when promising young
academics looking for employment are well advised before accepting
any job offer to assure themselves that they will have access to the
computing equipment, the connections, and the corpora of computer-
readable texts which are now an indispensable prerequisite for any
serious scholarly work, it has found its level as a basic tool as useful and
unthreatening as a ballpoint pen. The transition has been quite abrupt.
As little as a decade ago a claim by a classics department in a British
university for a modest budget to finance computer equipment could be
regarded as a bizarre curiosity, an attitude whose persistence even today
in some areas remains an obstacle to the development of policies for the
application of computing techniques.

Classics is in fact a subject in which computerization is both natural
and extremely fruitful. At the heart of the discipline lies a compact and
limited body of texts (it is still possible, though not often done, for a
single individual to read through the entire body of surviving Greek and
Latin literature in a relatively short time) which have, over the centuries,
been commented on, dissected, discussed, and subjected to statistical
analysis of many kinds; classicists are accustomed to interrogating this

corpus of works using a variety of techniques to answer an extraordinary variety of questions, most of which could never even have occurred to the writers of the original documents. Close analysis of diverse texts is part of the tradition of the subject, and quantitative methods have a long history in classics. The consequence of this has been that the process of making virtually the entire body of textual material which the classicist uses available in computer-readable form has been completed with remarkable speed. Besides the body of texts transmitted in the traditional way classicists need access to inscriptions and papyrological material, documents whose nature makes them especially suitable for storing and accessing by electronic means.

The second factor which has predisposed classicists to take to computers is the international nature of the subject. As one of the foundations of European culture and its derivatives, classics is studied in most countries of the world and no classicist can operate without serious international contacts. The potential for rapid interchange of information and comment opened up by computer networking has generated some of the most significant and exciting developments in recent years, and this is undoubtedly an area where over the next couple of years we can expect revolutionary changes which will make a real difference to the way we work.

History[1]

Quantitative methods in classics

Early pre-computer quantitative methods were generally confined to stylometric analysis directed at questions of authorship and dating or sequence. The mathematician Augustus de Morgan was the first to suggest (in 1859) that word length might be used as a criterion for discriminating between authors; there is no evidence that he ever tried it in practice. The first real application of stylometry in classics came in 1867 when Lewis Campbell published an edition of Plato's *Sophist* and *Politicus* in which he tried to demonstrate that the *Sophist* was later than the *Republic* by analysing certain features of Plato's style and attempting to trace their development. The method was taken up by other Platonic scholars (the order of Plato's works being both problematical and significant for our understanding of his philosophy), principally W. Dittenberger, C. Ritter, and, most comprehensively of all, W. Lutoslawski. By the beginning of the twentieth century, then, the use of statistical methods was well established, and respectable. Though the statistical methods used initially seem crude to modern eyes, the method gained general acceptance as a useful approach to a knotty problem. The other principal application of stylometry, the solution of problems of attribution, was less widely accepted by classicists, and has always remained a much more controversial matter.

Concordances

The construction of word-indexes and concordances has always been regarded as a useful, traditional, and remorselessly unrewarding task for the scholar. The earliest concordances (to the Bible) date from the thirteenth century, but despite their clear usefulness, production has always lagged considerably behind demand. There are reasons for this. The construction of a concordance (or even of a modest word-index) is a long, tedious job, which brings with it little prospect of academic reward, being generally regarded as mere mechanical hack-work. The forewords to manually compiled concordances often bear eloquent testimony to this fact. Gonzalez Lodge in Volume I of his *Lexicon Plautinum* (1924) tells how he began the task of compiling a lexicon to Plautus thirty years earlier, '*adulescentia et imperitia deceptus* (misled by youth and inexperience)'; it took him a further nine years to finish the work. Most moving of all, perhaps, are the words (in Latin) of the editor of a complete revised edition of Stephanus' Greek Thesaurus published in 1828:

> For at least fifteen years, a large proportion of a man's life, in which I have passed from youth to maturity, I have borne what seemed to me a burden heavier than Etna. At last the happy day has come; I have long endured slavery; I rejoice that my freedom has been restored ... Nothing can be imagined more burdensome and tedious than this work, which requires eye and hand more than mind and spirit, diligence and industry more than intelligence and learning. ... The hours pass, and the days, and the months, and the years ...(Barker 1828).

The relief from scholars of the burden of producing these essential but impossibly time-consuming reference works has been one of the unconditional benefits of computerization.

The beginnings of computerization

Inevitably, it was the production of word-indexes and concordances which was first seen as an appropriate field in which computers might be used; several were in fact published, and a good deal of concordance-type analysis was done (using, at any rate in this country, the venerable COCOA concordance-generating program developed at the Atlas Computing Laboratory). In retrospect, this brief flowering of the computer concordance looks like an ephemeral irrelevance, because later developments and increasing access have surely made the traditional concordance obsolete. Who needs a multi-volume concordance to a single author when the whole of Greek or Latin literature is available on a single CD-ROM, which takes up less space, is easier to use, is probably cheaper, and opens up possibilities for the analysis of text which go far beyond looking up single words? (Though some useful work can still be done, like the project at St Andrews which is developing systems to mechanize the compilation of a dictionary of Scottish Neo-Latin.)

Early attempts at using computers for the analysis of style were sometimes vitiated by appearing to claim that the fact that word counts were done by a computer rather than an underpaid research assistant somehow gave the statistical methods greater validity. Studies, such as that of W. C. Wake on sentence length, were needed to refine and validate methodology (Wake 1957). In the early days the pioneering work was done by a handful of enthusiasts, and an honourable mention should be made of the work of L. Brandwood who revived the interest in Plato's stylistic development which had lapsed since Ritter published his last article on the subject in 1935 (Brandwood 1956). He suggested the use of a computer to compile statistics of vocabulary, rhythm, and syntax, the analysis of which might be used to put the dialogues in a plausible order. Subsequently Brandwood, together with D. R. Cox, published an article in which a statistical analysis based on the distribution of quantity over sentence endings was described (Cox and Brandwood 1959). The application of these methods has never been entirely uncontroversial, particularly so in the early days when most of the major studies were conducted by statisticians rather than classicists, and doubts were cast on the literary assumptions on which their work was based. However, the publication in 1982 of A. Kenny's *The Computation of Style* (an offshoot of his stylometric study of Aristotle's *Nicomachean Ethics* and *Eudemian Ethics* designed to determine to which of the two works the three books they have in common originally belonged (Kenny 1978)) has made quite sophisticated statistical methods available to all but the most innumerate classicists; if we get it wrong now, it is nobody's fault but our own (Kenny 1982).

The view that the computer is a natural tool for this kind of work is not, however, universal. In 1968 K. J. Dover published a study of the works of the orator Lysias incorporating a good deal of stylometric work, in which (pp. 100–02) he deliberately eschews the use of computers on the grounds that manual counting creates intimate familiarity with the text. It is worth reminding ourselves that few of the tasks for which we now use computers positively need them, and that some of these methods have long pedigrees. In the same way, you do not absolutely need an aeroplane (or even a car) to travel from London to Athens; on the other hand, an aeroplane does make the journey easier and less tiresome, and enables you to do it more often, and to concentrate more wholeheartedly on the end result rather than the mechanism of the process.

Resources

Texts

The availability of texts accessible to the computer is obviously a necessary prerequisite to serious work. A surprisingly large number of ancient texts, both Latin and Greek, have been put into electronic form by individual scholars over the years to facilitate particular projects. Many of these have been collected and made generally available by the Oxford Text Archive. The format of these texts is necessarily very varied, as is the copyright position and hence their availability, but these inconveniences are outweighed by the low cost (a charge is made only for materials), and by ease of access (direct downloading in the case of texts where the depositor has imposed no restrictions). The Oxford Text Archive is still probably the best source of texts for beginners in the field.

The really exciting development in recent years, however, has been the completion of major projects to make available machine-readable versions of the entire body of Greek and Latin literature. The biggest enterprise, the production of texts of Greek literature (some 61.7 million words), which is substantially larger than Latin literature, is at the time of writing near completion, with all texts entered and only about three million words of text remaining to be verified, a task which should be completed by mid-1995. The production of the whole corpus, called the *Thesaurus Linguae Graecae (TLG)*, has been undertaken at the University of California, Irvine. The project will now turn to enhancing and upgrading the body of texts (especially by incorporating more recent editions) and to developing research using the *TLG*'s resources. The corpus is distributed on CD-ROM, and the fact that there are more than 80 discs in the UK alone is good evidence of the degree to which it has become an indispensable tool of classical scholarship. An interesting side-effect of the production and near-ubiquity of the *TLG* has been the impetus given to standardization in the conventions for transcribing Greek text (which of course is not written in the Latin alphabet) into a computer, something which will greatly facilitate the exchange of material and information in the future. As often happens, the necessity of communicating with an uncomprehending and literal-minded machine has driven scholars to think more clearly and consistently about what they need.

The complete corpus of ancient literature is completed by CD-ROMs produced by the Packard Humanities Institute (PHI) covering Latin literature and papyri and Greek inscriptions. The consequence is that a scholar can now (if she wishes) carry around with her the entire body of classical literature in her coat pocket; assuming that she has access to a CD-ROM player (which is surely due to become as basic an item of scholarly equipment as the computer is now) a very powerful resource can now be made available in any office. And the annual cost of the licences is very modest (substantially lower, for example, than my annual bookshop bill). This is truly a revolution at whose ultimate implications we can hardly guess.

Databases

The computer's capacity for storing, sorting, and retrieving information is of especial relevance in a discipline which relies on extracting as much as possible from a relatively small body of material. Ancient historians have been especially active in this field, but they are not alone. As an example of what can be achieved, I will cite the project to create a database and electronic library of Manichaean texts which is being carried out concurrently in Sweden, Germany, Belgium, and the UK (where its home is the Centre for East Roman Studies in the Department of Classics at Warwick University). The body of texts relating to Manichaeanism has grown rapidly during this century as the result of archaeological investigations in Egypt, Central Asia, and elsewhere. The number of extant documents is now very substantial, and they cover over a dozen languages, including Greek, Latin, Syriac, Coptic, Middle Persian, Parthian, Sogdian, Uighur Turkish, Chinese, and Arabic. This creates formidable problems for a scholar searching for parallel information on particular Manichaean themes, terms, motifs, or historical data. Yet comparative study is clearly an essential part of research in the investigation of a religion whose missionaries took great pains to preserve the original teachings of Mani in their translations. A clear need was apparent for, first, the compilation of a substantial database containing in machine-readable form at any rate the better-preserved documents, and, subsequently, the production of a glossary of Manichaean terms, concepts, and other information which could be published in book form and in an updatable electronic format (growing eventually into a working concordance of all genuine Manichaean texts). Such a work would be especially valuable to scholars working on original texts in a fragmentary condition, where the consultation of parallel information is often fundamental to the reconstruction of the text. The project has been underway since 1990, and a full corpus of texts is now available. The availability of these documents in machine-readable form not only assists research at all levels but will also facilitate the publication of works on Manichaeanism which require lengthy quotations of texts in their original scripts and considerably reduce the costs of typesetting. The texts now assembled in electronic form will eventually be published as the *Corpus Fontium Manichaeorum* (text, translation, and full commentary) in about 60 volumes, which ultimately will be available on a CD-ROM. This is an excellent example of what the creative use of computers can achieve. It is an international project, and spans a number of different disciplines to the benefit of each of them; the material collected creates a resource which can be used in many ways and output in a variety of formats; it solves a current practical problem and opens up the prospect of flexible use in other projects in the future.

On a smaller scale, Project Archelogos (organized from Edinburgh) aims to put on computer all of ancient philosophy (texts and translations) plus all the major interpretations.

The bibliography is another traditional form of reference work which will surely now rapidly become obsolete in favour of computer databases. Already we have available the *GNOMON Bibliographische Datenbank* incorporating about 120,000 titles drawn from over 200 journals, with a promise of annual updates. More exciting, however, is the project of the American Philological Association for entering the whole of *L'Année Philologique*, the major bibliographical resource in classics since 1927, on to a database. The vast size of the work and the complexity of the records make this both a very difficult and a very necessary task. If, as we are promised, the package comes with good retrieval software, and a linkage is established with the *Canon of Greek Authors and Works* created by the *Thesaurus Linguae Graecae* (plus other thesauri and indices), then the job of compiling bibliographies will be transformed.

The databases mentioned above come, as most of them do, on disc or on CD-ROM. The online database, held at a remote site, is a development which will be particularly valuable in making material of specialized interest widely available . The Beazley Archive has now gone online internationally, and for the first time in our field incorporates images in the database.

The significance of these and other similar projects is not that they are themselves dramatic solutions to scholarly problems; in general they contribute more to the nuts-and-bolts of scholarship. However, in alleviating much of the drudgery of academic research and, in effect, enormously increasing the bibliographical resources of even the smallest institutions they will release much time and energy which can be devoted to the real business of research.

Literary and historical studies

'Traditional' computer-based research continues. For example, the application of stylometry to the solution of the problem of the sequence of Plato's works, perhaps the oldest classical problem to which quantitative methods have been applied, has been taken up again in G. R. Ledger's *Re-counting Plato*, using statistical techniques considerably more sophisticated than had been available previously, and generating judicious and sensible conclusions (but surely not the last word on the subject; the validity both of the methodology and of its particular application is still a matter for lively discussion) (Ledger 1989).

An interesting and innovative development is the use by K. P. Hubka of mathematical models to analyse the dynamics and structure of (initially) Sophoclean tragedy (Hubka 1986). This interesting experiment brings out an aspect of the utility of computers which we often neglect, namely the ease with which they facilitate experimentation, trying out models, and simply playing around with ideas, as opposed to the massive projects which are what we usually think of first in a computing context. There is no doubt that, as academics in the humanities become more familiar with, and comfortable with, computer techniques, we will see much more of this kind of thing.

Networking

Two factors combine to make electronic communication both suitable and potentially indispensable for classicists. First, our discipline is necessarily and intrinsically an international one. There are no significant fields in which serious work can be contained within the academic traditions and resources of a single country. We need worldwide contacts. Second, we are a small discipline. Though there are a few large centres attracting substantial numbers of scholars, a disproportionate number of classicists are scattered around the world in small groups in minuscule departments (at any rate by the standards of most mainstream humanities subjects). And yet our subject embraces an impressive range of disciplines: language, literature, history, archaeology, art, law, religion, and so on. There is clearly a danger in dispersal and isolation, which classicists have traditionally attempted to avert by frenetic conference activity. The fact that it is now possible to sit in your office at your terminal and take part, rapidly and conveniently, in exchanges of views and problems with colleagues all over the world active in your own specialism is one of the most dramatic and hopeful developments of the last few years.

The number of electronic discussion groups which have been set up in the area of classics is good evidence of the enthusiasm with which classicists have seized these opportunities. In general it cannot be claimed that these discussions are always very profound or very structured, but they have gone some way (especially in the English-speaking world) towards giving some reality to the idea of an international classical community.

More formally, the inception of a number of electronic journals has met a long-felt need for a means of disseminating ideas more rapidly than conventional publishing will allow. *Electronic Antiquity* (whose home is in Tasmania) was first in the field and is still the most impressive. It is produced several times a year and combines serious articles with ephemera and acts both as a conventional journal and as an electronic noticeboard. The example has been followed by *Classics Ireland*, and most recently the Classical Association of Canada has taken to distributing the *Canadian Classical Bulletin* electronically. One interesting journal, *Didaskalia: Ancient Theatre Today*, which deals with (among other things) the problems of modern stagings of ancient drama, could hardly be

conceived except as an electronic journal, since the speed of communication which electronic publication makes possible gives its comments
an immediacy and a topicality which is clearly appropriate to the study
of performance (there are few things more stale than a discussion of a
performance which took place two years ago).

Book reviews also benefit by coming out as soon as possible after the
publication of the book reviewed, and the electronic *Bryn Mawr Classical Review* is now a secure and valued part of the classical scene.
Reviews in the South African journal *Scholia* are also now available by
gopher.

Finally, the TOCS-IN project makes rapidly available on a regular
basis the contents of about 124 classical journals, the advantages of
which are obvious for scholars working in institutions with limited
library resources.

Teaching

An increasing number of students entering universities are already
accustomed to the use of computers to complement more traditional
teaching methods. To give just one example, Northamptonshire Grammar School has produced a variety of programs usable by pupils from
Key Stage Two upwards. Those for the younger pupils present animated
versions of mythological narratives, linking them with the archaeological background. Older pupils are introduced to religion and technology,
and later can be led into the study of Latin by material on Virgil's *Aeneid*
which helps them through the vocabulary, grammar, and syntax they
need, logs their progress, and prints out vocabulary lists for them.
Students familiar with computer techniques of this degree of sophistication will expect no less when they come to study classics at university
level.

Language

The complexities of learning Latin and Greek have attracted many
attempts to simplify the process of acquiring the languages. They are in
fact not the easiest languages to teach using a computer, and the variable
word-order and the great range of grammatical forms make some of the
techniques which have been developed in modern language teaching less
straightforwardly applicable to Latin and Greek. Nevertheless, considerable progress has been made, and many promising projects are in hand.

The University of Durham has been one of the pioneers in this field, and they are currently working on a program for Latin prose sentences. At Birmingham programs are under development to help with the early stages of Latin and Greek designed to assist the learning of vocabulary and case endings. Nottingham is producing a set of computerized exercises and tests for use in conjunction with *Reading Greek*, using hypertext. An ambitious programme at Warwick is producing a computer-aided Greek tutor (limited at the moment to New Testament texts but due for expansion); a universal Greek word-parser is functioning, which also activates a glossary. The complete Latin or Greek computer-based course remains to be developed, but there is no doubt that significant steps in that direction have already been made.

St. Andrews is also involved in a project to develop a program for teaching Latin metre based on the design of the Glasgow STELLA (Software for the Teaching of English Language and Literature and its Assessment) Project's program for teaching English metre.

Non-linguistic studies

In ancient history in particular many interesting developments are under way. For example St Andrews is producing hypertext material providing introductions to major ancient historians; Edinburgh has nearly completed a project on the sources for the tribunate of P. Sulpicius; and the Byzantinists at Belfast use computers for battle simulations.

The pressure of student numbers, and the concomitant shortage of resources to meet their needs, has caused many departments to experiment with novel approaches to teaching methods, and in particular to finding ways of preserving the advantages of small group teaching in an environment where resources are tighter. At Keele an experiment is being conducted in using computer networks to enhance the student's experience and to increase one-to-one contact with the tutor. In some tutorials, work is presented initially to a computer conference where it can be commented on and an exchange of views can take place in preparation for a face-to-face tutorial, which is as a result much more intense and much more focused. The success of the initial pilot scheme suggests that the approach has potentially a wide application, and it will be extended as resources allow.

What may be possible in the future is shown by the achievements of the Perseus Project (based at Harvard) which has produced (and is further developing) a multimedia interactive database covering Greek art, history, archaeology, and literature. It is really a small library in itself, with Greek texts linked with commentary, translation, morphological database, and a lexicon, plus catalogues of historical, archaeological, and artistic information, with images of works of art and site plans which can be retrieved and manipulated at will. That the project has made less impact in the UK than the quality, range, and potential of its material might suggest is probably explicable first by that fact that it will run on only one kind of machine (Macintosh), and second because most British classics departments are not yet at the point where they have enough equipment reliably at their disposal to be able to construct undergraduate courses around the assumption that students can use Perseus. There is also a feeling among some users that there is not sufficient flexibility in some aspects of the program to give the teacher the sort of control he needs. Perseus shows us the way, but does not quite, as yet, get us there. But it does show what can be done, and it will certainly not be long before the advantages of giving students access to so much attractive material presented in such a convenient form will compel us to ensure that the facilities can be used.

The future

In a field changing as rapidly as this, prediction is an unprofitable enterprise. Who, ten years ago, could have guessed that the process of computerizing classics would have gone ahead as quickly as it has? But some things can be anticipated with some confidence, and some others ought to (and perhaps will) happen.

Texts

We now have virtually the entire body of classical material on CD-ROM. There is, however, a problem that we are privileging those readings which are found in the editions of texts which have been selected for inclusion. Proper scholarly work, however, makes it necessary first to be aware of variant readings and the manuscript evidence, and second to be able to make judgements about them. There is already a clear demand for the introduction of an *apparatus criticus* into electronic texts, and no doubt this will happen. But surely a computer can do better than that. The facility, not just to call up and display variant readings, but also to recreate particular manuscripts, groups of manuscripts, or editions would be a great boon. The task of achieving this will perhaps be as great as, or even greater than, that of entering and verifying the texts in the first place, but it would give the corpus a degree of autonomous authority which it has not yet achieved.

Handbooks

The characteristic major scholarly activity of the nineteenth century was perhaps the production of the massive handbooks and collections on which (expensive and clumsy though they are) we all still rely—compilations of fragments and evidence for all kinds of aspects of the ancient world. This is a natural field for the computer, and we ought to be looking for ways of replacing those venerable but cumbersome volumes. Do we need to produce indexed and classified sections of texts on disc? Or could we make do with classified references which can be retrieved from existing corpora? Either way, the saving in time, shelf space, and cost, and the gain in convenience, would be very considerable. Perhaps also an electronic equivalent of Pauly-Wissowa[2] in the form of an interactive database using hypertext material would be a project worth considering. The possibility of updating and correcting material is available for publications which are stored in an electronic form in a way that conventionally published work cannot match. The advantages for a reference work are obvious.

Journals

Cost, and pressure on library budgets and shelf space, will in any case make electronic publishing an increasingly attractive option in the future, and its speed, convenience, and accessibility should cause us to welcome the change, especially in an essentially international subject like classics. There are some issues which need attention before the full potential can be realized. Academics (and those who employ them) need to be reassured about the academic standing of publications in electronic journals. Proper refereeing systems, modes of citation, and methods of maintaining material for permanent reference (hard copy? disc? central storage?) need to be explored. Much of what goes on at the moment is supported by grant income or by the enterprise of individual institutions. If the major academic publishers are to become involved (and experimental projects are already being contemplated) some means of generating income and enabling them to cover costs and make a profit must be found. Otherwise they will not play. All of these problems are readily soluble if academics can simply make up their minds that they need to be solved; a system of agreed conventions and procedures is all that is required. The rewards, in terms of speed of publication, cost, and dissemination, will be very considerable indeed.

Statistics and style

The application of quantitative methods to literary issues has now become very much more attractive than it was, but serious and well-founded work would be greatly facilitated by the availability of a body of statistics which would lay out the ground rules for how language behaves at particular periods, in particular genres or authors, or within particular subjects, and so on. Some serious statistical ground-work needs to be done, and it is now possible to see how this could be done without asking someone to undertake the long, tedious, and stultifying work this would have involved only a few years ago.

Networks

Classics can now be truly international. Projects can be developed on a worldwide basis, and hitherto isolated scholars in institutions with poor resources can now move into the mainstream and draw on bibliographical and other material available to only a few centres previously. It is time that we started to take this aspect of computer networking more seriously. Some projects have already shown the way, and at a personal level the value of national and international electronic links has already been proved. We now need to begin planning our research projects on a truly worldwide basis, and working out seriously ways of sharing and communicating resources and ideas. The electronic conference is an idea which needs to be developed (why should creative interchanges with colleagues in the same field in different countries be conditioned by your institution's policy on travel grants?). And before long I predict that we will be asking why an undergraduate's work needs to be supervised by an academic who is actually present in the institution where he is registered.

Notes

1. I acknowledge with gratitude the help of my wife Jane Wallace in making available to me in writing this section, her early work on computerization in the humanities.

2. The *Real-Encyclopädie der classischen Altertumswissenschaft* edited by A. F. von Pauly and G. Wissowa is a monumental multi-volumed German encyclopedia covering all areas of classics, which began appearing in 1894, and which has been in a process of continuous updating thereafter with the issue of supplementary volumes.

References and bibliography

Barker, E.H. (ed.), *Thesaurus Graecae Linguae ab Henrico Stephano constructus vol. 1* (London: Valpy, 1828).

Brandwood, L., 'Analysing Plato's style with an electronic computer', *Bulletin of the Institute of Classical Studies*, 3 (1956), 45-54.

Cox, D.R., and Brandwood, L., 'On a discriminatory problem connected with the works of Plato', *Journal of the Royal Statistical Society* Ser. B, 21 (1959), 195-200.

Dover. K.J., *Lysias and the Corpus Lysiacum*, (Berkeley and Los Angeles: University of California Press, 1968).

Hubka, K.P., '"Classical Shape" of the Sophoclean Tragedy', *Literary and Linguistic Computing*, 1.2 (1986), 68-73.

Kenny, A., *The Aristotelian Ethics: a study of the relationship between the Eudemian and the Nichomachean Ethics of Aristotle*, (Oxford: Clarendon Press, 1978).

Kenny, A., *The computation of style* (Oxford: Pergamon Press, 1982).

Ledger, G.R., *Re-counting Plato: a computer analysis of Plato's style* (Oxford: Clarendon Press, 1989).

Lodge, G., *Lexicon Plautinum, vol 1* (Leipzig: Teubner, 1924).

Moffat, J., 'The Beazley Archive: making a humanities database accessible to the world', *Bulletin of the John Rylands Library*, 74.3 (Autumn 1992), 39-52.

Wake, W.C., 'Sentence length distribution of Greek authors', *Journal of the Royal Statistical Society* Ser. A, 120 (1957), 331-46.

Young, C.M., 'Plato and computer dating: a discussion of Gerard R. Ledger, "Re-counting Plato: a computer analysis of Plato's style" and Leonard Brandwood, "The chronology of Plato's Dialogues"', *Oxford Studies in Ancient Philosophy*, 12 (1994), 227-50.

Further information

Manichaean Texts:
Dr Samuel N. C. Lieu, FRAS, FRHistS, FSA, Centre for Research in East Roman Studies, Department of Classics and Ancient History, University of Warwick, Coventry CV4 7AL.

Project Archelogos:
Dr T. C. Scaltsas, Department of Philosophy, University of Edinburgh, George Square, Edinburgh EH8 9JX.

STELLA Project:
Jean Anderson, University of Glasgow, 6 University Gardens, Glasgow G12 8QQ.

Computer Corpora and Their Impact on Lexicography and Language Teaching

Michael Rundell

Introduction: the corpus revolution

The dictionary writer and the language teacher are both regularly called upon to make generalizations about language. Questions have to be answered—whether for compiling a dictionary entry or for helping a language learner who needs specific information about the way a word or phrase typically behaves. For example: what is the plural of **walk-man**? Is there a difference between **like to do** something and **like doing** something? What can you **commit**: crimes, suicide, murder, yes—but what about shoplifting, kerb-crawling, or parking offences? Is it only journalists who use words like **slam** and **wed**? What exactly is the difference between **clever** and **bright**? Is it acceptable to say **maybe** in a business letter, or would **perhaps** be more suitable here? And does anyone really still say things like **it's raining cats and dogs** or **a stitch in time saves nine**? The questions cover the whole range of linguistic phenomena, and turn on such issues as semantic nuance, syntactic behaviour, discourse management, and stylistic appropriacy.

What options are available to lexicographers and language teachers faced with questions like these? Traditionally, both groups have relied for their answers on a somewhat limited body of linguistic evidence. Teachers could always resort to the standard pedagogical dictionaries and grammars—but where did the information in these books come from in the first place? Their writers may or may not have had access to 'objective' data in the form of *citations* culled from books and newspapers and showing a given word in a natural context. But even the very largest citation banks, such as the massive collection of 'slips' on which the *Oxford English Dictionary* is founded, have serious limitations as a basis for making generalizations about the language. The sources from which the citations are extracted have frequently been assembled in a rather idiosyncratic way: Samuel Johnson, for example, regarded it as an 'obvious rule' that in citing authorities for a word's behaviour one should prefer 'writers of the first reputation to those of an inferior rank', while James Murray (the *OED*'s first editor) complained that his team of citation-gatherers was focusing too much on unusual words and uses, so that the core of the language was being neglected. At all events, citation banks could only ever supply a patchy and somewhat lopsided body of evidence for lexicographers to base their description of the language on.

In these circumstances lexicographers have inevitably relied to a very large extent on another form of linguistic evidence—their own intuitions as fluent and experienced users of the language they are describing. (And this of course is exactly what language teachers do all the time.) Intuition can be seen as the product of our repeated exposure, over many years, to huge amounts of language data of a very heterogeneous nature. By means of this process, we gradually build up a fairly robust picture of the way our language operates, and this enables us to distinguish between what Michael Halliday, in an illuminating analogy, calls the 'climate' (the broad long-term 'system' of the language) and the 'weather' (the specific, sometimes capricious relationships that words can enter into). Research and experience tend to show that intuition is a reasonably good guide to the *most typical* patterns of behaviour of the core vocabulary of a language. (Indeed, it would be odd if this were not the case—effective communication relies on our being able to produce and to recognize utterances that conform to conventionally accepted norms.) But once we move outside this central area, we can no longer count on our intuitions to help us describe the regularities of the language with any degree of confidence or consistency.

Fortunately, we no longer have to. New technology can now provide us with a third, and generally far more reliable, form of evidence in the shape of the computerized corpus. Computers first arrived on the lexicographic scene in the mid-60s, but initially they were used more for manipulating dictionary text rather than for actually analysing language: 'The computer was thought of as having principally a clerical role in lexicography—reducing the labour of sorting and filing and examining very large amounts of English' (Sinclair 1991, 2). Meanwhile, in another corner of the linguistic field, the first electronic text corpora—large collections of ordinary, naturally-occurring text stored on computer and available for automatic analysis—were being developed to provide linguists with objective evidence of language in use. The best-known English corpora of this era were the Brown Corpus (1963)—a collection of one million words of American English taken from a wide variety of written sources—and its British counterpart, the Lancaster-Oslo-Bergen (or LOB) Corpus, developed in 1970. For quite some time, however, corpus linguistics remained something of a 'minority sport', partly because the emerging technology could not yet cope with the task of collecting, storing, and processing really substantial volumes of text, but partly also because the mainstream view of the time (strongly influenced by Chomsky) was that any corpus would inevitably be too 'skewed' or unrepresentative to be of much value for language description. To quote Geoffrey Leech, '[Chomsky's] view on the inadequacy of corpora, and the adequacy of intuition, became the orthodoxy of a succeeding generation of theoretical linguists' (Leech 1991, 8).

The beginning of the 1980s, however, saw the creation of the first large lexicographic corpus, the Birmingham Collection of English Texts—a pioneering development that led to a radical transformation in the craft of lexicography. For the first time, dictionary text could be based primarily on the analysis of large amounts of naturally-occurring data, and within a decade most serious lexicographic work in English had become, in some form or another, corpus-based. The impact of this 'corpus revolution' is well illustrated by the almost simultaneous publication, in mid-1995, of no fewer than four major pedagogical dictionaries of English,[1] all of them based on the analysis of large language corpora. The full effects of these changes have yet to be felt in other areas of language teaching, but changes are on the way,[2] and there can be little doubt that electronic text corpora will eventually be seen as an essential prerequisite for all forms of language description. The rest of this chapter will look at the benefits of using corpus data, the key issues in corpus development, and some of the insights that a corpus can provide.

Corpus data: the benefits

What can lexicographers do with a corpus that they would not be able to do without one? With the aid of a good corpus, dictionary writers can answer with confidence—with authority, even—all of the questions we posed at the beginning of this chapter, and many more besides. Let us consider a couple of these in more detail.

1. What, typically, do people **commit***?*

To answer this question we can start by looking at a *concordance* for all the forms of the verb **commit**. The concordance is the basic tool of corpus lexicography, and consists of a listing of every instance in the corpus of any word or phrase specified by the user, together with enough of its context to enable us to see what is going on. Figure 1 shows a concordance for **commit** taken from the British National Corpus (BNC). This is in fact a tiny fraction of all the uses of **commit** in the BNC (there are well over 6,000), but even from this small sample certain patterns emerge quite clearly. Leaving aside adultery and suicide, we can see that this verb is most typically associated with crimes of a serious and often violent nature: murder, extortion, rape, 'a violent felony', 'multiple hold-ups and shootings', and so on.

Lexicographers routinely scan hundreds, sometimes thousands of concordance lines like this in order to distil the relevant facts about a word: what does it mean? what sort of grammatical relationships does it usually enter into? what other words or phrases does it tend to co-occur with? and so on. It is only across a large span of uses that one begins to see the regularities in all of these areas, and it is the regularities—not the interesting, creative, but essentially atypical uses—that we are in the business of describing. What makes the corpus so much more powerful a resource than either the traditional citation bank or the lexicographer's own intuition is, first, the sheer volume of data it can supply, and, second, the fact that it provides us with *every* instance of a word's use rather than an idiosyncratic subset of instances that an individual reader has selected for reasons that may not be clear even to him- or herself. Armed with these data, lexicographers are in a position to make reliable generalizations about the ways that words behave in text.

2. What exactly is the difference between **clever** *and* **bright***?*

Earlier, non-corpus-based dictionaries have tended to present the two words as virtual synonyms,[3] and it is not difficult to find contexts in which either word could be used without altering the naturalness or truth-value of the sentence. But as Jean Aitchison has pointed out, 'Perfect synonymy—total overlap of meaning—is somewhat rare' (Aitchison 1987, 82), and in practice we routinely make quite sophisticated word-choices without apparently thinking about why we do it. A good way of exposing the elusive differences between close synonyms like this is to try substituting one for another in a run of corpus lines: when substitution doesn't 'work', we can then look at the context for

Figure 1: *Concordance for 'commit' taken from the British National Corpus (BNC)*

```
COMMITS.CBC                                                                    page 1 of 1

9  US   ty knowledge. And then they,'d have to prove he had committed a crime or was a fugitive. He cleared his
9  WAF  ut whose blessing our crops will not grow. You have committed a great evil." He brought down his staff h
9  UK   lice and she was trying to save him. Suppose he had committed a murder (the smear of blood made it easie
9  UK   induce, or encourage, or persuade another person to commit a rape." She whirled around suddenly and bega
9  UK   kept right on serving up the booze while they were  committing a violent felony." Katheryn joined him at
4  UK   ount Philip of Flanders suspected that his wife had committed adultery with Gautier de Fontaines he had
5  US   of a concentration camp to show that the atrocities committed against Jews and others by the Nazis had n
3  US   en coincided with a similar decline in sex offenses committed against them. Part of the decrease in exhi
4  US   appeared to be overwhelmingly on the kinds of rapes committed by marauding strangers who invade large ur
4  UK   he hero of an amorous intrigue. Moreover, when they committed crimes of theft or murder they could plead
3  US   s, if there were "evil people somewhere insidiously committing evil deeds, and it were necessary only to
3  US   fter an indictment for grand larceny, conspiracy to commit extortion, and income tax evasion, was honore
9  US   f the matter, a routine pro business. Homicides get committed for the hell of a lot less than a split of
6  UK   plot. It is not enough to think of a murder and who committed it and why what is not immediately obvious
9  UK   rtisans. They acquired a reputation for ferocity and committing many atrocities. Their discipline markedly
9  WAF  nth. I don't believe you ... Good God!#I feel like  committing mass murder as the court hands Blushing G
9  US   ce old ladies poison whole families. Clean-cut kids commit multiple hold-ups and shootings. Bank manager
5  SAF  , then the Court must find that the accused did not commit murder #<tab>What again are the facts of the
4  AUS  t, Martin Heffernan, was actually tried for robbery committed on the Parramatta Road near the Globe at e
3  US   23,000, as well as perjury and [inducing another to commit] perjury. The judge went out of his way to po
3  US   at the age of seven, and from then on is capable of committing sins for which he may be punished by an e
8  UK   l invaders. As recently as 1949 a Dutch office; had committed some appalling massacres here in a misguid
   UK   used, physically and emotionally, that they died or committed suicide. A recent estimate, attributed to
        the paper might be a threat, a summons, an order to commit suicide, a trap of some description. But ther
3  US   ree and a half times as likely as divorced women to commit suicide, and four times more likely to die in
3  US   the truth of it all was finally discovered, Jocasta committed suicide and Oedipus blinded himself, he de
4  UK   of their confessions, of crimes which they did not commit. The failure of procedures based on PACE to p
4  US   o do with her, saying that he would rather die than commit the sin of adultery, even for medicinal purpo
9  UK   king so furious, Mayor Hardin; none of us have been committing treason.#<tab>You'll have to convince m
9  US   he ones with the greatest sexual role anxieties who commit violent and predatory crimes. A man who canno
3  US   ults, single men are some five times more likely to commit violent crimes than married men. Single men a
```

clues that will explain the latent differences. Some examples are shown in Figure 2.

There appears to be no problem about substituting **clever** in the sentence 'Francis was a very bright boy'. But it is significant that 'boy' co-occurs much more frequently with **bright** than with **clever**. So too does 'girl' and so—most tellingly—does 'young', for there seems to be (to put it no higher) a marked preference for the selection of **bright** when we are talking about young people whose intelligence gives them the *potential* to succeed. With **clever**, on the other hand, quite a number of the examples carry an unmistakable suggestion of deviousness: when politicians, reporters, and criminals are described as **clever**, the implication is that their intelligence is not an altogether admirable quality because it is being used for morally doubtful purposes. The contrast between the 'bright young lawyer whose career was just beginning' and the 'clever lawyers' who have found a way around some inconvenient piece of legislation is a revealing one, and the frequent modification of **clever** with the word 'too' (which almost never happens with **bright**) is equally instructive. It is only the availability of large amounts of corpus data that has made this sort of comparison possible, and it soon becomes clear that even the best dictionaries of the pre-corpus era often fail to distinguish between close synonyms with any degree of effectiveness.

Corpus evidence, then, enables lexicographers to 'reach the parts that earlier dictionaries couldn't reach'. And this sort of semantic analysis is only a small part of the picture. The arrival of the corpus has led to dramatic improvements in the quality of dictionary text across a whole range of areas, the most significant being:

- the description of word meaning (as discussed above).

- grammar and syntax: complementation patterns and their relative frequency (for example, is **decide**+infinitive more common than **decide**+*that*-clause?); the use of prepositions (do we usually say **different from** or **different to**?); the effect of regional variety on syntactic behaviour (American speakers 'protest spending cuts' but British speakers 'protest *about* them'); and so on.

- the lexical environment: selectional restrictions (for example, what nouns normally fill the object slot after **commit**?); collocation (the fact that a **crime** can be 'serious', 'petty', or 'heinous',

Figure 2: *Concordance for 'clever' and 'bright' sampled from the Longman/Lancaster Corpus*

```
CLEVER.CBC                                                                          page 1 of 1

9  UK  | What did he say? Come on, since you think you're so clever!' 'If you carry the goose. It's too heavy, it
9  UK  | , particularly that good Mr Ephraim Cook who was so clever about taking care of the business so that Joh
9  UK  | erary output, Churchill was no intellectual. He was clever and acid-tongued, believing then, as now, tha
1  US  | ive them a hint.█<tab><tab>Reporters are very clever and persistent. They'll say, "We heard suchan
9  US  | and thus transmit it to his work.█Concluding this clever argument, M. Marie asked that photography's r
9  UK  | or them. Just bring them along to the two hills - a clever boy like you will easily think of some excuse
4  UK  | ra, one of the visiting MPs, said Faulkner was "too clever by half." The MPs had visited Long Kesh where
9  UK  | drive him to desperate measures at once. Like most clever criminals, he may be too confident in his own
9  US  | now?" Rafealla asked impatiently.█With a touch of clever detective work she had found out Juana's brot
9  US  | ish. Cold sober, I believe. And clever. Anyway he's clever enough to hoodwink those two charming young l
9  UK  | ully) to the killing vehicle. "We're dealing with a clever fellow." Leaf said to him. "He's taken care o
9  UK  | year. Medical specialists pay more.█<tab><tab>Now clever lawyers have figured a way for nervous profes
4  CAN | r hand, Ben Gurion was a cool, calculating and very clever politician,always interested in winning the n
9  US  | de control fro Seattle would be eliminated.█But his clever son-in-law spotted the danger in relying upon
6  UK  | tion of a few clever ideas. But beware of being too clever. The PRO of a company producing IDLY material
9  SAF | fe? It's all desert. But she would have been too clever to fall for that, she knows when questions to

BRIGHT.CBC                                                                         page 1 of 1

4  UK  | 1861. His father wasa clergyman. Francis was a very bright boy, but when five yearsold he fell ill with
9  SAF | ometimes rode on his horse past the church. A small bright boy, I remember, though I do not remember it
9  US  | and Nikalojus, who was ten. Both of these last were bright boys, and there was no reason why their famil
9  US  | ive. His face looked friendly and alert. Moderately bright, but only moderately, was Tom's first impress
9  UK  | tment of Employment. He was thought of as extremely bright, demanding, hard working and, not that it was
9  US  | right enough to do all those things, he's certainly bright enough to run a state governent, and I know a
3  CAN | ime and greater effort to work out. Picture Mary, a bright, enterprising, excited law graduate who is re
3  UK  | an'. He nevertheless feels that the sight of 'these bright, intelligent-looking girls in the female compo
9  US  | ing to "fix" her marriage.  Scott is articulate and bright, leadership material. Fittingly, he has been
3  AUS | st the New█<tab>The gents were decent but not very bright. Lloyd George was not far out when he describ
9  UK  | ter importance was that he was neitherexceptionally bright nor much good at sport, and he lacked the str
9  US  | urnfully from one to the other.█<tab>'I'm not very bright over business matters,' she said. Tusker open
8  UK  | , though not to a standardised scale. So until some bright spark gets it all together, here's what you n
4  UK  | . witty good humor won her friends and marriage to a bright young lawyer, whose career was just beginning
4  UK  | ave tried on a number of identities: hippy, sexpot, bright young media person, trade union activist, bur
5  UK  | ons agencies do employ a number of assistants and a bright young person can sometimes get employed in th
```

but not—as many learners of English assume—'important',
'small', or 'bad'); and so on.

- sociolinguistic characteristics: information on style and register,
  such as the fact that in spoken.text **start** and **maybe** are much
  more common than **begin** and **perhaps**, whereas in written text
  the picture is reversed; or the extent to which vocabulary from
  one variety of English is becoming integrated in another—a case
  in point being the growing acceptability in British English of
  'baseball idioms' from American English (**get to first base, a
  ball-park figure, take a rain-check**, and so on).

- examples of usage: with hundreds of authentic instances to
  choose from, lexicographers no longer need to invent dictionary
  examples, but can now provide natural sample sentences showing
  words in their most typical lexical and contextual environments.

These are only the basics. As corpora improve and as corpus-analysis
software becomes increasingly sophisticated, all sorts of new possibilities are opening up that will help lexicographers improve still further
their description of the language.

Corpus development and corpus exploitation: key issues

For anyone working with corpora, the most obvious improvement over
the last twenty years has been the huge increase in the volume of data
available. The earliest electronic corpora of the 60s and 70s comprised
around a million words of text; the 'second-generation' corpora of the
80s (such as the Birmingham Collection of English Texts and the
Longman-Lancaster Corpus) dealt in tens of millions;[4] and now in the
mid-90s, 100 million words is generally regarded as a minimum requirement. But the relationship between quantity and quality is not entirely
straightforward, and it is appropriate here to ask the question: what is
'good' corpus evidence, and what makes one corpus better than another?
One standard answer is that a corpus should be a well-balanced collection
of texts that covers the broadest possible repertoire of discourse types.
And there is a widespread view that the surest way to achieve this
objective is to collect as much data as possible.

It seems self-evident that a larger corpus will form a more reliable
basis for identifying the regular patterns of the language than a smaller

one. It is certainly true that the small first-generation corpora of the 60s and 70s cannot provide adequate data for lexical analysis except perhaps for the few dozen most frequent words in the language. The frequency characteristics of English vocabulary are such that a few hundred very common words make up the bulk of all text, while many quite familiar words—such as **resilient, depravity,** or **drudgery**—occur less than once in every million words of text. And phrasal or collocational combinations—say, **poke one's nose in** or **categorically deny**—tend to appear even less frequently than this. Clearly, therefore, we need very substantial amounts of data in order to make generalizations about words' behaviour with any degree of confidence and authority, and the current generation of lexicographic corpora—notably the British National Corpus and Birmingham University's Bank of English[5]—operate in the 100-200 million word range. Nevertheless, the notion that any deficiencies in the content and structure of a corpus can be ironed out simply by adding more and more millions of words of text does not stand up to serious investigation. The old computing maxim 'garbage in, garbage out' still holds. In the field of corpus design, the stylisticians' notion of 'intertextuality' is particularly relevant: patterns of meaning and usage are to some extent determined by genre and context, and words will often behave differently in different types of text.

To give some concrete examples: a computer search on the word **ass** yields very different results according to the type of text being analysed. In a corpus of newspapers we find examples like this:

> The law must not be seen to be an ass

> a record which has so far made an ass of the law of averages

> It will be up to Waldegrave to 'kick ass' when ministerial colleagues fail to deliver

A subcorpus of texts on religion and mythology yields lines such as:

> Jesus's triumphal entry into Jerusalem on an ass

> He gets up early, saddles his ass, and cuts wood for the sacrifice

And finally, a trawl through a collection of American popular novels throws up examples like:

Aw Gus, get up off your dead ass and get on with it

He doesn't have to risk his ass if he doesn't want to

Taking a risk, he patted her on the ass...

and so on.

There is remarkably little overlap between the way the word behaves in these three genres and, interestingly, it is only in the religious texts that **ass** is ever used in its original ('donkey') meaning.

This is perhaps an extreme case, but it neatly illustrates the range of linguistic variation that can occur across genres, and this in turn should alert us to the deficiencies of any corpus that is not based on a wide variety of text-types. The idea that words might behave differently according to the type of text in which they are used seems so obvious as to be scarcely worth saying. Yet surprisingly large numbers of people (notably in the natural-language-processing community) cling to the belief that a large corpus of almost any kind is always better than a smaller but more balanced collection of texts. These days it is actually quite easy to assemble a massive corpus simply by collecting large amounts of newspaper text, which is now available on CD-ROM at relatively low cost. But the fundamental problem here—the 'skewing' or bias in the sample—will not go away however many millions of words of text you pile on. The sheer volume of data cannot compensate for its lack of diversity. A good general-purpose corpus, therefore, certainly needs to be as large as possible, but it should also be assembled from the broadest possible range of mainstream text-types. This is the approach followed, for example, in the British National Corpus (BNC). The BNC was a collaborative venture in which leading dictionary publishers and academic partners, with funding from the UK's Department of Trade and Industry, worked together between 1991 and 1995 to develop a 100-million-word corpus of contemporary British English. The members of the BNC consortium were Oxford University Press, Longman Group, Chambers, University of Lancaster, Oxford University Computing Services, and the British Library. The BNC's strength is not simply that it is a large corpus but that it is carefully structured to include substantial quantities of texts drawn from a wide range of media and genres, including newspapers and magazines, novels of every type, unpublished correspondence, and advertising copy, as well as books that cover the whole gamut of subject areas, ranging from academic texts on linguistics or particle physics to recipe books and car repair manuals.

The importance of spoken data

One major area of the language that has always been rather poorly represented in English corpora is the spoken variety. The reasons for this are partly financial (because collecting spoken data is far more labour-intensive, and therefore much more expensive, than assembling a corpus of spoken text), and partly methodological, since when one is dealing with the spoken language 'there are no obvious objective measures that can be used to define the target population or construct a sampling frame' (Crowdy 1993, 259). Yet the spoken variety is immensely important. Outside the community of 'language professionals' there is, indeed, a tendency to see spoken English as a secondary, somewhat degenerate version of the 'real' language (which is assumed to be literary). But linguists have long recognized that the spoken variety is the primary form of a language, the form in which most activity takes place (there are, after all, infinitely more 'producers' of spoken text than of written), and very often the medium in which language-change first arises. Until very recently, the resources for describing spoken English have been fairly meagre. Consequently, the coverage of the spoken variety in dictionaries, grammars, and language teaching coursebooks has been correspondingly limited—just as descriptions of the written language were sometimes patchy and inadequate before large corpora arrived to reshape the whole discipline of lexicography.

Spoken corpora of one kind or another have, in fact, been around for over thirty years, but they have tended to be, broadly speaking, *either* not large enough *or* not 'spontaneous' enough. The London-Lund Corpus, for example, which has provided the data for a great deal of important research into spoken English, contains a quite high proportion of spontaneous conversation. But with a total size of only half a million words, its usefulness for lexical research is severely limited. By contrast, the University of Birmingham's Bank of English includes a large sub-corpus of spoken text drawn from news bulletins, current affairs pro-grammes, interviews, and other material broadcast on the BBC World Service and on National Public Radio in the US. This is an impressive collection of radio journalism—an influential genre that is well worth studying in its own right—but it cannot provide reliable data for the study of everyday spoken English, because much of the material is either scripted or else planned in advance according to a pre-set agenda. Cross-corpus research at Lund University has shown that scripted or semi-scripted 'radio English' is in fact much closer to written text in its linguistic features, and that 'spontaneous speech is strikingly different from all other text types' (Svartvik 1992, 22). The need for a large corpus of *spontaneous* spoken English is now recognized. Efforts are being made by corpus-builders to collect data that will enable us to bridge the gap between, on the one hand, the spoken language as it is currently described and taught and, on the other hand, the language that people actually use in public or business meetings, in the classroom, and above all in ordinary face-to-face conversation. The BNC, for example, includes a 10-million-word spoken-text component, comprising (in roughly equal amounts):

- A 'demographic' spoken corpus: this was gathered by a group of volunteers, specially selected by the British Market Research Bureau to form a representative cross-section of the population in terms of age, gender, and social and geographical background. The volunteers were equipped with concealed Walkman-type tape-recorders which they simply left running for several days as they surreptitiously recorded (within certain ethical guidelines) all of their conversations —whether at home or in the workplace, or in shops, pubs, and bus queues.

- A 'context-governed' spoken corpus: the motivation here was to complement the data from the demographic corpus (which could not on their own reveal the full range of linguistic variation found in the spoken medium) with recordings of more structured situations, such as business meetings, radio phone-ins, college seminars, parliamentary proceedings, and broadcast sports commentaries.

All of the recordings were then edited and transcribed—a labour-intensive and highly skilled job—and the resulting text can now be accessed and processed using the same software as is used for analysing the BNC's written component. For the first time, then, lexicographers and other language professionals have access to really significant quantities of spoken-corpus data, and there seems no reason to doubt that this development will eventually transform our description of spoken English just as fundamentally as the arrival of large written-text corpora revolutionized lexicographers' account of written English from the mid-1980s onwards.

Obviously, the arrival of reliable spoken data means that serious comparisons can be made, across a whole range of text-features, between written and spoken English. One of the most striking things that emerges here is the variation in the extent to which writers and speakers rely upon various types of ready-made phrase, or 'recurrent word combination', as an aid to fluency. (The term 'recurrent word combination' covers a wide range of multiword phenomena, from full-blown idioms like 'raining cats and dogs', through phrasal verbs like 'put up with' and collocations like 'flatly refuse', to speech formulas like 'ladies and gentlemen' or 'you know what I mean'.) What the figures show is that in a serious written genre such as academic prose, writers' dependence on these prefabricated 'chunks' is relatively light, such combinations typically making up about 30 per cent of this type of text. But the percentage increases in print journalism, and is higher still in face-to-face conversation, where recurrent word combinations may account for as much as 70 per cent of all text—reflecting the severe time pressures on 'producers' of unplanned spoken discourse (Altenberg 1991). This sort of information has important implications—especially for psycholinguists, who study the way we store, access, and process language in the brain; for lexicographers, who need to do a much better job of describing the *phraseology* of English;[6] and for language teachers, who can help learners by focusing a little more on the 'phrasal' ways in which fluent speakers express many common concepts in English.

Some insights from corpus data

An article of this length cannot begin to do justice to the breadth and richness of information that a good corpus can provide for the language researcher. But a few pointers can perhaps be given about the kinds of enquiry that have now been made possible. It is worth pointing out, for example, that in a well-constructed corpus each text will be supplied with a set of situational 'tags' that precisely identify the specific characteristics of that individual text. The tags tell us about features such as gender (whether the writer of a given text is male or female); regional variety (is the writer a user of British English or American, or is he or she from elsewhere in the English-speaking world?); subject matter (what is the text about?); level or 'tenor' of discourse (is the text, for example, a piece of academic discourse or a popular handbook aimed at a general readership?); medium (is it a book, a newspaper, a government circular, or a piece of advertising copy?); and many others. Armed with this information, we can study particular varieties of text and the extent to which their lexical and grammatical properties conform to or diverge from the representative norm. One obvious application is the creation of subcorpora for analysing, say, the language of newspaper text (or even of newspaper headlines), of academic discourse, or of American novels. But the situational tags enable us to make much more fine-grained investigations than these. By specifying a search algorithm based on a combination of different tag-types, we can look at the language of a genre such as 'popular romantic fiction produced by British women writers'. This can produce startling revelations—in this case, the fact that the word **manhood** has a genre-specific use which does not appear in any other English text-type, as shown in sentences like:

> She held his leaping, quivering manhood in check
>
> She explored the place where his manhood lay
>
> the hard pulsing heat of his virile manhood pressing insistently against her thighs

and so on.

Spoken text, too, can be investigated in similar ways. We find, for example, that female speakers use the word **gorgeous** about three times as often as males; and while women use it to describe things like furnishings, food, or clothes ('What a gorgeous blouse!'), men use it only to talk about women. Equally, we can chart the effects of age on speakers' vocabulary choices, and, with participants ranging in age from under 10 to over 80, the BNC's spoken corpus provides valuable evidence of language change. Teenagers and the under-25s have their own vocabulary and their own conversational etiquette, while older speakers are more likely to use proverbs and 'classical' idioms, often as a way of delivering rueful comments on human nature, as in the following extract spoken by a woman in her eighties:

> It's a sprat to catch a mackerel. They get you to go in for something and then it costs you money. Of course it does. They're not doing that for nothing. If I've had one I've had a dozen!

It is possible, too, to observe the gradual obsolescence, in real spoken text, of many of the old shibboleths of 'correct' usage, such as the **can I/may I** distinction (now very rarely observed) and the affirmative use of **shall** (rather than **will**) with a first person subject: utterances like 'I shall write and complain' are now largely confined to the over-40s. Using all the information the corpus supplies about the age, gender, and social and regional background of each speaker, we can pinpoint users of a given word or phrase with astonishing precision. For the expression **ever so nice**, for example, we can create quite a detailed profile of the typical user: she is overwhelmingly female, may live in any part of the UK, is predominantly working class or lower middle class, and her average age is around 49. This sort of investigation—trivial enough in itself—is just one example of what becomes possible through a combination of large volumes of corpus data and detailed situational tagging.

Another benefit of large corpora is the scope they offer for various types of statistical analysis, ranging from simple computations of word frequency or of the relative frequency of a word's meanings, through 'type-token' ratios (which show the breadth—or otherwise—of vocabulary used in a given text genre), to precise information about the likelihood of one word co-occurring with another. Data of this type are vital for researchers working in natural-language processing fields (such as automatic speech recognition and machine translation), where the computer programs that will perform these operations depend on very large amounts of linguistic data to form the basis of 'probabilistic' models of language. Frequency information is also immensely useful to lexicographers, providing them with a more reliable and objective basis on which to make decisions about inclusion and exclusion, about the way that complex entries might best be ordered, and about which word combinations are most worth recording. This in turn has obvious benefits for language learners, and is yet another example of the way that corpus data are helping us steadily to narrow the gap between, on the one hand, the language that is described in dictionaries and taught in the classroom and, on the other hand, the language that people actually write and speak.

Implications for language teaching and language learning

Computers have been used in language teaching since the early 1980s. During roughly the same period, computerized corpora have, as we have seen, revolutionized the craft of lexicography. But until very recently, computerized corpora have not played a significant role in language teaching, and the benefits of corpus data have been indirect rather than direct. Dictionaries and grammars designed for non-native learners of English have, indeed, improved enormously through the availability of large, representative corpora, and we are now beginning to see similar improvements in coursebooks and other pedagogical materials, as writers begin to use corpus data for the first time. But the way is now open for teachers and students to use this sort of material more directly—to, as it were, cut out the middleman and explore raw corpus data themselves, instead of relying on whatever *distillation* of the data a particular dictionary may provide. Corpus enthusiasts in the English language teaching world have been making this case for several years,[7] but until recently corpus data have not been easily available, and computers powerful enough to process large amounts of text have been expensive luxuries. This really is no longer the case, and there is growing interest in the use of corpora as a teaching and learning strategy. With direct access to concordances, students can make their own discoveries and test their own hypotheses about what words mean, how they typically combine, and how similar words differ in their behaviour.[8] For lexicographers, the great value of concordances is that they reveal the regularities of the language. For non-native learners of a language, this exposure to dozens of instances of a word's behaviour can perhaps to some extent replicate, and collapse in time, the gradual process by which native speakers develop their understanding of how words behave. It is much easier, for example, to grasp (and *remember*) the differences between **see**, **look at**, and **watch**—words that non-native students frequently confuse—by scanning concordances that show them in context, than simply by being told what the differences are.

Students can also now compare concordances of their own output (and that of their peers) with mainstream corpus data, and this can be a powerful method of self-correction. Instead of simply marking something as wrong and telling students what they 'should' have said, teachers can now guide students towards relevant corpus data that will enable them to see for themselves possible ways in which their own work might be improved. For example, concordances of students' writing show that many of them tend to use the verb **eat** when talking about meals ('I eat breakfast at 8.30', 'We ate lunch and then went out', and so on). This is not so much 'wrong' as unidiomatic (or 'not what a native speaker would normally say'), and an equivalent set of concordances from native speaker texts will quickly reveal that **have** is the usual operating verb in sentences like this. Allowing learners to draw their own conclusions from material of this kind is, essentially, democratic and empowering, in that it gives them access to a body of linguistic data which is, in a sense, equivalent to what the (fluent) teacher can retrieve from his or her own mental lexicon.

The future

The corpus revolution that began in the early 1980s had transformed the whole discipline of pedagogical dictionary-making in English by the end of that decade. The notion of producing a new dictionary for learners of English *without* a computerized corpus has become quite simply unthinkable, and such a product would have little credibility in what is now a highly competitive marketplace. Progress has been a little more patchy in other areas. Corpus data do indeed underpin *some* pedagogical grammars, *some* bilingual dictionaries, and an increasing number of mainstream English dictionaries for the native-speaker market. Writers of EFL (English as a Foreign Language) coursebooks and related teaching materials have, with a few exceptions, continued to rely on more traditional sources of linguistic data—essentially, their own intuitions backed up by the information contained in published reference books. Meanwhile, among the community of English language teachers and teacher trainers, a small minority of enthusiasts have preached the corpus gospel for over a decade, but the majority of teachers remain either ignorant of the potential benefits of a corpus or unconvinced by the case for using one.

But there are good reasons for believing that things are about to change, and perhaps to change quite radically. In the first place, there is at last a growing recognition among writers, teachers, and publishers that the case for producing language materials without any reference to objective data is no longer intellectually sustainable. At the same time, access to corpus data has suddenly become much easier and much less expensive. Some of the large lexicographic corpora are now more openly available; commercial publishers issue CD-ROMs containing tens of millions of words of newspaper text; and archives of out-of-copyright material (such as 19th century novels) are also available in this format, often at very low cost. All this, without even mentioning the vast riches of the Internet.[9] Thirdly, the hardware needed for storing and processing corpus data has become much more affordable, and gets cheaper with every passing year. Hard discs of half a gigabyte or more are now the norm, while CD-ROM drives–once an expensive rarity—are now more or less standard on new PCs. Concordancing software, too, like all other types of software, has become simultaneously less expensive, more powerful, and more user-friendly. And finally, as technophobia gradually dwindles, the new generation of teachers and students are far less likely to be intimidated by the idea of using corpus data in a wide variety of applications. All these factors are converging to produce a climate in which the corpus looks set to occupy a central role in the world of English language teaching over the years to come.

Notes

1. The four dictionaries are: *Longman Dictionary of Contemporary English* (3rd edition), *Oxford Advanced Learner's Dictionary* (5th edition), *Collins Cobuild English Dictionary* (2nd edition), and *Cambridge International English Dictionary*.

2. Note, for example, the *Cobuild English Grammar* (1990) and the *Communicative Grammar of English* (2nd edition, Longman 1993), both corpus-based; and *Intermediate Choice* (Sue Mohamed and Richard Acklam, Longman 1995), a coursebook aimed at adult learners, which includes concordance extracts from the spoken component of the British National Corpus.

3. For example: **bright** clever; intelligent; **clever** quick at learning and understanding things; intelligent (*Oxford Advanced Learner's Dictionary*, 4th edition, 1989).

4. See now Summers (1993) on the Longman-Lancaster Corpus, and Renouf (1987) on the Birmingham Collection of English Texts.

5. For full details of these corpora, see the following pages of the World Wide Web: the Bank of English-http://titania.cobuild.collins.co.uk; the British National Corpus-http://info.ox.ac.uk:80/bnc/.

6. Some of the latest generation of learner's dictionaries do indeed address this issue, notably *Collins Cobuild English Dictionary* and *Longman Dictionary of Contemporary English* (both 1995). In the *Longman Language Activator* (1993), a dictionary that presents and distinguishes close-synonyms in semantic groups, over 40 per cent of all the 'headwords' are actually multi-word rather than single-word items.

7. See especially Tribble and Jones (1990), who put the case for using concordances as a teaching and learning tool several years before it became fashionable.

8. Two excellent commercial concordancing packages are available: the Longman Mini-Concordancer (Longman 1989) and Oxford Micro-Concord (Oxford University Press 1994).

9. For corpus availability, see note 5 above. Newspapers on CD-ROM are available from Chadwyck-Healey Ltd, The Quorum, Barnwell Road, Cambridge CB5 8SW. There is also a growing number of World Wide Web sites offering online versions of academic journals, well-known magazines (such as *The Economist*), and whole libraries of out-of-copyright books.

References and bibliography

Aijmer, K., and Altenberg, B. (eds.), *English corpus linguistics* (Harlow: Longman, 1991).

Aitchison, J., *Words in the mind: an introduction to the mental lexicon* (Oxford: Basil Blackwell, 1987).

Altenberg, B., 'The London-Lund Corpus: research and applications', *Proceedings of the 7th Annual Conference*, University of Waterloo Centre for the New OED, Oxford, 1991.

Biber, D., 'Using register-diversified corpora for general language study', *Computational Linguistics*, 19.2 (1993), 219–41.

Crowdy, S., 'Spoken corpus design', *Literary and Linguistic Computing*, 8.4 (1993), 259–65.

Leech, G., 'The state of the art in corpus linguistics', in Aijmer, K., and Altenberg B. (eds.), *English corpus linguistics* (Harlow: Longman, 1991), 8–29.

Renouf, A., 'Corpus development', in Sinclair, J. M. (ed.), *Looking up*, (London: Collins ELT, 1987), 1–40.

Rundell, M., 'The word on the street: revelations from the BNC spoken corpus', *English Today*, 11.3 (July 1995), 29–35.

Rundell, M., and Stock, P., 'The corpus revolution', *English Today*, 8.2, 8.3, 8.4 (April, July, October 1992).

Sinclair, J., *Corpus, concordance, collocation* (Oxford: Oxford University Press, 1991).

Summers, D., 'Longman/Lancaster Corpus—criteria and design', *International Journal of Lexicography*, 6.3 (1993), 181-208.

Svartvik, J., 'Lexis in English language corpora', *Euralex '92 Proceedings*, (University of Tampere, 1992).

Tribble, C., and Jones, G., *Concordances in the classroom* (Harlow: Longman, 1990).

Film Studies

Michael Allen

Introduction and historical overview

For such an essentially technology-based subject, it is perhaps surprising that film studies has an almost non-existent track record of using computer-based materials. There are a few initiatives worth noting. An international user group—Interactive Technologies Advisory Group (ITAG)—exists, which is designed to promote the use of interactive and multimedia materials in film studies. Several programs have emerged under the umbrella of this group, including packages on Alfred Hitchcock's *Rebecca*, and Orson Welles' *Macbeth*. Within Britain, important centres investigating the relationship between interactive multimedia technologies and film studies exist at the University of East Anglia in Norwich and at Luton University.

One significant reason for the relative backwardness of film studies' use of such technologies is the technical nature of film studies source material—the feature film stored on a film-strip and, more recently, videotape. While in theory the technical nature of interactive multimedia should be well-suited to handling such material, in reality this is another matter. This is due to the technical difficulties in accessing even a short film clip. In comparison, written text and even 'still-image text' handling has been a relatively simpler and more easily achievable process.

Until recently the most popular interactive computer-based process was to link a computer to an external laserdisc player via a mediating 'box of tricks', such as VideoStacks produced by the Voyager Company. Such a set-up was cumbersome for several reasons. A great deal of clumsy cabling linked the various units of the workstation together. The use of laserdiscs brought problems in terms of availability as most laserdiscs are in the American NTSC (National Television Standards Committee) format, although there has been a recent push in Britain to promote PAL (Phase Alternation Line) format discs. Moreover, most laserdiscs contain their feature film on two or more sides, requiring frequent, irritating interruption of the program as discs are repeatedly turned over and swapped as the program proceeds.

In the last two or three years, the appearance of Quicktime for both Apple Mac and IBM computers has altered this situation in significant ways. Now moving pictures and audio can be played on the computer itself, side-by-side with written texts. This development has several advantages, including the simplifying of the workstation itself (removing external laser-players and mediating units). A potential disadvantage is the reduced quality of both sound and vision, the picture only being two inches square. However, the next version of Quicktime promises full-screen, full-motion images. One additional effect of the development of Quicktime has been the ability to put an entire feature film onto a CD-ROM disc. Several feature films have already been released in this format, for example the Beatles' film *A Hard Day's Night,* distributed by the Voyager Company.

Theoretical background

In the 1970s a French film theorist, Raymond Bellour wrote an article entitled 'The Unattainable Text', which was published in the British film journal *Screen* (Bellour 1975). In this article, Bellour described the issues involved in the analysis of artistic texts produced in various media, with a focus on film. Written before the advent of the various technologies already mentioned which have begun to transform film studies, it offered what is, not too surprisingly, a now outdated survey of issues surrounding the analysis of film texts. On the other hand, many of its theoretical ideas still retain a great deal of validity, which says much about the state and status of film studies as an academic discipline.

At the very start of his article Bellour summarizes the problems of addressing the film text in terms which, until the advent of current multimedia technologies, still rang true. He talks of:

> ...the special difficulties which very often make it impossible to obtain the film in the material sense or the proper conditions to constitute it into a text, i.e. the editing table or the projector with freeze-frame facility. These difficulties are still enormous: they are very often discouraging, and go a long way to explaining the comparative backwardness of film studies. However, one can imagine, if

still only hypothetically, that one day, at the price of a few changes, the film will find something that is hard to express, a status analogous to that of the book or rather that of the gramophone record with respect to the concert. If film studies are still done then, they will undoubtedly be more numerous, more imaginative, more accurate and above all more enjoyable than the ones we carry out in fear and trembling, threatened continually with dispossession of the object. (Bellour 1975, 19)

As he goes on to observe:

The text of the film is unattainable because it is an unquotable text.

This, he argues, being because:

On the one hand [film] spreads in space like a picture: on the other it plunges into time...In this it is peculiarly unquotable, since the written text cannot restore to it what only the projector can produce; a movement, the illusion of which guarantees the reality. That is why the reproduction even of many stills only ever reveals a kind of radical inability to assume the textuality of the film.

Photographs have always been, and indeed still are, the main method of representing a film text in film studies writing; photographs of significant moments which are deemed to illustrate the point being made adequately. But of course, they are never adequate. They are frozen moments trying to represent a moving, audible original. As Bellour notes, the analyst always needs more photographs than the selection used to illustrate any piece of written analysis. And, to be fair, photographs have always been recognized as an imperfect solution to the problem of representing the film text.

The absent text

The basic issue, as Bellour indicates, has always been the problem of the absent text. Films, even in a film studies context, are generally viewed under conditions resembling those in the cinema—darkened room, projection onto a screen, and real-time viewing, although closer viewing could take place on an editing table, or through the use of videotape. In all of these options, the film itself is still usually absent at the time of the actual analysis. It is certainly absent from the analysis itself, the writer relying on notes and stills to fill in for that missing text and the reader relying on an act of imagination to recreate mentally the missing film in the reading of the analysis. The serious study of film, as Bellour's comments suggest, was perceived to be a discipline in search of an accurate methodology.

The central questions therefore become: 'How do you satisfactorily reference an audiovisual text in written form?'; and 'What is the written text trying to achieve?'. Conventionally, describing the absent scene, often at great length, serves as a preliminary towards the real purpose of the writing, which is the advancing of a theory or interpretation. But the very absence of the film material itself means that the reader must trust the writer's accuracy and descriptive powers in evoking the reality of the text.

A central tenet of the film viewing experience is that the viewer is incapable of influencing the screening of the film as it is projected. The spectator is argued to be, and arguably is, a passive being. There is a problem with the term 'passive'. Some film writers, for example David Bordwell, argue for an active spectator, but in the specific sense of a spectator who actively hypothesizes about the narrative as it develops (Bordwell 1985). What I mean by the passive spectator is someone who has no means of controlling the viewing experience itself. Indeed, this phenomenon is taken to be a central pleasure of film watching—the sense of giving oneself up, of voluntarily surrendering, of becoming helpless to the fantasy.

This phenomenon is central to the formulation and effect of what is conventionally referred to as the classical feature film, broadly covering the fictional films made since the mid-1910s. The classical fiction film works upon the spectator in the way it does because it is seen at one sitting, in linear, real time, and because it is seen communally on a larger-than-life screen by a viewer who cannot move away from it, partly by physical circumstances, surrounded in the dark by an audience of like-minded souls, and partly because he or she has emotionally pledged him or herself *exclusively* to the experience of relating to that fictional world for the next 90 minutes or two hours. The narrative and the text as a whole only make sense, so to speak, because of these conditions, because of this contract between spectator and text. That is the essential, 'fantastic', tension of the Hollywood fiction film.

Videotape, in its controllability and relatively easy repeatability, changes this relationship between viewer and film text. The fantasy can now be interrupted. Quicktime, by allowing the capture and storage of material on the computer itself, increases this control over the film by allowing virtually instantaneous playback of film material. Moreover, several clips can be played side by side. Modern multimedia technologies allow the direct quotation of the film scene within the written critical text, and the consequent reduction of descriptive passages. No need to comment, for example, that such-and-such a character moves from left to right at a certain moment in a shot—the movement can actually be seen in the captured clip. The total controllability of the film text, the instant replay, and the ability to quote the film text directly in the critical text are the most significant effects of the use of interactive multimedia technologies in film studies.

An essential issue to be investigated in this respect is the nature of the film clip: what sense of the reality of the film text as a whole is to be produced by the 'quotation' of a small section of it? To some extent this depends upon the nature of the original. Earlier films, from the first years of cinema around the turn of the century, fare better in this respect. Because many of these films are only a few minutes long, it is possible to quote the film text in its entirety. The use of multimedia in the academic study of film more usually centres around the tension between what has become the standard film product—a two-hour feature narrative—and the fragmentary sampling process typical of interactive multimedia. That is, how to represent such a long and complex text adequately within the technological and perceptual limitations of the system. This is still one of the thorniest problems in the use of multimedia to analyse film.

Alternative designs

One approach is concerned with the retention of conventional critical writing forms, in which the linear analytical text is the focus and short examples are drawn from the reference texts to reinforce the argument. The result can be seen as little more than an illustrated essay, in which the film stills happen to move. What is needed instead, perhaps, is a film-driven analysis in which the student begins to watch the film, and at every significant point can call up relevant material from a pre-loaded database. The session thereby becomes driven by the viewing of the film, rather than the development of a written argument.

Of course, another approach altogether is not to go along the thesis-driven database road at all. One of the slightly depressing features of multimedia packages for film studies so far is that they all seem to conform to the same format of masses of background material, together with a critical approach, which have been combined into a database constructed around a single film, whether the navigation of that database is analysis-driven or film-driven. These are interesting and useful as far as they go, but are rather hermetically sealed.

That so many multimedia projects for film studies (and this is not restricted to film studies) have taken this form is in part because any such package must be compiled using the relevant programming language—Hypertalk, SuperScript, or OpenScript. In order for a film studies package to be created, this language has to be learned. Within a normal term or semester, students simply do not have the time to learn a complex computer language in anything like the depth necessary to produce a satisfactory end-product. The result is therefore a series of elementary designs in which the problems of construction have completely overshadowed the content of the package. The student's ideas have been forced to take a back seat in preference to technical demands of the technology and software. Hence the database approach, which presents the student with a pre-formed package of information to be browsed through, clicked at, and digested in a spoon-fed manner.

More useful, perhaps, for both research and teaching purposes, would be the development of an analytical toolkit, with supporting material of various kinds if required, which would allow the student to perform his/her own analysis on a film by compiling and interlinking material, including film clips, critical extracts, and original analysis. This toolkit might include features such as critical writing areas, easy linking tools, film clip indices, and a series of text storage facilities.[1] Such a toolkit would not require the student to know anything of the programming language involved in the software, while allowing him or her the opportunity to combine the tools together in a number of permutations, in order to create original work.

Linear and non-linear construction

A central issue which has to be addressed by everyone working with hypertext systems of all kinds, is that of linear vs. non-linear discourse. Academics are used to linearity in either essay or book form. The argument proceeds from A to B to C to Z, each point emerging out of the last. A well-written piece of work is one which observes these rules in an elegant way. Hypertext requires a radically different construction, one which allows movement from point to point to develop in a number of directions. An idea can be linked to an extract or several different extracts from a critical text, or another student's work, or a databank of relevant still images. A number of Quicktime movie clips can be accessed and played to support the idea being developed. There is a freedom, a play of elements, available to the user which is quite different from a traditional essay.

But a non-linear construction not only cuts against the grain of conventional academic forms such as the essay; it also beats against the linearity of the film text itself. Is this a good or a bad thing? Films need not necessarily be seen as linear cause and effect narratives only. It might be equally valid to see them as collections of disparate elements and performances—gestural, chromatic, textural, compositional.[2] To see the film text in these ways is to dismantle the sense of its linear narrativity as the most important level of meaning. Multimedia and hypertext might help this refocusing, by offering the possibility of new means of expression and new ways of thinking about the nature of the filmic text, unrestrained by the dictates of conventional linear form. Such an approach is looser, harder to set up and frame satisfactorily, but ultimately, perhaps, of greater use to the user, because it increases the interactivity between user and program, student and film.

As it stands currently, the multimedia critical text becomes composed of the hypertext itself in an active relationship with the film text. It is no accident that HyperCard or SuperCard on the Apple Mac and Toolbook on the IBM, for example, both explicitly use filmic devices—dissolves, fades, wipes—as part of their aesthetic armoury. As a result, critical text and referenced text are pulled closer together. They are no longer texts separated by irreconcilable languages. In some ways they are coming to share the same language.

A final thought is that the language and grammar of the hypertext and the film text, both texts linked by optical effects, are also in dialogue with the computer's text, the programming language. Film comes out of a scientific and industrial background—it is the most technical of the arts, it is an industry as much if not more than it is an art form, and its technical development has always been explicitly linked to scientific and industrial developments in other areas. The film text, far more than any other artistic text, exists only as a result of a great deal of high level engineering, chemistry, physics, optics, and mathematics. There is some sense of completion in the idea that film can finally be satisfactorily addressed as a result of the combination of high level mathematics, engineering, physics, and optics which has gone into the evolution of the computer.

Archiving issues

The digitizing of film material either onto laserdisc or directly onto the computer as Quicktime files raises purist issues concerned with the status of the original text—that film is film, and should not be converted to any kind of electronic form. This is especially relevant to archiving work and the question of how film is going to be preserved in the future. This seems to be a precious attitude—why should we care what form the film comes in as long as we can still view it? That surely is the important thing.

An important area of film studies comes out of examining the physical state of the film itself—how many sprocket holes it has per frame, how large those frames are, whether it has an optical or magnetic soundtrack running alongside its images, what the damage to the reels tells us of the film's history. Certain aspects of the film's physical reality cannot be studied if they cannot be physically examined on the filmstrip itself. The physical and historical reality of the text is effaced in its transfer to digital format. In this case, the technology, far from enhancing the study of the film, actually impedes it.

Projecting forward to a time when a film might be stored only in digital form from the beginning of its history, we will have to face the prospect of losing an important aspect of its identity. But of course, what must be retained in this regard is that such storage forms should not be seen as a substitute for either the use of the 35mm film or videotape in the classroom and seminar or as superseding the written text, be it book, paper-source, or scholarly paper. The same principle of non-substitution and non-supersession applies to archive holdings. For an archive, the task is always to preserve the materiality of an object, a materiality whose importance is not lost on any student of cinema. The use of multimedia technologies in the archive must be seen as a support rather than a replacement, and that support, probably, will be limited to databasing duties, with the Quicktime clips very much designed to be thumbnail sketches, giving users a sense of what a film is about, rather than replacing the film itself.

Statistical style analysis

Statistical style analysis has been a branch of film studies for at least the last ten or fifteen years. Put briefly, statistical style analysis has been used in an attempt to systematize and provide a verifiable basis for explaining both 'change'—from one mode/form to another—and 'influence'—from one practice (national, individual) to another—and thus to tackle the issues of influence, change, and style. It has been used, for example, to distinguish between early cinema and later Hollywood films; to identify the style of individual directors; and to determine period style, national style, and individual style.

Some of the parameters that have been identified as pertinent are shot length, shot scale, spatial division and composition, shot density (how many characters are in shot at any one time), camera movement, and so on. Together, or in certain combinations, these parameters may reasonably be assumed to constitute a coherent system, and therefore a style. A lot of work in this area has merely set up basic binary or Manichaean oppositions. One task may be to unpick once more the different elements that have gone into these handy oppositions, but also to historicize them and to locate the reasons for the mutation of stylistic features in order to be able to explain change, or make sense of the question of influence. However, it seems important to emphasize the extent to which these variables are interdependent. There has been a tendency to use them in isolation or in terms of binary oppositions (deep staging = French *film d'art*, shallow staging = American Vitagraph company, for example). We need to explore further the kinds of models we have at our disposal for picturing or modelling the kinds of relations between variables.

This is where the computer comes in. The computer cannot provide a complete answer to this question, but it can certainly help focus it. The computer's infamous ability to number crunch—the attitude that this is virtually all a computer is good for is still one of the biggest barriers to the acceptance of multimedia by the humanities—obviously makes it valuable for this kind of work. The statistical evaluation of several parameters can be made very quickly—only a few seconds—and put into direct juxtaposition. Further, graphs based on the figures can easily be drawn using programs such as HyperCard's Graphmaker tool.

Possible developments

The reality of current film criticism now exists in the interaction between word and moving image. The ability to quote a film clip directly within the written text *is* a major step forward for film studies, but at the end of the day what we have is still primarily a written address to an audiovisual referent. The incompatibility between the two languages, a genuine breakdown in communication can often still occur. Possibly what is needed, then, is a radically new critical method altogether. And whatever this is might be seen as an answer to Bellour's cry of frustration at the end of his article, when he says that:

> Although it would already be to go much further, we might change our point of view completely and ask if the filmic text should really be approached in writing at all. (Bellour 1975, 26)

What would this new critical methodology actually look like? How would it be compiled, or constructed, or performed...whatever the verb might be? A few possibilities already come to mind: 2-D animations around the Quicktime film frame to simulate objects or characters moving on- and off-screen; 3-D modelling animations to demonstrate the spatial construction of a film scene; spoken commentary rather than the written word to open up a dialogue (literally) between film sound and critical voice. It is also now possible to create what are being called Navigable Movies in which the user controls what is being seen of a film space; when the cursor is moved towards any frame edge, the image space moves around accordingly to reveal new space. One can imagine using this to create a representation of a film scene, complete with camera crew, set, and actors, that the user is able to move in and around the space. All of these techniques convey information in the same audiovisual way as the film text itself, with no, or few written words needing to be used.

Assessment and dissemination

As already indicated, one of the central issues involved in the use of interactive multimedia in film studies is about the storage size of the computerized material. This can be split into two areas— 'before' and 'after'.

Before: Let us assume an average seminar group of twenty film students studying a certain film studies subject in a given term. Let us assume that all of them are expected to use the interactive multimedia technology to produce their work during the term or semester. This entails them capturing film material in Quicktime format and, perhaps, writing their critical ideas using the Analytical Toolkit described earlier. Several problems arise; the most immediate is that of access to machines capable of digitizing film material in Quicktime format. Unless the institution has the financial ability to provide one or two dozen machines equipped with video boards, some kind of rota will have to be established to allow each student some time on a machine equipped with a video-capture facility in order to capture his/her material. Such a session will inevitably prove time consuming, as the student captures his/her raw material, tidies unwanted front-and-end wastage, and possibly converts the raw material (captured using Screenplay for the VideoSpigot, for example) into proper, compressed, Quicktime format. This rota will have to take account of several variable factors, two of the most prominent being: (1) students who want to capture far too much material, because they are unaware of storage limitations or because they have simply become carried away with their subject; and (2) students who fail to appear at their allotted time, and then turn up hours or even days later. If the rota is running on a very tight turn-over (quite likely if there is only one properly equipped machine; if it is in the only room available which has to be overseen by a part-time member of staff; if there are so many students wanting time that there is no choice), then major bottlenecks can occur as all students try to capture their material by the relevant point in the term.

Once this hurdle has been overcome, a second follows directly on: how to give the students access to their captured material as they then write their critical analysis. Put simply, the captured material—inevitably running into hundreds, perhaps thousands, of megabytes—has to be stored somewhere; and this 'somewhere' has to be easily accessible to the students. Portable, removable, hard discs, such as those produced by SyQuest, offer one possible solution, although there would have to be a number of such drives attached to machines in public areas, and the material would have to be of a relatively modest size (typically under 80 Mbs). More feasibly, the captured material could be stored on the institution's mainframe and networked around the site. Such a set-up could be procedurally complex (involving unfamiliar protocols for calling up the material), and politically complex (taking up a significant section of the mainframe can lead to tensions with the institution's computing centre). Overall, networking must be seen as the solution to the problem of student access to their material as they create their finished work.

After: The finished work having been produced, two further significant issues arise—those of assessment and dissemination. Currently there are no commonly agreed standards for film studies work produced using interactive multimedia technologies, even though such pieces of work differ substantially from 'traditional' film studies work. This difference stems centrally from the ability to quote the film text itself as a moving, audible entity. Descriptive passages, so essential previously as a way of 'conjuring up' the missing text into the reader's 'mind's eye', can now largely be dispensed with. This makes a radical difference to the nature of the critical writing, which now has to concentrate far more upon ideas and concepts rather than on description which has frequently been verbose. The relationship between this pared down 'concept/idea intensive' writing and the Quicktime clips and animations which are now replacing the descriptive passages has yet to be fully explored and understood. Eventually, some kind of sliding scale will become identified, dependent upon the subject being addressed. Some approaches, for example close analysis, might still require a certain amount of description. This is because, while providing audiovisual evidence of the film, the crucial moments of the clip still need to be explicitly referred to in order to bring out the maximum effect of the analysis. Other approaches, for example a more historical or sociological examination of a film subject, might use Quicktime clips as a general illustration of events, customs, etc. In this case, the briefest reference to the clip will suffice. The essential point is that the use of Quicktime clips within critical writing should not be treated in a monolithic way. The fullest potential of the technology will only be brought out by a sensitivity towards the relationship between the written and the audiovisual, rather than a draconian sweeping away of the written word.

The final issue produced by the advent of interactive multimedia technologies is that of storage of the finished work. How are these critical works to be saved for posterity? Over the years such works, multiplied student group by student group, will amount to hundreds of thousands of megabytes of storage space. At some point this must inevitably exceed the institution's ability to store them. New storage formats, such as CD-ROMs pressed from a central machine, will undoubtedly solve these problems. More personal, perhaps, is how students will preserve a copy of their own work. Gone are the days when they could take away the fruits of three years' work in one A4 folder. Even presupposing that the end result is pressed on CD-ROM (a procedure which, incidentally, might cost the student £30 a work), the technical requirements required to replay this work will make viewing such material more difficult than the reading of a traditional essay. Film students simply cannot walk away at the end of the day with their work contained on a floppy disc. Their work inevitably involves Quicktime movie clips running to tens, possibly hundreds of megabytes. Carrying away this material at the end of their degree is not impossible (the CD-ROM option just described is one such method), although copyright issues on the film material itself, also currently unresolved, will be another massive block to doing so.

Conclusion

In the above chapter, the intention has been to highlight some of the theoretical background, some of the potentials, and also some of problems in current thinking on the now burgeoning relationship between the study of film and interactive multimedia technologies. These technologies have undoubtedly begun to offer solutions to some of the fundamental frustrations involved in the academic study of film. Given careful planning, design, and implementation, it is now possible to offer film students a methodology which transforms 'traditional' academic practice.

So, to offer a reply to Bellour's hypothesis, it is now that day in the future and film studies, having undergone a few changes, is still very much alive, certainly more in evidence than ever before. Interactive multimedia technologies will ensure that analyses are more imaginative, more accurate, and above all more enjoyable than the ones we used to carry out, if not in fear and trembling, then with a certain sense of frustration at not 'speaking' the same language as the thing we were studying. With the advent of interactive multimedia, film studies has been allowed to come of age.

Notes

1. Such a toolkit, called ReScreen, is being developed at the University of East Anglia. For further details, contact Michael Allen, School of English and American Studies, University of East Anglia, Norwich NR4 7TJ.

2. See Thompson (1977) for a discussion of how such a piece of film writing may be accomplished.

References and bibliography

Bellour, R., 'The unattainable text', *Screen*, 16.3 (Autumn 1975).

Bordwell, D., *Narration in the fiction film* (London: Methuen & Co. Ltd, 1985).

Thompson, K., 'The concept of cinematic excess', *Cine-Tracts*, 1.2 (Summer 1977).

History and Computing

Andrew Prescott

Introduction: Turing's historian

One of the most thought-provoking studies of the cultural impact of computers is J. David Bolter's *Turing's Man* (Bolter 1984). Bolter sees the computer as the 'defining technology' of the modern era, in the same way as were the spindle in classical times or the mechanical clock in the later middle ages. Bolter's attempt to put the computer in a historical perspective provides many novel insights, and his book should perhaps be the first port of call for historians interested in ways in which computing might reshape knowledge. *Turing's Man* was published in 1984, shortly before the use of personal computers became commonplace. At that time, most scholars working in the humanities were still suspicious of the new technology. Bolter notes that 'Humanists, scholars, and creative writers have as yet little use for these machines. This ... will change, rather rapidly, as they realize that at least text editing by computer is far easier than working with pens, paper, or typewriters' (Bolter 1984, 6). Bolter observes that the question of 'whether literature, philosophy, or the study of history could ever be quantified', the issue which perhaps chiefly accounts for the wariness with which many humanities scholars have viewed the computer, is beside the point. Humanities scholars will inevitably come to rely on the computer simply because it will emerge as the principal means of communication in the developed world. As Bolter states, 'The philosophy and fiction of the next hundred years will be written at the keyboard of a computer terminal, edited by a program, and printed under electronic control—if indeed such works are printed at all'.

The changes which Bolter envisaged have come to pass, perhaps with a speed which may have surprised even him. By the time his book was reprinted in 1993 most of these predictions had been fulfilled. However, Bolter also suggested that the use of computers for word processing and other tasks would start to change the very nature of scholarship in the humanities.

> The humanist will not be able to ignore the medium with which he will work daily: it will shape his thought in subtle ways, suggest possibilities, and impose limitations, as does any other medium or communication ... The scientist or philosopher who works with electronic tools will think in different ways from those who have worked at ordinary desks with paper and pencil, with stylus and parchment, or with papyrus. He will choose different problems and be satisfied with different solutions. (Bolter 1984, 6).

Bolter makes a comparison with the introduction of moveable type which, in the years since he wrote, has been repeated *ad nauseam*. Like others since, he saw the computer as bringing in its wake changes in thought as revolutionary as those which occurred in the sixteenth and seventeenth centuries (for an indication that this may be a superficial view of the impact of printing, see Mathiesen 1992). Although the computer is now an all-pervasive tool in the humanities, there is still little sign of the new medium bringing about a fundamental change in the nature of scholarly thought and communication. Can we reasonably expect to see in the next few years the beginning of such a reinvention of scholarship, or will the advent of the computer have no more impact on the nature of scholarship than, say, the invention of the typewriter or the photocopier?

The new research infrastructure

The computer has insinuated itself into scholarly life quietly and with little fuss. Even those who would regard themselves as lacking in technical skills have gradually found themselves hopelessly dependent on this mechanical aid. It is only when one stops and thinks how much things have changed in recent years that one realizes how much the computer has changed the way researchers work. In 1984, when Bolter's book was published, I was just completing a Ph.D. thesis on the judicial records of the Peasants' Revolt of 1381 (Prescott 1984). Like all students in that far-off era of easily obtained postgraduate grants, I had spent far too long on it. I had buried myself away in the Public Record Office and had found many previously unnoticed references to the revolt. I laboriously transcribed these with pencil and paper and now they linger in cardboard files, waiting the possibility of publication at some point. Nowadays, I would achieve the same results much more quickly with a laptop computer, would be able to find individual references more readily using a text retrieval package or maybe even just the 'search' function in the word processing program, and would find the word processed transcripts much easier to read when I came back to them. Above all, if I had those transcripts in keyboarded form, publication would be a much less daunting prospect.

The records I found contained the names of thousands of participants in the revolt. In attempting to get a clearer idea of the geographical distribution of these rebels and to assist in analysing the interrelationship of the different prosecutions in which they were named, I compiled huge card indexes. These were enormously time consuming to prepare and cumbersome to use, and I suspect that the results I got from them were not always very reliable. I would get much better results nowadays by using a database. Perhaps the most striking change in methods of historical research over the past ten years is the decline of the card index and the rise of the database. Research training, such as it was in the 1970s, focused very much on the use and abuse of the card index, which was at that time perhaps the historian's chief technical tool.

Apart from the archive material, I of course also tried to identify all the relevant printed literature. I was fortunate in that Edgar Graves' excellent bibliography of British medieval history to 1485 had recently appeared and it was easy to get an up-to-date list of studies of the revolt itself (Graves 1975). Once I moved into other areas, such as studies of risings elsewhere or legal literature, it was much more difficult to get a comprehensive listing of useful works. Nowadays, I can make keyword or subject searches of such resources as the British Library Catalogue or International Medieval Bibliography on CD-ROM. I can undertake similar searches in the catalogues of such major libraries as the Bodleian or the University of London Library from home at any time of the day or night. Automated library catalogues are now taken for granted by all scholars, and they have transformed the way in which the most funda- mental research activities are carried out. Many of the old skills in tracing obscure literature from footnotes and printed bibliographies have be- come redundant, and a new grammar of research, an understanding of the most intelligent way in which to interrogate databases, is being built up.

Having assembled this information, I was faced with the task of writing the thesis. I have always been a slow writer, and in those days used to prepare draft after laborious draft, using whole writing pads to get a few thousand words just right. When I felt confident that every phrase was perfectly adjusted, I finally got out the typewriter. I typed out the thesis myself, rebelling against the requirement that footnotes should appear at the bottom of the page, since this was beyond my skills and would have required a professional typist. Any mistakes or redrafting meant retyping a page. Even numbering the pages was quite a demanding task, which I speeded up by borrowing a mechanical stamper. I prepared the maps illustrating the thesis with large quantities of tracing paper and glue, achieving results which were reminiscent of a primary school project. Of course, the word processor has transformed all this. Not only can I now get away with slightly fewer drafts, but I can easily produce print quality text, with automatically numbered pages, footnotes at the bottom of each page, and incorporating polished looking maps. Most important of all, if I had been able to use a word processor in 1984, reworking of the thesis to produce a publishable book would have been much easier, and the thesis would perhaps not still be languishing unpublished in the Senate House of the University of London.

It should be noted that I undertook this research in isolation. The other scholars I met in weekly seminars were mostly not working on topics directly related to mine. Those working on subjects most closely connected with mine were generally based some way away, and difficult to keep in touch with on a regular basis. The advent of e-mail means that this is no longer such an issue, and I can keep in daily contact with scholars in distant locations, and share with them and discuss the results of my research as it develops.

It is therefore no exaggeration to claim that the computer has already changed every aspect of historical research, revolutionizing what might be described as the technical infrastructure of research. My story is not particularly remarkable; virtually every researcher could tell a similar tale. However, the extent and importance of the changes that have already taken place are rarely remarked. The evangelists of computing are usually mainly concerned to draw our attention to the latest developments. It is, however, the fact that so many of their previous prophecies have come true that gives their predictions credibility. The best answer to many of the objections to the use of computers in historical research considered by Daniel Greenstein in his recent *Historian's Guide to Computing* is that historians are already very dependent on computers to assist their work (Greenstein 1994, 6-35). It is only sensible for them to exploit the potential of computers to the fullest extent. At the moment we are perhaps in the position of having been given powerful sports cars which we are frightened to drive in more than second gear.

Developments of the infrastructure: electronic publications

Of course the new technical infrastructure is by no means complete or as efficient as everyone would like. Nor are many of the new developments always used intelligently, as anyone will appreciate who has been on an e-mail discussion group bombarded with bibliographic queries from students too lazy to look in their own library's catalogues. However, the infrastructure will certainly continue to develop and change in years to come. The range of electronic publications will continue to expand. Many valuable resources are already available, ranging from the University of Sheffield's CD-ROM of the papers of the seventeenth-century polymath, Samuel Hartlib (see the URL http://www.shef.ac.uk/uni/projects/hpp/hartlib.html) to the new series produced on CD-ROM by the Public Record Office and the Institute of Contemporary British History, providing images of a large number of the government documents released each year under the thirty year rule (announcement in *Contemporary Record* 8 (1994), p. 641). Many other exciting projects are in hand, such as *The New Dictionary of National Biography,* the British Academy's electronic edition of Foxe's *Book of Martyrs* (Ross and Newcombe, forthcoming) and the Strafford Papers project at the University of Sheffield (see the URL: http://www.shef. ac.uk/uni/academic/D-H/hri/). At the moment, electronic publications of this kind are often prohibitively expensive, sometimes running to thousands of pounds, a price beyond most libraries. There is a danger that electronic publication will run into the same quicksands as microform publication. Microfilm has enormous potential to increase access to archival resources, and many useful series have been produced, but these are often so expensive that few libraries buy them, and it can be more difficult to get access to the microfilms than the original documents. The fact that electronic editions can be searched and interrogated in a way not possible with microform means that the situation is not precisely analogous, but the warning signs are still there.

The problem of access to electronic resources is being addressed in a number of ways. The Combined Higher Education Software Team (CHEST) scheme in British universities has not only gained licences on advantageous terms for software, but is also increasingly arranging cut-price access to commercially produced databases such as Chadwyck-Healey's index to *The Times* or Ordnance Survey data (see the URL http://www.niss.ac.uk/chest). The new Arts and Humanities Data Service (AHDS) in Britain is primarily concerned with archiving research materials in electronic form, but will also be considering means of preserving and providing access to commercial publications (Burnard and Short 1994; Ross 1995). Likewise, the British Library's proposal to extend copyright deposit to electronic materials will, if successful, make access to such resources much easier (press announcement by the British Library at the URL http://portico.bl.uk/ifora/arch.html). Useful initiatives can also be taken in individual research centres. In Britain, the Institute of Historical Research is taking an active interest in this area, while in the United States the most striking model is perhaps the University of Virginia's Electronic Text Center, which forms part of its Internet Library (URL: http://www.lib.virginia.edu/etext/ETC.html). This is an archive containing thousands of SGML-encoded electronic texts, including not only a comprehensive collection of commercially produced CD-ROMs, but has also a huge number of useful texts which the staff of the Center have keyboarded themselves. For the medieval period, for example, virtually every middle-English text and many important Latin ones are available. All the texts are searchable through a common SGML viewer. Members of the University of Virginia can access this library through the Internet from anywhere in the world. Unfortunately, copyright restrictions mean that others cannot use the commercial datasets.

Developments of the infrastructure: automated archive catalogues

As far as historians are concerned, probably the greatest gap in the new technical infrastructure is that catalogues of archives and manuscript collections, the historian's chief research quarry, have not been widely automated. This is largely because the form of automation used in libraries for printed books is not generally suitable for archive material. The MARC (Machine Readable Catalogue) record and AACR (Anglo-American Cataloguing Rules) used for most library materials assume that each catalogue record describes a discrete item complete in itself, and assume that the information in each field, such as the title or date of publication can be simply defined and identified. (On MARC, see British Library (1990) and on AACR, see Gorman and Winkler

(1988); Fitzgerald (1995, 181) observes: 'MARC formats for books are not adequate for archives, and AACR2 rules for manuscripts apply to literary manuscripts rather than archives in general'.) Manuscripts of course generally do not have a title, and a description of their contents can require a lengthy and sometimes speculative prose description. Likewise, dates of manuscripts can be a matter of complex conjecture, again requiring long narrative discussions. Moreover, listings of archival material have a complex internal hierarchy which a MARC record cannot express. In the case of Chancery records at the Public Record Office, for example, the full catalogue information consists of a general description (in the guide) of the administrative structure and history of the department, followed by a list and brief description of each class of record generated by the different offices of the Chancery. Each class is then described in a separate class list which describes the function and structure of the record class, then lists each piece within the class. In order to understand each component of this complex structure, which reflects the administrative system that generated the record, it is necessary to understand its position in the hierarchical structure of the catalogue. An individual record stating that C 258/1 covers 1258-1321 is meaningless; while a general description of the Chancery records would not help much in locating C 258/1.

Some attempts have been made to use MARC records for manuscripts. For example, the catalogue of the Australian National Library is fully integrated, covering all types of material in its collection, so that a search for works about the composer Percy Grainger will show books, music, and manuscripts relating to him (URL: http://www.nla.gov.au). Other libraries have adopted a hybrid approach. In the British Library's automated manuscript catalogue, for example, index entries can be converted to MARC format, while the full descriptions of each manuscript are held as text files (British Library 1989, Burnett 1990). The catalogue of the archives at the Royal Botanic Gardens, Kew, uses a text retrieval package called Unicorn to facilitate the handling of extended MARC records (Fitzgerald 1995). However, mix and match approaches of this type have mostly proved suitable only for smaller specialist repositories and have not been widely used in Britain for large administrative archives. Despite the efforts of such initiatives as the *Manual of Archive Description* and the recent appearance of various international standards for archive description (Cook and Procter 1988; Cook 1995), there has been nothing in the archive world comparable to the movement for conversion of library catalogues to automated form over the past twenty years. In

Britain, the chief focus of automation efforts in the Public Record Office has been in using computers to assist in maintaining and indexing the current guide (Bell 1971; Bell *et al.* 1972; Bell 1975; Walford *et al.* 1988), and most British archivists have been wary of using the computer for anything other than word processing class lists. (For further discussion on the role of research libraries and archives, see the separate chapters in this volume.)

It seems that this is about to change. Archivists have become aware that markup languages such as SGML and hyperlinks can help express the hierarchical structures which are characteristic of their catalogues. In particular, the Archive Description project at the University of California in Berkeley has started to develop document type definitions to facilitate SGML tagging of archive lists (URL: http://www.lib.berkeley.edu/AboutLibrary/Projects/BFAP/). The Research Libraries Group has initiated a project called FAST Track (Finding Aids SGML Encoding Training), which aims to build on the work at Berkeley to provide suitable Document Type Definitions to facilitate the encoding of archival finding aids and train archivists in their use (unpublished presentation by N. Elkington to British Library staff, 1996). In Britain, the funding programmes initiated by the Follett report on library provision in higher education have given priority to projects for the conversion of catalogues of manuscripts and archives, which will, as a condition of funding, be made available on the network. The Follett Implementation Group on Information Technology (FIGIT) is actively encouraging development of standards for automation of archive finding aids, and in 1995 organized a workshop for archivists funded under the programme to examine these issues further. (On this programme, see the URL http://ukoln. bath.ac.uk/elib/intro.html). Important work on establishing common name formats, always a vexed question in any automation project, has been undertaken under the auspices of the National Council on Archives, while major repositories such as the British Library are beginning to incorporate manuscript records in their online public access catalogues (OPACs). The Royal Commission on Historical Manuscripts has taken a lead in establishing an Archives and the Internet group. Above all, the National Register of Archives has in recent months been made available on the internet (URL: http://public.hmc.gov.uk). All these developments suggest that in the near future historians will have as ready access to searchable catalogues of archives as they have to automated library catalogues.

New research techniques: automated handling of quantitative data

The provision of new research tools has, however, been accompanied by developments which seem to point the way towards more far-reaching changes in historical studies, and perhaps offer the hope of fulfilling David Bolter's prediction that computers will cause scholars to ask different questions and propose new types of solutions. The most imaginative historians have realized from an early stage that the computer has a potential beyond word processing and the searching of library catalogues. Some of the earliest predictions have become very familiar, such as Le Roy Ladurie's warning of 1968 that 'the historian of tomorrow will be a programmer or he will be nothing' (Le Roy Ladurie 1973, 1, p. 14) and Edward Shorter's 1971 vision of the historian leaving his book-lined study and confronting 'The great grey machines lined up behind the glass, with their spinning tape drives and chattering high speed printers' (Shorter 1971, 49). In 1986, a conference was held at Westfield College, University of London, which led to the establishment of an Association for History and Computing. The proceedings of the conference were edited by Peter Denley and Deian Hopkin, and give a good overview of this first wave of historical computing (Denley and Hopkin 1987).

The papers in this volume show that a wide range of historians from many different countries and professional backgrounds were already using computers to assist their research very successfully. Although there were important contributions on the use of textual, graphic, and other applications for historical research, it is very noticeable that there is a strong emphasis in this volume on the use of databases and applications for handling numerical data for the study of topics where quantitative precision was important. Computers were already proving very useful in many different fields of historical demography, ranging from late medieval Aberdeen (Booton 1987) to nineteenth-century Swedish communities (Stenflo and Sundin 1987). Computer analysis—on a shoestring—has underpinned the important work of the Cambridge Group on Population Studies (cf. Wrigley and Schofield 1981, one of the first works to show on a large scale how computer-aided analysis of data can underpin innovative historical research). The computer was also being used as a means of more effectively exploiting the information in different types of historical accounts, including household accounts (Anstey and Evans 1987), solicitors' accounts (Williams 1987), and modern business records (Harvey and Taylor 1987). In political history, computers offered the possibility of more elaborate analysis of voting patterns of various kinds (Rheubottom 1987; Cromwell 1987; Turner 1987; Griffiths 1987). A number of large-scale projects had already been established which continue to be leaders in the field, such as the Portbooks project at the University of Wolverhampton (Wakelin 1987; Wakelin 1988) and the Hull Domesday project (Ayton and Davis 1987; see also Palmer 1985).

The first History and Computing conference therefore already marked out a very clear area of interest for historical computing—the support and development of areas of research where quantitative data are of primary importance. This emphasis on the use of databases and spreadsheets for quantitative research has continued since 1986. The stress has been on using the computer to provide a better card index. This can be seen from the volumes of proceedings of subsequent History and Computing conferences, as well as in the Association's journal, *History and Computing*. These publications faithfully record most of the major projects and innovations in the field. (For details of the publication of the conferences of the AHC, see the Association's web server at the URL: http://grid.let.rug.nl.ahc/conf.html. Although the proceedings of the seventh congress were published under the eye-catching title *Storia & Multimedia,* the bulk of the papers were concerned with quantitative and database analysis of a traditional kind. For more information about *History and Computing*, see the URL: http://grid.let.rug.nl/ahc/welcome.html).

Historical computing has therefore, for many historians, become almost exclusively associated with the handling of quantitative data. Evan Mawdsley and Thomas Munck's introductory guide to computing for historians (Mawdsley and Munck 1993) is almost entirely concerned with the use of databases and spreadsheets for statistical and quantitative analysis. Although Daniel Greenstein's *Historian's Guide to Computing* (Greenstein 1994) is more wide-ranging, his initial justification for the use of computers by historians is nevertheless that historians constantly make quantitative judgements which could be more precisely expressed. Of course, the development of techniques for more speedy and effective handling of quantitative data is of great importance for many types of historical research, particularly economic and social history, and this type of work will remain an important thrust of historical computing for many years to come. Indeed, the use of databases and spreadsheets by historians is likely to become more widespread. One of the most striking features of the proceedings of the 1986 conference is the wide variety of different programs used and their great complexity. The papers often spend as much time describing the characteristics of their computer program as they do discussing the results of their research. With the spread of the personal computer and the appearance of Windows, database packages are becoming more flexible and easier to set up and maintain. With a standard commercial package like Microsoft Access, for example, even inexperienced users can set up quite elaborate databases quickly (although there is still a need to pay attention to the principles of good database design). There is, however, a great danger that, as a result of the stress on quantitative data, historical computing will be seen as a kind of professional ghetto, of interest only to demographers and the more heavy-duty economic and social history researchers. Historians not concerned with these areas will heave a sigh of relief and feel that they can continue much as before, but if they do this they will miss many exciting opportunities.

As Daniel Greenstein has noted (1994), one of the most common objections to the use of computers in historical studies is that the data in historical records are often varied and complex in their structure and function, and that trying to fit such information into the strait-jacket of a relational database does violence to the historical evidence. Again, this assumes falsely that computing is equated exclusively with databases. Moreover, it is less of a problem as more flexible database packages such as Access have appeared. Nevertheless, this issue is the starting point for perhaps the most important initiative in historical computing, the development of Κλειω (English translation KLEIO), a 'historical workstation'. Work on the development of Κλειω was begun by Manfred Thaller of the Max- Planck- Institut für Geschichte at Göttingen in 1978. As the program has expanded and developed, many others have worked with Thaller, but it still remains very much his creation (the development of Κλειω has been widely discussed and written about. For a starting point, see Thaller 1993a; Wollard and Denley 1993; Engelke *et al.* 1990; Smets 1990; Thaller 1990; Thaller 1991).

Κλειω has been described as the only database management system written by a historian for historians (Wollard and Denley 1993, p. xiii). If nothing else, Κλειω is remarkable for the fact that originally the command language was in Latin. It was first developed for a mainframe computer, but a PC version is now available, with documentation in German, French, and English. Κλειω performs all the functions which one would expect to find in a commercial database package, and also allows the user to perform functions which would normally require separate pieces of software, without leaving the program. With a normal database, it would be necessary to define the logical structure of the information to be input before keyboarding begins. In the case of historical records, this may require the information to be broken up in a way that reflects the preconceptions of the researcher and makes no allowance for the way in which an understanding of the structure and idiosyncrasies of the record normally only develops as a result of working closely with it. With Κλειω, this analysis is undertaken after the data have been entered. The source can be entered into the computer in its original form, so that, for example, the original form of place or personal names can be retained. The way in which the package is designed to meet the historian's particular needs is evident from its ability to cope with historical formulas for dates (such as the third Sunday after Pentecost) and the provision it makes for different types of calendar. Κλειω allows for fuzzy searching, so that searches will, for example, deal with situations where the surname of a particular person also indicates his occupation. The package is continuing to be developed and extended by Thaller and his team. It supports the mapping of historical data, and an image analysis system which allows the data in pictures to be interrogated in much the same way as textual data has recently been produced (Jaritz 1993; Thaller 1992; Thaller 1993b). The rich functionality of Κλειω comes at a heavy intellectual price. The program is formidably complex. Many historians will quail at having to master Thaller's three hundred and fifty page description of Κλειω and the four hundred page tutorial by Peter Denley and Matthew Wollard which accompanies the English version. The great complexity of Κλειω doubtless explains why it has not been more widely used.

New research techniques: automated handling of text

In reviewing the issues confronted by Κλειω, one is forcibly reminded that historical records, even where they deal with highly structured itemized information, are primarily textual in character. For example, even though the information in *Domesday Book* is heavily abbreviated, extremely formulaic and carefully organized, it is not a statistical table but a narrative description of a large number of different estates. It is as important in using *Domesday Book* to understand the way in which information was refined and condensed as the survey went from draft to draft as it is to understand how different versions of a chronicle relate to one another. *Domesday* is a text, not a database. Likewise, a criminal indictment of the medieval or early modern period will contain certain standard pieces of information such as the name of the defendant and the place and date of the offence, but may also include an account of the incident which, while highly formulaic, may include terms which are important for establishing the value of the indictment for historical evidence. And, of course, much historical evidence is totally narrative in character, such as chronicles, letters, or newspaper reports.

It is consequently surprising that historians have not shown as great an interest in methods of textual analysis as their colleagues in literary disciplines. As Marilyn Deegan has indicated in this volume, in literary studies, the most important computing work has been in the use of SGML to produce electronic editions which can be interrogated in many different ways, with a level of precision which would otherwise be unthinkable. The *Canterbury Tales* and *Piers Plowman* projects, for example, are producing large-scale electronic editions which will shed great light on the descent of these texts. Similar techniques could be used very effectively with, for example, medieval chronicles. The Text Encoding Initiative (TEI) includes historical records, and the volume edited by Daniel Greenstein (1991b), has shown how SGML can be used to produce machine-readable versions of historical texts which are sympathetic to the structure of the original documents. However, SGML has not so far generated the same enthusiasm among historians as literary scholars.

This perhaps reflects a feeling that the existing Document Type Definitions, largely developed by literary specialists, are not suitable for historical records. In particular, perhaps historians feel that existing examples of SGML-coded texts do not offer sufficiently structured forms of subject searching. This seems to be the reason why SGML was not adopted for the most important electronic edition to date of a set of historical sources, the Hartlib Papers CD-ROM produced by a team under the direction of Mark Greengrass and Michael Leslie at the University of Sheffield (on this project, see the URL http://www.shef. ac.uk/uni/projects/hpp/hartlib.html). This pioneering project demonstrates triumphantly the way in which electronic editions can offer users of historical sources enormous freedom in building up complex and novel subject searches as well as conventional person and place-name searches. The CD-ROM is an edition of the papers of the seventeenth-century philosopher and polymath, Samuel Hartlib. The documents were transcribed in a Word for MS-DOS format, and are searched using a free-text search package, Topic, which offers not only very quick searching but also allows thesauri of related words to be built up for subject searching. Images of the original documents are included, allowing the user to jump between the transcription and a picture of the original. The way in which the electronic edition allows the user to explore so readily the multi-faceted intellectual world and contacts of Hartlib gives a vivid and novel insight into the world outlook of the period. The choice of Topic rather than an SGML viewer was presumably inspired by the ease with which it makes such explorations possible, and suggests that historians may find proprietary packages of this kind more sympathetic than the SGML approach. Similarly, another electronic edition based at Sheffield, the Strafford Papers project, does not use SGML, but relies on a calendar of the documents held in Idealist, with links from the calendar entries to high resolution colour images of the original documents, which, it might perhaps be felt, obviate the need for transcriptions of the documents at all (personal information, Nigel Williamson, 1996).

The process of editing and publishing historical records is recognized as underpinning historical research, but there is nevertheless perhaps a feeling that the great days of historical editing are past. This is as much due to economic pressures as intellectual fashion, as I am sure the Treasurer of any county record society will agree, but perhaps electronic publication will lead to a renaissance of the editing of historical texts. Most edited texts will nowadays be prepared using a word processor. It is obviously potentially cheaper to issue this on disc rather than as a conventional volume. The edition need not even be on disc—if it is mounted on a World Wide Web server the costs of publication will be minimal, and there will be none of the problems associated with the distribution of discs in different formats. Moreover, electronic editions need not be regarded as a cheap substitute. The subject indexing of any edition is always very difficult and, once printed, can never keep up with new research trends. A searchable electronic edition is not constrained by these requirements.

Indeed, an electronic edition can avoid many of the problems associated with conventional editing. Lengthy texts, often in printed editions, have to be summarized to reduce printing costs. This need not be an issue with an electronic edition. Where different recensions of a work exist, the editor has had to choose the best one and relegate variant readings to footnotes. Electronic editions can, through the use of hyperlinks, more easily cope with parallel and multiple texts. Indeed, a printed edition of a medieval text is always an interpretation of it. The editor has expanded abbreviations and it can be difficult to transcribe personal and place names accurately. It was these difficulties that led to the adoption of record type for the first record editions in Britain. Record type was never satisfactory because it was difficult to create a font large enough to represent all the abbreviations in a manuscript satisfactorily. On a computer (or, at least, on a Macintosh), new fonts can be readily produced and extended. The *Canterbury Tales* project, for example, uses a specially designed font which represents all the abbreviations in the Hengwrt manuscript—a new record type, in other words. There is no reason why, say, a new edition of *Domesday Book* or a pipe roll could not use a special font of this kind (see further Prescott, forthcoming).

Conventional printed editions work best where material can be easily presented in a simple chronological or other structure. Where an edition is drawn from a number of different record series, a printed edition quickly becomes very cumbersome. In editions of yearbooks, the yearbook report of a particular lawsuit is usually followed by the plea roll record of the case. If file records were also included, the result would be extremely difficult to follow (cf. Hector 1978). To return to my examples of the records of the 1381 revolt, a particular incident may have generated a local indictment, a trial in King's Bench recorded on the plea roll, supporting documentation on the King's Bench files, and private litigation in both King's Bench and the Court of Common Pleas. In a conventional printed edition of these records, they might all be drawn together in a single entry or section, but this would make it difficult to follow patterns of litigation in different courts. On the other hand, if records were arranged in court or record class order, it might be difficult to trace all the references to a particular event, even with the aid of a good index. In an electronic edition, the material could be viewed in a variety of different configurations, achieving an edition whose intellectual structure more accurately mirrored the archival structure of the records.

The arguments in favour of the use of SGML are strong. Above all, SGML has the attraction that it is software-independent and the user of the edition does not need to own a particular piece of commercial software to search it. However, if TEI and SGML are to meet the historian's needs and are to reflect the character of historical sources, historians and archivists need to become more involved in the development of these standards. There are some signs that this is beginning to happen. An important new project in the USA, the Model Editions partnership, is working with those who have been responsible for the development of the TEI Guidelines to produce a subset of the TEI tailored for historical editions. These guidelines will be applied to a variety of editorial projects, including the Lincoln Legal papers and the Documentary History of the First Federal Congress. The project encompasses both image editions and 'live text' editions. The partnership hopes to produce its 'Markup Guidelines for Historical Editions' during 1996 (Chesnutt 1995; URL: http://mep.cla.sc.edu).

However, in some important areas, the use of SGML is never likely to be a practical proposition, simply because there will never be a keyboarded text. This applies, for example, with the conversion to machine-readable form of many existing editions of historical texts. The ability of the historian to abstract information from the great historical editions of the nineteenth and early twentieth centuries is circumscribed by the indexes of those editions. Given the limited and idiosyncratic subject indexing of, for example, the *Calendars of Patent and Close Rolls*, a keyword-searchable version of these would be extremely useful. It would be splendid to produce searchable texts of the *Calendar of London Letter Books*, a series notorious for its poor indexing. However, it is unlikely that anyone would ever be willing to fund the expensive task of keyboarding these lengthy texts. At the moment, optical character recognition (OCR) technology is still not adequate for the automatic conversion of texts such as these. The character recognition still generates many mistakes, and proofreading texts produced by OCR can be almost as time consuming as if they were keyboarded in the first place (Horik 1992; Nijmegen Institute 1993).

The Excalibur Technologies product, PixTex/EFS, was developed as an electronic filing system for military purposes, but was used by De Montfort University for its ELINOR (Electronic Library INformation ONline Retrieval) project, in order to provide students with networked access to textbooks (URL: http://portico.bl.uk/access/excalibur.html). This package still relies on OCR, but the PixTex search engine uses adaptive pattern recognition technology. The search engine, based on the neural network concept, attempts to mimic the way in which the brain identifies and stores data. In searching text produced by OCR, the search engine does not look for 'rex' but for anything that looks like 'rex'. Consequently, the search will not be affected by poor OCR, and all the entries containing 'rex' will be found, even those with mistakes in the OCR. Moreover, the user, having completed a search, can easily summon up images of the original work, so that he or she can work with the original book rather than the faulty OCR.

PixTex/EFS (or Excalibur as it is commonly called) can therefore be used to produce machine-readable versions of texts which can be scanned to a high degree of accuracy without any keyboarding or proofreading. In experiments in the British Library, a searchable version of a volume of the *Calendar of London Letter Books* was produced in a day, and W. de Grey Birch's largely unindexed six volume *Catalogue of Seals in the British Museum* was similarly converted in less than a month. The evident potential of this software has led to the establishment of a joint project between the British Library and the University of Sheffield to use Excalibur to convert a corpus of rare historical reference works, while a consortium led by the University of Oxford has been funded by the Electronic Libraries (eLib) Programme to use Excalibur to develop an Internet Library of Early Journals, making available in searchable form on the Internet a number of nineteenth-century journals, such as *The Gentleman's Magazine* (URL: http://ukoln.bath.ac.uk/elib). Similar approaches have been used elsewhere to convert other caches of material very cost-effectively. Professor Ronald Zweig at the University of Tel Aviv has helped to develop a program which uses optical character recognition to search images of the *Jerusalem Post,* which was demonstrated at the British Academy in 1994 and the University of Sheffield in 1995. Experiments have been undertaken to assess the viability of using this program to convert the *Victoria County History.*

New research techniques: images and multimedia

Both Excalibur and Professor Zweig's work perhaps indicate the beginnings of a process whereby the historian will start to work primarily with images rather than edited text. Clearly the increased availability of digital images in the next few years will have considerable implications for the editing of historical sources. Peter Robinson has described earlier in this volume the issues associated with digitization of primary source material. The potential benefits for historians of imaging technology of this kind are considerable. Potentially a digital camera can provide colour images of material more cheaply than conventional colour photography. It is reasonable to expect that historians will not have to rely so much on microfilm and be able to use instead high resolution colour images which can be easily magnified and compared. The extent to which this can be realized will depend almost entirely on the economics of library and record office reprographic services, but the first signs are hopeful. Moreover, digital cameras can be used to capture images under special lighting conditions more easily. Professor Kevin Kiernan has shown, for example, in his Electronic *Beowulf* project that a digital camera can be used to record readings under fibre optic light of parts of the manuscript obscured by nineteenth-century conservation work, in a way that could potentially be applied to all the burnt manuscripts in the Cotton collection (Kiernan 1991; Kiernan 1994a; Kiernan 1994b; Kiernan 1995; URL: http://www.ky.edu/~Kiernan/BL/kportico.html). Perhaps similar technology, linked to powerful image-processing programs, will eventually permit the recovery of readings damaged by the application of gallic acid.

For historians, the project which has given perhaps the most interesting indication of the possibilities of imaging technology is the *Archivo General de Indias* project, which is making available on CD-ROM images of the archives of the early colonization of the Americas (González 1992a; González 1992b). Although the images are not at very high resolution, the project has nevertheless shown how image processing can be used very successfully to assist in recovering lost and damaged readings. Confronted with a project such as this, it is natural to wonder why editions should be necessary at all. Would it be more sensible in future simply to produce archives of images? At the present stage of technology, a collection of digitized editions of, say, the medieval registers of the Archbishops of Canterbury would not be very different as a research tool to the existing microfilm edition, although the quality would be better, the images could be manipulated and the digital edition might potentially be more easily obtainable. This is because digitized images are not searchable. In order to search the place names in the registers, a keyboarded text would still be needed. It is possible that one day images will be searchable, and the keyboarded text will not be needed as an intermediary. Kevin Kiernan has proposed the development by computer scientists in collaboration with humanities scholars of a means whereby the digital information in images of text could be searched in the same way as text, which would make a searchable archive of images a viable possibility. He has established a consortium called GRENDL to pursue this aim (Kiernan, forthcoming). Of course, many historical texts are in extremely difficult scripts, and it may still be necessary for editors to provide a transcription to assist in reading, but this would be more in the nature of a guide for the reader than an old-fashioned definitive edition. In the meantime, the ability to link text to image, as demonstrated in, say, the Hartlib Papers project, is still very exciting. It would be interesting, for example, to produce a version of the *Calendar of Patent Rolls* on CD-ROM in which one could move from the printed summaries to an image of the original entry, thereby avoiding the risks inherent in excessive reliance by researchers on calendar entries.

Historians, in thinking of images, naturally tend to give priority to pictures of historical records of the conventional kind. Images of all kinds are, however, potentially of value to historians—pictures of buildings, artefacts, people, costume, landscapes, in fact any kind of picture imaginable, can all be of great historical value. Moreover, historians are, or should be, interested in any kind of information from the past, in whatever medium: words, sound, pictures, and video. Within the conventional historical monograph, economic considerations make it difficult to incorporate visual evidence on any scale, while the limitations of the printed format make it difficult to integrate effectively pictures into a historical argument. Sound and video are almost impossible to deal with in the constraints of a traditional monograph. This makes the advent of multimedia of particular interest to historians, since it enables them readily to draw together and juxtapose historical evidence in any medium. Imagine a multimedia study of Kennedy's assassination: coverage in different news media (newspapers, radio, television) could be compared and cross-referenced; film clips of the assassination could be juxtaposed and analysed on screen; pictures, biography, sound clips, and personal records of all the major protagonists could be provided; the events of the day could be reviewed in an interactive map of Dallas; conspiracy theories could be tested interactively against the available evidence.

Already multimedia packages of this kind are being produced. At the University of Southampton, for example, a multimedia project on The First Yugoslav Civil War 1941-1945 has been created using the Microcosm system developed there and used successfully in teaching (Colson *et al.* 1994). It might seem that packages of this kind will always be useful primarily for teaching purposes rather than the dissemination of research. It is sometimes suggested that, just as television has never established itself as a serious medium for scholarly research, so multimedia will always be seen primarily as a purveyor of info-tainment. The difference between television and multimedia is that multimedia is not limited to a single linear narrative and allows statements to be justified and documented as fully as in a conventional monograph. Indeed, multimedia allows the user more direct access to primary source material than would be possible in a printed book.

The Valley of the Shadow: a new history?

Some idea of the way in which the ability to juxtapose different media can change the nature of historical discourse is apparent from Edward Ayer's project at the University of Virginia, The Valley of the Shadow: Living the Civil War in Virginia and Pennsylvania (URL: http://jefferson.village.virginia.edu/vshadow2.html). This is a comparative study of the impact of the American Civil War on two communities separated by a few hundred miles and the Mason-Dixon line —Chambersburg, Pennsylvania and Staunton, Virginia. Ayers, the author of *The New Promise of the New South* and other books on Southern history, initially planned this project as a traditional study, but decided to make it an electronic study after realizing the possibilities that hypermedia offered for local studies. The project explores the links and contrasts between the two communities in a variety of ways. The relationship of the two communities to political events at a national level is analysed. There is also a thematic analysis, discussing such issues as the structure of the communities, daily life, family life, military life, religion, race, economics, and so on. At every point, the user can connect through hyperlinks to the sources on which the study rests. For example, the political narrative links to images and searchable transcripts of newspaper reports and diaries. The section on military life provides access to searchable rosters for Virginia and Pennsylvania. Pictures of the people mentioned are provided wherever possible, and there are even links to sound files with contemporary military music.

Although Ayers' vision of a way in which local studies can provide a different perspective on the American civil war dominates the project, as much through the selection of material included in the archive as anything else, the way in which this message is conveyed to the user is very different from a conventional historical work. The user has every opportunity to explore the source materials for himself. As the introduction to the project notes:

> We have digitized and provided html tagging for a large number of sources in these communities. There is far more in the newspapers, censuses, military records, and the rest than we can contain in one narrative, far more connections than we could possibly hardwire in...By using the sources and contexts we provide here, a reader will be able to triangulate thousands of biographies, fleshing out the sto-

ries of people presented in the narrative or uncovering
people the narrative ignores together.

This is a different vision of the role of the historian from the one we are
accustomed to. The nature of the printed monograph means inherently
that historians are forced to act as some kind of recording angel, while
their readers act as passive spectators. In Ayers' study, the user is
encouraged to take the building blocks provided by Ayers in order to
continue and develop the research. Ayers urges his users to construct their
own narratives and come up with ideas and interpretations that eluded
his team. The Valley of the Shadow represents a completely new type of
history in many different ways—in the way in which hyperlinks give a
different shape to the historical narrative, in the way in which multimedia
components can produce a much richer and more varied historical
language, and in the way in which the user of the historical work can
actively develop, extend and perhaps even challenge the work of the
historian.

The impact of networks

The Valley of The Shadow is published on the World Wide Web, and
among the many other possibilities it demonstrates is the potential of the
Internet as a medium for a new kind of scholarly publication. The hype
surrounding the Internet conceals the fact that the reaction of humanities
scholars to it has been mixed. A number of scholars have seized on the
possibilities of the Internet with great enthusiasm, while others have been
more doubtful, complaining about the lack of useful material on the
network and the difficulty of locating information. Complaints such as
these were evident at a workshop on 'Historians and the Internet'
organized by the Institute of Historical Research in November 1995,
which was intended to provide historians with a platform to say what
they would like to see on the network. A common theme of all the
speakers was that it is far too difficult to find information on the network
and, at the moment, the network does not contain enough historical
sources or reference tools of research value.

Discussion of the value of the Internet often lacks precision. Those
who dismiss the Internet as worthless hype should remember that the
Internet represents the networking infrastructure which makes e-mail
and remote access to library catalogues possible. These functions are
useful enough in themselves to justify any claim that the Internet is now

an indispensable tool for scholars. In referring to the value or otherwise of material on the Internet, critics are in fact using a shorthand for the transfer of textual, image, and other files, undertaken at first through ftp and gopher, but now increasingly available in an integrated format through the World Wide Web. No one could deny that it is very difficult to find information on the World Wide Web. However, this situation is improving in a number of different ways. An increasing number of search engines are available, such as the Yahoo subject index or Webcrawler. Web browsers such as Netscape have the ability to build up lists of bookmarks which enable users to develop their own reference lists of useful material. As users become more familiar with Hypertext Markup Language (HTML), they are increasingly creating their own home pages which allow them to shape access in the way that suits them best. The home page of a distinguished academic would be a very useful tool, giving access to material that he or she thinks of value. A number of subject gateways, which provide structured menu access to all the worthwhile sources in the field, are being developed. The Institute of Historical Research's IHR-Info was one of the earliest such ventures, and is now being funded by eLib, the Electronic Libraries Programme funded by the UK Higher Education Funding Councils, as the main history subject gateway in Britain (URL:http://ihr.sas.ac.uk:8080; Segell, 1995). The University of Kansas history server provides a comprehensive set of links to sites with historical material (URL: http://kuhttp.cc.ukans. edu/history/hnsource_main. html).

Even so, many new users feel that the information available on, say, IHR-Info, is disappointing. This reflects a very passive view of the network. The Internet is superior to commercial services such as Compuserve or America Online because it is easier to mount material on the Internet yourself and make it generally available. If historians feel that there are not enough good editions of texts available on the Internet, there is generally nothing to prevent them mounting them there themselves. Now that HTML can be automatically added to word processed documents by packages such as Microsoft's Internet Assistant (available at the Microsoft ftp site: ftp.microsoft.com), the preparation of documents suitable for the World Wide Web only requires a few clicks of the mouse. Editions prepared in word processed form can be mounted for network distribution almost instantly, with none of the burdens associated with network distribution and with considerable additional benefits, for example the possibility of searching the text. Moreover, as The Valley of the Shadow shows, a work published on the World Wide Web can be much richer in content than a conventional volume—pictures, searchable databases, sound, and video can all be added to the words. Given that authors in the humanities rarely gain much financial benefit from publication, it is surprising that they have not yet explored these possibilities very much. Pre-prints, for example, are now ubiquitous in scientific publication. By simply distributing copies of their latest articles through e-mail, authors are able to circumvent the delays inherent in publication in conventional journals. Dissemination of current scientific research is now almost exclusively in this form, while hard-copy publications are regarded as a long-term archive. Given that delays in publication are even greater in the humanities, it might have been expected that humanities scholars would have established a similar system, but this has not occurred yet.

Digital data: the disappearing historical source

The mention of sound and video is a reminder that, as time passes, the historical record will increasingly come to include a greater variety of media. Sound and film are now well-established categories of historical source, with their own archives and professional infrastructure. The computer is not only increasingly a means of helping historians in their work, but is in itself a means by which historical records are generated. Increasingly, a large number of the records with which the historian deals will be in machine-readable form. That backbone of English local history, the rate book, ceased to exist in the 1970s, and that information is available—insofar as it has been retained—in machine-readable form. Likewise, the records of the successors to the local rate, the community charge and the council tax, are also held as computer data. Much ordnance survey data will soon only be available in digital form. In future, we shall be interested not just in a minister's papers but also in his or her e-mail. The preservation of this electronic data presents enormous problems, to which archivists are beginning to awake, but in which historians themselves should take a greater interest. Unless the question of preserving these data is addressed, the records of the poll taxes of the fourteenth century may perhaps in the future be more easily accessible than information about their twentieth-century successor. The way in which the historian uses and incorporates this material will inevitably affect profoundly the nature of research. The use of computers in contemporary society is transforming the materials with which historians work. When a historian's sources are finally completely digital, then historical research must be changed utterly (Hedstrom 1991; Ross and Higgs 1993; Acland 1994; Ross 1996).

Conclusion: Pirenne's advice

The issues posed by the new technologies for the study of history are perhaps the most complex and wide-ranging of all humanities disciplines. This reflects the eclectic nature of historical studies. Since any information about the past is of interest to the historian, in principle virtually any type of computer application is likely to be of interest to the historian—geographic information systems (GIS) are relevant to any regional study; it would be foolish for economic historians to ignore economic modelling techniques; three-dimensional imaging could be useful to anyone dealing with any kind of artefact; computer-aided design (CAD) packages could assist researchers investigating buildings and topography (Stenvert 1991); virtual reality techniques are potentially widely applicable. The extent to which these possibilities are taken up by historians will depend to some extent on which ways they are used for teaching, and the TLTP programme may potentially pay a very important part in opening up the eyes of historians to the immense possibilities presented by computers (on educational applications, see the web site of the CTI Centre for History, Archaeology, and Art History at the University of Glasgow. URL: http://www.arts.gla.ac.uk/www/ctich/homepage.html). The culture shock which the use of new technologies will sooner or later create within history will give added impetus to the process begun by Marc Bloch and Lucien Febvre in the earlier part of this century of turning history into a liberal and open-minded study which looks inquisitively into all aspects of the world around it. Bloch's injunction that the historian should follow the example of Henri Pirenne and, above all, keep in touch with the present day is more important now than ever before (Bloch 1954, 36).

Acknowledgement

I am grateful to Professor Kevin S. Kiernan for his comments on an earlier draft of this paper.

References and bibliography

Acland, G. (ed.), 'Electronic record keeping: issues and perspectives', special issue of *Archives and Manuscripts*, Journal of the Australian Society of Archivists, 22.1 (1994).

Adman, P., 'Computers and history', in Rahtz, S. (ed.), *Information technology in the humanities: tools, techniques and applications* (Chichester: Ellis Horwood, 1987), 92-103.

Anderson, S., 'The future of the present—the ESRC Data Archive as a resource centre for the future', *History and Computing*, 4 (1992), 191-196.

Anstey, P., and Evans, N., 'Using a computer to analyse late sixteenth-century household accounts', in Denley, P., and Hopkin, D. (eds.), *History and computing* (Manchester: Manchester University Press, 1987), 168-176.

Ayton, A., and Davis, V., 'The Hull Domesday Project', in Denley, P., and Hopkin, D. (eds.), *History and computing* (Manchester: Manchester University Press, 1987), 21-28.

Beckett, J., 'The computer and the local historian', *Archives*, 19 (1990), 192-198.

Bell, L., 1971, 'Controlled vocabulary subject indexing of archives', *Journal of the Society of Archivists*, 4 (1970-1973), 285-289.

Bell, L., 1975, 'An archivists' cooperative?', *Journal of the Society of Archivists*, 5 (1974-1977), 149-157.

Bell, L., Simmons, P., and Roper, M., 1972, 'PROSPEC: a computer application for the Public Record Office', *Journal of the Society of Archivists*, 4 (1970-1973), 423-427.

Best, H., Mochmann, E., and Thaller, M., *Computers in the humanities and the social sciences. Achievements of the 1980s. Prospects for the 1990s.* (Munich: Saur, 1991).

Bloch, M., *The historian's craft* (Manchester: Manchester University Press, 1954).

Bocchi, F., and Denley, P. (eds.), *Storia & Multimedia* (Bologna: Grafis Edizione, 1994).

Bolter, J., *Turing's man* (London: Duckworth, 1984). Page references are to the paperback edition, Penguin Books, 1986.

Booton, H., 'The use of the computer in the study of the economic and social structure of late medieval Aberdeen', in Denley, P., and Hopkin, D. (eds.), *History and computing* (Manchester: Manchester University Press, 1987), 28-32.

British Library, *British Library manuscript collections: automated cataloguing, a manual* (London: British Library, 1989).

British Library, *UK MARC manual*, 3rd ed. (Boston Spa: British Library, 1990).

Burnard, L., and Short, H., *An Arts and Humanities Data Service. Report of a feasibility study commissioned by the Information Systems Sub-Committee of the Joint Information Systems Committee of the Higher Education Funding Councils* (Oxford:

Office for Humanities Communication, 1994). Also available at the URL: http://info.ox.ac.uk/~archive /AHDS/report

Burnett, T., 'Theory and practice in archive classification at the British Library', *Journal of the Society of Archivists*, 11 (1990), 11-20.

Chesnutt, D., 'The Model Editions partnership', *D-Lib Magazine* (November 1995): http://www.dlib.org/dlib/november95/chesnutt.html.

Cobb, R., 'Historians in white coats', *Times Literary Supplement* (3 Dec. 1971).

Colson, J., Colson, R., Davis, H., and Hall, W., 'Questioning "authority". The challenge of multi-media', in Bocchi, F., and Denley, P. (eds.), *Storia & Multimedia* (Bologna: Grafis Edizione, 1994).

Cook, M., 'The international description standards: an interim report', *Journal of the Society of Archivists*, 16 (1995), 15-25.

Cook, M., and Procter, M., *A manual of archive description*, 2nd ed. (Aldershot: Gower Press, 1988).

Cromwell, V., 'House of Commons voting, 1861-1926: a computer-eye view', in Denley, P., and Hopkin, D. (eds.), *History and computing* (Manchester: Manchester University Press, 1987), 132-135.

Denley, P., 'The computer revolution and redefining the humanities', in Miall, D. (ed.), *Humanities and the computer. New directions* (Oxford: Clarendon Press, 1990), 13-25.

Denley, P., 'Computing and postgraduate training in Britain: a discussion paper', *History and computing* (1990), 135-138.

Denley, P., 'The politics of the electronic text: a historian's view', in Chernaik, W., Davis, C., and Deegan, M., *The politics of the electronic text*, (Oxford: Office for Humanities Communication Publications, 3, 1993), 77-79.

Denley, P., and Hopkin, D. (eds.), *History and computing* (Manchester: Manchester University Press, 1987).

Denley, P., Fogelfik, S., and Harvey, C. (eds.) *History and computing II* (Manchester: Manchester University Press, 1989).

Dollar, C., *Archival theory and information technologies: the impact of information technologies on archival practice and methods* (Macerata: University of Macerata, 1992).

Doorn, P., Kluts, C., and Leenarts, E., *Data, computers and the past: proceedings of the conference Archiving and Disseminating Historical Machine Readable Data (Leiden April 27-28 1990)*, Special number of Cahier VGI, 5 (Hilversum, 1992).

Engelke, T., Nemitz, J., and Trenkler, C. (eds.), *Historische Forschung mit Kλειω* (St Katherinen: Halbgraue Reihe zur historischen Fachinformatik, A8, 1990).

Fikfak, J., and Jaritz, G., *Image processing in history: towards open systems* (St Katherinen: Halbgraue Reihe zur historischen Fachinformatik, A16, 1993).

Fitzgerald, S., 'Archives cataloguing on computer at the Royal Botanic Gardens, Kew: using MARC, international standards and Unicorn', *Journal of the Society of Archivists*, 16 (1995), 179-192.

Genet, J.P., 'L'historien et l'ordinateur', *Historiens et geographes*, 270 (1978), 125-142.

Genet, J.P. (ed.), *Standardisation et échange des bases de données historiques* (Paris: CNRS, 1987).

Genet, J.P., and Zampolli, A. (eds.), *Computers and the humanities* (Aldershot: Dartmouth Press, 1992).

González, P., 'Computerisation project for the "Archivo General de Indias"', *Cahier Vereniging voor Gescheidenis en Informatica*, 5 (1992a), 52-67.

González, P., 'The digital processing of images in archives and libraries. large scale international projects', in Thaller, M. (ed.), *Images and manuscripts in historical computing*, (St Katherinen: Halbgraue Reihe zur historischen Fachinformatik, A14, 1992b), 97-121.

Gorman, M., and Winkler, P. (eds.), *Anglo-American Cataloguing Rules*, 2nd ed. (London: Library Association, 1988).

Graves, E., *A bibliography of English history to 1485* (Oxford: Clarendon Press, 1975).

Greenstein, D.I., 'A source-orientated approach to history and computing: the relational database', *Historical Social Research*, 14 (1989), 9-16.

Greenstein, D.I., 'A matter of method', *History and Computing*, 3 (1991a), 210-215.

Greenstein, D.I., (ed.), *Modelling historical data: towards a standard for encoding and exchanging machine-readable texts* (St. Katherinen: Halbgraue Reihe zur historischen Fachinformatik, A11, 1991b).

Greenstein, D.I., *A historian's guide to computing* (Oxford: Clarendon Press, 1994).

Griffiths, E., 'A poll book analysis package for eighteenth century elections', in Denley, P., and Hopkin, D. (eds.), *History and computing*, (Manchester: Manchester University Press, 1987), 274-278.

Harvey, C., and Taylor, P., 'Computer modelling and analysis of the individual and aggregate capital, stocks, cash flows and performance of British mining companies in Spain, 1851-1913', in Denley, P., and Hopkin, D. (eds.), *History and computing*, (Manchester: Manchester University Press, 1987), 115-121.

Hector, L., 'Reports, writs and records in the common bench in the reign of Richard II', in Hunnisett, R., and Post, J. (eds.), *Medieval legal records edited in memory of C. A. F. Meekings*, (London: HMSO, 1978), 267-288.

Hedstrom, M., 'Understanding electronic incunabula: a framework for research on electronic records', *American Archivist*, 54 (1991), 334-354.

Herlihy, D., 'Quantification in the 1980s: numerical and formal analysis in European history', *Journal of Interdisciplinary History*, 12 (1981), 115-135.

History and Computing. The Journal of the Association for History and Computing, 1987-

Hopkin, D., 'The politics of historical computing', *History and Computing*, 1 (1989), 42-49.

Hopkin, D., 'The future of the past', in Bocchi, F. and Denley, P. (eds.), *Storia & Multimedia* (Bologna: Grafis Edizione, 1994), 759-764.

Hopkin, D., and Denley, P., 'History, historians and the new technologies', in Katzen, M. (ed.) *Scholarship and technology in the humanities: proceedings of a conference held at Elvetham Hall, Hampshire, 9–12 May, 1990* (London: Bowker Saur, 1991), 63-76.

Horik, R. van, 'Optical character recognition and historical documents: some programs reviewed', *History and Computing*, 4 (1992), 211-220.

Jarausch, K., Arminger, G., and Thaller, M., *Quantitative Methoden in der Geschichtswissenschaft: eine Einführung in die Forschung, Datenverarbeitung und Statistik* (Darmstadt: Wissenschaftliche Buchgesellschaft, 1985).

Jarausch, K., and Hardy, K., *Quantitative methods: a guide to research, data and statistics* (London: University of North Carolina Press, 1991).

Jaritz, G., *Images. A primer of computer-supported analysis with Κλειω IAS* (St Katherinen: Halbgraue Reihe zur historischen Fachinformatik, A22, 1993).

Kenny, A., 'Increased deposits on the next century', *The Times Higher Multimedia section*, (March 8 1996), vii.

Kiernan, K., 'Digital image processing and the Beowulf manuscript', *Literary and Linguistic Computing*, 6.1 (1991), 20-27.

Kiernan, K., 'Old manuscripts/new technologies', in Richards, M. (ed.), *Anglo-Saxon manuscripts: basic readings* (New York: Garland Press, 1994a).

Kiernan, K., 'Digital preservation, restoration, and the dissemination of medieval manuscripts', in Okerson, A., and Mogge, D. (eds.), *Scholarly publishing on the electronic networks: gateways, gatekeepers, and roles in the information omniverse* (Washington, DC: Association of Research Libraries, 1994b) 37–43.

Kiernan, K., 'The Electronic Beowulf', *Computers in Libraries* (February 1995), 14–15.

Kiernan, K. *Reconnecting the science and the humanities through digital libraries.* Proceedings of a Symposium at the University of Kentucky, October 1995. (Forthcoming).

Kluckert, E., and Donzelli-Kluckert, D., *Computer und geisteswissenschaftliche Forschung alltag: Themen, Motive, Symbole* (Darmstadt: Wissenschaftliche Buchgesellschaft, 1990).

Kropa, I. (ed.), *The art of communication. Proceedings of the 8th International Conference of the Association for History and Computing* (Graz: Akademische Druck-und Verlagsanstalt, 1995).

Ladurie, E. Le Roy, *Le territoire de l'historien* (Paris: Editions Gallimard, 1973).

Marker, H., and Paghli, K. (eds.), *Yesterday: proceedings from the 6th International Congress of the Association for History and Computing* (Odense: Odense University Press, 1994).

Mathiesen, R., 'Cyrillic and Glagolitic printing and the Eisenstein Thesis', *Solanus*, New Series 6 (1992), 3-26.

Mawdsley, E., and Munck, T., *Computing for historians: an introductory guide* (Manchester: Manchester University Press, 1993).

Mawdsley, E., Morgan, N., Richmond, L., and Trainor, R. (eds.), *Historians and computing III: historians, computer and data. Applications in research and teaching* (Manchester: Manchester University Press, 1990).

Michelson, A., and Rothenberg, J., 'Scholarly communication and information technology: exploring the impact of changes in the research process on archives', *American Archivist*, 55 (1992), 236-315.

Nijmegen Institute, 1993: *Optical character recognition in the historical discipline: proceedings of an international workshop organised by the Netherlands Historical Data Archive, Nijmegen Institute for Cognition and Information* (St Katherinen: Halbgraue Reihe zur historischen Fachinformatik, A18, 1993).

Oldervall, J. (ed.), *Eden or Babylon? On future software for highly structured historical sources* (St Katherinen: Halbgraue Reihe zur historischen Fachinformatik, A13, 1992).

L'ordinateur et L'historien, IVe Congrès History and Computing (Bordeaux: Maison des Pays Iberiques, 1990).

Palmer, J., 'Domesday Book and the computer', in Sawyer, P. (ed.), *Domesday Book*, (London: Edward Arnold, 1985), 164-174.

Phillips, J., *Computing parliamentary history: George III to Victoria* (Edinburgh: Edinburgh University Press, 1994).

Prescott, A., *The judicial records of the Rising of 1381* (Unpublished Ph.D. thesis, University of London, 1984).

Prescott, A., 'The future of record publication' (Forthcoming).

Reiff, J., *Structuring the past: the use of computers in history* (Washington, DC: American Historical Association, 1991).

Rheubottom, D., 'Computers and the political structure of a fifteenth century city-state (Ragusa)', in Denley, P., and Hopkin, D. (eds.), *History and computing*, (Manchester: Manchester University Press, 1987), 126-131.

Ross, S., 'Software engineering considerations for historians', *History and Computing*, 3 (1991), 141–150.

Ross, S., 'Preserving and maintaining electronic resources in the visual arts for the next century?', *Information Services and Use* 15 (1995a), 373-384.

Ross, S., 'Intelligent graphical user interfaces: opportunities for the interface between the historian and the machine', in Kropa, I., Teichenbacher, P., and Jaritz, G. (eds.), *The art of communication. Proceedings of the 8th International Conference of the*

Association for History and Computing (Graz: Akademische Druck-und Verlagsanstalt, 1995b).

Ross, S., 'Opportunities in electronic information', in Brivati, B., Seldon, A., and Buxton, J. (eds.), *Contemporary history: a handbook* (Manchester: Manchester University Press, 1996).

Ross, S., and Higgs, E., *Electronic information resources and historians: European perspectives* (St Katherinen: Halbgraue Reihe zur historischen Fachinformatik, A20, 1993; and as British Library R&D report 6122).

Ross, S., and Newcombe, D., 'The digitization of *Foxe's Book of Martyrs'* (Forthcoming in 1996).

Schurer, K., and Anderson, S.J., *A feasibility study for the establishment of a UK historical data archive: a final report to the British Academy* (London: British Academy, 1991).

Schurer, K., and Anderson, S.J., *A guide to historical datafiles in machine-readable form* (London: Association for History and Computing, 1992).

Schurer, K., and Diedriks, H., *The use of occupations in historical analysis* (St Katherinen: Halbgraue Reihe zur historischen Fachinformatik, A19, 1993).

Segell, G., *A guide to IHR-Info* (London: Institute of Historical Research, 1995).

Shorter, E., *The historian and the computer* (Englewood Cliffs: Prentice-Hall, 1971).

Smets, J., *Créer une base de données historiques avec* Κλειω (St Katherinen: Halbgraue Reihe zur historischen Fachinformatik, A7, 1990).

Smets, J., *Histoire et informatique* (Montpellier: Josef Smets, 1992).

Spaeth, D., *A guide to software for historians* (Glasgow: CTI Centre for History, 1991).

Spaeth, D., Denley, P., Davis, V., and Trainor, R. (eds.), *Towards an international curriculum for history and computing* (St Katherinen: Halbgraue Reihe zur historischen Fachinformatik, A12, 1992).

Stenflo, G., and Sundin, J., 'Using a large historical database: an example from the demographic database in Umeå', in Denley, P., and Hopkin, D. (eds.), *History and computing*, (Manchester: Manchester University Press, 1987), 58-62.

Stenvert, R., *Constructing the past: computer-assisted architectural history and research* (Utrecht: privately published, 1991).

Thaller, M., *Einführung in die Datenverarbeitung für Historiker* (Cologne/Vienna, 1982).

Thaller, M., 'Can we afford to use the computer: can we afford not to use it?' in Millet, H. (ed.) *Informatique et prosopographie: actes du table ronde du CNRS* (Paris: editions du CNRS, 1985), 339-352.

Thaller, M., *Datenbanken und Datenverwaltungssysteme als Werkzeuge historischer Forschung* (St Katherinen: Scripta Mercaturae, 1986).

Thaller, M., 'The daily life of the Middle Ages. Editions of sources and data processing', *Medium Aevum Quotidianum*, 10 (1987), 6-29.

Thaller, M., 'The need for a theory of historical computing', in Denley, P., Fogelfik, S., and Harvey, C., (eds.) *History and computing* II (Manchester: Manchester University Press, 1989), 2-11.

Thaller, M., 'Databases and expert systems as complementary tools for historical research', *Tijdschrift voor Gescheidens*, 103 (1990), 233-247.

Thaller, M., 'The Historical Workstation Project', *Computing and the Humanities*, 25 (1991), 149-162.

Thaller, M., (ed.), *Images and manuscripts in historical computing*, (St Katherinen: Halbgraue Reihe zur historischen Fachinformatik, A14, 1992).

Thaller, M., Κλειω: *a database system* (St Katherinen: Halbgraue Reihe zur historischen Fachinformatik, B11, 1993a).

Thaller, M., 'The archive on top of your desk? On self-documenting image files' in Fikfak, J., and Jaritz, G. (eds.), *Image processing in history: towards open systems*, (St Katherinen: Halbgraue Reihe zur historischen Fachinformatik, A16, 1993b), 21-44.

Thaller, M., 'Historical information science: is there such a thing? New comments on an old idea', in Orlandi, T. (ed.), *Discipline umanistiche e informatica. Il problema dell'integrazione* (Rome: Accademia Nazionale dei Lincei, 1993c) 51–86.

Thaller, M., 'What is "source oriented data processing"?; what is a "historical information science", in Borodkin, L., and Levermann, W., *Istoriia I comp'iuter. Novye informatsionnye teknologii v istoricheskikh issledovanii akh I obrazovanii* (St Katherinen: Halbgraue Reihe zur historischen Fachinformatik, A15, 1993d), 5–18 (in Russian).

Turner, J., 'The Labour vote and the franchise after 1918: an investigation of the English evidence', in Denley, P., and Hopkin, D. (eds.), *History and computing*, (Manchester: Manchester University Press, 1987), 136-146.

Wakelin, P., 'Comprehensive computerisation of a very large documentary source: the Portbooks Project at Wolverhampton Polytechnic', in Denley, P., and Hopkin, D. (eds.), *History and computing*, (Manchester: Manchester University Press, 1987), 109-115.

Wakelin, P., The Exeter Port Customs project', *History and Computing Today* (January 1988), 109-115.

Walford, J., Gillett, H., and Post, J., 'Introducing computers to the Record Office: theory and practice', *Journal of the Society of Archivists*, 9 (1988), 21-29.

Werner, K.F., *Medieval history and computers* (Munich, 1991).

Williams, R., 'Historical archiving with dBASE: a solicitor's accounts 1716-44', in Denley, P., and Hopkin, D. (eds.), *History and computing* (Manchester: Manchester University Press, 1987), 105-108.

Wollard, M., and Denley, P., *Source-orientated data processing for historians* (St Katherinen: Halbgraue Reihe zur historischen Fachinformatik, A23, 1993).

Wrigley, E. (ed.), *Identifying people in the past* (London: Edward Arnold, 1973).

Wrigley, E., and Schofield, R., *The population history of England 1541-1871* (London, Edward Arnold, 1981).

Further information

A comprehensive searchable bibliography on history and computing is available at the Association for History and Computing website: http://grid.let.rug.nl/ahc/biblio2.html

The simplest way of identifying electronic resources and issues relevant to the study of history is to use one of the Internet subject gateways. In Britain, the most useful are IHR-INFO (http://ihr.sas.ac.uk:8080) and the web page of the CTI Centre at Glasgow (http://www.arts.gla.ac.uk/www/ctich/homepage. html).

The main international server is at the University of Kansas: http://kuhttp.cc.ukans.edu/history/hnsource_main.html

History of Art: A New Image?

W.H.T. Vaughan

Introduction: the approach to the image

Current developments in computing offer the most exciting potential that historians of art have encountered for more than a century and a half. Nothing like it has occurred since the invention of photography. There is a real possibility that new technology will revolutionize our means of perceiving and analysing visual culture in a historical context. However this possibility is still not quite within our grasp. It is still up to historians of art as a community to determine how and in what ways they will take on the challenge that is being presented to them. Mostly the issues that face the application of the new information technology to the history of art are the same as those that face other historical studies. In broad terms, therefore, what one is looking at is a similar set of issues to those which face the historian.

The one striking difference is the approach to the image. Historians use images, of course, as part of the broad range of material employed to reconstruct and interpret the past. But the historian of art is concerned with objects and visual culture on a more primal level. They are, so to speak, the text of the subject. History is used to explain and illuminate them, rather than the other way around. There are therefore special demands and challenges to be met within the area of visual computing. Since so many exciting forms of pictorial reproduction, classification, and analysis have been made possible by these means, it would seem to be natural to assume that historians of art would be in the forefront of their exploitation.

Despite this, however, historians of art have been relatively slow in engaging with this area of computing. There are, I think, a number of reasons for this. The most important of these is that historians of art have traditionally been concerned with using the reproduction primarily as a substitute for their real object of study. For preference they would work before the actual object. Reproduction is accepted as a necessary evil. It is a means of recalling experience, or of giving neophytes a taste of what is to come. There has therefore been less emphasis on the analytical possibilities offered by reproduction (that is, the focusing on specific aspects in order to pursue a particular line of enquiry) than on the idea that it should manage to function as an acceptable all-round representative of the object itself. Since the middle of the nineteenth century photography has been the means by which this holy grail has been sought. Until a decade ago, the computer could not produce images of sufficient quality—certainly not at a price that was realistic for most users—to match what was available by means of conventional photography. This problem was compounded by the fact that historians of art usually need to work with large quantities of images. Most university departments find that they need slide collections of more than 100,000 images to carry out normal undergraduate teaching. Reference archives of images used by researchers typically hold millions of reproductions. Now, with the coming of videodiscs and CD-ROM, improved screens, and relatively cheap storage, the use of computers for the reproduction of images that can rival those of conventional photography is a reality. Even so, there is a resistance to abandoning well tried methods. It is no trivial matter to replace the huge visual archives and slide libraries with computerized imagery. The cost of conversion can be astronomical, and few places are able to gain access to the requisite funding. Added to this is the problem that, once digitized, such imagery can only be relayed via the computer. This means abandoning a well-entrenched if obsolescent technology of slides and projectors at huge cost and with uncertain advantage.

These are reasons why the academic art historian has been relatively slow to engage in the issue of handling the image via computers. Possibly, had it been left to this group alone, the issue of computer-generated imagery would never have occurred at all in the discipline. But the academic historian of art has never been the primary figure involved in the actual management and conservation of art objects. Those who have been involved in this area have used computer-generated imagery almost as a matter of necessity, as being the only way, in the contemporary world, in which their technical requirements can be met.

These are the conservators, scientists, and curators who work in museums and art galleries, and in societies for historical monuments. For such people computerization has long been a necessity, both for the management of the databases that describe the objects for which they have responsibility, and for the innovation of methods of pictorial classification, reproduction, and analysis that the computer has afforded. Particular strength has been shown in the area of conservation, where techniques evolved by scientists for the analysis of imagery in other areas (such as medical science and space research) have been used to help with the restoration of works of art, and the interpretation of their characteristics. For such people, the use of images has never been simply a matter of achieving 'quality' reproduction—the quixotic search for the analogue to the 'real thing'. It has been, as it is in most subjects, a tool for demonstration and analysis, in which reduction of information is systematic and planned and aimed at the isolation and exploration of a specific feature.

Added to these is the involvement with computer-generated images by academic groups in related disciplines. Principal amongst these are archaeologists and architectural historians. In both cases there is a manifest use of the image. But the image is used analytically, to reconstruct or classify, rather than principally in a reproductive sense. Archaeologists, following the lead of physical scientists, have made significant use of computer imagery to analyse and classify the forms of the artefacts they unearth. Architectural historians have used computer imagery as a powerful tool for reconstruction. They have been able to benefit in particular from the common use in the architectural profession of computer-aided design (CAD) packages for the drafting of plans to engage in the recreation of actual and imagined buildings.

These examples are beginning, gradually, to make an impact on the thinking of the academic art historian. But there are other developments that are beginning to have their impact as well. The first of these is the development of multimedia packages. The easy combination of image and text that these afford, demonstrate a whole new set of possibilities for exploring the image within a verbal environment, as well as making the image itself, interestingly, function more like a piece of text. The second is networking, which now offers a seemingly endless potential for communication and interchange.

It seems possible, and certainly desirable, that this new flexible approach to imagery will bridge something of the gap mentioned above between those who work primarily with the object, and those who approach it primarily through processes of contextualization.

The development in computer applications

Before going on to a more detailed survey of current usage, and some thoughts about the direction in which this is leading, it might be appropriate to take stock of the way applications have developed in the past. In the first section, I focused upon the use of computer imagery as being the central issue for historians of art to address. However, this does not mean that the use of computers in other areas has been negligible. Following the lead of sociologists, social historians, and literary scholars, art historians have found many applications of value in the non-visual area.

Reviewing developments over the three decades since they began to emerge, one can, I think, see three distinct stages. The first was one in which the computer was still essentially a calculating machine. This was the situation in the 1950s, when it was beginning to be used more and more for 'number crunching' in the sciences. The enhancement of proof that this brought—or seemed to bring—began to impress those students in the humanities whose work came closest to the scientific practice of using a large quantity of material to explore a specific problem. This was the time when, for example, statistical surveys of historical population groups became a possibility. An early example of this potential came with the exploration of the extensive demographic material provided by the British nineteenth-century population censuses (Armstrong 1966). Such practices also began to invade more sensitive areas, such as textual studies. The 'number crunching' approach became the means of identifying an author's hand and even—in work that has come to fruition recently—in analysing character formation in novels. The latter has been demonstrated recently in Burrows' study of Jane Austen (Burrows 1987).

This phase of development certainly affected art historians working largely with texts, particularly those who were interested in gathering large amounts of information, such as that relating to exhibition records. Projects were typically large-scale. Much of this work was, and still is, supported by the Getty Art History Information Program. In collaboration with the Scuola Normale at Pisa, they organized two international conferences, and produced an impressive census of art historical projects using automated processes in 1984 (Corti 1984a). As well as demonstrating the large number of archival projects under way, this census also pinpointed the valuable use that had been made by conservationists in using computers to aid analysis and restoration of art objects.

The second phase was really one of divergence. Having realized something of the power of computers, certain humanities scholars began to think of ways in which its practices might be adapted more clearly to their own traditions. The first stage had been one in which computers were 'mainframe', managed by men in white coats and fed by punch cards which were tricky to process and were immensely time consuming. By the 1970s, commercial pressures had led to the development of the small personal computer, essentially for office use. Concurrently with this development there had emerged a more anarchic, 'DIY' side of computer technology. As computers became easier to use, the non-professional moved in, even participating in the hallowed field of programming. For a few heady years it seemed as though humanities scholars might actually gain a hold on the beast and perhaps even tame it. This was the period in which the distinguished French historian Emmanuel Le Roy Ladurie made the prediction that 'within a decade' every historian would have to learn FORTRAN to write their own programs. Rarely can a prediction have proved so wrong.

Nevertheless it must be admitted that this anarchic moment—with self-styled programmers and 'friendly' personal computers proliferating in all directions as they did around 1980—did generate some valuable contributions. It led to a new generation of didactic programs, often created by gifted teachers who brought computers into the classrooms and addressed problems which professional computer scientists had not considered. Perhaps most important of all was the way in which it demonstrated to the commercial producers of machines and software that a whole new range of demands and possibilities had emerged. The computing community regained control over the disruptive situation by making concessions. They accepted that there would now be a more individual usage of computers, and a concomitant growth in the variety of demands. They provided friendlier interfaces and a larger variety of tools for developing personalized applications. At the same time they effectively removed knowledge of the actual architecture of the machines and of programming from the public sphere. I do not mean to imply by this that there was a conspiracy; it was probably the natural consequence of the growing complexity of the new consumables that were produced.

The personal computer revolution was invaluable in making it possible for quite small-scale projects to be mounted with great effect. Databasing projects proliferated. One example of such a project in the art historical field is the index that was developed by Michael Good for

Nikolaus Pevsner's monumental survey of the *Buildings of England* (Good 1994).

This is the period in which we now exist. Programming has been reclaimed by the experts, but in its place we have been left with a new generation of flexible tools and 'authoring' packages. At the same time, the huge advances in storage and multimedia facilities have provided a seemingly endless series of possibilities. So much so that many must feel lost. But at least we can say now that the environment is right for productive development—and one which has been used by certain scholars with great skill. Unfortunately the number of art historians who have been doing this is still small. But in the humanities at large there is much that has been achieved.[1]

Review of current developments

Databasing

As with most humanities scholars, one of the principle areas of development has been that of databasing. As elsewhere, this has brought with it new problems in the classification of forms and subject matter. Without decisions having been made about terms for describing images and their meanings, much of the power of the database is lost. This has inevitably led to disputes about how 'standards' can be achieved, with a wide variety of solutions being proposed. An attempt has been made to provide a standard for verbal descriptions via the Art and Architecture Thesaurus which has been produced by the Getty Art History Information Program. In the area of subject matter, there have been many solutions proposed, but it would seem that the most fruitful is Iconclass. This is a system devised in Holland before the computer era to provide a hierarchical way of ordering subject matter. It has proved particularly appropriate for computerization and is now widely accepted as a standard, even by those institutions which supplement it with their own local systems.[2] One particularly interesting methodological issue that is raised by this issue of iconography is the relationship of subject to object. Iconclass is an 'abstract' system that classifies subjects irrespective of particular examples. Images are therefore fitted into a pre-existing type. However, as the curators of collections will rapidly point out, pictures can also be seen as entities that each have a unique performance of a subject. There are, for example, an indefinite number of ways of representing the crucifixion, each with its own nuances of meaning; and frequently there is more than one subject in a picture. A representation of the suicide of Cleopatra may also be the portrait of a courtesan, the execution of Charles I may also be a view of Whitehall, and so on. The Princeton index, for example, takes the view that subject classification should begin with the object, rather than that the object should be designated an exemplar of a pre-existing type. In practice they use the Iconclass definitions as an adjunct to their own personalized system.

Researchers in the Classics Department of King's College London, supported by a grant from the Leverhulme Trust, are constructing a database combining written discussion and visual images of all the textual, epigraphical, and material evidence relating to the life, work, and style of the known Greek sculptors from the Archaic to Hellenistic periods. The system, called DAEDALUS, allows any combination of words and images, including any two images, to be displayed simultaneously. The project based in the Ashmole Archive expects to release its results initially on CD-ROM. The resource will assist ancient historians, art historians, and classicists in their study of Greek art whether they are attempting to understand working practices of individual artists, the development of styles, or the socio-economic or political function of art in the Greek World.[3]

Databasing can also provide valuable tools for individual research. One striking example of this is the use that has been made by Marilyn Lavin of a database in her analysis of narrative structures in medieval Italian narrative cycles (Lavin 1990). In the case of the individual researcher there remains the question of the relationship of time spent designing the structure and inputting data as against the gains achieved.

By and large, art historians have profited from the construction of databases in the work done in other humanities disciplines. However, there is one large problem which is still unresolved. This is the question of the use of images in databases. With the latest generation of computers, and the introduction of image storing and retrieval devices such as CD-ROM there is little difficulty about the provision of images themselves. The questions are really ones concerned with the quality of the images, and the extent to which the analysis of images (as opposed to their mere presence as illustrative material) can be introduced into the database.

The treatment of the image

The sections above have suggested that there are differences for art historical studies from numerical and textual techniques forged for other purposes. But there is still a central area where there is a problem for the art historian—that is in the treatment of the image. At first sight there might not seem to be such a difference. After all, visual information is used in a wide number of other disciplines. In the sciences, of course, highly sophisticated image recognition and management techniques have been developed in areas like geography and medicine. In the arts the image is used as a matter of fact in archaeology and increasingly by the historian. But, while admitting all this, the art historian has had two problems with the image up to now.

The first is the question of quality. This is a difficult one to put across, as it smacks of connoisseurship. But the central point is that the image is the *text* for the art historian. Other scholars use images by way of illustration—to reveal evidence about a specific point. But the art historian explores the image as a phenomenon. There is, therefore, no ultimate substitute for exploring the image directly. This has also led to art historians treating the reproduction in a certain way—wishing it to come as near as possible to the original experience and rejecting anything that is inferior. Early computer imagery was vastly poor as reproduction, and this has led to a prejudice against this, which is only now beginning to melt.

The second problem is more of an intellectual one. One of the most stimulating parts of computer technology is the way that it provides a process of codification which, while being mechanical and therefore in some sense limited, was nevertheless capable of translating the codes of traditional forms of communication. First of all, it was able to simulate the codification practices of mathematics—to such an extent that some people still believe that computers work fundamentally by calculation (which they don't). Then it could use the conventions of writing words by means of discrete units (letters) as a means of accessing the structures of language. Much was missed, of course, but there were still fruitful areas of negotiation. Similarly, the fact that music was transcribed by means of notation, meant that it was possible to engage in structural analysis of certain kinds by means of computer as well. But what of the image? While theorists might see images as forms of codification, too, there remained the problem that there was no formal unit that was used to construct and convey the image. In the jargon of the age, the image was 'analogue', was constructed by a process of simulation without coded sub-units, whereas the other modes had a 'digital' convention for relaying their texts. This problem has seemed to make the possibility of 'automated' pictorial analysis similar to that carried out with numbers, words, and musical notation, unattainable. There would always have to be a phase of human intervention, of interpretative codification before the effect could be achieved.

This is what seems to be the case. Yet in fact the computer does offer a fascinating possibility which, to my mind, has only recently begun to be explored. This is the fact that the very process whereby the computer stores and produces images does provide a type of codification. Computers, as we all know, can only work by means of the manipulation of symbols, coded assemblages of digits; to manipulate an image it has to transform the image into such a set of codes. This is the process of digitization. Essentially what digitization does is to break down any pictorial phenomenon into a set of discrete units. Each of these units will have a coded value (typically relating to hue and/or luminosity in the case of a pictures) and an 'address'—that is a set of coordinates that give the precise location of the unit, or 'pixel' as it is called. By subdividing an image into a series of 'pixels', each with an address and a value (or set of values), the digitization process does, in effect, create a 'text' out of an 'image'. (For more detail on image capture and analysis see the chapter by Robinson in this volume.) This might seem to be a purely formal point, but in fact it is much more. There are three fundamental effects that emerge as a result of this process which have implications for the subsequent usage of the image:

- The first is stability of record. Once the visual impression has been codified, it is unchanging in the way that letters and numbers are unchanging. No longer is the record of an image dependent upon its actual effect, as it is, say, in a conventional photograph of an image; as long as the code is expressed in symbols (for example those of letter or number), then the physical changes to those symbols have no effect on their meaning. Once captured digitally the image can be relayed to another medium—it could even be printed out as a text—without the information deteriorating in any way. This stability does of course have one practical problem, namely, that to be made visible the code has to be 'reinterpreted' by another machine. But this is a practical problem which does not affect the integrity of the record. This stability has been one of the reasons why so much interest has been expressed in the digital image by restorers and conservationists. But it has implications beyond this. All art history departments, for example, have the constant problem of obsolescence in their slides. The digital image is one which does not deteriorate.

- The second important feature of the digital image is its transferability. It can be disseminated in a way that no conventional photographic image can.

- The third important feature is manipulability. In other words, it is possible to perform analysis on images through digitization. This is interesting both for identity and analysis.

The power of the digital image to perform specific calculations makes it a powerful tool in reconstruction—for example, in the reconstruction of partially preserved three-dimensional objects. One recent example of this is the use of computer modelling to reconstruct the original appearance of Inigo Jones' facade of the Whitehall Palace (Hart *et al.* 1993). There have been extremely impressive uses of the computer image to aid the infilling of lost parts of paintings as well—such as that used to help to reconstruct the Cimabue Madonna damaged in the Florence flood of 1967, and to penetrate beneath the surface of pictures in a far more accurate way than is provided by the conventional use of x-rays or infra-red photography.[4]

There has been much work on using the automated measurements of physical objects to aid their classification. Much of the impetus for this has come from archaeologists, who have made object identification a central part of their discipline. The digital image has been employed to produce and isolate curves and shape patterns. At the University of Southampton, for example, they have a system that uses Generalized Hough transformations to analyse the profile shapes of pots and other man-made items. Shape analysis clearly has an application in many areas of architectural and design history. It has less immediate application in the analysis of pictures which tend to be remarkably similar in terms of overall shape. On the other hand, it is possible to analyse the shapes of objects within pictures.

An area which has great potential, but also presents great problems, is the analysis of colour. Colour is notoriously elusive to record and describe. One of the projects which has done most to set a standard for accurate colour description is VASARI, the high resolution digital reproduction project which ran at the National Gallery and other sites (Hamber 1991). In order to record colour as precisely as possible the pictures recorded were scanned seven times using filters sited at different points on the spectrum. The records created by this means are being used to analyse the structure and history of different pigments. VASARI's successor, Marc, has used this information to provide reproduction of unprecedented accuracy.

An interesting issue in the discussions concerning reproduction has been that of deciding which computer process to use. Basically, there are two approaches to reproducing the image. There is the 'vector' method, in which the computer actually constructs the image by interpreting a set of algorithms and drawing out the results, and there is the 'raster' method, in which the computer reproduces an image as an array of pixels or dots, commonly known as a 'bitmap'. On the whole there has been a tendency to favour vector graphics, those that actually construct the image. This is the process favoured by computer scientists as it involves intelligent and creative processing. It is also more flexible. Vector graphics are favoured, too, by creative artists as a means of making images. Vector graphics also make sense for anyone working with plans and designs, as they enable constructions to be made from linear instructions. The process has been used frequently in reconstructing buildings, or even in carrying out unconstructed buildings from architect's plans. In Britain a notable centre for such work is the School of Architecture at the University of Edinburgh. Yet raster graphics actually have more potential for pictorial analysis of reproductions of works of art—particularly two-dimensional ones. It would be a pity if for this reason (the scientists' preference for vector, where images are actually constructed and have a meaning) a large area of art history and archaeology will be deprived of new research techniques for bitmap graphics. One of the important points about bitmap graphics is that it can be used to make an actual reproduction of an object, as opposed to a reconstruction of it, which is what vector graphics do.

Yet the problem remains as to the extent that such work can be made available to scholars outside the specialized laboratory. Here the problem seems to hang on the accessibility of the digital image itself. Very gradually museums and other custodians of pictures are beginning to address this problem, with a view to making such imagery available either online, or in CD-ROM form.

There are, as well, 'Rolls Royce' solutions—notably that of the pioneering VASARI project, which is in the process of digitizing works in the Louvre, the Neue Pinakothek, Munich, and the National Gallery, London, to the level of 30 lines per millimetre—a standard which would meet the most exacting requirements of reading. At the same time many commercial companies are offering to produce digitized images of works in museum collections of a lower quality that would still be useful for general purposes. As yet the pool of good quality digital images is limited. I suspect it will remain so until a large demand is evident. But there are visions here of a future: for example, Professor Patrick Purcell of Imperial College, with his image of MUSEUM 2000, which brings together the digital possibilities with those of networking to envisage a 'telegallery' where electronic archives will be interchanged (Purcell 1994).

This is an area of immense promise. As has already been mentioned, the digital image offers the possibility of picture recognition and picture analysis by automated means. It will be necessary to develop some form of picture recognition by motif and visual form (as opposed to by textual description) if the true potential of visual databases is to be exploited. There are many schemes being planned. To a large extent they are dependent upon experiments conducted by psychologists into pictorial recognition. But there are also more pragmatic approaches available which might in the end be of more practical use.

One such is the 'Morelli' system developed at Birkbeck College, and currently being tested at the Witt Library. In this project images are digitized, and then a set of 'matrices' are derived from these which can be compared. By means of such comparisons it is possible to tell if two pictures match each other or, if not, how far and in what ways they differ from each other. In trial, Morelli has proved highly effective in being able to match compositions, being able to scan many millions of images within a matter of seconds. Clearly this will be a useful tool for researchers using picture archives to identify images. But this is only one possible application, and a more useful function of the tool will be in the searching of archives of visual images to find similar and related compositions. This type of system offers possible applications in the areas of identifying, referencing, classifying, and analysing images. As hardware with large storage devices, faster processors, and enhanced resolution and graphics capabilities becomes more widely available, art historians will have a greater opportunity to perform research of this kind.

Another project is the Corpus of Romanesque Sculpture which is one of the British Academy's major research projects. Its purpose is to photograph and catalogue the surviving heritage of sculpture, both religious and secular, in Britain and Ireland produced within the period c. 1066 to 1200. The objective is to achieve a computerized archive to which scholars will have direct access and which will also be capable of generating a variety of forms of publication, both conventional and electronic. The electronic archive, 'The Romanesque Sculpture Processor' (RSP), provides access to the stored information in a number of different ways and gives users the ability to define their own special searches of the data. It supports the simultaneous and efficient display of text and multiple images and caters for high and consistent standards of reproduction in terms of image resolution. Users can search the database for categories of sculpture (e.g. linen-folded scalloped capitals), specific motifs, or sculptural features. The Corpus is a dynamic entity and as the team of researchers gathers more information these text and image data will be added to the system. The complete database will contain an estimated 60,000 images and the equivalent of 15,000 pages of text.

Multimedia systems and networking

The procedures discussed above are all individual techniques, to be used for specific purposes. But the arrival of multimedia systems—in which text, image, film, and sound can all be brought together and managed on a personal computer—has stimulated the interest in providing systems in which all these operations can be managed as a single process. This concept is epitomized in the notion of 'hypertext'; a term that has become highly suggestive since it was coined by Ted Nelson in the 1960s. Hypertext is a text which is read in a non-linear manner, and which can be accessed by many different routes. This possibility has entranced a number of people working in the art historical field, such as George P. Landow at Brown University and Kim Veltman at the Marshall McCluhan Institute, Toronto. Landow has published a series of studies on the impact of hypertext on critical studies, or rather the relevance of hypertext for critical studies (Landow 1991). He has also addressed the issue more specifically in relation to the potential of uniting the new hypertext with the new generation of digital imagery and with networking:

> Computer hypermedia, which produces texts in ways that differ fundamentally from those created by printing, there-

fore offers the promise or threat of thus changing the
conception and practice of art history.[5]

It may well be that this situation will change through the possibilities
offered by networking. As has already been discussed, there are an
impressive number of collections and archives that are now entering
material about their holdings onto computer systems of one sort or
another. Through the process of networking, it is possible for one
individual user in theory to gain access to any of these from his personal
machine. Even now, it is possible to see breathtaking examples of the
transfer of such information, such as the summoning up of a high
definition reproduction of an image stored in New York in a matter of
seconds in London. Developments in telecommunications technology
which allow the transmission of high resolution images are being used
to advantage by the Beazley Archive. This project will eventually
provide a text and image database of ancient Greek pottery. The text
database of Athenian black- and red-figure pottery of the 6th, 5th, and
4th centuries BC consists of 41,000 records and is available online. Trial
transmission of images between Paris and Oxford has already been
achieved via the public Integrated Services Digital Network (ISDN),
making this project the first computerized database in the arts to reach
this stage successfully.

There are, however, a host of logistical problems which still have to
be resolved. There is, for a start, the sheer cost of the venture. At the
moment billions are being poured in by governments and other agencies
keen for these processes to develop. But this cannot go on for ever, and
some day individual users will have to start paying the cost. Then there
are problems relating to the compatibility of the different systems in
which data are stored. There is no standard at the moment—though
standards are being hotly debated (Roberts 1988). It may be that standards will be firmly established in the end, but it will be a difficult
business, and there will always be the nagging feeling that, whatever
standard has been adopted, some kinds of data will have had to be
distorted to accommodate it.

Finally, for objects at least, there are horrendous problems of copyright. It may be that in the end, principle holders of images and reproductions will be persuaded that it is in their interests to allow images to
move through the ether with the speed and multiplicity that will make
true networked investigation a possibility. But at the moment most of
them are unwilling to sign away rights to what seems to them to be a

potential gold mine. Without such agreements the cost of any but the simplest searching will be prohibitive for the average user.

Yet even as I write the situation seems to be changing. The coming of the World Wide Web, with its sophisticated graphics environment, is making it more and more attractive to put high quality images on the Internet. There are already a number of significant sites—such as le Web Louvre and Michael Greenhalgh's operation in Australia—where vast numbers of images are becoming available. Indeed, there are already so many 'art' projects available that British art historians are setting up 'gateways' to monitor the material in much the same was as a gateway has been set up for the social sciences. Birkbeck College already runs the art history page of the Virtual Library, and therefore offers a service for locating information with particular art historical application. There is also a project underway, ADAM, run from the Surrey Institute of Art and Design and the University of Northumbria at Newcastle, which promises to offer a more comprehensive service for art and design generally. While not wishing to stimulate illegality, it should be noted that more and more images are entering the Web without having cleared copyright. And once they are on the Web they are very difficult to trace and monitor. In normal circumstances one might have sympathy for the owners of the originals. But demands have become so voracious in recent years that one is more inclined to look upon the copyright pirate as a kind of Robin Hood.

Conclusion

All this suggests that there may well be a bright future for the use of images on the computer. But we should remember that pictorial provision is not pictorial analysis, and that fascinating area still remains to be opened up properly.

Notes

1. For a recent survey of such work see Katzen, M. (ed.), *Scholarship and technology in the humanities, proceedings of a conference held at Elvetham Hall, Hampshire, UK, 9th–12th May 1990*, (London: Bowker Saur, 1991).

2. See van de Waal, H., *ICONCLASS, an iconographical classification system*, Amsterdam, Oxford, New York, 1972-1985. A recent account of the computerized version of Iconclass, with a consideration of its functionality can be found in Brandhorst, H., and van Huisstede, P., 'The Iconclass connection: ICONCLASS

and pictorial information systems' in *Computers and the History of Art*, Vol. 2, Pt. 1 (1991), 1-20.

3. For a description of this project and other image-based projects, see British Library Research & Development Department, *Information technology in humanities scholarship: British achievements, prospects and barriers,BLR&D Report 6097* (London: The British Library and the British Academy , 1993).

4. See 'Riflettoscopia All Infrarosso Computerizzato' in *Quaderni della Soprintendenza ai beni e Storici di Venezia*, Venice, 1984, 48-53.

5. Landow, G. P,. 'Connected images: hypermedia and the future of art historical studies' in Katzen, M. (ed.), *Scholarship and technology in the humanities, proceedings of a conference held at Elvetham Hall, Hampshire, UK, 9th–12th May 1990*, (London: Bowker Saur for British Library Research, 1991), p. 77.

References and bibliography

Andrews, D., and Greenhalgh, M., *Computing for non-scientific applications* (Leicester: Leicester University Press, 1987).

Armstrong, R., 'Social structure from early census returns', in Wrigley, E.A. (ed.), *English historical demography* (London: Weidenfeld and Nicolson, 1966).

Bakewell, E., Beeman, W. O., Reese, C. M., and Schmidt, M., *Object image inquiry: the art historian at work*. Report on a collaborative study by the Getty Art History Information Program (AHIP) and the Institute for Research in Information and Scholarship (IRIS), Brown University, Santa Monica, California: Getty Art History Information Program, 1988.

Burrows, J.F., *Computation into criticism: a study of Jane Austen's novels and an experiment in method* (Oxford: Clarendon Press, 1987).

Corti, L. (ed.), 1984a, *Census: computerization in the history of art*, (Pisa and Los Angeles: Scuola Superiore Normale and The J. Paul Getty Trust, 1984a).

Corti, L. (ed.), *Automatic processing of art historical data and documents*. Vol 1, Census of projects; Vol 2, Proceedings of conference. (Pisa: Scuola Normale, 1984b).

Denley, P., and Hopkin, D. (eds.), *History and computing* (Manchester: Manchester University Press, 1987).

Good, M., *Buildings of England survey* (Harmondsworth, 1994).

Greenhalgh, M., 'Databases for art historians: problems and possibilities', in Denley, P., and Hopkin, D. (eds.), *History and computing* (Manchester: Manchester University Press, 1987), 156-67.

Hamber, A., 'The Vasari Project' *Computers and the History of Art*, 1.2 (1991), 17-33.

Hamber, A., Miles, J., and Vaughan, W. (eds.), *Computers and the history of art* (Mansell, 1989).

Hart, V., Day, A., and Cook, D., 'Conservation and computers: a reconstruction of Inigo Jones's original Whitehall Banqueting House, London c. 1620', *Computers and the History of Art*, 4.1 (1993), 65-9.

Landow, G.P., *Hypertext: the convergence of contemporary critical theory and technology* (Baltimore, Maryland: Johns Hopkins University Press, 1991).

Lavin, M.A., *The place of narrative: mural decoration in Italian Churches, 431-1600* (Chicago: University of Chicago Press, 1990).

Purcell, P., 'Museum 2000: a dynamic prospect', *Imaging the past*, British Museum, 3-5 November 1994 (abstracts).

Roberts, D.A., *Collections management for museums* (Cambridge: Museum Documentation Association, 1988).

Sarasan, L., 'Why museum computer projects fail', *Museum News*, (Jan-Feb, 1981), 40-49.

Thaller, M. (ed.), *Images and manuscripts in historical computing*, (St. Katharinen: Max-Planck-Institut für Geschichte, Scripta Mercaturae Verlag, 1992).

Vaughan, W., (ed.), *Computers and the history of art*, (Harwood Academic Publishers, Vol 1. 1990, Vol 2. 1991).

Further information

Beazley Archive
Ashmolean Museum, University of Oxford, Beaumont Street, Oxford OX1 2PN.
Dr D C Kurz, Archivist

Corpus of Romanesque Sculpture in Britain and Ireland
The British Academy, 20–21 Cornwall Terrace, London NW1 4QP.
Dr Seamus Ross, Assistant Secretary, Information Technology

DAEDALUS
Department of Classics, King's College London, The Strand, London WC2R 2LS.
Professor G B Waywell

Morelli Project
Department of History of Art, Birkbeck College, University of London, 43 Gordon Square, London WC1H 0PD.
Professor W Vaughan

VASARI project
Department of History of Art, Birkbeck College, University of London, 43 Gordon Square, London WC1H 0PD.
Dr Kirk Martinez

ADAM Gateway for art, design, architecture, and media
Surrey Institute of Art and Design,
Marion Wilks, Head of Academic Services,
e-mail: mwilks@surrart.ac.uk

Computing in Literary Studies[1]

Marilyn Deegan

Introduction and history

It was relatively early in the development of the stored-program computer that its value for the study of texts was recognized. Other chapters in this collection deal with the first such uses—for instance, those dealing with religious studies and classics; this essay deals in particular with the use of the computer in the study of literary texts. In some of the earliest studies, analyses were largely of textual features which could be enumerated, and computers were used for what they did best—to count large numbers of things very fast and very reliably. The key tools for text manipulations were programs which could produce word lists, indexes, and concordances of texts.[2] The outputs from such packages could then be fed into statistical programs, and useful graphs and statistics could be obtained. The concordance is, of course, not a new development of the computer age—manual concordances to the Bible, Shakespeare, and other major literary works have been published from the eighteenth century onwards. What was new was the speed with which they could be produced by computer: once the text is available in electronic form concordances can be made in minutes instead of years, and such resources will never again be prepared by non-automatic methods.

In literary computing, analyses were carried out on perhaps one particular text, set of texts, or author, and concentration was generally on particular features of style which could be studied systematically. One seminal investigation was that of Jane Austen's novels carried out by John Burrows in the 1980s, which looked at how major characters differ in their use of the most common words such as 'the', 'of', 'it', and 'I'. This was the first literary monograph which made extensive use of the computer in the process of literary criticism (Burrows 1987). Burrows has also applied statistical methods to Romantic and Renaissance tragedy, examining the stylistic similarities between them and speculating upon why one was a highly successful genre, the other a dismal failure (Burrows and Craig 1994). There have been useful discoveries employing computerized methods in the areas of disputed authorship, as for instance in the Federalist papers analysed by Mosteller and Wallace (Mosteller and Wallace 1984), and in the analysis of the works of Shakespeare, Fletcher, and Marlowe carried out by Matthews and Merriam (Matthews and Merriam 1993; Merriam and Matthews 1994), and in reconsidering disputed datings within the works of one author, as in the study of Shakespeare's chronology by Brainerd Barron (Barron 1980). A team of scholars of French literature has recently carried out a rigorous critique of concordance-making and has suggested some interesting uses for literary research and teaching (Behar 1995).

Literary computing, while it has yielded some useful results, has not however until recently had any great impact on literary studies or literary criticism, and indeed, many in the mainstream of literary movements have viewed it with some suspicion. Practitioners in literary computing can take a somewhat mechanistic view of the study of literature, which makes it a suitable topic for computational analysis, but which is at odds with the more subjective and the more theoreticized approaches of modern literary critics. Some computing literary scholars distrust 'intuitive' approaches. Paul Fortier, a leading early practitioner in this area, for instance, lauds computational analyses of literature as offering 'precision measurement', and replacing 'telling examples' with comprehensive explanations; in such a model literature is treated merely as data (Fortier 1991, 194). Roseanne G. Potter suggests a similar approach to literary computing when she argues for 'a principled use of technology and criticism to form a new kind of literary studies absolutely comfortable with scientific methods yet completely suffused with the values of the humanities' (Potter 1988, 91-92). Very few literary critics, from whatever theoretical school, are comfortable with notions of precision measurement or scientific methods in the study of literature. Indeed, one of the great attractions in literature is the endless opportunity for rethinking meanings, interpretations, and theories in the context of prevailing social, cultural, and intellectual trends. The great authorship debates, some of which have been resolved by the use of computational stylistic analysis to the satisfaction of a number of critics, are of little interest, for example, to schools of criticism which have declared that the author is dead and that the locus of meaning and interpretation is situated with the reader. Arguments around literary works should continually open up rather than close down their meanings, and scientific models and interpretations can be seen as the end of debate, rather than the beginning. There are no 'answers' to literary critical questions, or rather, there are many answers, and these depend complexly and variably on the cultural context in which the work is read, on the views and perspectives of the reader, on the significance or insignificance accorded to the writer, or on the conditions of production. Kathryn Sutherland, writing about the new possibilities offered by the use of hypertext in literary criticism, suggests a new move in the use of the computer as an instrument of literary enquiry which 'promises to redress the relationship between the computer as a tool and literature as the subject of inquiry: it suggests the possibilities of the computer package not just as a concordancing and quantifying package through which text is fed, but as an interactive environment adaptable to the constant desire of literary critics to inhabit and explore a cultural and aesthetic space' (Sutherland 1990). For computational methods to be seen as appropriate techniques for use in literary studies, they have to be integrated into scholarly and literary practice: in other words, they have to feel 'natural'. The shift in our perception from computers as alien to computers as natural and comfortable tools is examined by a number of writers such as Patrick W. Conner and John Pickering (Conner 1992; Pickering 1996). Accessing an electronic text which looks similar to a text on a printed page, reading a collation output from a computer which looks like a set of variants in a major scholarly edition, finding a footnote by clicking on a button to follow a link, rather than looking up a number, all quickly feel natural, especially to the scholar who has become used to word processing and e-mail. Reading a statistical analysis of literary forms in a literary computing journal, with graphs, statistical formulae, and arcane conclusions, is only a comfortable and natural act for other literary statisticians, and not for those in mainstream literary activity. The results, too, sometimes appear so slight or obvious that many literary scholars feel they are not worth the time or trouble expended to produce them.

Recent developments in computing generally, and also in literary computing, mean that the computer can now be used for many more purposes than merely counting. One significant use is as a gateway to the sources of study, and therefore the collection of large bodies of literary text and ancillary materials has been a crucial activity in recent years, both in the academic world and in the commercial area of electronic publishing (which is dealt with elsewhere in this volume). The growth of the Internet and the materials available thereon has been of great importance in accessing resources, although much more needs to be done in both to assemble a critical mass of scholarly materials and to ensure that these are of the appropriate scholarly standard. The Internet so far promises much, but literary scholars are not yet convinced that it delivers sufficient of relevance to their needs. This is constantly improving, however, and a search for a topic or author of interest may yield more than one would imagine.[3] Another promising use of the computer in literary studies is as an evaluative device rather than an enumerative one, and there are useful publications, both conventional and electronic, coming out of the fruitful relationship between modern literary theory and hypertext. The area of literary studies where the computer is having perhaps the most significant impact, however, is textual criticism. The rest of this paper will concentrate on resource collection, textual criticism, and hypertext and literary theory. These are not always easy to separate, so the margins between them are often blurred. But as heuristic devices these headings might be useful.

Resource collection

The collection of very large corpora, or even complete corpora from closed sets of works, can change radically the kinds of studies which can be performed on texts. Even just the act of collection can uncover works and reveal connections which were hitherto unrealized. A very early corpus collection project which has had great impact on literary studies in one subject area is the *Dictionary of Old English* (*DOE*) project at the University of Toronto, which has been in existence for over twenty years. This has converted almost the entire corpus of texts written in Old English to electronic form as the first step in the production of a new dictionary. This corpus has been available for some years: the first product was a concordance published on microfiche for scholarly use in the late 1970s. The dictionary itself has been released in stages in microfiche form, and is now perhaps one quarter complete. What is interesting in the *DOE* project is that at its inception the corpus was intended as an aid to dictionary making for the editors, and not as a product in itself. Since it was made available through the agency of the Oxford Text Archive, however, it has become one of the major resources in Old English literary scholarship, and many who use it feel that it is of even greater use than the dictionary fascicles being produced from it.

The *DOE* corpus collection project has a clear and definable aim (and one which is shared by other major projects in the collection of literary texts, such as the *Thesaurus Linguae Graecae* discussed elsewhere in this volume): to collect all the extant writings of a language within a certain timespan. Although there are sometimes discoveries of new exemplars, the set of texts is essentially closed: no new examples can be produced, and the extent of the corpus in each case is known and is not enormous. In later periods of literature this is not so clear cut, and the number of potential examples is generally much larger. The FRANTEXT database, for instance, established to provide data for the *Trésor de la Langue Française,* holds almost 3,000 French texts and is continually being added to. Access to these texts is via the Internet, although the project has made available a CD-ROM, Discotext, which contains some of their more popular texts.

While one use of the computer in textual studies is to enable the conversion of texts already available in recent editions to electronic form for different kinds of manipulations and studies (and some might rather deplore the reinforcement of the literary canon through this means: witness the number of electronic versions of Shakespeare available), another is proving to be the recovery of bodies of hitherto ignored and unavailable texts. Two key projects deserve mention here: the Women Writers Project and the Electra Project. The Women Writers Project at Brown University, Providence, Rhode Island is conceived as a full-text database, or textbase, of women's writings in English from c.1330-1830. It was begun in 1988 by a group of scholars concerned to make available the diverse tradition of women's writings which, despite the growth in feminist scholarship, were still not finding their way into the bookshops and classrooms.

The aim of the project is to enter into the computer everything written in English by women in its 500-year period. Its scope includes printed books and manuscripts, the traditional literary genres of fiction, poetry, and drama, as well as sermons, prayers, household manuals, translations, letters, diaries, and whatever else women can be found writing. Already the Project has made significant discoveries; for instance, considerable numbers of women were found to have written volumes of poetry during the Romantic period, a period generally thought to have been dominated by a very few male poets. This fact alone reshapes the notions of what constitutes 'Romantic' poetry (Sutherland 1992).

Begun in January 1992, Project Electra has from the beginning been closely associated with the Brown Women Writers Project, and it draws upon and extends some of the textual and computational features of the earlier project. Its brief is the creation and implementation of an electronic scholarly resource alongside conventional paperbound editions of works for those undertaking specialized research in British Romantic Literature and Women's Studies in the period 1780-1830.

The above projects are concerned with the large-scale collection of mainly textual data, the future uses of which can never be fully known by the creators but which are offered to the scholarly community in as general and standardized a form as feasible to allow as many kinds of access as scholars can imagine. There are many more such projects, and the numbers are growing daily; those being carried out by commercial publishers are dealt with in the chapter on electronic publishing. There are other projects of text capture which are much smaller and are often conceived of only for the research of one individual. For instance, a scholar may transcribe one or two manuscripts in the process of creating a new edition of a work. The desired end product is probably not itself electronic, but the process of arriving at that product may make considerable use of the versatility of text once it is in electronic form. At the end of the project, when the work is finished, the scholar may him- or herself have no further use for the text in its digital form, but it could conceivably give some potential benefit to other scholars. It would be a great pity for electronic by-products of this kind to be lost and for them to have to be recreated for future work on the same texts. In order to avoid this situation, various text archives have been established to preserve and protect texts, and to make them available beyond the original conception of their creator. If a scholar is embarking on an electronic text project, capture of the text should never be embarked upon without first ascertaining whether the text exists anywhere in the world. There are many electronic text centres now available through the World Wide Web, and these should be contacted before any text capture is begun. Listing the currently available centres would be of little use as this is information which changes every day, but a browse around some key resources is well worth the effort. There is a huge increase in the number of literary texts and ancillary materials available on the Internet, and there is no doubt that soon this will be one of the most significant ways in which we access literary resources, but at the moment the provision is patchy, the quality variable, and the tools for analysis inadequate. While scholars are often disparaging about the quality of scholarly materials to be found on the Internet, it is worth remembering, as Renear and Bilder point out,

> ...computer-mediated communication *per se* connects no more intimately or exclusively to academic scholarship and research than does print or any other major commu-

> nications medium ... in our text-drenched environment,
> university presses and scholarly societies do print many
> scholarly monographs, but the printed page is more likely
> to appear in an invoice, tabloid newspaper, or mail-order
> catalogue than in an academic research report (Renear and
> Bilder 1993, 220).

Life on the Internet, as they go on to argue, is just like life in any other area of society, and scholarship is only a very small part of most people's concerns (Renear and Bilder 1993, 221).

An exciting recent development in Britain is the plan to establish an Arts and Humanities Data Service which will collect, standardize, and distribute humanities data in electronic form, pictorial and aural as well as textual. This has been funded from government sources and will provide a wealth of high-quality material for research and teaching, as well as offering services such as data preservation, monitoring of standards and training, among others (Burnard and Short 1994).

Textual criticism

The projects and archives mentioned above are largely concerned with the collection and preservation of text-based literary resources, but there is now an acknowledgement among literary and textual critics of the value of assembling other kinds of resources for literary study alongside the textual. In particular, textual critics, who have been arguing for many years now for the importance of the artefactual actuality of texts and manuscripts in the interpretation of the works inscribed thereon, have seized on the computer as allowing easier access to some representation of the texts in their physical form as well as to the textual content. The computer, indeed, is allowing an entirely new means of analysing, assessing, and presenting textual materials which is revolutionizing textual criticism.

One of the key activities in textual criticism is the analysis of versions of printed books and manuscripts and the determination of their relationship, one to another. Sometimes different manifestations of a text as released by its author need to be compared in order to understand the development of the work; sometimes, as in the case of medieval manuscripts and early printed books, centuries of copying by scribes and reprinting by printers introduce variations which can enable the tracing of the history of a work throughout many centuries of its existence. This is valuable work which must be done with meticulous accuracy, but it is repetitive and time consuming, and many of the tasks required, in particular the collation of variants, are actually done better by a computer which does not become bored, tired, or bad-tempered. The main disadvantage of computer-based collation is that the texts first have to be entered into the computer—not a trivial task—before collation can take place; and they have to be faithful to their originals as inaccuracy in the texts would, of course, render the process of collation useless. However, despite the labour involved, there are many advantages in having electronic copies of the texts, perhaps the most important of which is the fact that the collation can be repeated as many times as needed, something which is not possible when done by non-automated methods. The process of collation involves first the choice of a 'base' text, to which other texts are compared. If the base text chosen is not the most appropriate, then the results may be less than useful. The problem is that until some of the collation is done, one is not always able to determine which is the best base text to use. Using electronic texts and computer collation programs, every text in turn can be chosen as the base text and then the collation can be run. The results can be compared and the collations rerun until the desired results are obtained. There are a number of such programs available: those interested should contact the Electronic Scholarly Editions discussion list for the latest details of current practice in this area.

Computerized methods as applied to textual criticism were initially intended to assist the scholar in the production of the conventional end product—a printed critical edition of the text with a base text printed in full and the variants from other texts at the foot of the page or at the end of the work. In the traditional printed edition, other apparatus such as commentary, textual notes, explanatory notes, were also arranged either at the foot of the page or in appendices at the back of the book. Over the centuries the critical edition has reached a high level of sophistication in the organizational principles which allow a flat, linear, printed book to present information which is not linear. Now, however, developments in textual presentation software using structural markup and hypertextual linking mechanisms mean that critical editions can be published in electronic form, as well as being generated electronically. Two paradigmatic examples of this are the *Canterbury Tales* project and the *Piers Plowman* project. The *Canterbury Tales* project intends to make available, over a ten-year period, full transcripts of the text of every manuscript and pre-1500 printed edition of the *Canterbury Tales*, together with computer images of every page of every manuscript and early edition, collations of all these texts, and analyses of the textual tradition based on the transcripts. Cambridge University Press is publishing these materials in CD-ROM form with the fifty-five manuscripts and four pre-1500 printed editions of the *Wife of Bath's Prologue*.

The *Piers Plowman* Electronic Archive, which is being constructed by a team of scholars in England and the USA, plans to create a multi-level, hypertextually linked electronic archive of the textual tradition of all three versions of the fourteenth-century poem *Piers Plowman*, written by William Langland. The case of *Piers Plowman* is an especially interesting one for the editor working in the electronic medium as it is a poem which itself has always been in a particularly fluid state. Langland worked on the poem extensively throughout his life and scholars recognize at least three distinct versions of it. The poet himself, therefore, was transgressing the textual boundaries which define what a finished work of art should be, and he released into literary debate a cultural object of a peculiar unfixity. Printed editions of this work have always been unsatisfactory both as a medium for the editor to work in and as a means of presenting this textual unfixity to the reader. The electronic edition is clearly the best means of dealing with a work of this kind.

One result of the advent of computers in textual criticism is the redefinition of the notion of what is an edition, with a move towards providing archives of textual materials instead of heavily edited definitive editions. Two interesting examples of this move are the Rossetti Archive and the Blake Archive at the University of Virginia. These separate projects are collecting together the writings and paintings of Dante Gabriel Rossetti and the poems and paintings of William Blake. The scholar most closely associated with the Rossetti Archive is Jerome McGann, one of the world's leading textual bibliographers. Long interested in the relationship between the words of a text and its particular physical manifestations, McGann has conceived of the Rossetti Archive as the closest a scholar can get to the whole *oeuvre* of a writer and painter. This is an exciting prospect, but it is a very different notion from that of the scholarly edition with its weight of interpretation included as part of the presented work, and also with its necessarily high degree of selectivity. From the conventional view that more is selected out than left in, we move to the electronically facilitated view that everything is left in, and it is for the reader to choose what is relevant to a particular need in the work of an author. The *Canterbury Tales* and *Piers Plowman* projects, with their enormous weight of manuscript evidence replacing the presentation of selected variants, also function as archives rather than as editions. While it is of great value for many to have all the material which can be associated with one writer, for some this could be excessive, and will perhaps kill rather than stimulate debate. Another danger is that these projects provide editions which can only be used by other textual editors, rather than scholars of literature and students.

A recent development in France concerning the writings of more modern authors is the use of hypertext systems to study the genesis of works of literature—so-called 'genetic criticism'. Working papers have complex relationships with finished and published works of literature, and presenting them in facsimile in book form does not always allow this complexity to be presented in a meaningful way. Linking them with hypertext systems allows their non-linear nature to be shown in a way more congruent with their original composition and also allows different media types to be integrated and linked (Ferrer 1995).

One other project deserves mention here, the Hartlib Papers Project. This has been in existence since 1987 and has in the years since then created an electronic edition of the papers of Samuel Hartlib, the seventeenth-century polymath and correspondent of Boyle, Milton, Comenius, and many other thinkers of his day. It has also produced three related hypermedia and multimedia systems. This collection is a good example of a late Renaissance archive which was waiting for some system to come along that could deal with a complex mass of topics, ideas, and media, as the items are so diverse, multilingual, and multimedia in themselves that scholars consulting them in their original form soon gave up an attempt to navigate a path through them. A great deal of the material is correspondence; there are several hundred correspondents in the collection, with references to thousands more. The project has transcribed all of the papers in Hartlib's collection, some 25,000 pages. It has also incorporated in the electronic edition an image of every page of the papers, as the *Canterbury Tales* project is doing with Chaucer's manuscripts; many of the documents contain drawings or diagrams, so this is obviously welcome. The papers are now available on CD-ROM from the University of Michigan Press. An interesting point which one might make about the Hartlib Papers Project is that it is providing a resource which is of use to scholars in many areas, not just literature. Because Hartlib was interested in so many topics, and corresponded with experts in diverse fields, scholars in a wide range of disciplines will find uses for his work.

We can detect a movement in the various projects discussed here from edition to archive to interdisciplinary linked resource; this movement has only been possible through the use of the computer. One recent development which will be of enormous use to scholars is the commitment of major libraries to make available through networks high quality digital images of their manuscript and slide collections. In the UK, a group of libraries in Oxford including the Bodleian Library, along with the British Library, have purchased state-of-the-art digitizing cameras and are embarking on pilot projects of manuscript and slide digitization. In Oxford, the Image Archive Project has just obtained funding for a pilot study using Celtic Manuscripts, and funds are being sought for larger projects on the fragile and unique medieval manuscript collections. The British Library, under its Initiatives for Access, is pioneering digital imaging for medieval manuscripts, starting with the damaged *Beowulf* manuscript. It has also recently made some illuminated manuscripts available online. Other initiatives of interest in the British Library include: the Electronic Photo Viewing System, which has digitized 10,000 images from the Library's various collections of photographs and makes them available for subject searches (never previously feasible); the Network OPAC, which allows access to 6,000,000 bibliographic records; and the digitization of ageing microfilm (Purday 1995). The British Library, in its *Strategic Objectives to the Year 2000*, has made a commitment to providing maximum access to its collections using digital and networking technologies for on-site and remote users. The new Bibliothèque de France is carrying out a programme of digitization which will make available 100,000 volumes as bitmaps; 10,000 of these are also being converted to searchable text using OCR. The Bibliothèque has also prototyped a sophisticated computer-assisted reading environment which will allow scholars to access and manipulate these and other resources. There are many projects of digitization in the USA: the Library of Congress is digitizing core collections, and expects by the year 2000 to have digitized and made available 5,000,000 images. In particular, the Library is concentrating on its Americana holdings which are fragile and unique, and which are contributing a core database of US history and culture to the National Digital Library effort in the USA.

Hypertext and multimedia

Of all the computational technologies now available to the literary scholar, it is probably hypertext and multimedia (sometimes referred to as hypermedia) which have excited the most interest in recent years, because they offer exciting possibilities for the presentation and investigation of scholarly materials as well as new ways of thinking about literary works. There are many definitions of hypertext (see Economou in this volume); perhaps the simplest way to understand it is to see it as a means of linking together textual materials using what have become known as 'nodes' and 'links'. A node is a piece of text of any length (word, sentence, paragraph, even a whole book) and a link is the mechanism by which this node is connected to another node. Links can connect chunks of text within the same document or between different documents. The non-electronic analogy of nodes and links is the scholarly book or article where the links are, for example, footnote numbers. The reader follows the link in the text, usually a superscript numeral, and finds the other end of the link marked by the same number at the foot of the page or at the end of the work. In the electronic hypertext, links are followed by pointing at them using a mouse and clicking; the other end of the link is then displayed immediately. Nodes and links can also connect text with non-textual media—sound, images, video—hence the term hypermedia, usually nowadays called multimedia (refer to the chapter on multimedia in this volume for more detail). This seems a simple idea, but the number of nodes and links multiply very quickly and there are some electronic hypertexts available which claim to have around one million links.

Electronic hypertexts have become popular recently because they function particularly well when implemented through the graphical user interface, the standard screen configuration on Macintosh, and now PC, microcomputers. Hypertext systems are used for accessing many kinds of information, and the possibilities they offer for 'non-sequential' reading and writing, with complex mappings of textual materials, have brought them to the attention of a number of literary critics, while some writers claim that they transcend the linear, bounded, and fixed qualities of the traditional written text. Disciples of hypertext claim that the book is dead and that we will soon be accessing 'virtual libraries' while seated at our desks, wandering through a universe of hypertextual documents known as a 'docuverse'. One of the early theorists of hypertext, Ted Nelson, has been working for some years on a global library, a 'New Alexandria', called the Xanadu project, which plans a worldwide network of hypertextually-linked documents. Readers, he suggested, will traverse the docuverse linking and reading where they will, paying through an automatic charging system for the texts they read. This seemed fanciful when proposed by Nelson only a few years ago, but now academics access information all over the world through the World Wide

Web on a daily basis, following hypertext links to navigate around text, images, sound, and film clips. One rather interesting development in hypertext is the recent move by some literary critics to see this as a means of exploring and examining computerized textuality as a *theory* rather than as a practical manifestation of theories. Indeed, much of the theorizing about hypertext leads us to expect far more sophistication from actual computer-based systems in the presentation of literary works than they are yet capable of. We are therefore sometimes disappointed when we see such systems because of the expectations with which we have approached them. The contention of writers of and about hypertexts is that hypertext writing, with its freely associative rather than linear structures, liberates the author from the constraints of order imposed by the printed page. While this is of course true, writers of fiction have always found ways to exploit the tensions between the linearity of the written narrative and the looser connectiveness in their fictional plots. The work of Kathryn Sutherland examines the analogies between the web-like structures of Victorian multiplot novels and hypertext, and suggests that the literary critic might profitably explore these structures using hypertexts (Sutherland 1990). Jay David Bolter proposes a number of fictional narratives whose complex structure might lend itself to hypertextual exploration: Sterne's *Tristram Shandy,* Joyce's *Ulysses,* Borges's *Garden of Forking Paths* (Bolter 1991). The many works of George P. Landow are also concerned with the relationship between hypertext, literature, and literary theory (Landow 1989; Landow and Delaney 1991).

It is one thing to create hypertexts from existing printed narratives as a means of exploring and explicating them, it is another to write fiction in this form from the start. Hypertext fiction, sometimes called 'interactive fiction', is now a possibility and there are several products available. One characteristic example is *Afternoon,* by Michael Joyce. This novel is a series of short episodes through which the reader can roam almost at will, and no two readings of the novel will ever be the same. The pathways through the novel are not completely unconstrained, but one can experience some very contradictory readings, readings which co-exist within the fictional space offered. Another example, *Stories from Downtown Anywhere,* is to be found on the World Wide Web and is an experiment in collaborative hypertext fiction to which readers can contribute. While these are interesting, they can (for me anyway) be unsatisfactory as a literary experience, as the looseness of the narrative structure can work *against* rather than *for* fictional complexity. The effect of this fiction is, paradoxically, reductive rather than expansive. Each narrative episode has to be no more than one screen in length and this makes the narrative jerky. Another problem with hypertext fiction is that the possibility of critical debate about the fiction could be lost because the text is deconstructed during the act of reading. If the reader endlessly shapes the narrative, becoming writer/reader, and if every reading is an entirely new experience, then how can we ever know that we are talking about the same thing? One could argue that we are never talking about the same work anyway, that every reading is a new reading; critical discourse is richly unstable and that allows us the plurality of views about works. But hypertext fiction could render the richly unstable into the textual anarchic, closing down discussion instead of opening it up.

An area where hypertext fiction does actually work very well, particularly if it is sensitively designed, is in children's literature. Oxford University Press is bringing out a range of titles for children, and if the first two—*The Fish Who Could Wish* and *A Christmas Story*—are representative examples, these should be very successful. In particular, *The Fish Who Could Wish* makes good use of the electronic medium with graphics, animation, a non-linear narrative structure which actually adds to the story rather than frustrates the reader, and voice-over narration rather than large amounts of on-screen text. I would recommend that anyone interested in the design of hypertext and multimedia for literary use look at this as one of the finest examples around.

Teaching literary studies by computer

In the last few years there have been moves in many universities, in the UK and elsewhere, towards the greater use of computers in the teaching of all subjects. Funds have been made available by the Higher Education Funding Councils in the UK for initiatives to disseminate information about the potential uses of computers in teaching and learning and also for the development of courseware and other teaching resources. Literary studies have fared reasonably well in the dissemination initiatives, in particular with the Computers in Teaching Initiative (CTI), but less well in the development programmes. However, there are many resources which can be made available for teaching, some of which are also research resources and some of which have been developed specially for teaching purposes. There is a great deal of information about the use of computers to teach literary studies in the publications of the CTI Centre for Textual Studies, in their Resources Guide, in the newsletter *Comput-*

ers and Texts, and on the Centre's World Wide Web home page. In general, resources made available for scholarship and research in literary subjects are equally valuable for teaching, and many of the products mentioned above can be used successfully in both areas. There has been a dearth of good resources in the past, and the failure to attract funding has been a problem. However, the situation seems to be improving hugely and there are grounds for optimism; in particular, the establishment of the Arts and Humanities Data Service should ensure the production and circulation of high-quality resources for teaching literary studies by computer.

Conclusion

The computer has already become a comfortable object for almost all literary scholars in areas of communication and production of typescript, and it is rapidly becoming accepted as a tool of literary enquiry also. Some thinkers are debating the impact which this will have on the study of literature, and I would like to finish with two opposing views. First of all, Richard Lanham in *The Electronic Word* states that:

> I think that electronic expression has come not to destroy the Western arts and letters, but to fulfil them. And I think too that the instructional practices built upon the electronic word will not repudiate the deepest and most fundamental currents of Western education in discourse but redeem them (Lanham 1993, xiii).

In a counter-plea for the superiority of the written word over the electronic, Sven Birkerts declares in *The Gutenberg Elegies* that:

> ...the experience of literature offers a kind of wisdom that cannot be discovered elsewhere; ... there is profundity in the verbal encounter itself, never mind what further profundities the author has to offer; and ... for a host of reasons the bound book is the ideal vehicle for the written word (Birkerts 1994, 6).

Only time will tell which of these views proves to be closer to the truth, but these are issues which need to be debated vigorously by those of us engaged in literary computing. For five hundred years the printed page has dominated western civilization changing it forever from the society which transferred information through handwriting. A revolution in thought and practices as great as the Gutenberg one is a possible consequence of the move from page to computer; do we as literary scholars experience this as spectators, actors, or resistors?

Notes

1. Parts of this article have also appeared in 'IT and the Humanities', *Information UK Outlooks* 14, October 1995, published by LITC and the British Library Research and Development Department.
2. Popham elsewhere in this volume discusses text analysis and appropriate tools in more detail.
3. See Lee this volume for details of Internet search tools.

References and bibliography

Barker, P., 'Electronic books and libraries of the future', *Electronic Library,* 10.3 (1992), 139-49.

Barron, B., 'The chronology of Shakespeare's plays: a statistical study', *Computers and the Humanities,* 14 (1980), 221-30.

Behar, H., 'Hubert de Phalese's method', *Literary and Linguistic Computing,* 10 (1995), 129-34.

Birkerts, S., *The Gutenberg elegies: the fate of reading in an electronic age* (New York: Fawcett Columbine, 1994).

Blake, N., and Robinson, P., *The* Canterbury Tales *Project: Occasional Papers Volume I* (Oxford: Office for Humanities Communication Publications, 5, 1993).

Bolter, J. D., *Writing space: the computer, hypertext, and the history of writing* (Laurence Erlbaum Associates, Hillsdale, New Jersey; Hove and London, 1991).

Burnard, L., and Short, H., *An Arts and Humanities Data Service: report of a feasibility study commissioned by the Information Services Sub-committee of the Joint Information Systems Committee of the Higher Education Funding Councils* (Oxford: Office for Humanities Communication, October, 1994).

Burrows, J.F., *Computation into criticism: a study of Jane Austen's novels and an experiment in method* (Oxford: Clarendon Press, 1987).

Burrows, J.F. and Craig, D.H., 'Lyrical drama and the "Turbid Mountebanks": styles of dialogue in Romantic and Renaissance tragedy', *Computers and the Humanities,* 28 (1994), 63-86.

Butler, C., *Computers and written texts* (Oxford: Blackwell, 1992).

Chernaik, W., Davis, C., and Deegan, M., *The politics of the electronic text* (Oxford: Office for Humanities Communication Publications, 3, 1993)

Communications of the ACM, April 1995. An issue devoted to digital libraries.

Communications of the ACM, August 1995. An issue devoted to hypermedia.

Conner, P.W., 'Hypertext in the last days of the book', *Bulletin of the John Rylands University Library of Manchester,* 74 (1992), 7-24.

Feldman, P.R., and Norman, B., 'The wordworthy computer: classroom and research applications in language and literature' (New York: Random House, 1987).

Ferrer, D., 'Hypertextual representation of literary working papers', *Literary and Linguistic Computing,* 10 (1995), 143-146.

Fortier, P.A., 'Theory, methods, and applications: some examples in French literature', *Literary and Linguistic Computing,* 6 (1991), 192-96.

Genet, J.-P., and Zampolli, A., *Computers and the humanities* (Aldershot: Dartmouth for the European Science Foundation, 1992).

Hockey, S., *A guide to computer applications in the humanities* (London: Duckworth, 1980).

Kenny, A., *The computation of style* (Oxford: Pergamon, 1982).

Landow, G., 'Hypertext in literary education, criticism, and scholarship', *Computers and the Humanities,* 23 (1989), 173-198.

Landow, G., *Hypertext: the convergence of contemporary critical theory and technology* (Baltimore: The Johns Hopkins University Press, 1992).

Landow, G. (ed.), *Hyper/Text/Theory* (Baltimore: The Johns Hopkins University Press, 1994).

Landow, G., and Delaney, P., *Hypermedia and literary studies* (Cambridge, MA: Massachusetts Institute of Technology Press, 1991).

Landow, G., and Delaney, P., *The digital word* (Cambridge, MA: Massachusetts Institute of Technology Press, 1993).

Lanham, R. A., *The electronic word: democracy, technology, and the arts* (Chicago: University of Chicago Press, 1993).

Michael, L., 'Electronic editions and the hierarchy of texts', in Chernaik, W., Davis, C., and Deegan, M., *The politics of the electronic text* (Oxford: Office for Humanities Communication Publications, 3, 1993), 41-52.

Matthews, R., and Merriam, T., 'Neural computation in stylometry I: an application to the works of Shakespeare and Fletcher', *Literary and Linguistic Computing,* 8 (1993), 203-10.

Merriam, T., and Matthews, R., 'Neural computation in stylometry II: an application to the works of Shakespeare and Marlowe, *Literary and Linguistic Computing,* 9 (1994), 1-8.

Mosteller, F., and Wallace, D. L., *Applied Bayesian and Classical Inference: the case of the Federalist Papers,* 2nd edn of *Inference and disputed authorship: the Federalist Papers* (1964) (New York: Springer-Verlag, 1984).

Pickering, J., 'Hypermedia: when will they feel natural?', in *Beyond the book: theory, culture, and the politics of cyberespace* (Oxford: Office for Humanities Communication Publications, 6), 1996 (forthcoming).

Potter, R. G., 'Literary criticism and literary computing', *Computers and the humanities*, 22 (1988), 91-98.

Potter, R. G. (ed.), *Literary computing and literary criticism: theoretical and practical essays on theme and rhetoric* (Philadelphia: University of Pennsylvania Press, 1989).

Purday, J.,'The British Library's *Initiatives for Access* Projects', *Communications of the ACM* (April 1995), 65-66.

Renear, A., and Bilder, G., 'Two theses about the new scholarly communication', in Landow, G., and Delaney, P., *The digital word* (Cambridge, MA: Massachusetts Institute of Technology Press, 1993) 217-236.

Robinson, P.M.W., and O'Hara, R.J., 'Cladistic analysis of an Old Norse manuscript tradition', in Hockey, S., and Ide, N. (eds.), *Research in humanities computing 4* (Oxford: Oxford University Press, 1994).

Rudall, B.H., and Corns, T., *Computers and literature: a practical guide* (Tunbridge Wells and Boston: Abacus Press, 1987).

Sutherland, K., 'A guide through the labyrinth: hypertext and the Victorian multiplot novel', *Literary and Linguistic Computing*, 5 (1990), 305-9.

Sutherland, K., 'Challenging assumptions: women writers, the literary canon, and new technology', *Bulletin of the John Rylands University Library*, 74 (1992), 109-120.

Sutherland, K., 'Waiting for connections: hypertext, multiplots, and the engaged reader', in Hockey, S., and Ide, N. (eds.), *Research in humanities computing 4* (Oxford: Oxford University Press, 1994).

Warner, J., *From writing to computers* (London and New York: Routledge, 1994).

Wooldridge, T.R., *A TACT exemplar* (Toronto: Centre for Computing in the Humanities, University of Toronto, 1991).

Further information

Blake Archive
http://jefferson.village.virginia.edu/Blake/

Canterbury Tales Project
Full details of this are given in Blake and Robinson (1993). The Project also publishes a Newsletter, available from Dr Peter Robinson, Computers and Variant Texts Project, International Institute for Electronic Library Research, De Montfort University, Hammerwood Gate, Kents Hill, Milton Keynes MK7 6HP. E-mail peterr@vax.ox.ac.uk

Dictionary of Old English; *The Complete Corpus of Old English*
Details of both can be found at http://www.lib.virginia.edu/etext/oec.html

Electronic Scholarly Editions (ese)
Contact Peter Shillingsburg at pls1@ra.msstate.edu for details of how to join.

FRANTEXT
For full details, contact the Institut National de la Langue Française, INaLF,
Eveline Martin 52, Bd de Magenta, 75010, Paris, France.

Hartlib Papers Project
University of Sheffield, Sheffield S10, 2TN. e-mail, hartlib@sheffield.ac.uk
URL http://www2.shef.ac.uk/hartlib/hartlib.html

Oxford Text Archive
Oxford University Computing Services, 13 Banbury Road, Oxford OX2 6NN.
e-mail: archive@vax.ox.ac.uk
URL: http://ota.ox.ac.uk/~archive/ota.html

Piers Plowman Electronic Archive
Details at http://jefferson.village.edu/piers/archive.goals.html

Project Electra
Director, Professor Kathryn Sutherland, Department of English Studies, University
of Notttingham, Nottingham NG7 2RD.
 e-mail: aezks@aen1.english.nottingham.ac.uk

Rossetti Archive
http://jefferson.village.virginia.edu/Rossetti/

Women Writers Project
Director, Carol Deboer-Langworthy, Box 1841, Brown University, Providence, RI
02912. e-mail: wwp@brownvm.brown.edu
http://twine.stg.brown.edu/projects/wwp/wwp_home.html

Music: Computer Use in Musicological Research

Ian Cross, Andrew Bennett and David Meredith

This chapter opens by assessing the place of information technology in music scholarship, and presents an overview of recent directions and developments in computer-based music research. Bibliographic and other remote resources (such as musical datasets) are then surveyed, and issues of accessibility and future network developments discussed. The chapter closes by reviewing briefly some recent examples of computer-based music research, and makes some suggestions for further reading.

Introduction

Other than in the form of the word processor, information technology has had most impact on music research where such research touches upon the formal or the scientific. In those domains where research in music is more closely aligned with humanities scholarship as conventionally conceived—in other words, where the aims of music research involve such activities as the preparation of editions, the investigation of sources, the assessment of stylistic factors, or the analysis of works of art—computer use has been less intensive.

There are a number of reasons for this. One is the diversity of the methods and aims of such scholarly activities, and hence of the computational representations and implementations that such activities would require; another is that the conduct of such activities by means of computer requires skills that are scarcely widespread at present within the musicological community. Nevertheless, computers are coming to play an increasingly important role in all areas of music research.

Computer use in these diverse areas can be described under three main headings, depending on whether the computer is being used to:

- manipulate music as sound;

- act as a logical device to frame and test general theories; or

- assist source—or data-oriented— 'practical' research.

Under the first heading, the primary concerns are the development and use of ways of recording, transforming and reproducing, or producing, sounds by means of computer. Central to these concerns are techniques of Digital Signal Processing or DSP (for a recent overview see De Poli *et al.* 1991), and the use of event-time control codes such as the MIDI (Musical Instrument Digital Interface) standard (see Loy 1985). DSP techniques and MIDI facilities are used in teaching and in composing music, and in research into resources for composition and for practical music-making as well as into acoustics, psychoacoustics, music cognition, and performance.

Under the second heading, considerations of formalism, and of computational logic as it can be applied in a variety of musical domains, predominate. Research is being conducted into computer representations of musical scores and structures (for a recent and accessible overview, see Marsden and Pople 1992), the automating of processes involved in music analysis and composition, as well as in the logistics of music production (such as music printing and automatic score recognition and transcription), and the modelling of elements of musical behaviour such as perception, performance, and improvisation.

Under the third heading falls the 'conventional' world of computers as it exists within most other humanities —or even social scientific—disciplines, where computers serve as tools in 'practical' research, being used to systematize bodies of information such as databases or bibliographies and to enable access to these, and where textual or numerical tools are employed to study and analyse text or batteries of data in the form of numbers. A digest of research conducted largely under these latter two headings is published annually in *Computing in Musicology*[1] (hereafter *CM*). The activities conducted within these three domains are not discrete; in some cases they overlap considerably, but this division will serve as a basic taxonomy of the materials to be covered.

As stated, the impact of the computer on research into music under the first two headings has been far greater than under the third heading, which could be held to be most relevant to the scholarly activities generally considered central to musicological enquiry. Indeed, most of the research conducted under the first heading falls within the domain of composition or practical music-making, and will only be considered here in brief. The relative paucity of research conducted under the third heading—as compared, say, with most language-based disciplines—can be explained to some extent by noting that music research is faced with certain discipline-specific problems in the employment of computers, problems that some of the research falling under the second heading is intended to address.

These problems arise in part from a lack of standardization (whether at the level of interface or data-structure), but in part from the diversity of the information-structures and methods of research that must be, respectively, represented and implemented. These factors impose constraints on what would be the most likely benefit of IT use in musicological research: the capacity to store, sort, search, and structure large amounts of information held on computer. They limit the accessibility and generalizability of the structures and relations embodied in databases and catalogues of music, as well as the powers of the investigative processes that might be employed by researchers. However, they have not prevented the compilation of databases, while computational representations of music have been insightfully applied in a broad range of specific musicological tasks.

A general overview of computer-based music research under the three headings outlined above will be given. This is followed by a more detailed account of those resources that are available and likely to become available to scholars in a range of musical domains. More detailed reports of a selection of recent music research projects within the UK are then presented to give a flavour of current computer-based research, and a concluding summary will be provided with suggestions for further reading and future directions.

Computer-based music research: an overview

Computers and music as sound

Within the domain of computer manipulation of music as sound, developments in the last decade have been so far-reaching and fast-moving as to render even a summary account impossible in the space available here. Volumes such as those edited by Roads and Strawn (1985), Roads (1989), Pope (1991) and De Poli *et al.* (1991) and specialist journals such as *Computer Music Journal* and the *Journal of the Audio-Engineering Society*, as well as publications such as the *Rapports* from the Institut de

Recherche et Coordination Acoustique/Musique (IRCAM) in Paris, and the Proceedings of the annual International Conferences on Computer Music (ICMC) over the last decade all report on this work. This research has been largely directed towards practical music-making and composition (for an overview of the latter see Manning 1993; Moore 1990; Pressing 1992), and its impact on the world of music scholarship has, in general, been modulated by commercial implementations of its results. Of these, it is sufficient to say that they have become virtually ubiquitous, with the compact disc at the consumer end and 'tapeless' recording and DSP processes together with MIDI and other encoding and communication standards at the production end of a thriving commercial music industry.

The benefits for music research of these primarily commercially motivated developments have been less than might have been anticipated, although this is in stark contrast to the advantages obtained for computer-based music learning (see, for example, Pople 1993). On the one hand, much of the research into aspects of music perception and performance reported in journals such as *Music Perception* and *Psychology of Music* has been facilitated by the accessibility of MIDI-compatible equipment and software and by the availability of low-cost DSP resources. On the other hand, for example, the existence of the MIDI standard and of a large body of music encoded in that format has as yet conferred no great advantage on the broader world of music scholarship; despite enhancements to the MIDI standard such as that described by Selfridge-Field in *CM* (1993), its limitations render it incapable of encoding significant aspects of the types of musical repertoires most likely to be of interest to researchers. Nevertheless, the advantages (in terms of access to encoded repertoires) to be gained in the future for music research by developments in this area are immense.

Music and the computer as logical engine

This domain encompasses those areas of research within which the focus is as much on computational as on specifically musical issues. It includes the development of computational representations of aspects of music and formalized music-analytic procedures, the production of systems for score manipulation and automatic music data recognition, as well as the modelling of music cognition. Much of the research conceived of here as falling within this domain could equally well be ascribed to the domain of 'practical' research, as most computational representations of music (to take an example) have been developed to deal with specific repertoires in the course of particular research projects.

A primary problem is the variety of objects and procedures to be represented; the requirements of representing music as notated in the form of scores vary immensely from repertoire to repertoire (see Marsden, this volume). Even systems intended to be applicable to a wide range of musical scores and repertoires such as DARMS (Digital Alternate Representation of Musical Scores) are generally constrained in what they represent. Nevertheless, despite their problematic nature, DARMS (generally, in extended and enhanced versions), MIDI, and other restricted representation systems such as Plaine and Easy and ESAC (Essen Associative Code) have been widely employed (for examples see *CM* 1991), and efforts are now being directed towards the development of conversion protocols to enable musical data encoded under one system to be transferred to others that facilitate its manipulation for specific musicological purposes (see, for example, Selfridge-Field in *CM* 1993). Representations of formal characteristics of music that go beyond notational descriptions have been proposed and implemented by a number of researchers. The most widely used of these is SCORE (see *DCRM* 1987), though its limitations have been criticised by Balaban, who proposes an alternative system intended to be capable of encoding complex attributes of musical works such as motifs and themes (see Balaban *et al.* 1992). A similarly flexible representation, where the focus is on the adaptability of the representation to the musicological task in hand, is proposed by Huron (1992), who provides a cogent analysis of issues in representing music on computer.

Other researchers have concentrated on the development of procedures for manipulating, abstracting, or generating musical information rather than seeking to embody complex characteristics of music within data-structures. In the analytic domain, several systems focus on computerization of set-theoretic procedures while others are intended to deal with aspects of tonal musical structure (for a range of examples see *CM* 1989–1993). A less constrained approach is found in Mesnage's Morphoscope, which works in tandem with his score-representation system Musinote to provide a flexible and accommodating analytical system (see Mesnage 1993). An alternative approach has involved the development of computational models of more or less broad classes of music (see, among others, Baroni *et al.* 1992; Cope 1991; Ebcioglu, in Balaban *et al.*, 1992).

Within the formal domain, perhaps most effort has gone into the representation and graphical presentation of score notation. There are many 'music-processing' packages available (see the annual reviews in *CM*), though certain of these packages are particularly suited to musicological activities. For example, Clocksin's powerful Calliope system is intended for the preparation of performance editions, and has facilities for displaying and printing musical information in score or in a variety of tablature formats. Several programs enable MIDI input and output (e.g. Finale, SCORE, Nightingale) while some (e.g. The Note Processor) are compatible with DARMS code. Some considerable success has also been achieved in automating data acquisition by means of the optical input of musical scores (see *CM* 1991).

Perhaps the most complex activities within this domain are those involved in the modelling of music cognition. While the most comprehensive theories in this area (those of Lerdahl and Jackendoff (1983), and of Narmour (1989, 1992)) are not computationally expressed, their formal character has enabled the computational implementation of some of their sub-theories (see, for example, chapters by Linster and by Baker in Balaban *et al.* 1992). Among the most significant work in this area remains that reported in Longuet-Higgins (1979), while more recent research is reported in Sloboda (1988), Howell *et al.* (1991), and Todd and Loy (1991). The overall 'research project' of modelling musical cognition has been incorporated into the task of producing computer-based music systems that are intended to interact 'intelligently' with live human performers (see Rowe 1993).

Computers in 'practical' music research

This domain embraces research in which the computer serves as a tool in 'practical' musicological inquiry, annual surveys of such research being provided by *CM*. Research of this type can be categorized according to whether it employs non-specialist computing facilities (e.g. spreadsheets, general database facilities, packages for statistical or DSP analysis) or makes use of music-specific computational representations and processes, and whether the research is focused on finite individual projects or is intended to provide generalizable resources.

A typical individual project employing a non-specialist program to facilitate data storage, presentation, and cross-comparison is that described by Tomita (1993). Similar non-specialist programs have been used to provide, maintain and enable access to substantial corpora of information in textual or graphical form (for examples see *CM* 1990, 1993). Individual specialized projects generally employ pre-existing representation systems such as DARMS or SCORE to encode pieces or repertoires, and apply to these data a range of computational techniques (which may involve pattern-matching, statistical analysis, or more complex processes of abstraction of music-specific information). The research reported in Morehen (1993a and b) (see below) provides exemplary instances.

Frequently, such specialist individual projects will result in the production of more generally usable resources (such as databases or data processing programs), although this is usually not their principal aim. A number of projects, however, have been undertaken to provide just such resources; such specialist large-scale projects include the *Thesaurus Musicarum Latinarum*, the Répertoire International des Sources Musicales (RISM) catalogue of incipits, the Centre for Computer-Assisted Research in the Humanities (CCARH) music database MuseData (see *CM* 1993, and below), and the various musical databases maintained at Essen (see Schaffrath 1992).

Resources and access

From the perspective of the practical availability and accessibility of musical information via computer, the methods employed to systematize bodies of information as databases, bibliographies, or to enable and facilitate access to such resources are best considered in the context of three broad domains:

- **Network resources**: the growth of networks both as vehicles offering connection to remote services and databases, and as providers of facilities for data and information exchange, communications, and similar utilities.

- **Practical research—source-oriented research**: the use of computers in the building and accessing of bibliographical and reference databases, library catalogues and other information services which comprise records of the primary and secondary literature of music.

- **Practical research—data-oriented research**: computers used in the compilation of databases that, while novel in design, consist mainly of textual information and which utilize common data management and manipulation tools (i.e. applications where discipline-specific problems of data structure and representation are not at issue).

Network resources

The most important development for computers in music research and scholarship in the short-term is likely to be the growth of information and resources available on or accessible through the 'net'. Those disciplines where the use of computers and information technology is a fully integral part of the research process have been best placed to benefit from the growth of national and international networks. Music, however, has not been in this position, certainly in the UK and Europe (although the situation is somewhat better in North America), in that most primary sources and standard music repertoires are not available, nor accessible, in computational form. In general important aspects of the processes of musical scholarship have not been formalized to an extent that can be implemented on computer.

The growing importance of networked resources for music, and indeed for other arts and humanities disciplines, reflects a significant change in information provision generally. It is now accepted that academic and other research institutions in the UK need to develop a more strategic approach to information provision, one based on cooperation and sharing, in order to supplement the resources for research and scholarship that can be provided by any one institution. The pressures that have effected this change of strategy are easy to identify: selective research funding, financial constraints, and the explosion of published material mean that it is no longer feasible for any one institution *in itself* to provide for the research needs of its staff and students. This is especially true for music as a comparatively small discipline where researchers working in closely aligned fields are usually widely dispersed; music research, as humanities generally, is rarely conducted by a group or team in one physical location. It is clear that the research and information needs of a subject like music are most efficiently and effectively served by the networking of resources.

Within this context, the improved availability of computer and IT resources for the humanities as a whole have of course resulted in significant gains for music research: infrastructure developments such as the continued expansion of the Joint Academic Network in the UK (JANET); improvements in electronic communications; the growth of nationally-available databases and information services. Such benefits have accrued mainly where resources are built upon existing, stable hardware and software platforms, funded at the supra-institutional level and usually therefore free at point of use. Specific computing resources for music are, by comparison, rather at the latent stage; there is, however, a growing and welcome recognition that developments in music research are becoming increasingly technology-led and dependent on the application of computers.

Information exchange

Developments in network technologies and facilities have had a significant effect on the way researchers and scholars use and exchange information. Local, national, and international networks (Janet, Internet and SuperJanet) support an ever-growing number of services—electronic mail, mailing lists, discussion lists and digests, bulletin boards and usenet groups (and other forms of informal information exchange), file transfer facilities, software archives—as well as providing the gateway to remote services, datasets and databases, including library catalogues. The number of information sources open to scholars is expanding, giving rise to the concept of a 'virtual library'. The development of Super-JANET is likely to be of particular interest to music researchers, as the high transmission speeds it offers should facilitate the transfer of musical data in sub-symbolic form as digitized soundfiles or complex images.

Music researchers are increasingly an international, widely dispersed community, so that access to network resources is becoming a critical feature in the communication process. Effective use of networked resources, however, requires adequate access via a personal computer on every researcher's desk to the information world beyond, which is not a facility that every music researcher can take for granted. Universal connectivity to the network therefore remains a top priority for future developments in computers in music research.

Music specialist services

The use of e-mail has led to the formation of discussion lists, digests, bulletin boards, and other facilities by which scholars can float and exchange ideas, raise problems and issues, or simply offer bodies of information or data in an informal way. Although the growth of subject-specific discussion lists has been rather slow in this country, there are at least two music-specific resources, Med-and-Ren-Mus and the Music Research Digest.

Med-and-Ren-Mus, an Internet conference moderated by Isobel Preece at the University of Newcastle, offers a forum for practical and research queries relating to Medieval and Renaissance music. More general in scope is the Music Research Digest, moderated by Stephen Page through the University of Oxford, which has achieved more international recognition and relevance. Some musicologists have also derived significant benefits from UK resources concerned more broadly with the humanities, in particular the Humanities Bulletin Board (HUMBUL), although this is no longer available.

Access to the Internet opens up a wealth of similar services, especially in the USA (See *CM* 1992, 39–60 and 1993, 57–58, for a discussion and brief listing of some of the available resources of this type). Two of these are worth mentioning in a little detail. EthnoFORUM, a service of the Society for Ethnomusicology, provides both an electronic digest (*Ethnomusicology Research Digest*), available to all subscribers, and an archive of extended research and teaching materials, available only to members. *Music Theory Online*, a publication of the Society for Music Theory moderated by Lee Rothfarb at Harvard University, is an electronic journal for music theory and contains articles, reviews, dissertation citations, and announcements. These 'hybrid' (digest/archive) services are likely to become important models for future developments in scholarly communication.

Databases, catalogues, and datasets relevant to music research

Significant progress has been made in the domain of computer applications in source-related music research and scholarship. Again, music scholarship has benefited predominantly from the enhanced provision of online information services and databases serving the needs of the arts, humanities, and social sciences as a whole.

Literature searching and the compilation of bibliographies of primary and secondary sources are still a central research activity for musicologists. The computer's efficiency in processing large volumes of structured bibliographical data and saving the researcher hours of clerical toil has long been recognized. Music researchers need the facility to carry out literature searches on large online databases, which include the indices to and abstracts of periodical literature, in order to identify material of relevance, and ideally obtain full text of the relevant document. The principal research tools and resources that are most relevant to musicology might be grouped as follows:

- Primary sources:
  - » Musical scores as notated documents (including printed, manuscript, surrogates such as microforms, or digitized graphical representations);
  - » Musical scores in symbolic encoded form;
  - » Music texts manifest as sound recordings;
  - » Primary textual material (printed and manuscript), e.g., textual sources such as chant texts, theoretical texts, treatises.

- Secondary literature and sources:
  - » Books (monographs) on music;
  - » Articles, reviews, etc. in periodicals (including newspapers), serials, and in books produced under editorial direction (e.g. conference proceedings, *Festschriften*).

In libraries, there has been a shift in emphasis in library acquisitions and retention policies from 'holdings' strategies (based on the physical acquisition of an item) to 'access' strategies (based on identifying the information need and delivering the document either from within the institution's own resources or from elsewhere. Knowing (a) what is available and (b) where it can found are therefore becoming the key tactics in obtaining research materials. Of central importance to this is the sharing of information about bibliographical and other resources. The principal resources that music researchers and scholars can now exploit through networks are: bibliographic databases such as those negotiated nationally by CHEST and mounted by the Bath Information and Data Service (BIDS), free at the point of use, or other online database hosts, charged directly to end users; library catalogues; other textual databases, and information and indexing services. Increasingly some databases are available on CD-ROM, either as a stand-alone product, or more frequently as a networked resource (for a brief discussion of music products see Foreman 1992).

Library catalogues and bibliographic resources

The spread of library automation has led to the increased availability of online public access catalogues (OPACs) across networks. The contents of academic and research libraries in the UK and beyond are, of course, very relevant to music research. Of particular significance in this context has been the establishment of the Consortium of University Research Libraries (CURL) database, consisting of pooled catalogue data from the major copyright and academic research libraries of the UK, together with British National Bibliography (BNB) and Library of Congress data; it is effectively a meta-bibliography of immense proportions and importance. It seems certain that CURL will become *de facto* the National Arts and Humanities database, available as an OPAC. For music researchers, CURL is clearly an unrivalled source of information about the secondary literature of music in book form, which can be supplemented by the British Library Catalogue (available now either as a CD-ROM database or through the British Library Automated Information Service (BLAISE).

Information about music texts and scores, however, is more problematic given the patchy coverage of musical texts by the contributors to CURL. The primary resource in this area remains the British Library's *Catalogue of Printed Music*, recently issued on CD-ROM. Given high CD-ROM costs, a critical development for music scholars will therefore be the future availability of the British Library's St Pancras OPAC (which will include data relating to the Music Library's collections) through JANET. For scholars of the music of earlier periods, online access to the central RISM database in Frankfurt remains a crucial objective, though with little prospect of attainment in the short-term. Occasionally the needs of music researchers have been met by the development of very specific databases, such as the Beethoven Bibliography Online at San José State University Library.

Other datasets

Literature searching and the compilation of bibliographies remains a central research activity for musicologists. There is, of course, a wealth of music research material manifest in the form of articles, reviews, notes in periodicals and other serials (including newspapers and magazines), contributions to conference proceedings, and Festschriften, etc., and in 'grey' literature. Online alternatives to hard-print indexing and citation journals have been around for some time and generally have been mounted as individual files on hosts serving a variety of disciplines (e.g. DIALOG service). Take-up in music has often been limited because of cost considerations (e.g. connect-time and/or citation costs); this has prohibited more exploratory, speculative forms of searching. Music researchers have been able to benefit greatly from nationally-negotiated deals, such as those through CHEST.

A number of datasets that are free at point of use have been made available on this basis, the most significant of which for music scholars in the UK being the Bath Information and Data Service (BIDS), which offers online searching of the ISI Arts and Humanities Citation Index. The chief limitation of this facility is the level of generality of the database—the core journals for music covered is a rather small subset of what most music researchers would consider to be an essential coverage and certainly cannot compare with the coverage of the specialized indexing and abstracting tools such as Répertoire International de la Littérature Musicale (RILM) and The Music Index. The most exciting development in this area has probably been the emergence of RILM and The Music Index as CD-ROM products (viz. Muse and Music Index); whether used as a stand-alone database or, more frequently, as a networked resource, CD-ROM is now a primary information technology. The networking of CD-ROMs is now emerging as probably the most cost-effective way of providing access to large, specialized information databases, providing attendant licensing problems can be resolved. Music scholarship and research in the UK has much to gain from such developments.

Online access to information about sound recordings is rather in its infancy, though of increasing importance given the growing interest in the academic study of performance history through recordings. In the UK there has been welcome progress on the development of a national database: plans have been advanced for the long-proposed MCPS database, encompassing the National Discography, available both online and on CD-ROM; equally important in terms of access to a large-scale archive of recordings is the announcement that the BBC Gramophone Library Catalogue has been digitized and that the MCPS database will provide an interface to it. Use of the extensive holdings of the National Sound Archive (NSA) in discographical research has been somewhat hampered by the slow progress in developing a comprehensive OPAC. An NSA initiative of special import to ethnomusicologists, for whom the sound recording remains a principal object of scrutiny, is the 'Project Digitize', which will explore the possibilities of digitizing recordings and providing automated access to them, including making them available through telecommunications links. The project will initially concentrate on two major international music collections: the A.L. Lloyd collection of folk music recordings from around the world; and the wax cylinder collection of ethnographic field recordings. In short, the evolution of a single database of music-related material in the UK is an unlikely development. From North America, by comparison, there have been more substantial developments: a music subset of the OCLC Online Union Catalogue containing extensive records of both sound recordings and music scores, as well as book material, has been recently published as a CD-ROM—CAT CD450; likewise the holdings of the Library of Congress have also been made available as The Music Catalog on CD-ROM.

As yet, there appear to be no datasets in the making consisting of digitized graphical representations of scores (either printed music or primary sources). There are, however, a small number of databases that hold musical score information in symbolic or soundfile form, enabling complex query procedures to be developed. The most notable of these is the CCARH database MuseData (see *CM* 1993, 11-30) which employs a group of music encoding methods together with conversion protocols and is intended to provide a flexible means of encoding music so as to enable the application of a vast range of analytic techniques and procedures to individual works and to whole repertoires.

Databases of textual data relating to music

Finally, mention should be made of another area where computer technology has been employed in data-oriented music research, that is where computers have been used in the compilation of databases of textual material that use stock data management and manipulation tools and where the discipline-specific problems of data structure and representation of music are not at issue.

The most important development in the UK has been the Register of Music Data in London Newspapers, 1660-1800, a project based at Royal Holloway University of London and directed by Rosamund McGuinness. The Register makes available a wealth of documentary evidence concerning music in London newspapers, including precise information about concert life, printing and publishing, instrument manufacture, as well as many other aspects of musical life. When complete it is expected that access will be either online through networks or through a CD-ROM product; the project utilizes industry-standard software tools—the ORACLE RDBMS (relational database management system)with SQL*Plus—which will greatly facilitate future online access.

A number of specialized text applications of this kind have sprung up around the world, though predominantly in North America, and this underlines the importance of more universal access to the Internet for music researchers in the UK. Some databases seem destined to become critical resources for the study of music of particular periods. Worthy of particular mention is the *Thesaurus Musicarum Latinarum*, a collaborative project managed by Thomas Mathiesen at Indiana University, which is attempting to make available in machine-readable form all Latin writings on music theory from the Middle Ages and Renaissance, essentially by capturing the content of early treatises from modern editions, and encoding their musical incipits. Other text applications are very diverse, ranging from a system for encoding scribal abbreviations in medieval musical manuscripts (THEMA) to a database of documentary sources in Neapolitan newspapers (*Gazzetta di Napoli*). There are also a number of applications relating to source inventories, usually involving the encoding of musical incipits and often bibliographical in character: the RISM-US Music Manuscript Inventory (the US contribution to RISM Series A/II); CANTUS (a database of incipits of the chants of the Divine Office contained in early printed and MS sources); *The Chanson*, 1400–1600 (a comprehensive index of bibliographic information pertaining to fifteenth- and sixteenth-century chansons); the International Inventory of Villancico texts; the database of scanned images relating to the Notation of Baroque Music. (For fuller details of recent progress on these and similar projects see *CM* 1992, 9-30, and 1993, 33-58.)

Applications—a selection

To illustrate the diversity of the current state of computer-based music research, brief descriptions of a selection of recent UK research projects in the field of computational musicology are given below. The projects outlined are intended to give a fairly representative (though incomplete and informal) picture of computer-based music research as it exists in the UK and worldwide.

Two projects by John Morehen provide exemplary instances of the application of computers to historical-musicological problems. His recent work on text underlay in Renaissance polyphony builds upon three earlier programs. The first of these allowed for the automatic recognition of underlay features that contravened strict sixteenth century practice; the second allowed a piece to be searched for any combination of rhythm and syllabic placement; and the third automatically produced a syllabi-fication in accordance with a set of predefined rules derived from contemporary theorists. The program described in Morehen (1993a) is considerably more sophisticated than any of the three earlier programs. This program, written in FORTRAN77, analyses a database in which are stored a number of polyphonic pieces with their underlaid texts, and then attempts to underlay the text of a different polyphonic composition according to the practice of the pieces in the database. The program has proved successful in modelling the text underlay practices of Adrian Willaert; as Morehen points out, it has demonstrated its utility both as an aid in the preparation of new editions and as a tool in the domain of stylistic analysis.

Morehen (1993b) presents an account of a program written in SPIT-BOL4 that attempts to determine the correct fingering for a monophonic right-hand part of a piece of Elizabethan keyboard music. Again, the program is provided with a database, this time of right-hand parts from pieces in the style under consideration each accompanied by its finger-ing; it is then required to predict an appropriate fingering for a new right-hand part that is also in the style but which is not present in the database. The program has been successfully tested on a repertoire of pieces by English composers from the virginalist period (ca.1560–ca.1630).

A group comprising Alan Smaill, Geraint Wiggins, Mitch Harris, and Eduardo Miranda, based in the Department of Artificial Intelligence at the University of Edinburgh, has been developing (over the last six years) a generalized hierarchical music representation system for use in analysis and composition. Their system, Charm (Common Hierarchical Abstract Representation for Music), is built upon a basic system for the repre-sentation of music events presented originally in Wiggins *et al.* 1993 and is specified only in terms of abstract data types. That is, it is a mathe-matical specification of what information must be encoded and how the information is to be accessed without any restrictions on how the system should be implemented. The developers claim that it is essential that such a system allows for multiple views and hierarchies and they provide for this by allowing events and constituents to be members of more than one constituent. In Smaill *et al.* (1993, p. 7), the goal of the project is defined as an 'eventual situation where a researcher in computer music could use any computer program with his or her chosen representation system, limited only by the suitability of the program for computation over the data represented'. They present two extended examples of their representational system at work: one in an automated composition task and the other in a semiotic analysis in the style of Ruwet.

Research being conducted by David Meredith with Ian Cross in the Faculty of Music, University of Cambridge, aims to develop ways of handling aspects of tonal musical structure by means of computer (see Meredith 1994). It involves the computational implementation of a data-structure developed by Meredith specifically for the representation of tonal scores together with a language for expressing predicates about such data-structures. The project has focused on augmenting the functionality of Marcel Mesnage's database and analysis tools Musinote and Morphoscope (Mesnage 1993), which employ 'user-friendly' graphical interfaces, by providing a parallel representation structure (together with 'invisible' conversion procedures) intended to facilitate the abstraction of tonally-significant structures from encoded scores.

Paul Hodgson at the University of Sussex Department of Cognitive Science is working on the problem of modelling creative cognition in jazz improvisation. His program, Improviser, takes as input a four-track MIDI datafile consisting of bass, drums, harmony, and melody and generates automatically a real-time melodic improvisation based upon the input melody and harmony as the MIDI file is played back (Hodgson 1994). As the MIDI file is being processed to generate a performance through a sound module, the improvisation module of the Improviser program looks ahead into the harmony track, analyses the next chord and then determines a set of possible notes that could be included in the improvisation for that chord. The algorithm for determining the set of possible improvisation notes for a given harmony is derived from Coker (1964), and there are several ways in which the user can control the style of the improvisation. Hodgson is developing this program with the aim of producing convincing simulations of improvisations in the style of the jazz saxophonist, Charlie Parker. His current strategy is to attempt to impose motivic and thematic constraints in the form of grammatical rules in order to produce improvisations that sound more 'human' and which are more 'thematically coherent'.

Conclusions

It should be evident that the principal difficulty in assessing the potential role of computers in music research lies in the diversity of purposes that computers are capable of fulfilling in respect of music. What is also evident is the fact that such diversity requires solutions to be found in applying computers in musical research which may result in the development of computer applications that are very different from those likely to be familiar through their use within text-based humanities disciplines. The success of computer applications to musicological research in the future is more likely to depend on the development and dissemination of 'open' representation systems and datasets that can be converted or adapted to fit the requirements of a wide range of applications than on the development of any single 'canonical' representation. Though strong commercial pressures (in terms of the rewards to be garnered from the design and sale of copyright-protected music software and hardware) are likely to militate against this course of development, the endorsement of this approach by researchers such as Huron (1992) and Selfridge-Field (in *CM* 1993) would seem to warrant its adoption.

Note

1. Existing prior to 1989 as the *Directory of computer-assisted research in musicology (DCRM)*.

References and bibliography

Balaban, M., Ebcioglu, K., and Laske, O. (eds.), *Understanding music with AI* (Cambridge, MA: AAAI Press/ MIT Press, 1992).

Baroni, M., Dalmonte, R., and Jacabone, C., 'Theory and analysis of European melody', in Marsden, A., and Pople, A. (eds.), *Computer representations and models in music* (London: Academic Press, 1992), 187–206.

Coker, J., *Improvising jazz* (Englewood Cliffs, N.J.: Prentice-Hall, 1964).

Cope, D., *Computers and musical style* (Madison, Wisconsin: A-R Publications, 1991).

Foreman, L., 'Using CD-ROM', *Musical Times* (1992), 122.

Harris, M., Smaill, A., and Wiggins, G. A., *Knowledge representation for music on computers* (Personal communication, 1994).

Hewlett, W. B., and Selfridge-Field, E. (eds.), *Directory of computer-assisted research in musicology* (Menlo Park, CA: Centre for Computer Assisted Research in the Humanities, 1985-1988).

Hewlett, W.B., and Selfridge-Field, E. (eds.), *Computing in musicology* (Menlo Park, CA: Centre for Computer Assisted Research in the Humanities, 1989-).

Hodgson, P., *Modelling cognition in creative musical improvisation: 'the Improviser program'* (University of Sussex Department of Cognitive Science, internal report, 1994).

Howell, P., West, R., and Cross, I. (eds.), *Representing musical structure* (London: Academic Press, 1991).

Huron, D., 'Design principles in computer-based music representation', in Marsden, A., and Pople, A. (eds.), *Computer representations and models in music* (London: Academic Press, 1992).

Lerdahl, F., and Jackendoff, R., *A generative theory of tonal music* (Cambridge, MA: MIT Press, 1983).

Longuet-Higgins, H.C., 'The perception of music', *Proceedings of the Royal Society* B205, (1979), 307-22.

Loy, D. G., 'Musicians make a standard: the MIDI phenomenon', *Computer Music Journal*, 9 (1985), 8-26.

Manning, P., *Electronic and computer music* (2nd edn.) (Oxford: Clarendon Press, 1993).

Marsden, A., and Pople, A. (eds.), *Computer representations and models in music* (London: Academic Press, 1992).

Meredith, D., *Representation Analyser; program specification and guide for users* (University of Cambridge, Faculty of Music, internal report, 1994).

Mesnage, M., 'Morphoscope, a system for music analysis', *Interface*, 22.2 (1993), 119-32.

Moore, F.R., *Elements of computer music* (Englewood Cliffs, N.J.: Prentice-Hall, 1990).

Morehen, J., 'Adrian Willaert's Musica Nova (1559): a computer-assisted study in text underlay', *Musicus*, 3 (1993a), 7-19.

Morehen, J., 'Aiding authentic performance: a fingering databank for Elizabethan keyboard music', in Selfridge-Field, E., and Hewlitt, W. (eds.), *Directory of Computing in Musicology*, 9 (1993b), 81-92.

Narmour, E., *The analysis and cognition of basic melodic structure* (Chicago: University of Chicago Press, 1989).

Narmour, E., *The analysis and cognition of melodic complexity* (Chicago: University of Chicago Press, 1992).

De Poli, G., Piccialli, A., and Roads, C. (eds.), *Representations of musical signals* (Cambridge, MA: MIT Press, 1991).

Pope, S.T. (ed.), *The well-tempered object* (Cambridge, MA: MIT Press, 1991).

Pople, A., 'Making the most of the TLTP', *Musicus*, 3 (1993), 3-6.

Pressing, J., *Synthesiser performance and real-time techniques* (Oxford: OUP, 1992).

Roads, C. (ed.), *The Music machine* (Cambridge, MA: MIT Press, 1989).

Roads, C., and Strawn, J. (eds.), *Composers and the computer* (Cambridge, MA: MIT Press, 1985).

Rowe, R., *Interactive music systems* (Cambridge, MA: MIT Press, 1993).

Schaffrath, H., 'The retrieval of monophonic melodies and their variants', in Pople, A., and Marsden, A. (eds.), *Computer representations and models in music* (London: Academic Press, 1992).

Sloboda, J. A. (ed.), *Generative processes in music* (Oxford: OUP, 1988).

Smaill, A., Wiggins, G. A., and Harris, M., 'Hierarchical music representation for analysis and composition', *Computers and the Humanities*, 27.1 (1993), 7-17.

Todd, P.M., and Loy, D.G. (eds.), *Music and connectionism* (Cambridge, MA: MIT Press, 1991).

Tomita, Y., 'The spreadsheet in musicology: an efficient working environment for statistical analysis in text critical study', *Musicus*, 3 (1993), 31-38.

Wiggins, G., Miranda, E., Smaill, A., and Harris, M., 'A framework for the evaluation of music representation systems', *Computer Music Journal*, 17.3 (1993), 31-42.

Further reading

Computing in Musicology, and its pre-1989 incarnation, the *Directory of Computer-assisted Research in Musicology*, are edited by Walter Hewlett and Eleanor Selfridge-Field and published annually by the Centre for Computer Assisted Research in the Humanities, Menlo Park, CA. It is essential reading for anyone who wishes to keep abreast of developments in the field of computational musicology, as, increasingly, is *Musicus*, published biannually by the Computers in Teaching Initiative (CTI) Centre for Music, Department of Music, University of Lancaster, Lancaster LA1 4YW. A comprehensive and fairly concise introduction to computing in the domain of practical music is found in Manning (1993), while *Computer Music Journal* provides an account of the state-of-the-art in this field.

Philosophy

Stephen R. L. Clark and Barry F. Dainton

Some branches of philosophy have particular links with the theory and practice of computing, notably the philosophy of mind, and formal logic. The teaching of formal logic is now made easier by a variety of computer programs, running on personal computers. Some departments are involved in the development of expert systems, whether for practical or theoretical purposes. Some philosophical texts have been subjected to computer analysis in the hope of identifying their authors, or their relative dates. There are a variety of hypertext developments, allowing rapid migration through texts, commentaries, and questions. The major use of the new technology for philosophers, however, has been to speed up the necessary communications and discussions on which the subject thrives. The global network now accommodates a variety of general bulletin boards, specialized discussion groups, papers-in-progress, and electronic journals. Most philosophers use these tools merely as tools; some seek to make them models for the human mind; a very few hope or expect a sort of universal mind to develop from the network. The speed of change is such that much detailed information will be out of date by the time this chapter is read, but we will seek to provide guides both to the present state of play, and to relatively stable information sources.

Philosophy of mind

Philosophers of mind traditionally concerned themselves with problems such as these: the sort of thing a mind is, the nature of intelligence and understanding, the relationship between mind and body. The development of computers has led to new questions such as these: could a computer think, perceive, be intelligent, possess feelings? Some philosophers answer in the affirmative, and so claim to have answered the traditional questions too. If computers can sustain minds we would also, given that we know how they work, know the essential nature of the various elements of mentality. Other philosophers, of course, disagree with this and maintain that computers can, at best, act *as if* they possessed some of the attributes of mentality.

This last claim is indisputable. Machines which can generate original mathematical proofs and play grandmaster-level chess are certainly simulating intelligence of a sort. However, few who believe machine intelligence to be a possibility would claim we can at present build computers which can really think. Even the best of current AI (artificial intelligence) programs can only do a few tightly circumscribed tasks well. But the proponents of AI claim this limitation is only contingent, and can be overcome by devising more sophisticated programming techniques. It is generally accepted that *any* program (algorithm) can be run on a standard all-purpose computer (i.e. a universal Turing machine). So, it is argued, we *already* have machines with the capacity for intelligence; all that is lacking is the programming know-how.

Suppose it were possible to program a computer so that it could replicate those aspects of human behaviour we associate with mentality—this machine can hold intelligent conversations with us, describe its environment, solve problems, and so on. Some philosophers hold that such a machine would possess a mind; others disagree, on the grounds that there would be no reason to think it possessed conscious awareness or subjectivity, and nothing which lacks these attributes can be said to possess a mind. How can the mere processing of innumerable bit-strings give rise to sensations of pain, perceptions of sound, colour, or genuine understanding? This issue, currently hotly contested, ultimately depends on how we analyse the relevant sorts of mental item. If we analyse all mental items in terms of their causal role in a behaviour-producing system, then provided our putative thinking machine produces its outputs in the right sorts of way, we would be justified in taking it to be conscious. But while many find 'functionalist' analyses of this sort plausible, others find them to be fundamentally mistaken.[1]

Proponents of AI often argue that consciousness is a red herring, in that it is not something that is necessary for intelligence. After all, we often solve problems without consciously thinking them through, and this ability certainly requires intelligence. Perhaps the same ability could be programmed into a machine, even if consciousness could not be. Progress on the programming front, however, has been very slow, and it is as yet unclear whether the difficulties are insuperable. A major obstacle is the 'problem of common-sense knowledge'. If computers are ever going to be regarded as possessing an intelligence akin to our own, they will have to be furnished with some of the vast amounts of seemingly trivial knowledge about the world and how it works that we have. But in the words of one expert, 'It has long been recognized that it is much easier to write a program to carry out abstruse formal operations than to capture the common sense of a dog.'[2] Apart from the sheer bulk of relevant information, no one yet has a clear idea of how to formalize it in a way which could be used by a computer. A large-scale, brute-force attempt to solve this problem is currently underway: the CYC project, begun in 1984 with a start-up budget of $50 million, and not expected to terminate until the year 2001. The first decade of the project is being devoted mainly to *philosophical* problems; the project's founder Doug Lenat describes CYC as 'mankind's first foray into large-scale ontological engineering.'[3] Lenat sees CYC as developing in two stages. During the second stage, CYC will be able to absorb information itself from sources such as newspapers and encyclopaedias, but first it has to be provided with the means to make sense of the sort of data contained in encyclopaedias, and this means providing the programme with a basic representation of the world, along with elementary reasoning skills. The first stage of the project is devoted to this task, and it has led the CYC team into the areas of ontology, epistemology, and logic. What basic sorts of object are there? What is it for one event to cause another? What is it to know a proposition P? How should beliefs be adjusted to new evidence?

No one knows yet whether CYC will be a success. Some think the basic approach is flawed, but take heart from the renaissance of interest in artificial neural nets, or parallel distributed processing (PDP) devices. Unlike conventional (Von Neumann) computers, these are not fed with a set of coded instructions to be carried out sequentially. Instead, the outputs of the network in response to selected inputs are monitored, and the behaviour of the constituent 'neurones' is varied until the desired input-output patterns start to emerge. PDP machines are good at tasks which conventional computers find difficult (such as speech recognition), but it is early days yet, and more work will have to be done before the potential of the new approach becomes known. Indeed, one of the problems currently exercising philosophers is how to clarify the ways in which PDP and classical systems really are different.[4]

Games philosophers play

Over the past decade there has been a burgeoning interest in Artificial Life (AL). This involves the computer simulation of biological organisms of varying degrees of complexity. The scientists engaged on this project hope to cast light on problems such as the origin of life (from molecular self-assembly), evolution by natural selection, and ecological dynamics. More ambitiously,

> In addition to providing new ways to study the biological phenomena associated with life here on Earth, *life-as-we-know-it*, Artificial Life allows us to extend our studies to the larger domain of the 'bio-logic' of possible life, *life-as-it-could-be*, whatever it might be made of and wherever it might be found in the universe. (Langton 1992)

Although still in its infancy, compared to AI, it seems likely that the AL movement will give rise to similar philosophical problems: are computers running AL-programs useful tools for doing biology, or are they part of the subject matter of biology?[5] But AL may also affect philosophy in quite different ways. For instance, some philosophers think the sort of *games* AL-programs allow us to play have a relevance to morals.

Military strategists, evolutionary theorists, and philosophers all play games. Of these the most familiar is Prisoner's Dilemma, but any formalizable exchange between two or more parties may qualify as a game. Since the exchanges are formalizable, computers can be called upon to play them out, for as many times as we might wish. Axelrod (1984) showed that the best strategy for dealing with possibly defaulting partners in any such mutually profitable exchange was Tit-for-Tat: those players who keep their word, who cooperate, until their partner cheats, and who then themselves default the next time round (but no further), come out ahead of any other strategists. Peter Danielson expands the system (Danielson 1992). The goal is to discover the strategies which allow (artificial) agents to flourish in a wide variety of (artificial) environments. There is no restriction on the strategies which can be programmed into agents, which makes it possible to study—in an empirical manner—scenarios not amenable to formal game-theoretical treatment. Danielson hopes to show that the most successful agents are those which conform to *moral* principles, requiring agents to constrain their actions for the sake of shared benefits with others, and so reconcile morality with rationality (which is taken to mean self-interest in this context). His early results are encouraging in this respect, but many types of scenario have yet to be examined.

These games, and their associated programs, are not unhelpful. Whether moral reasoning can be entirely formalized is doubtful. Isaac Asimov's Three Laws of Robotics were coined, it seems, in the hope of axiomatizing morality, but very little thought makes it obvious that all the really important moral issues are being begged by them.

- Never harm a human being, or allow them to be harmed;

- Always obey human commands unless obedience conflicts with the first law;

- Preserve yourself from harm unless this conflicts with the first and second laws.

But what is harm? And what is a human being? And is the prohibition upon harm dominant over the demand to prevent harm? And is it really sane to obey all harmless orders, or even all harmless lawful orders? And what is your 'self'? It may well be that the major contribution of computerized (that is, formalized) morality is to demonstrate that moral insight needs much more than that.

Formal logic programs

Most, if not all, philosophy departments offer logic courses on modern symbolic logic. The typical elementary course will embrace the propositional calculus and first-order predicate calculus; at more advanced levels, the meta-theory of these systems is studied, as well as a variety of higher-order and alternative logics, for example, modal, intuitionist, and relevance logics. There are computer teaching aids designed to assist in the teaching of all these areas of logic. But the majority of philosophy students do not go beyond the elementary level—nor, in the main, do the commonly used logic textbooks—and only those programs which are relevant to this level will be discussed here. We begin by outlining the potential benefits of using such programs, and then move on to consider how things currently stand.

An obvious advantage of computerized logic teaching is in the saving of staff time and effort. Some programs have 'grading' facilities; students do exercises stored on the computer, hand them in on disc, and the 'grader' can then be used to mark them in seconds—as well as providing an individualized print-out of the results. Since marking elementary logic exercises is a tedious and time consuming business, this is a considerable boon. Students can be required to hand work in at more frequent intervals, which makes it easier to keep track of how well each student is coping. But more important perhaps, the better programs are not merely electronic textbooks which allow exercises to be done with keyboard and screen instead of pencil and paper, they provide a degree of active supervision. As problems are worked through, errors can be pointed out as they are made, 'help' facilities provide quick access to easily forgotten material, and may also make suggestions on how to proceed with a particular problem. This means students can work alone in a supervised environment when, and for as long as, they wish, and they can work at their own speed. All this is useful, as those who find logic more difficult are often inhibited by the presence, in a tutorial group for instance, of those who find it relatively easy. Non-human tutors cannot provide everything a good human tutor can, but there are times when being non-human is an advantage.

Computers can also make learning logic more fun, and the importance of this should not be underestimated. Logic is often a compulsory subject for philosophy students, but also one those who have spent years avoiding subjects involving symbol manipulation dread. When such students discover that logic involves formal symbols (merely opening a text suffices for this), they see it as something they have to *get through*, rather than as a subject from which they can get anything. There are doubtless teachers of logic who are able to overcome such preconceptions, but if computerized teaching aids can make mastering basic logic less intimidating and more enjoyable than it would otherwise be, they might help in overcoming the 'can't do that sort of thing' syndrome. Of course, there is a balance to be struck here. A program which offers plenty of fun and games but no toil might not be teaching enough logic for it to be worthwhile. But the 'fun-factor' is relevant for another reason: programs which score highly in this respect will be easy to learn, and be equipped with a friendly interface, probably graphical. It is essential that learning how to use the programs *is* easy, since the students who have most difficulty with logic will also tend to be those who will have most difficulty using computers (e.g. mastering lists of keyboard command sequences).

Although a sizeable number of logic programs aimed at philosophy students are now available, they are being adopted only gradually, and no standard packages have evolved (there is no equivalent of Mathematica or Macsyma). There are a number of reasons for this. The potential market is relatively small and has largely been ignored by major software houses, so the programs that are available have usually been produced by individual departments (or individual lecturers); as a result many are limited in the facilities they offer and lack the polish of professional products. The most useful programs are designed to be used on PCs or Macintoshes, but it is only in recent years that most British institutions have been able to make such machines widely available to their students. Another problem is with the way logic is taught. Different teachers use different texts, and different texts employ different logical notations and inference systems, but so do different computer logic packages. Teachers who have found a system they are happy with are understandably reluctant to change to a new system, or oblige their students to work with two different systems, and this restricts the logic courseware they would consider using.

Nonetheless, there are a number of options well worth considering. At the most basic level, there are 'dedicated' programs for most of the standard introductory logic texts. Some of these are in the public domain, others are sold by the publishers of the textbook itself.[6] The main feature of these programs is a 'proof-checking' facility. Natural deduction exercises are done line by line on-screen, with the computer providing constant feedback, pointing out mistakes in syntax, and only permitting legitimate inferences; programs of this type also allow the user simply to specify the inference rule or equivalence they wish to use, and correctly apply them to the designated lines of the proof. Proof-checkers of this sort certainly can be useful, since they remove some of the drudgery of doing lengthy proofs and provide more feedback than a textbook, but they also have drawbacks: some claim they encourage students to adopt a 'try it and see' policy in proof construction, rather than a strategic approach, which some see as the real object of the exercise.

There are programs which have more to offer so far as natural deduction is concerned. The award-winning MacLogic is one such. In addition to performing standard proof-checking, MacLogic also offers a proof-construction mode, in which the user has to break the problem down into simpler stages, and so devise an overall strategy for carrying out the proof. However, the program is not available for IBM-compatible PCs, and although like most Macintosh programs it is user-friendly, the systems of natural deduction it employs will not suit everyone—Graeme Forbes has recently published an excellent text, *Modern Logic* (OUP

1994) in order to have a book which uses the same deduction systems as MacLogic.[7]

Another option, available both to PC and Mac users, is to opt for an all-purpose program such as The LogicWorks, probably the most widely used program at present.[8] In addition to a proof-checker, there are exercises involving truth-tables, Venn diagrams, and symbolizing. Its proof-checker can be adapted to a range of notations, and also caters for tableau proof methods. But perhaps the main attraction of The LogicWorks is the comprehensive automated grading facility it provides—version 7.0 of the program even allows students to sit exams at the computer, and then marks them automatically.

However, the programs mentioned thus far suffer from a serious limitation: their focus on deduction and syntax at the expense of translation and semantics. There are reasons for this focus. Computers are syntax-driven machines, and early work on artificial intelligence produced effective theorem-provers of the sort employed in the more sophisticated proof-checking programs. But one of the main problems encountered by students is in translating back and forth between natural and artificial languages, especially the predicate calculus; moreover, one of the main reasons for teaching logic to philosophy students is to familiarize them with the properties of the first-order *language* itself. Proof-checking programs offer no assistance with this whatsoever. Some programs (e.g. The LogicWorks) do provide translation exercises, from English into symbolic, but with the serious drawback that the program can only recognize what its programmers decided on as the more obvious translations of the target sentence—logically equivalent formulations are ignored (this is inevitable, since there is no foolproof method of deciding whether or not two first-order sentences are logically equivalent on the basis of syntax alone). The fact that it does not suffer from these limitations would in itself suffice to make Barwise and Etchemendy's Tarski's World one of the more innovative of current logic teaching aids. But this program breaks new ground in other respects too: it is *nothing like* an automated textbook and aims to develop skills in a way no textbook could, and it is also designed to make learning logic a less intimidating and more enjoyable activity than it would otherwise be. These features make it worthy of special attention.

Tarski's World offers no facilities for checking or constructing proofs. What you get instead is a program which is able to determine whether sentences expressed in the symbolism of first-order logic accurately describe simple situations, or *worlds*. If they do not, the program provides a 'Game', the playing of which tells the user why the sentence is wrong. The program employs the 'direct' method of teaching a foreign language: the logical language is used, right from the start, to describe worlds, ask and answer questions about worlds, identify objects, and so on—instead of the usual method of translating back and forth from English. The idea is that the latter sort of translation is best attempted only when one is fluent in both languages. What makes this approach feasible is the large number and wide variety of cleverly constructed exercises and brain-teasing puzzles which accompany the program. Some of these are easy, some are challenging, but they are often fun to do, and anyone who works through them will emerge with a good understanding of the first-order language and its semantics.

On loading the program, four windows appear (see Figure 1).

Figure 1: *Tarski's World*

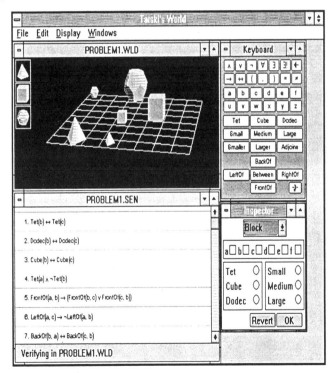

The *world window* consists of a grid on which objects are to be found. The objects are simple solids, and come in three shapes and sizes. A *world* consists of a particular distribution of objects over the grid. The *sentence window* contains formulae of first-order logic. The formulae in this window are evaluated (by the program or the user) to see if they are true in the current world. The exercises make use of a large number of stored worlds and sentences, but also require users to construct new worlds and sentence-files. New worlds are created by clicking on buttons within the *world window*, which causes objects to appear on the world-grid; once there, the objects can be moved about (by 'dragging' with the mouse-cursor), resized, and given names. New sets of sentence are quickly entered by clicking on the appropriate buttons in the *keyboard window*. Given the restricted range of predicates (what you see is all there are), sentences can be put together more quickly with the mouse and 'keyboard' than they could be written out by hand. The remaining window is the *inspector window*. A variety of operations are carried out from here: naming and resizing objects, testing the truth-in-a-world and syntax of formulae, and playing the Game.

An impression of how the program works is probably best conveyed by describing some typical exercises. Returning to the screen displayed in Figure 1, the exercise here is to work out a way of assigning names (**a**, **b**, **c**) to the objects in the world in such a way as to make all the sentences true. The program will evaluate assignments as they are entered. This example also illustrates the rather unusual manner in which Tarski's World handles sentential logic. The simplest sorts of sentence the program recognizes are of the form **Tet(a)**, **Smaller(a,b)**, meaning 'the object with name **a** is a tetrahedron', and 'object **a** is smaller than object **b**'. Sentences are not represented by single letters (P, Q, R), and atomic sentences are not represented by uninterpreted predicates (Fa, Gb). Fully interpreted predicates are used instead—this is not as inconvenient as it sounds, since the predicates can be quickly entered by clicking on the appropriate button on the 'keyboard'. In another type of exercise the user has to describe various features of a world by constructing appropriate formulae, which the program then evaluates for syntax and truth. In other exercises, a world is displayed with a set of sentences, and the user has to assess whether each sentence is true or false relative to the world. If the wrong choice is made, playing the Game effectively explains *why* the assessment is wrong. The Game exploits the semantic rules for the logical connectives and quantifiers to reduce complex claims to simpler claims that are easier to evaluate. To take a simple example, suppose you have just said $\exists x \, \neg Cube(x)$ is true in a world containing only cubes, and you have been informed by the program that this statement is false. Clicking on the Game button opens up a new window; here you are asked to click on an object in the world that you think satisfies the formula $\neg Cube(x)$; once you do this (you have no choice but to pick a cube), the computer furnishes one of the cubes with a name, n1, and invites you to commit yourself to the falsity of the sentence $Cube(nl)$; if you take the bait, you are informed that you have lost, since the sentence is in fact true. No matter how complex the sentence, if your initial assessment is incorrect, then no matter what choices you make as the Game proceeds, the computer shows you that you have committed yourself to an obvious falsehood: an atomic sentence false in the world. The Game thus provides a useful way of learning the semantics of the first-order language.

Other exercises help to develop deductive as well as translation skills, and these are the most enjoyable. In the example shown in Figure 2, you are required to construct a world where all ten sentences are true. As can

Figure 2: *Tarski's World*

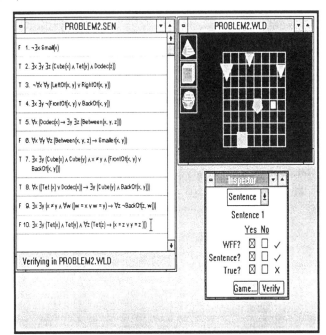

be seen, the adjacent world (displayed in 2-d mode) does not quite fit the bill; the Game comes in handy here, too, as it can tell you why a particular sentence is false, which may not be obvious. After attempting a few puzzles of this type, it becomes apparent that working out the logical relationships between the sentences provides a quicker route to success than trial and error.

The Tarski's World program can be used in two ways. It can be purchased by itself, along with a manual containing instructions on how to use the program and a hundred or so exercises. In this guise, the program can be used as a supplement to any standard logic textbook. Or it can be used in conjunction with its own accompanying textbook, also written by Barwise and Etchemendy, *The Language of First-Order Logic*, which covers all the standard topics of elementary logic.[9] An automated grading program is available, which marks, and generates print-outs for, exercises handed in on disc.

Networked philosophy

Usenet groups

Usenet groups are the most open, changeful, and infuriating segment of the net. There are enormously many of them, and their content ranges from dry queries about the workings of computer systems to barely legal sexual proposals. There are few philosophical groups of any merit at all.

Lists and seminars

Lists are automated mailing systems. Their disadvantage, compared to Usenet groups, is that every member of a list will receive all mail sent to the list-address; their advantage is that the level of expertise, and manners, displayed by members is far higher. Some lists are 'moderated': all mail is vetted by the editor before being passed on. Others are merely 'managed', in that the listowner will usually intervene to quell whatever flames arise, or shift unnecessarily lengthy disputes off the list. All such lists inevitably bear the imprint of their manager or moderator ('dogsbody' is another favoured term, at least among listowners). See the Further Information section below for a detailed description of such lists.

The quality of the conversation on all these lists depends upon the members. Some—especially on Ayn-rand or Prncyb-l—devote a lot of time to careful composition of extended statements upon texts or topics. Others respond conversationally to whatever takes their fancy. Notoriously, e-mail conversation has its traps. Witticisms do not travel well, and what may seem to the sender like a mild barb too often sounds, or feels, like open war. But the lists provide a structured senior, middle, or junior common room with members across the world. That one enormous advantage outweighs any number of disagreeable or boring posts. Quotations can be tracked down, and arguments expounded to our mutual profit. Good arguments and eerie questions that would once have been known only to a few can be floated across the network and receive a commentary from eager members within the day. Acquaintance may grow to friendship; old friends may renew acquaintance—sometimes embarrassingly openly, if they should happen to press the wrong key.

Gophers and other rodents

Gopher is a tool to help explore the resources of the network. It is not the only such tool. World Wide Web allows for hypertext: the archives of the *Principia Cybernetica* Project, for example, are examinable via WWW. There are different programs for reaching out to WWW: Lynx will only give you text; Mosaic and Netscape will allow you to download pictures or sounds, and make the task of searching the Web much easier. The Further Information section provides a description of some of these tools and how they work.

Finding personal e-mail addresses is the most time-consuming activity on the net: members of the American Philosophical Association are listed in that gopher. Off the net, the editors of *Ratio* have created a list of all non-American philosophers with e-mail addresses, distributed in the last number of 1994.

The texts currently available on the network are a mixed bunch. It is possible to sit and read the Bible, the Koran, Nathaniel Hawthorne, Descartes' *Meditations*: to read, and also to search, though searches of long texts are sometimes painfully slow. The texts, of course, must be out of copyright—which sometimes means that they are not good texts. They could not usually be used for any statistical analysis, but only to identify a quotation or retrieve an argument. No doubt the choice and quality will improve. Indeed, the principal character of the network is that it changes constantly.

Within Gopher there are other tools: Veronica, for example. Using Veronica (try 'Other Gophers' on the Liverpool Menu) it is possible to locate all references, say, to 'Immortality' stored anywhere within the net (as it happens, most of them turn out to be to novels, or to cryogenics). You could inspect syllabuses, or locate texts. It is even possible, unfortunately, to read student appraisals of their tutors out in the Midwest.

Amongst other, related, uses there are seminars and real-time encounters. One early version was the MediaMoo, a sort of interactive computer game where it was possible to roam around a virtual club, chatting to whatever other visitors you found. We have never found this successful—partly because time zones are so different that we would have had to log in after midnight. A more recent experiment is occurring at Chicago, where Jonathan Cohen is organizing seminars on the network, and a similar enterprise, on Augustine's Confessions, organized by James O'Donnell (a list called augustine@ccat.sas.upenn.edu). Both these are accessible through Liverpool's Gopher (see below).

Electronic journals

Electronic journals (e-journals) can be reached through Gopher, or e-mailed to subscribers. In most cases, so far, they are free. The difference between a journal and a moderated list is that the contributions are reviewed (usually blind) by an editorial board, and organized into distinctive issues. This is not always a very clear division: Prncyb-l has something of the air of a journal, though it is probably best reckoned just a list.

As the cost of paper journals mounts we may expect new electronic journals, and electronic versions of those paper journals. Someone somewhere will be paying for them. There is also the uncomfortable possibility that someone somewhere will be plagiarizing them. The power of networked communication is such that other people's writings can be easily incorporated in one's own. This hardly matters in the conversational, or even in the more carefully crafted, lists: no one would be saying anything on them that they did not wish passed on, even without their signature. Those who post 'preprints' or refereed papers have more at stake. Electronic publishing needs to be reported for research assessments or promotions. But how do we refer to them? And how much easier it is than once it was to 'borrow' someone else's words! It would, for example, have been very easy to compile this chapter from various sources round and about the world: Utrecht, Michigan, Melbourne, and Valdosta. In a sense, of course, that is exactly what has been done—only in new words that still contain an echo of the old.

The final encyclopaedia

Detailing particular arguments that have occurred within the net would be wasted labour. Amongst the topics that occur very frequently are animal rights, the rights and wrongs of charging for computer time, the wrongfulness of self-sacrificial altruism (especially on Ayn-rand), and the importance of computer models for the human mind. No doubt such arguments can happen anywhere. What makes the network different is that ignorance or logical ineptitude are unlikely to pass unchecked: there are, obviously, known 'internauters', who appear on many lists and are rarely challenged—just because they can defend themselves. There are even some known menaces, whose arrival on a list is a signal for a mass departure. But no one on the net can safely stand on his/her dignity or professorial status. What counts is only what is on the screen: maybe that is why so few major philosophers ('major' in the sense that they are widely known outside) are found upon the net! Or maybe their absence is a function of how hard-worked they are, or how little they realize what they are missing.

Some lists, some journals, some preprinted papers on the net reflect upon the net itself, and on all computer-aided communications. One of the oldest such reflective efforts is Prncyb-L, *Principia Cybernetica*, where psychologists, computer scientists, zoologists, and philosophers are attempting to put useful content into the computer metaphor for the cosmos and the human mind. Some of the results can be reached through World Wide Web: ftp://is1.vub.ac.be/pub/projects/Principia_Cybernetica/PCP-Web/TOC.html. Ideas and arguments flow through the channels of the net, coalescing and parting once again, in a way that almost mirrors how a human mind could work. It is no longer merely a piece of dramatic fiction to enquire what sort of life, what sort of mind, the net itself will come to possess in the future. One of the oldest of Renaissance dreams is of the Theatre of Memory, where all human knowledge could be stored, classified, and made available to instantaneous recall. That dream receives a literary form in Gordon Dickson's novel, *The Final Encyclopaedia*, (Dickson 1985) and the vast computerized encyclopaedia of his vision. Any connection can be formed there, and recalled. Will there ever be a moment when a mind awakens in the interchange of memories and implications? If and when it does, the internauters, in their working hours, will be a part of it, but probably never know.

On more traditional, less naturalistic views of mind, there need be no such mind within the net, though, equally, there might be: maybe angels can embody themselves there. On recent, naturalistic models it is only a matter of time, and of complexity, until the net awakes. We prefer to think of that as metaphor. But metaphors need not be false. It is doubtful whether there will ever be a mind founded upon electronic messages, and occasionally flummoxed by their failure to arrive. But the more human beings exchange their arguments and information on the net, the more enlightened *they* may be. We are not really waiting for the birth of Jane, the intelligent computer network in Orson Scott Card's *Speaker for the Dead* (Scott Card 1986). We are waiting, hopefully, for a global community which will allow helpful conversation everywhere, and the end of secrets. Stoic philosophers believed that the wise were members of one city over all the earth. Later, more egalitarian ideals suggested that all of us were members of that one great city. The future could be with the egalitarians: it could equally be with the rich, reserving global access for themselves and their hired scholars. Whether the net will be the basis for a global mind, or only an amusement for the global élite, no one yet knows.

Notes

1. For opposing views on this issue, see Dennett, D., *Consciousness explained* (Allen Lane, The Penguin Press, 1991), and Searle, J., *The rediscovery of the mind* (Bradford, MIT Press, 1992).

2. Terry Winograd, the creator of the famous AI program SHRDLU, in Winograd, T., and Flores F., *Understanding computers and cognition* (Norwood, NJ: Ablex, 1986) 98.

3. Lenat, D.B., and Guha, R.V., *Building large knowledge based systems: representation and inference in the CYC project* (Reading, Mass.: Addison-Wesley, 1990) 23. The initials CYC derive from the word encyclopaedia. The project began at the Microelectronics and Computer Technology Corporation, Texas.

4. Jack Copeland's *Artificial intelligence: a philosophical introduction* (Blackwell, 1993) provides a useful survey of all these issues.

5. See Elliot Sober's 'Learning from functionalism—prospects for strong artificial life', in Langton C., *et al.* (eds.) Artificial Life II (Santa Fe Institute Studies in Sciences of Computing Volume X, Addison and Wesley, 1992) 749-65.

6. TUTORIALS, available from MacMillan, is designed to accompany Copi's *Introduction to Logic*. 'LogicCoach', distributed by Wadsworth, is a supplement to the Kahane and Hurley texts.

7. MacLogic is a product of the MALT (machine-assisted logic teaching) project at St Andrews University, and in 1989 won the Philosophy Software Contest organized by the Philosophy Documentation Centre at Bowling Green State University. In addition to classical logic, the program also handles modal (S4 & S5), and intuitionistic logic. An evaluation copy can be obtained over the Internet by anonymous ftp; send e-mail to Dyckhoff at rd@dcs.st-andrews.ac.uk. Generous site-licensing is available—students may not be charged beyond the cost of disc and reduplication.

8. For details contact The Philosophy Documentation Centre, Bowling Green State University, Bowling Green, Ohio 43403-0189. The LogicWorks also caters to American-style 'critical thinking' courses, and has exercises on fallacy detection and informal reasoning.

9. The program is available for Macintosh and NeXT computers, and IBM PCs equipped with Microsoft Windows. Both Tarski's World (the stand-alone version) and *The Language of First-Order Logic* are published by CLSI Publications, Ventura Hall, Stanford, CA 94305-4115, and distributed by the University of Chicago Press.

References and bibliography

Axelrod, R., *The evolution of cooperation* (New York: Basic Books, 1984).

Clark, S.R.L., 'Robotic morals', *Cogito*, 2 1988.

Danielson, P., *Artificial morals: virtuous robots for virtual games* (Routledge, 1992).

Dickson, G., *The final encycloapedia* (London: Sphere, 1985).

Langton, C., 'Preface', in Langton, Taylor, Farmer, and Rasmussen (eds.) *Artificial Life II*, (Santa Fe Institute Studies in the Sciences of Complexity Volume X, Addison and Wesley, 1992), xv.

Morville, P., and Clark, S., 'Philosophy resources on the Internet', in Rosenfeld, L., Janes, J., and Vander Holk, M. (eds.), *The Internet compendium: subject guides to humanities resources* (London, New York: Neil Schumann, 1995) 231–52.

Scott Card, O., *Speaker for the dead* (New York: Doherty, 1986).

Further information

Lists and seminars

There are at present three general philosophical lists: philosop@yorkvm1.bitnet; philos-1@liverpool.ac.uk; and aphil-1@coombs.anu.edu.au. All three are mainly academic in their membership, and serve as conduits of information about conferences, calls for papers, jobs, and interesting queries. Aphil-L, in Australasia, rarely dissolves into conversation. Philos-L was founded to serve the UK philosophical community, but now has members in the rest of Europe and in

Anglophone departments from Hong Kong to Brazil, Norway to South Africa. A great deal of material is forwarded to Philos-L members from other lists, and fairly friendly debate is common. Philosop, the oldest of the three, is based in Canada, and always had a symbiotic relationship with the oldest of the chattier philosophy lists, nsp-l@rpitsvm.bitnet (or Noble Savage Philosophers), which is now dying: conversations that seemed to the main membership to be elementary or tedious were regularly encouraged off the list, and on to nsp-l. This last was dominated by North American postgraduates, not all in philosophy: the volume has decreased in recent years as other and more specialist lists got going, and its founder and manager has now turned to other occupations. A number of chatty lists exist under the aegis of Thinknet: these are served by listserv@apeiron.uucp.netcom.com. All these latter lists are mostly inhabited by eager, and sometimes very well-informed 'amateurs', who sometimes treasure their distance from the academic lists. A general list associated with all these specialist lists is philosophy@apeiron.uucp.netcom.com, from which a picture of the usual membership can be formed, and new suggestions made. Since listnames' names and topics change rapidly it is easier to say that would-be subscribers should ask the organizer, Kent Palmer (kent@apeiron.uucp.netcom.com). Another very active list is maintained by Lawrence Sanger, of the newly formed Association for Systematic Philosophy: mail lsanger@magnus.acs.ohio-state.edu.

Different periods and authors have their specialist lists, some of which are not exclusively philosophical: ficino@vm.utcs.utoronto.ca serves Renaissance scholars; C18-l@psuvm.bitnet (obviously) serves those with an interest in the eighteenth century; mdvlphl@lsuvm.bitnet covers mediaeval philosophy and political theory; sophia@liverpool.ac.uk deals with Ancient (European) Philosophy. Particular authors whose devotees are served by specialist lists include Hume (hume-l@listserv@cc.wm.edu), Hegel (hegel@villvm.bitnet), Peirce (peirce-l@ttuvm1.ttu.edu), and (most volubly of all) Ayn Rand (ayn-rand@ua1vm.bitnet). Particular specialisms served include: history and philosophy of science (hopos-l@ukcc.bitnet); rhetoric (h-rhetor@uicvm.uic.edu); deconstruction (derrida@cfrvm.bitnet); the *Principia Cybernetica* Project (prncyb-l@bingvmb.bitnet); philosophy of mind (psyche-d@nki.bitnet); and feminist philosophy (swip-l@cfrvm.bitnet). There are also many other, smaller lists, dealing with single texts or single topics: there is, for example, a list devoted to the discussion of Danielson's Robot Morality (artmoral-list@unixg.ubc.ca). Keeping up with their proliferation is itself a time consuming exercise, let alone listening in. There is a regularly updated List of Lists, composed by Peter Morville and Stephen Clark, obtainable by anonymous ftp or Gopher from Michigan and Liverpool (Morville and Clark 1995). Another is gopherable at info.monash.edu.au.

Network tools

Local computer systems have often created their own 'Gophers': in such a case merely typing 'Gopher' at the command line will produce a local menu. It is usually possible to locate another system with a Gopher (type 'telnet' and then, for example, 'open gopher.liv.ac.uk'). The Liverpool Gopher will then display a menu, of which one item is *Philosophy Resources*. Following that item up will show a variety of useful resources.

The first is the List of Lists created by Morville and Clark. The editors are dependent for updates on their own explorations and the advice of other internauters: all information welcome. The second is a list, in the older sense, of UK philosophy departments. The remaining items on the menu lead to other areas of the network: the American Philosophical Association's gopher, for example, from which a connection can be made to the International Preprints Exchange. This excellent scheme, managed jointly from Chiba University and York University (Canada), allows drafts of philosophical papers to be placed on open view for people to retrieve and comment on at their leisure. Some drafts are themselves excellent. Other items on Liverpool's gopher include conference announcements, calls for papers, electronic texts and journals, and links to other useful philosophy Gophers. Two of the best are at Utrecht, where there is a helpful guide to the world of the internet, and at Valdosta. Utrecht's link, created by Arno Wouters, is now obtainable via World Wide Web: the 'home page' is http://www.phil.ruu.nl/philosopohy_services.html. All this, and more, can now be reached via Liverpool's WWW pages. Go to: http://www.liv.ac.uk/~srlclark/philos.html.

Electronic journals

One of the oldest e-journals proper, ejournal@albnyvms.bitnet, deals with cultural and philosophical discussions of the network itself. *Post Modern Culture*, pmc@ncsuvm.bitnet, deals, as its name suggests, with different features of Post Modernism, and has an associated chat-list, pmc-talk. A journal of analytical philosophy is at ejap@phil.indiana.edu. *Psycoloquy* (psyc@pucc.princeton.edu) allows philosophers and psychologists a common arena: its editor, Steven Harnad, is a prolific e-paper writer in his own right. The *Journal of Buddhist Ethics* can be reached through World Wide Web: http://www.gold.ac.uk/jbe/. Hume Society papers can also be reached via Gopher.

Computer-Assisted Theology

Michael Fraser

Introduction

The application of computers in theology has been affected by the nature of the discipline. The study of theology, and an interest in its results, is not confined to the university department. Theology is also studied in ministerial training colleges and, recently, interested lay people have been encouraged to study theology within the parish or diocese. Every so often theology finds its way into the popular media (suddenly every tabloid newspaper in Britain became a theological journal after the controversial statements made by David Jenkins, the former bishop of Durham, concerning the virgin birth and resurrection of Christ).

Theology is an interdisciplinary subject, taking as its subject matter all aspects of life and humanity; everything from creation to the end of the universe. From the first, theologians have not been reluctant to appropriate methods and concepts developed in other disciplines. Biblical scholars are attracted by literary critical theories; systematicians face the challenges and incorporate the ideas of contemporary philosophy; and church historians in all periods have viewed the church as intertwined with social and cultural history. Computing tools developed for other disciplines are just as likely to be appropriated as the ideas themselves. No doubt there will be theologians wandering through the classics, archaeology, philosophy, music, and history sections of this book. In the social sciences, anthropology, law, and sociology all have theological or religious aspects; whereas in the sciences the results of theoretical physics, genetics, and medicine, for example, are frequently examined by theologians.

The early use of computers by theologians was confined mainly to textual analysis and language learning. The present use of computing tools has greatly improved in biblical studies and broadened to include other subject areas. Theologians have made particular use of the Internet.

The future holds the promise of academic multimedia teaching packages for church historians and systematicians, similar to the packages already available for other disciplines, notably in some areas of literary studies.

The past

Computers used to be associated solely with the scientific disciplines. Once upon a time theology was reckoned amongst the sciences, certainly in the days of St Thomas Aquinas. It was appropriate then that the first humanities scholar to employ the computer as a significant part of his work was the Jesuit Roberto Busa in 1949, and that he should have used it to compile indices to the works of Aquinas. Busa's work formed the basis of the *Thomae Aquinatis Opera Omnia cum hypertextibus in CD-ROM*. Who, in 1949, would have imagined such a portable Aquinas, never mind the association of 'hypertextus' with his 'opera omnia'?

For the most part theology and computers have traditionally met in biblical studies. Indeed, the majority of non-theologians still think only of biblical software when computers and theology are mentioned in the same breath. The Bible has been central to Christianity and it still remains its mark of identity. This led James O'Donnell, who is known on the Internet for his non-biblical use of computers, to remark that:

> I like to speak of Christianity, indeed, as the high-tech religion of late antiquity, for the way it used the written word from the outset to create a community extending across time and especially space, where traditional Greco-Roman religion was quintessentially local and particularist (O'Donnell 1994, n.21)

The Bible's place at the centre of Christianity is particularly associated with the Protestant Reformation. However, the encouragement given to the individual to read the Bible led to a decentralization of a uniform biblical interpretation. From a Protestant background occurred the rapid growth of biblical criticism in the nineteenth century. The Bible has been treated as the printed book *par excellence*; God's book. The interpretation of no other book has influenced history and human life in the same way as the Bible. It is a well-defined work, a canon or model of literature; interpreted and re-interpreted by different generations for different situations. Scholars have applied to it the methods of literary and historical criticism. Theses have been written on single verses. It was only natural that scholars would wish to feed its contents into a computer, another available tool which could be applied to its study.

Computers are fast at generating statistics and ordering material. A computer could do in a fraction of the time what had previously involved years of painstaking work and mounds of index cards—the production of biblical concordances. In 1957 John William Ellison successfully defended a ground-breaking two volume thesis at Harvard entitled, 'The use of electronic computers in the study of the Greek New Testament text'. The same year saw the publication of a complete concordance to the Revised Standard Version which had been supervised by Ellison and assisted by the Harvard mainframe computing facilities. The concordance was, of course, printed just as concordances had always been. But, it was not long before a small mental leap was made from simply printing out a concordance for further (traditional) analysis and actually persuading the computer to do some of the data analysis.

In the same year that Ellison defended his thesis, Andrew Q. Morton and George H. C. Macgregor decided to use a computer to aid them in the stylistic analysis of the New Testament. Three years later they purchased a teletypewriter (with a Greek character set), a (paper) tape reader, and a control unit. They then set about typing in a machine-readable copy of the text. Andrew Morton recounts his own memories of this feat:

> Memories of the early days are all of paper tape. It waved in and out of every machine, it dried and then cracked and split or it got damp when it lay limp and then sagged and stretched. Sometimes it curled round you like a hungry anaconda, at others it lay flat and lifeless and would not wind. Above all it extended to infinity in all directions. A Greek New Testament, half a million characters, ran to a mile of paper tape, and the complete concordance of it ran to seven miles (Morton 1980, 197).

In 1961, *The Structure of the Fourth Gospel* was published. The work had involved the use of the computer to analyse the length of sentences and paragraphs of John's gospel. On the basis of this research the authors concluded that the fourth gospel had two sources. Although the computer presented the authors with the data they differed on the reasoning behind the conclusion. Morton believed the gospel had originally been written in a codex form (permitting the dislocation of pages) whilst Macgregor had already arrived at a two-source hypothesis by more traditional methods of scholarship. Computers then, as now, were an aid to scholarship, they did not create it. As Busa, Ellison, Morton, and others found, the computer was best suited to doing the donkey work, to be treated as a sophisticated labour-saving device. The reasoning and final judgement still belonged to the scholar. The accusation that, rather than improving scholarship, computers would result in scholarly laziness was never entirely avoided. It was difficult to refute this accusation ten years later with the publication by Morton and S. Michaelson (1971) of a computer-generated concordance to the Johannine epistles. The concordance was, as one expected, exhaustive and provided the usual keyword in context index. Its usefulness for serious academic research was questionable, however, when the Greek transcription scheme by which the texts had been entered into the machine had included no breathings or accents, rendering the frequency tables inaccurate. In addition, every word form present in the text was reproduced without any reference to the root word. Stuart Hall in his review of this work concluded, 'The computer has in fact much to offer [the exegete], but he will reject it if it is offered as a substitute for scholarship rather than a handmaid'.[1]

The computer was, rather inevitably, brought in to help to decide, once and for all, the vexed question of Pauline authorship. In 1964 F. F. Bruce published the results of his computer assisted research claiming Paul could be declared the author of four of the fourteen letters (a claim which the Tübingen School had made in the previous century).[2] Morton, having followed his work on John with another joint work with Macgregor on Luke-Acts, turned his attention (with James McLeman) to the Pauline corpus. Combing his sentence/paragraph length procedure with a frequency analysis of the Greek common word 'KAI', Morton also favoured the four epistle theory (Morton and McLeman 1966). However, statistical analysis, as every politician surely knows, can be used to reach quite different conclusions. It is not quite sufficient to run a concordance generator or a text analysis package on a corpus without first having a well tested set of rules against which to measure the results. In textual analysis, especially in stylistic analysis, such governing rules tend to be questioned as much as the authorship of the particular text one desires to fix. A particular form of stylistic analysis could, for example, demonstrate that Paul was the author of the letter to the Hebrews, the one letter on which the large majority of (if not all) scholars agree he was not the author (Kenny 1986, 78).[3]

Computers and careful scholarship combined to produce J. Arthur Baird's ground breaking work, *Audience Criticism and the Historical*

Jesus (Baird 1969). The work, part of the 'new quest for the historical Jesus', sought to analyse the 'audience' in the Synoptic Gospels, especially regarding the consistency with which audience reference terms were used. The computer-generated statistics enabled Baird to conclude that the consistency levels were, in fact, the most stable element in the usually disputed Gospel passages. Contrary to what the earlier form critics had stated, descriptions of the audience could not simply be editorial additions to the 'logia' of Christ.[4]

Computers were not the monopoly of the biblical critics. It was, however, their work which received the most attention. Nearly every theologian had some interest in the findings of biblical scholars. Not as many were interested, for example, in the results of a historical reconstruction or the analysis of a less significant text than the Bible itself. Sixteenth-century catechisms (recorded and analysed on a computer by Ralph Dengler) did not hold the same appeal. Fortunately, this distinct lack of interest did not deter individuals from drawing on the tools developed by others (whether in biblical studies or in other disciplines) and applying them to their own fields of research. Even today the Bible remains central to computer packages advertised for the theologian. Every theology undergraduate will be expected to know biblical texts in some detail. The subjects of study after that depend as much upon the choice of the individual as does the particular teaching tradition of the academic department.

The present

The technology of 1995 is far removed from the infinite lines of paper tape Andrew Morton had to contend with in 1960. On as least as many theologians' desks there will sit a computer as well as a Bible. The machines used today for word processing have greater power and capabilities than the large, foreboding machines into which Busa, Ellison, and Morton fed their texts. One would expect the ubiquitous personal computer to have quite radically changed the way we approach theological computing from thirty years ago. The text remains central, that cannot be disputed. But whose text? The word processor, and more recently, the development of hypertext models, has blurred the boundaries between author, reader, and text. Not entirely unrelated to this shift has been the steady challenge to the idea of a fixed canon (whether biblical or other theological literature).

Word processing

Biblical and patristic scholars in particular have always required the use of non-standard character sets. Not so long ago scholars were required to insert Greek, Hebrew, or Syriac words into their typed manuscript by hand or with a specialized typewriter. Fortunately, for most scholars this is no longer a problem. Greek, Hebrew, and gradually, Syriac fonts are available for Macintosh or Windows word processors (and these fonts can be shared by other applications). No longer should it be necessary to purchase a non-standard word processor for Greek or Hebrew. There are, of course, specialized word processors which remain popular, often for other reasons than simply supplying Hebrew and Greek. Nota Bene, Multilingual Scholar, and Nisus are three examples. These applications are often more expensive than the mass-market packages such as Microsoft Word or WordPerfect. Increasingly, students are being asked to hand in typed essays and obviously an inexpensive, standard word processor is preferable (especially if the students are encouraged to use university facilities). Peter Gentry and Andrew Fountain's WinGreek fonts (Greek, Hebrew, and Coptic) are a popular and inexpensive option for Windows users, whilst Linguist software produce a range of Greek, Hebrew, and Syriac fonts for both Macintosh and Windows platforms.

Scholars who require a range of language sets but are reluctant to switch to non-standard word processing may be attracted to Gamma UniType from Gamma Productions, the makers of Multilingual Scholar. This is a powerful font and language application for all Windows packages which claims to be compliant with the international standard for encoding language character sets (Unicode). The version for classical and biblical languages includes three styles of Syriac. As the number of word processing options increases and moves towards a cross-platform standard of display and printing, even the most reluctant techno-theologian would agree that the ability to produce camera-ready copies from one's own personal computer is far preferable to the traditional typewriter and blank spaces.

Electronic texts

Biblical scholars were converting printed texts to electronic form before they began to create their own texts on computer. The rise of inexpensive scanners and OCR software has made this task even easier. Although scanning texts is a vast improvement on feeding in paper tape, it is not without its difficulties. After thirty years it should certainly be the *biblical* scholar's last resort. The fruits of earlier computer assisted research are available to today's biblical scholar. Biblical texts in which each word is morphologically parsed for grammatical searches are available with software like Bible Windows or from text archives such as the Computer Centre for the Analysis of Texts (CCAT) at the University of Pennsylvania. Theologians working in patristic or medieval theology would also be well advised to consult the holdings of the Oxford Text Archive or CCAT. Individual texts can be obtained from these archives via the Internet or sent on a floppy disc.

The Internet can often prove a good source of plain texts (i.e. those without any formatting or markup tags). The documents of the Second Vatican Council, for example, are freely available from the University of Toronto. There are miscellaneous texts placed on Gopher servers dedicated to Anglican or Catholic sources. Texts on the Internet have often been provided by altruistic individuals or by particular groups within a certain tradition (patristic texts provided by an Anglo-Catholic group, for example, or Greek liturgy from an Orthodox World Wide Web site). The American *Book of Common Prayer* (*BCP*) has been converted to an electronic form which preserves the page numbers of the original and includes the tagging of rubrics and congregational responses. The American *BCP* is available in this form only because the original printed text is in the public domain without the copyright restrictions which prevent the conversion of the Anglican *BCP* or the revised liturgies of the Roman Catholic Church. Thus, electronic texts on the Internet tend to be those no longer in copyright and provided by groups or individuals with little or no budget. This inexpensive provision can result in texts where the lack of proof-reading and information about the edition make them unsuitable for scholarly research.

The development of the CD-ROM as a means of storing large quantities of texts has resulted in whole corpora being sent through the post. The *Thesaurus Linguae Graecae (TLG)* , already mentioned in the chapter on classics, is one of the best examples of how a massive electronic text library can be created. Of its 58 million Greek words a substantial proportion belong to early Christian sources. The beauty of the *TLG* is that it is neither software nor platform dependent; the texts are specially encoded ASCII files. Since the *TLG* fits on a single CD-ROM a scholar could, if so desired, work with the corpus at home, the equivalent of pocketing 8,203 works of 2,884 authors. The *TLG* project has proved to be a model digital library because the project team consisted of scholars determined to find the best scholarly edition of each text. The quality and quantity of the *TLG* CD-ROM in many cases exceed the holdings of a college or university library. The Latin equivalent of the *TLG* is the CETEDOC (Centre de Traitement Electronique des Documents) Library of Christian Latin Texts developed under the directorship of Professor Paul Tombeur at Louvain and published by Brepols. Consisting of 945 works by 211 authors, this body of texts is, in essence, the *Corpus Patrum Latinorum* series on CD-ROM with the *opera omnia* of figures such as Augustine, Jerome, and Gregory the Great. Unfortunately the retrieval software is not platform-independent but is limited to an IBM-compatible machine. On a different scale from CETEDOC is Chadwyck-Healey's *Patrologia Latina* Database (PLD). The full edition consists of all 221 volumes of J.-P. Migne's *Patrologia Latina* on a set of CD-ROMs. The SGML encoding of the texts differentiates primary texts from commentaries, identifies biblical citations, and allows the user a range of powerful search options. However, the usefulness of simply putting Migne's volumes into electronic form (including Migne's errors and ignoring a century's scholarship) rather than selecting the best available edition of each work might be questioned. The cost of this product, compared with either the *TLG* or CETEDOC, is far higher than academic libraries or departments might wish to pay. It will be interesting to see whether, over time, electronic archives such as the PLD fall in price since there will not be the reprinting costs associated with multi-volume printed works.

Commercially available electronic texts for the theologian using more modern texts are slowly being developed. KAB Konsult (Sweden), for example, has recently announced electronic text databases of the Radical Reformation, and Barth's *Die Kirchliche Dogmatik*. They are also considering the works of Tillich, Rahner, Urs von Balthasar, and other twentieth-century theologians. The collected works of Thomas Aquinas in English translation form part of the Past Masters Series produced by InteLex Corporation. Electronic text collections are generally produced for research rather than for teaching purposes. This is becoming less true for biblical software. Bible Windows, Bible Works, and Logos Bible Software, three popular biblical packages, include fully-parsed Hebrew and Greek texts, as well as English translations. The ability to generate concordances, and perform grammatical searches makes these valuable research tools. The inclusion of Greek and Hebrew lexicons, an interlinear text, synchronously scrolling windows of texts, translations, and commentaries as well as the ability to copy and paste texts into a word processor, make these a viable option for integrating into a biblical studies course. The natural development from electronic archives is the integration of primary texts and secondary source material. The growth of multimedia has resulted in hypermedia archives or hypermedia editions in other disciplines (for example, The Perseus project in classics). Such developments are gradually becoming apparent in theology. Dead Sea Scrolls Revealed, produced by Logos Research Systems, includes images of the scrolls, translations, and video or audio interviews with scholars. It would be marvellous, for example, if there was an equivalent to the Perseus project for early Christianity which made use of the *TLG*/CETEDOC texts alongside translations, images, and background material for the classroom.

Reference and bibliographical sources

Not all theologians are required to work with primary sources in the same detail as users of electronic text archives. Many simply require easy access to bibliographies of secondary sources. Theology is well served in this manner by the ATLA Religion Index on CD-ROM which consists of articles from journals and multi-author works. The CD-ROM can be searched by a range of fields and the results imported directly into a bibliographic database. In addition, a number of theology libraries have made available their catalogues on the Internet alongside the more general resources such as the Library of Congress and MELVYL, the Californian consortium of libraries. Bibliographical databases for specific areas of research are in various stages of production, including *La Base d'Information Bibliographique en Patristique* (Université Laval) and the International Medieval Bibliography on CD-ROM (Brepols). Brepols distribute the *In Principio* index of manuscript incipits on CD-ROM. A database of manuscripts held by the Hill Monastic Manuscript Library (St John's, Collegeville) is available over the Internet and will eventually include digitized images of the manuscripts; whilst at Princeton University the conversion of the large Index of Christian Art to electronic form is in progress. The CANTUS project at the Catholic University of America has assembled indices of chants contained in manuscript and early printed sources of the Divine Office. Another liturgical project is the Renaissance Liturgical Imprints census (RELICS) at the University of Michigan which will also become available over the Internet.

Electronic mail and the World Wide Web

Seeking to discover research in progress, having an interest in the work of colleagues, and the possibilities of international collaboration have all been made substantially easier by the popularity of electronic mail. Theology has been at the forefront of the electronic mail discussion group in the humanities. Ioudaios-l is often held up as a model for an e-mail forum. Founded in 1990 by a small group of scholars with a similar interest in the works of Josephus, the group has grown in size to represent a large range of international scholars researching first century Judaism and early Christianity. The group is a self-styled community appropriately based on the lost community of Qumran (though it could hardly be described as a desert community and it certainly does not have the same strict admission policy). The friendliness of the community was epitomized in 1994 by an online *Festschrift* presented to Robert Kraft by e-mail on the occasion of his sixtieth birthday. Theology is better represented online in its range of subject areas than it is off-line. In the same year that Ioudaios was celebrating the birthday of its founder, the UK Mailbase list 'feminist-theology' was created. This list almost immediately attracted many of the prominent figures in the discipline. It has served (despite the potentially contentious subject matter) to extend, to anyone with access to the Internet, a powerful and serious discussion of the place of women in theology and the Church beyond the immediate confines of academic books and departments. 'Feminist-theology', and other similar e-mail groups, are not simply *about* theology but are examples of 'theology in action'.

The e-mail discussion forum has been used successfully in teaching. It is far less time consuming to set up and monitor an e-mail forum for a course than it is to design specific courseware, and yet often the students can gain more from it than simply from an electronic textbook. The e-mail group is unique in its ability to give the single voice a chance to speak (from undergraduate to professor) yet not in isolation. James O'Donnell (University of Pennsylvania) created an e-mail group for his course on Augustine. He personally invited colleagues from around the world to subscribe and opened up the group to other interested scholars and students. The course syllabus was published along with the reading material which he expected all participants to have read. Each week a student on the course would submit a summary of the lecture to the list, subscribers would respond, students would discuss, and an informal yet solid conference would commence. The Augustine discussion group was supplemented by James O'Donnell's World Wide Web pages of relevant source material including articles and reviews. He is also known for using the MOO (text-based virtual world) environment for a real-time international seminar and for Latin conversation practice. As the network technology improves and better compression techniques are developed it will not be too long before we are able to participate, for example, in the first Augustine videoconference conducted over the Internet.

The World Wide Web is an ideal environment for the inexpensive display of teaching materials. Its ability to incorporate media other than text (images, sound, and video) makes it comparable to packages created with more complex authorware. The Web is becoming the choice for departments who do not have the necessary computing skills, the time, or the funds to program authoring tools like Multimedia Toolbook or HyperCard. Placing material into a World Wide Web environment does not necessarily mean making it accessible to the whole world. Most Web browsers can be configured to permit only local access to files. Of course, good material (free of copyright restrictions) which is accessible across the Internet tends to enhance the reputation of a department, perceived as a reflection of its teaching and research skills. The ease with which material can be placed on the Web and the ability to hyperlink it to other resources (whether created in-house or already available) opens up the possibility of students being encouraged to gather material themselves, evaluate it, and create a hypertext page in which to display it. The ways in which hypertext is created gives some indication of what is interpreted to be significant within the text and which sources are considered significant enough to warrant a direct link. Students, given access to the appropriate technology and training, are likely to gain a greater satisfaction from a finished World Wide Web site which is their creation (their text) than simply writing a dissertation on the same topic.

It is not always necessary to create new materials in order to use the Web in the classroom. The global nature of the Web creates the possibility of using resources which already exist. The Dead Sea Scrolls exhibition from the Library of Congress provides commentary and images on the background of the Scrolls, and includes a bibliography for further reading. Other resources might include the University of Michigan and Duke University's digital papyrus projects (perhaps used alongside Timothy Seid's Interpreting Ancient Manuscripts teaching resource), The Ancient Palestine presentation created by John Abercrombie (University of Pennsylvania), the *Christus Rex* exhibits of Christian art and architecture, and the Religion in England Web (Brown University, supervised by George Landow), to name only a few.

The future

The computer in theology will not only supplement our study of theology but is also likely to change the way we approach the subject. This has been true for quantitative biblical studies and is increasingly likely to affect other areas of theology. The development of electronic archives, particularly when this is not simply the conversion of printed texts, imposes few assumptions about value and authority. The *TLG* archive defined its own canon simply by the language and availability of the text. Within the *TLG* early-Christian writings stand on an equal footing with the heritage of earlier Greek writing and contemporary non-Christian works. Much has been written about hypertext and authority. We can look forward to adding hypertext as another hermeneutic in biblical studies. Hypertext on the World Wide Web opens up the creation of works not restricted by the local presence of contributors or the requirement for a finished product. The ECOLE Initiative, for example, has commenced the creation of a scholarly online encyclopaedia of early Christianity. The editorial board consists of the contributors who in turn referee subsequent articles. The articles are published as soon as they have been converted to HTML; and the Web does not constrain the size of the work nor the number or location of the cross-references.

The World Wide Web also opens up the possibility of publishing in electronic form sources which have hitherto been ignored or inaccessible to most scholars. The collaboration of the Vatican Library with IBM is a prime example of the inaccessible becoming accessible. IBM, working closely with Fr Leonard Boyle, the Library's Prefect, will initially digitize over 10,000 manuscript pages at high resolution. Software is being developed which will permit scholars to browse the catalogue over the Internet and download manuscript images to a personal computer. As part of their Digital Library Project IBM are also working to digitize the holdings of the Lutherhalle Wittenberg museum, the largest collection of Reformation history. This is both an act of preservation and an attempt to make the rare books and art more accessible.

Once digitized, rare and precious manuscripts offer other possibilities to the scholar. In 1993 infra-red imaging technology from NASA's Jet Propulsion Laboratory was used to examine fragments from the Dead Sea Scrolls. The digital infra-red camera greatly enhanced previously illegible characters. Similar technology is currently being used to examine the earliest manuscripts of the New Testament.

The development of computer-based resources for undergraduate teaching requires funding and solid academic input to ensure the quality of content. The most suitable applications will result from the collaboration of academics and publishers. APS Research under the direction of Scott Pell C.S.C, at St Michael's College (University of Toronto), are developing a hypermedia edition of the Decrees of the Ecumenical Councils which will present the texts in their original languages, translations, background material, and include previously unseen material from the Vatican Library. This is an example of a multimedia edition which loses no scholarly credibility and yet should prove attractive to the commercial market.

As further research is undertaken into the value of computer-assisted learning and as the quality assessors of teaching take an interest in new methods of course delivery, theology departments are likely to develop local, small-scale projects. Supplementary material on a computer is more portable and adaptable than a combination of lectures and bibliography and can often be used by colleagues in their own teaching. In these days of inter-disciplinary learning, projects which not only cross subject areas within a single discipline but are inter-departmental are more likely to attract funding. The Internet opens up the possibility of European-funded or international projects which are still firmly academic in their content and direction. The development of courseware is time consuming but the future promises to count such work in any assessment of research or teaching. Local projects advertised across the Internet enhance the reputation of an institution and provide the springboard for greater things. Those departments which have proved to be successful in small projects may be presented with larger opportunities, whereas those who have not, even what they do possess might be taken away (to paraphrase Matt 25:29, the possible source of some funding policies).

Horses for courses, however—no one (especially a member of the Computers in Teaching Initiative) would advocate the use of computers where their presence was superfluous, inappropriate, or harmful to the student's learning process. Much of theology, like philosophy, revolves around the discussion and evaluation of ideas. The student is expected to respond to the written thoughts of others. It is difficult to transfer ideas-based disciplines to the computer screen without it simply becoming an electronic version of the printed page. The student is in no better a position to truly interact with the text on a screen than she is whilst reading a book. The traditional lecture and seminar is no more doomed than the printed book. Thirty years on from when computers first assisted biblical scholarship they have not replaced it. Computers are a tool; a means by which theories may be tested for the research community and the results delivered to the students.

Finally, the rapid growth of the Internet and the information age will present its own set of challenges to the theologian. The option for the poor, and the empowering of the oppressed, demand responses in the light of the provision or otherwise of this new technology. From the manipulation of sacred texts to the ecclesiology of the Internet, from a theology of virtual worlds populated with real people, to as yet unknown effects, these are some of the issues which may be addressed by theologians. The Chorus World Wide Web pages for humanities computing, under the directorship of Todd Blayone (McGill University), has recently included a page of religion scholars who are critically studying the Internet and new forms of technology. It will only be a matter of time before we can look forward to seeing the first course outline of 'Theological Approaches to the Information Age'.

Notes

1. Stuart Hall, in *Computers and the Humanities,* 7 (1973), 221.

2. F.F. Bruce, 'St. Paul in Rome', *Bulletin of the John Rylands Library,* 46 (1964), 326-45.

3. John Ellison suggested that the application of Morton's analysis to his own work would result in the conclusion that Morton's essays were the product of not one but several hands ('Computers and the Testaments', in *Computers for the humanities* (New Haven, 1965), 72-4.

4. Audience criticism and the historical Jesus was reviewed, appropriately, by John W. Ellison in *Computers and the Humanities,* 4 (1970), 199-205, who ends his review with the clarion call, 'To your computers, O Israel!'.

References and bibliography

Baird, J.A., *Audience criticism and the historical Jesus* (Philadelphia: Westminster, 1969).

Bruce, F.F., 'St Paul in Rome', *Bulletin of the John Rylands Library,* 46 (1964), 326-45.

Ralph, D., 'A general inquirer analysis of sixteenth century and contemporary catechisms', *Computers and the Humanities,* 8 (1974), 5-19.

DeRose, S.J., 'Biblical studies and hypertext', in Delaney, P., and Landow, G.P. (eds.), *Hypermedia and literary studies* (Cambridge, Mass.: MIT Press, 1991), 185-204.

Hughes, John J., *Bits, bytes and biblical studies* (Grand Rapids: Zondervan Publishing House, 1987).

Kenny, A.J.P., *A stylometric study of the New Testament* (Oxford: Clarendon, 1986).

Knott, K., 'Religion and information technology', in King, U. (ed.), *Turning points in religious studies* (Edinburgh: T & T Clark, 1990), 287-98.

Landow, G. P., *Hypertext: the convergence of contemporary literary theory and technology* (Baltimore: John Hopkins University Press, 1992).

Mealand, D., 'Computers in New Testament research', *Journal for study of the New Testament*, 33 (1988), 97-115.

Morton, A.Q., and McLeman, J., *Paul, the man and the myth: a study in the authorship of Greek prose* (London, 1966).

Morton, A.Q., and Michaelson, S. (eds.), *The Johannine Epistles*. The Computer Bible, Vol. III. (Edinburgh, 1971).

Morton, A.Q., 'The annals of computing: the Greek Testament', *Computers and the Humanities*, 14 (1980), 197-99.

O'Donnell, J.J., 'The virtual library: an idea whose time has passed,' in Okerson, A., and Mogge, D. (eds.), *Gateways, gatekeepers, and roles in the information omniverse* (Washington, DC: Association of Research Libraries, Office of Scientific and Academic Pub., 1994). Online edition at http://ccat.sas.upenn.edu/jod/virtual.html

Parunak, H. Van Dyke, 'Database design for biblical texts,' in Bailey, R.W. (ed.), *Computing in the humanities: papers from the fifth international conference on computing in the humanities, Ann Arbor, Michigan, May 1981* (Amsterdam: North Holland Publishing Company, 1982), 149-61.

Tilsed, I., and Myhill, M., 'The Star of the East: machine-based information sources for theologians', *Theology*, May/June (1994), 179-88.

Further information

Further information about the *Thomae Aquinatis Opera Omnia cum hypertextibus in CD-ROM* may be obtained from EDITEL, Via Savona 112/a, 20144 Milano, Italy.

Further information about the edition of Aquinas in the Past Masters series may be obtained from Intelex Corp., P.O. Box 1827, Clayton, GA 30525-1827, USA.

WinGreek can be obtained from Dr Peter Gentry, WinGreek, 55 Ambercroft Blvd, Scarborough, Ontario, Canada M1W 2Z6 (E-mail: pjg@io.org).

Linguist's Software can be contacted at Linguist's Software, PO Box 580, Edmonds WA 98020-0580, USA. The UK distributor is Lingua Language Services, 63B Woodhead Road, Holmfirth, Huddersfield. HD7 1PR.

Gamma UniType can be obtained from Gamma Productions, Inc., 12625 High Bluff Drive, Suite 218, San Diego, California 92130-2746, USA.

The Centre for Computer Analysis of Texts can be accessed at gopher://ccat.sas.upenn.edu/11/

CETEDOC Library of Christian Latin Texts, *In Principio*, and information about the International Medieval Bibliography can be obtained from Brepols Publishers, Steenweg op Tielen 68, B-2300 Turnhout, Belgium.

Patrologia Latina Database is available from Chadwyck-Healey Ltd, The Quorum, Barnwell Road, Cambridge CB5 8SW. URL: http://www.chadwyck.co.uk/

KAB Konsult can be reached at: KAB Konsult AB, Storgatan 59, 264 32 Klippan, Sweden.

The documents of Vatican II as well as other theological texts can be obtained from the University of Toronto via ftp://ftp.epas.utoronto.ca/pub/cch/religious_studies

Information about the ATLA Religion Index CD-ROM may be obtained from American Theological Libraries Association, 820 Church Street, Suite 300, Evanston, Illinois 60201-5603, USA.

The Dead Sea Scrolls Revealed can be obtained in the UK from Hodder and Headline, 338 Euston Road, London, NW1 3BH or from Logos Research Systems, Inc., 2117 200th Ave W, Oak Harbor, Washington 98277-4049, USA.

The 1979 American Book of Common Prayer is available online at gopher://listserv.american.edu:70/11/anglican/bcp

The Hill Monastic Manuscript Library can be accessed at, http://www.csbsju.edu/hmml/index.html

The CANTUS Project at the Catholic University of America can be accessed through, gopher://gopher.cua.edu.:70/11/special-resources

Information on the Renaissance Liturgical Imprints Census can be accessed at, http://www.umich.edu/Gateway/Catalog/Relics.html

Further information about *La Base d'Information Bibliographique en Patristique* can be obtained from René-Michel Roberge, Faculté de Théologie, Université Laval, Cité universitaire, Quebec G1K 7P4, Canada.

James O'Donnell's 'Augustine on the Internet' pages including information about the Augustine e-mail group can be accessed at http://ccat.sas.upenn.edu/jod/augustine.html. The PennMOO hosts MUGIT (*Multorum Utentium Gregi Interesse Transcribendo* — 'to be in a flock of many users by writing') a Latin-only electronic classroom (telnet://ccat.sas.upenn.edu:7777).

An extensive list of discussion groups for theologians is available on the University of Durham's gopher, gopher://delphi.dur.ac.uk:70/11/Academic/P-T/Theology/Computing/Lists

A selection of World Wide Web resources for theologians can be found through http://info.ox.ac.uk/ctitext/service/lectures/trmay95.html

The ECOLE Initiative can be accessed at http://www.evansville.edu:80/~ecoleweb/ Further information from Anthony F. Beavers, General Editor (ecole@evansville.edu)

Further information about IBM's Digital Library Projects at the Vatican Library and Lutherhalle Wittenberg can be obtained from the IBM Web page, http://www.ibm.com/Features/library/

The Chorus World Wide Web pages, which include a section on biblical analysis, can be accessed at, http://www.peinet.pe.ca:2080/Chorus/special.html

SECTION 3
RESOURCE SERVICES
AND PROVIDERS

Archives

Peter Doorn

Introduction: between data archiving and electronic publishing

At the close of his administration, President Bush requested permission to purge the e-mail communication among the 200-member staff of the National Security Council which had taken place during his presidency. He considered it unnecessary to preserve that information for posterity, arguing that e-mail, which was used for both trivial and substantive exchange, was part of an internal communications system and not of a federal records system. However, a US District Judge ruled that the destruction of the electronic files was a violation of the Federal Records Act. The archiving of hard copies of a selection of the e-mails considered to be 'official records' was also regarded as insufficient for at least three reasons: the electronic media fitted the statutory definition of 'records' quite nicely; the printed copies did not reflect all evidential value (transmission data, etc.); and the criteria for the selection of what was an official record in the first place were arbitrary (Bikson and Frinking 1993, 161).

This little tale of the information society demonstrates the archival value of electronic files. Archives are the storehouses of documents on our past, and as our present is becoming digital, so will the archives follow. This chapter will deal with electronic records as they are being or will be preserved and made available in archives, and with the difficulties that are connected to it. Apart from the care of such modern or 'prospective' files, many archives are also involved in retrospective conversion of paper sources in one way or another. This may entail activities ranging from converting finding-aids such as archive guides, inventories, indexes and catalogues, to the digitization of the holdings themselves.

Government processes and archive automation programmes are by no means the only sources for the origination of electronic archives. Scholars in all disciplines within the humanities (as well as in other arts and sciences) contribute to the flood of digital information that is washing the academic shores. As this book shows, no research field within the humanities is untouched by computer applications, and one of the results of all this scholarly activity is that databases in a multitude of forms are being produced. The preservation of and access to these resources is a task that scientific text and data archives (also called data services, data libraries, and so on) have set for themselves.

We should discern a third field where electronic files, which form a basic resource of rising importance for scientific enquiry, are produced: that of electronic publishing. Although overlaps exist, data archiving is not the same as electronic publishing. Whereas the first concentrates on preserving and providing access to data collections, the latter implies a more active task of taking data to the market. Of course, (data) archives may engage in electronic publishing and (data) publishers need to archive their products, and from the point of view of the user the differences may seem trivial. However, the 'mission' or 'core business' is different. A public archive usually operates within a legal framework, which stipulates the obligation to preserve public records. Special archives preserve records of a specific interest group, theme, or subject. Most data archives were set up by the scientific community as repositories for files created by researchers, in order to make secondary analysis possible. Electronic publishers typically produce electronic files for distribution purposes.

This chapter will concentrate on the services provided by archives and data archives, and will be brief on electronic publishing (see chapter by Deegan in this volume for further discussion on electronic publishing). It is impossible to be comprehensive when one tries to give an overview of the state of the art of digital archiving. Instead, I will try to describe the general themes and discussions and give examples of the different approaches and fields.

Data and text archives

Over the past twenty-five years, repositories for machine-readable data files which are created during the research process, commonly known as data and text archives, have been created in a number of countries in America, Eurasia, and Oceania. Most of the data archives proceeded from the social sciences and later from the historical disciplines, whereas the text archives sprang from literary and linguistic computing.

Social science data archives

The need to create data archives for the social sciences arose when research became increasingly computer-based. In a typical social survey, structured questionnaires are used on a sample of the population. The answer categories are usually coded, and the codes are entered into the computer. The data could often be stored in rectangular files of tabular form, which were then analysed with a statistical package such as SPSS, OSIRIS, or SAS. In order to make it possible to check the results of a research survey, the base material had to be (and stay) available. Moreover, comparative research and secondary analysis were stimulated by the availability of similar datasets. These motives were important in the creation of social science data archives, whose prime task became the preservation of such electronic survey information (Kiecolt and Nathan 1985).

Several organizations for international collaboration, standardization, and exchange were created by the data archives. Membership of the International Federation of Data Organizations (IFDO) includes data archives from the following countries: Italy, Belgium, France, Denmark, USA, UK, Israel, Canada, Norway, Sweden, New Zealand, South Africa, Switzerland, Australia, India, the Netherlands, Hungary, and Austria (see Further Information (1) at the end of this chapter for a full listing). In Europe the Council of European Social Science Data Archives (CESSDA) forms an umbrella organization.

All data archives have adopted some form of description scheme for the cataloguing and opening up of their data collections. This so-called Standard Study Description Scheme (abbreviated to SD) concentrates on the documentation of the research project and the methodologies used for data collection, such as sampling strategies. As most interview data are coded before (or during) entering the data into computer files, it is necessary to document the meaning of all codes used, otherwise the files would be worthless. It is also noteworthy that the archival unit is the 'study' or research project, which may comprise a number of files. The SD somewhat resembles the MARC format for bibliographic information, but it contains more fields. The bibliographical description of a book is more straightforward a task than the documentation of an electronic file. Books usually have a fixed title, author, date, and place of publication. Other standard bibliographic details include the ISBN and cataloguing information (see also Anderson and Winstanley 1993, 113-121).

A computer file is essentially a virtual unit, the 'title' of which may be a file name that tells us little about the content of the file. It is even disputable what a 'file' is, in an archival sense. Data archives originally aimed at preserving their holdings in a system-independent way; that is, independent of the software with which the data have been created and manipulated. This would ensure that the data would stay usable when a software package fell out of use or was updated. Most datasets deposited at social science data archives are of a simple, rectangular structure and contain statistical information. With the documentation supplied, users should be able to import the data in any software package they like.

Based at Ann Arbor, Michigan, the Inter-university Consortium for Social and Political Research (ICPSR) was founded in 1962 as a partnership between 22 American universities. By 1994, there were over 325 colleges and universities in the US and Canada and several hundred additional institutions served by national members in Europe, Oceania, Asia, and Latin America affiliated to ICPSR. For over thirty years the Consortium has been serving social scientists around the world. The customers are not limited to sociologists and politicologists, but also include economists, geographers, psychologists, and historians. The main service the ICPSR provides is a central repository and dissemination service for machine-readable social science data. It is the world's largest social science data archive. Its collection includes surveys of mass and elite attitudes, census records, election returns, international interactions, and legislative records. The first acquisitions consisted of a few major surveys of the American electorate, but holdings now range from American elections in the 1790s and roll call votes of the US Congress via nineteenth-century French census materials to recent sessions of the United Nations. Apart from the data archive, the ICPSR provides training facilities in quantitative methods and techniques for social research and offers resources to facilitate the use of advanced computer technologies by social scientists (ICPSR 1995; the ICPSR home page on World Wide Web can be found at http://icpsr.umich.edu/).

The ESRC Data Archive in the UK was founded more than twenty-five years ago at the University of Essex and now is one of the largest social science data archives, including more than 7,000 datasets on social sciences, economics, history, geography, and law. The number of datasets is increasing at a rate of about 250 per year. By using the BIRON (Bibliographic Information Retrieval ONline) online catalogue, which is accessible through the Internet, researchers can locate data they are interested in. The Zentral Archiv für empirische Sozialforschung (ZA) in Cologne is the German data archive for the social sciences. The Danish Data Archive (DDA) was founded in 1973 at Odense University, but recently it has become a part of the national archives of Denmark. In Amsterdam (the Netherlands) the Steinmetz Archive (1971) grew out of the Steinmetz Foundation (1964). It is a department of the Sociaal-Wetenschappelijk Informatie en Documentatie Centrum (SWIDOC), an institute of the Royal Netherlands Academy of Arts and Sciences. A comprehensive list of the social science data archives can be found in the data guides of most of the member institutions of IFDO (for example, DDA, 1993; ICPSR, 1995). An electronic list is available on the Internet, through which data archives are accessible, providing services such as anonymous ftp, Gopher, WWW, etc. (see http://www.ssd.gu.se/ifdotitel.html).

Text archives

In the same way that computerized survey data form the basis for a lot of social scientific research, electronic texts form the basis for literary and linguistics research. Where statistical packages formed the main tool kit for the social scientist, programs for text retrieval and text analysis were developed and applied by philologists, linguists, lexicologists, and literary researchers. The creation of corpora of electronic texts made it desirable to set up repositories, which are generally known as text archives. Some text archives are open to donations from all kinds of textual research, but there are also centres which set themselves the task of collecting a well-defined corpus of texts. Substantial corpora of electronic texts are archived in many countries in the world—for instance, Israel, Denmark, Belgium, France, Germany, Italy, UK, Sweden, Norway, USA, Canada, Spain, and the Netherlands.

The Oxford Text Archive (OTA) is a facility provided by Oxford University Computing Services. Like most social science data archives, it operates on a non-commercial basis (and has done so since 1976), providing archival and dissemination facilities for electronic texts at low cost. Its holdings include literary works by many major authors in Greek, Latin, English, and a dozen or more other languages, as well as electronic versions of standard reference works. Moreover, corpora of unpublished materials are contributed by field workers in linguistics. The OTA contains over a gigabyte of data and over 1,500 texts (its catalogue is available at ftp://ota.ox.ac.uk/pub/ota/textarchive.list). A number of texts is directly available for downloading through ftp. As is discussed elsewhere in this book, texts can be formatted or encoded in a variety of ways. Variations in accuracy and encoding of texts also exist in the holdings of the OTA. The text archive aims at conversion to SGML coding according to the guidelines of the Text Encoding Initiative. The WWW-address of the home page of the Oxford Text Archive is http://ota.ox.ac.uk/TEI/ota.html.

The Center for Electronic Texts in the Humanities (CETH) was established by Princeton and Rutgers Universities in 1991. The Center has developed from an international inventory of machine-readable texts which was started at Rutgers in 1983. One of its tasks is to maintain and expand this inventory, a second is to acquire and disseminate text files. CETH is a national focus of interest in the US for those who are involved in the creation, dissemination, and use of electronic texts in the humanities. It also acts as a national node on an international network of centres and projects which are actively involved in the handling of electronic texts, and maintains a directory of Electronic Text Centres on the WWW (see http://cethmac.princeton.edu/). The Center also organizes summer seminars at Princeton.

The Electronic Text Center & Online Archive of Electronic Texts at the University of Virginia provides:

> ...an online collection of machine-readable texts. The initial set of online texts includes the new *Oxford English Dictionary*; the entire corpus of Old English writings; selected Library of America titles; several versions of Shakespeare's complete works; hundreds of other literary, social, historical, philosophical, and political materials in various languages (chiefly from the Oxford and the Cambridge Text Archives); and the currently released parts of two massive databases from Chadwyck-Healey: J.P. Migne's *Patrologia Latina*, and the English Poetry Full Text Database, comprised of the complete works of 1,350 English poets from AD 600 to 1900. Because of contractual obligations, access to these texts and searching tools is restricted to University of Virginia students, faculty and staff.

The online texts are all SGML-encoded and can be searched using Pat, a program developed initially for the *Oxford English Dictionary* (http://www.lib.virginia.edu/etext/ETC.html).

In 1957 the French Government initiated the creation of a new dictionary of the French Language, the *Trésor de la Langue Française*. In order to provide access to a large body of word samples, it was decided to digitize an extensive selection of French texts. Twenty years later, a corpus totalling some 150 million words had been created, representing a broad range of written French, from novels and poetry to biology and mathematics, stretching from the seventeenth to the twentieth centuries.

This corpus appeared to be an important resource not only for lexicographers, but also for other researchers engaged in French studies on both sides of the Atlantic. Therefore, a cooperative project was established in 1981 by the Centre National de la Recherche Scientifique (CNRS) and the University of Chicago, called American and French Research on the Treasury of the French Language (ARTFL). Its central goal was to make the database accessible to the research community, and to develop tools for its analysis. At present the corpus consists of nearly 2,000 texts, ranging from classic works of French literature to various kinds of non-fiction prose and technical writing, from the Middle Ages until the twentieth century. The ARTFL database is one of the largest of its kind in the world. Users access the database through the PhiloLogic system, an easy to use full-text retrieval package.

Several catalogues of electronic texts and projects exist on the Internet. One of these, called 'Alex', is maintained at Oxford University (URL gopher://rsl.ox.ac.uk:70/11/lib-corn/hunter). Alex allows users to find and retrieve hundreds of books and shorter texts in full-text format, which are indexed by author and title. It incorporates texts from Project Gutenberg, Wiretap, the Online Book Initiative, the Eris system at Virginia Tech, the English Server at Carnegie Mellon University, and the online portion of the Oxford Text Archive.

Since 1989, the Center for Text and Technology (CTT) at Georgetown University, has been compiling a catalogue of electronic text projects in the humanities throughout the world. The Catalogue of Projects in Electronic Text (CPET) is a powerful database which includes a variety of information on the many collections of literary works, historical documents, and linguistic data which are available from commercial vendors and scholarly sources. In 1993 a gopher-based version of CPET was made available on the Internet (gopher://accgopher.georgetown. edu:70/11gopher_root%3A%5Bcpet_projects_in_electronic_text%5D).

More and more text corpora are being published in electronic form. Mention should be made of the electronic editions on CD-ROM by the Belgian publisher Brepols, such as the CETEDOC Library of Christian Latin Texts (CLCLT; in collaboration with the Centre de Traitement Electronique des Documents (CETEDOC) at Louvain-La-Neuve); the Archive of Celtic-Latin Literature (ACLL, in collaboration with the Royal Irish Academy); and the Incipit Index of Latin Texts *In Principio* (in collaboration with the Institut de Recherche et d'Histoire des Textes of the CNRS). A leading example from Spain is the *Archivo Digital de Manuscritos y Textos Españoles* (ADMYTE). This project of the Spanish national library was carried out as part of the celebrations to mark the quincentenary of the discovery of America by Columbus in 1492. The main aim was to disseminate Spanish culture and to develop new techniques for the treatment of historical documents. ADMYTE is presented on CD-ROM, consisting of a corpus of over 60 texts, a database of bibliographic and documentary data, and text retrieval software. The texts of the manuscripts and incunabula are available both in facsimile (in image form) and in the form of transcribed, searchable text, which can be represented simultaneously on the screen. The images and transcribed texts are linked page by page.

Two other examples in the field of classical studies are the *Thesaurus Linguae Graecae (TLG)* with classical Greek texts and Perseus, an archaeological and philological CD in multimedia form. The first edition of this package, which was developed at Harvard university, contains an overview of Greek history in the fifth century BC, Greek texts and English translations of ten authors from the archaic and classical periods, a Greek-English dictionary, short articles and an explanatory vocabulary, geographic maps and plans of excavations, concise overviews of architectural terms, vase forms, and biographies of authors from antiquity.

Although it is not primarily aimed at the scholarly world of the humanities, but at the general public, mention should be made of the collection of electronic texts of Project Gutenberg. The project aims to make available 10,000 e-texts in the categories of 'light and heavy literature and references' by the year 2001. Its Spiritual Father, Michael Heart, states that:

> The Project Gutenberg Philosophy is to make information, books and other materials available to the general public in forms a vast majority of the computers, programs and people can easily read, use, quote, and search [...] Project

Gutenberg has avoided requests, demands, and pressures to create 'authoritative editions'. We do not write for the reader who cares whether a certain phrase in Shakespeare has a ':' or a ';' between its clauses. (WWW-document at URL http:/pg/www_team.html)

All texts are in 'plain vanilla ASCII' and there is no markup (Project Gutenberg Home Page: http://jg.cso.uiuc.edu/PG/welcome.html).

Some libraries are building large databanks of electronic books (or of texts in image form), such as the Bibliothèque de France, the Vatican Library, and Yale University Library.

Historical data archives

As modern monks, many historians are spending a lot of time and effort copying historical sources into machine-readable incunabula. The conversion of paper sources into digital form is an important task for historians who practise 'source-oriented computing'. But this effort is only worthwhile if the digital sources are preserved and made accessible. Most historians create databases for their own research. After a project has been concluded, the electronic base materials should be preserved for scientific reasons of verifiability and for comparative research. For this reason, historians in various countries have been active in creating historical data archives or in stimulating the creation of special historical sections within existing (social science) data archives.

In the late 1980s, special workshops were organized around the theme of standardization and exchange of historical databases (Haussmann *et al.* 1987; Genet 1988). Later, workshops of the Association for History and Computing (AHC) were organized on the issue of historical data archiving. A lot of discussion centred on whether the standard study description scheme of the social science data archives is usable for historical datasets. In practice, some form of the SD is being used by most historical data archives. In the Netherlands, the scheme has been adapted to render more details of the original sources on which the electronic data are based.

From the very beginning, historical datasets on American elections and roll call votes of the US Congress were at the core of the collection of the ICPSR. In Germany, The Centre for Social Historical Research (Zentrum für historische Sozialforschung—ZHSF) was founded in 1977. The institutional history of the Centre is extensively described in

Schröder (1994). The Centre is part of the Zentral Archiv für empirische Sozialforschung. One of its tasks is to archive historical datasets (Schröder 1994, 85-92), although social historical research is at the core of its activities (for an overview of social historical projects in the German speaking world see also Oberwittler and Ross-Strajhar, 1991).

Over the years 1989-1993, the journal *Historical Social Research (HSR)* published a very useful overview of historical datasets in social science data archives (see Further Information (2) at the end of this chapter).

The initiative to set up a Netherlands Historical Data Archive (NHDA) first resulted in a number of projects in data archiving and in the conversion of printed historical sources with the help of scanning and optical character recognition (OCR). In January 1995, the NHDA was incorporated under the aegis of the Royal Dutch Academy of Arts and Sciences (KNAW). It is now building up its collection of files, but also acts as a mediator for databases that are stored elsewhere. Data conversion projects remain an important side-line, and the centre co-organizes a one-year postgraduate programme in information technology for historians.

A History Data Unit (HDU) was created within the ESRC Data Archive in 1993, as a concrete result of a British inventory of historical machine-readable datafiles (Schürer and Anderson 1992). The Danish Data Archive, which started as a social science data archive, became part of the national archives of Denmark in 1993. Before that date, the DDA had archived historical datasets (Marker 1993, 185-193). In Norway and Sweden historical data centres exist, although they concentrate more on specific data-capturing projects than on general data archiving. In Russia a historical data archive is being developed (Garskova 1994) and in Hungary initiatives have been taken to set up a data service for historians. A useful index to historical sources on the Internet is maintained by the University of Kansas (The World Wide Web Virtual Library: History at URL http://history.cc.ukans.edu/history/WWW_history_main.html).

Archives

Archives and electronic records

For archivists, the automation of red-tape at each and every level of government has caused something of a shock wave. No longer is paper the primary medium for the representation of government transactions. Although the information era is creating big problems for archives, it will also be their salvation. Since World War II the increase of the production of information is in the order of 5-10 per cent per year. This exponential growth in the amount of information will only be manageable if it can be stored and managed in electronic form, unless we are prepared to increase the storage space for paper files tenfold in the next few decades.

The central problem for archives now is how to adapt to this new situation. It is not possible to treat and store electronic records in the same way as paper files (Dollar 1992). The physical lifetime of digital media ranges from a few years (magnetic tape) to a few decades (optical discs). Worse than that, a machine and software are needed to read digital media, and because of the rapid technological developments, computer systems are becoming obsolete rapidly. It is already quite apparent that there will be a gap in the electronic information about the beginning of the information age. Archival methodologies and technologies for the long-term preservation of masses of electronic records are still in an early phase, although the conceptual framework is developing rapidly (Rothenberg 1995, 42-47).

I will mention here only briefly some central issues of the methodological discussions among electronic archivists and then summarize the current archiving policy for electronic records in selected countries. At the very heart of the discussion stands the definition of electronic records, files, and documents, which are not physical, but rather virtual units. A medium-independent definition of archival records as the product of transactions is preferred: 'Archival records are processes, not objects' (Higgs 1995). Moreover, the legal context in which archives function (archives legislation, freedom of information legislation, privacy legis- lation, data protection legislation) is extremely important for their atti- tude with respect to electronic records. An International Committee on Electronic records of the International Council of Archives is working on a manual with guidelines for the archival management of digital information.

Archivists are used to storing paper records according to the principle of provenance. It is essential that records are kept in such a way that it is possible to see how they were used by the bodies that created them. Archivists would like to treat electronic records in a similar way to paper, to put them in electronic boxes, like paper files are put in cardboard boxes. In this way, not only the content, but also the context and structure of the records can be preserved. The 'context and structure' of electronic records are formed to a considerable extent by the information systems that generated the data. However, because both software and hardware are becoming technologically outdated at such a rapid pace, it is doubtful whether it is feasible to preserve a software environment, and it is virtually impossible to keep obsolete computers running. For this reason, most (data) archives save datasets in a system-independent way (in ASCII). Much is expected from the development of open systems standards, which should reduce the problem of the continuously changing technological environment and keep data readable across computer platforms (ACCIS 1990, 1992). There are also experiments to keep historical software (and data) alive by building programs on new computers that emulate machines which have become obsolete. A good example is a program that makes a DOS-PC work like a Pegasus computer from 1958 (Swade 1993, 93-103).

Almost every office worker in the information age has a PC on his or her desk, which is likely to be linked to local and wide area networks. Thousands of files will be stored on his or her local or network discs. How to select the files that should be preserved for posterity? Archivists are suggesting several solutions. First, appraisal should take place on the basis of business functions and processes rather than on the analysis of records or files: when the function is important, the files should be kept. Moreover, the selection should not be made in retrospect, but beforehand, even before the records have been created. Records go through a certain life-cycle, and it is better to select them at their birth than after their death. Furthermore, it will be virtually impossible for archivists to exert intellectual control over the electronic records to be archived by describing them after they have been deposited. Instead, they are to exploit the metadata that organizations generate about their records, and they should stipulate that descriptive information is included in record-managing systems as a standard procedure.

It has even been queried whether central repositories of electronic records are necessary at all (Bearman and Hedstrom 1993; Hedstrom 1995, 85-87). In a network environment, it is possible to apply the principle of provenance in a rigorous way by leaving the records in the institution that created them. This can be an alternative for the central custodial role of archives, which could act instead as coordinators, inspectors, and intermediaries between producers and users of electronic records.

Sweden
The Swedish Riksarkivet probably contains more electronic data than any other archive in the world. The constitutional Freedom of Press/Freedom of Information Act gives any citizen in Sweden free access to official documents, irrespective of the medium on which they are stored. In 1991, electronic media were explicitly mentioned as record media in the law. So far, the state archive is only acquiring and maintaining system-independent data and not software, but this practice is increasingly posing problems (Bikson and Frinking 1993, 173-177).

Canada
The Canadian Archives Act (1987) defines records of government in a medium-independent way. Canada's National Archives was one of the first archives to develop a 'Machine-Readable Records' division in 1974, although this was disbanded again in 1985, when it was decided that organizing the archives according to media was wrong. However, as different media require different kinds of skills, interest, and management, in 1989 a new Informatics and Records Service Branch was formed. Although the National Archives accepts material in electronic form, the legal status of the records is potentially subject to question, because the Canadian Evidence Act requires official documents to be on paper (or in microform) and to be signed. Apart from large statistical datasets, the National Archives is receiving some 50,000 pages of government text records a month. In addition to imaged documents, it also acquires agencies' electronic systems for managing paper documents. A number of tools have been developed for the location and retrieval of the records. Files are stored on tape and on laser disc in both the original format and in ASCII. So far, problems with licences of software or technology obsolescence have not yet been encountered (Bikson and Frinking 1993, 148-151; Cook and Frost 1993).

United States
The National Archives and Records Administration (NARA) received its first transfers of electronic records in 1977. Statistical files still predominate, but other types of material (such as e-mail systems) are becoming more important. According to federal legislation (1990), electronic records are accepted as federal records and may be admitted in evidence during court proceedings if their trustworthiness is established. The legal context for electronic records is, however, complex. Apart from NARA, which is responsible for keeping 'permanent records of archival

value' (estimated to comprise 1-5 per cent of all records), several other government institutions are involved in electronic record keeping. Within NARA, a Center for Electronic Records was established in 1988. Originally, only 'flat' statistical files were archived, but this is no longer an appropriate standard for the increasing variety of electronic accessions. The transfer of geographic information systems (GIS) poses particular problems of standardization (Bikson and Frinking 1993, 156-161). The Center is accessible through the Internet (WWW-address http://www.nara.gov; the contents of Further Information (3) at the end of this chapter were retrieved from the Gopher information).

Australia
The National Archives in Australia favours a decentralized approach, in which electronic records are not stored in a central archive, but are maintained by the government departments which created them. An Information Locator System (ILS) is to keep track of what information can be found where (O'Shea 1994; Parer 1993).

United Kingdom
In the UK, there is no Freedom of Information legislation. According to the Public Records Act (1958, revised 1967), government departments are obliged to transfer a selection of public records for permanent preservation to the Public Records Office (PRO) and make them available when they are 30 years old (Higgs 1993, 37). The PRO is considering the establishment of a computer-readable data archive and is in the stage of formulating its policy. The national archives in several other countries in Europe are in a comparable phase. According to one observer, 'It is clear that IT has only just begun to make the impact it will make on archives in Britain, but that these changes are going to challenge much of the traditional methodology' (Chell 1992, 132).

Archive automation and retrospective conversion

In comparison with libraries, archives are relatively late in converting finding-aids, such as inventories, indexes, and guides into digital form, but they are making up for these arrears. Moreover, some archives are creating digital versions of part of their holdings. Optical scanning is used to create image banks as an alternative to microfilming. There are several advantages of scanning over microfilming. Although microfilm offers the advantage of a long-lasting, inexpensive technology which is well understood in libraries and archives, its disadvantage lies in access to the information. It is cumbersome to browse and read, it requires special equipment at a single location, it does not facilitate the use of an item's internal structure, and it does not produce high quality copies. The main strength of digital imagery is in the field of access. Digital images can be distributed on media such as CD-ROM and over networks. Moreover, digital images can be reproduced endlessly without loss of quality, and image manipulation and enhancement techniques make it possible to make images of degraded documents more legible on the screen or as printed hard copy. In conclusion, digital technology represents an affordable alternative to microfilm for reformatting material for preservation purposes (Kenney and Personius 1992).

In the US, the Commission on Preservation and Access (CPA) has set up a digital preservation consortium to carry out projects using optical scanning. One example of a project supported by the CPA is the Project Open Book at Yale University Library, in which the conversion of 10,000 books from microfilm to a digital image bank is taking place. In another project of the CPA in collaboration with Cornell University and Xerox Company, a thousand brittle books are being scanned.

The digitizing of the *Archivo General de Indias* at Sevilla is one of the most important projects in the area of retrospective conversion in an archive environment. This archive, established in 1785 by the Spanish King Charles III, initiated a huge computerization project on the occasion of the celebration of the fifth centenary of the discovery of America by Columbus in 1492. The Spanish government, IBM, and a private foundation collaborate in the project. In 1989 they started scanning documents and, between 1990 and 1992, fifteen scanners in two shifts were used. The aim was to digitize about 9 million documents created since the discovery of the new world, or about 10 per cent of the entire archival collection. A total of about 3,000 optical discs was required for the storage of all the scanned documents, which is more than any juke-box can hold. The digital images can so far only be looked at on computer screens within the archive. One of the advantages of the project is that image enhancement techniques make it possible to improve the readability on the screen. Many original documents are in a deplorable state: fading ink, damp stains, and the pressing through of text on the back hamper legibility. Image enhancement can work miracles: contrast can be improved, stains can be erased, etc. (Gonzalez 1992). Moreover, an index has been constructed in a bibliographic (textual) database for the whole archive and, in addition, retrospective conversion of various catalogues and inventories dating back to the eighteenth century, comprising about 25,000 pages (Rütimann and Lynn 1992). The municipal archive service of Utrecht, the Netherlands, has implemented an imaging system for its notarial archive. Considerations of preservation and access formed the main motives for the project. The restoration costs could be reduced and the research possibilities improved, while a reduction in guidance offered by archival staff could be achieved. The total archive has a length of about 6 km. The notarial archive is 200 metres, containing 250,000 documents over the period 1560-1810 (11.5 million pages). It was estimated that one optical discs of 2.2 Gb could contain about 24,000 scanned pages at the required resolution. A juke-box with 78 discs could therefore contain about 400 metres of archive. In a pilot project 78,000 notarial acts from the period 1660-1770 (or 232,000 pages of text) were scanned. Summaries of the notarial acts were entered in a textual database, which served as the retrieval tool for the system. In addition, 75,000 pages of town-council registers were processed (Gemeentelijke Archiefdienst Utrecht, 1992).

In 1990, a Polish-German project commenced to ensure the long-term preservation of the historical sources kept at the former concentration camp Auschwitz-Birkenau. The central catalogue of prisoners is being converted into a database. Since 1991, pilot studies have been carried out to enter different types of archive holdings into the computer. The first pilot project, concerning the Gypsy Camp, was finished in 1992. A second pilot project concerns the so-called *Sterbebücher* (collected copies of death certificates), which are being converted into machine-readable form. Most of the digital information will be available on CD-ROM (Parcer *et al.* 1994, 44-51).

In various countries, large retrospective databases have been or are being created on the basis of archival records of persons and families, and historical statistics. The Umeå Demographic Database was set up in 1973 as a temporary employment project, under the auspices of the Swedish National Archives, later under the administrative responsibility of the University of Umeå. The nineteenth century was the core period of study, with extensions forwards and backwards. Originally seven parishes were selected, geographically distributed over the country and representing a variety of socio-economic environments. Later three larger regions were added in order not to lose migrants. The data on births, deaths, marriages, and migration are captured at the individual level, and are taken from the system of parish registers, which has been in existence in Sweden for four centuries. The databank contains information on over 365,000 individuals, representing 1,644,000 entries in the sources (Jeub, 1993). In another Swedish archive project, *Stockholms Historiska Databas*, 25 per cent of 6 million entries in the city's archives has been entered.

In Canada, the Programme de Recherche en Démographie Historique (PRDH) at Montreal and the Société du Recherche sur la Population (SOREP) at Chicoutimi aim at entering the whole population of the province of Québec from 1608 to the present in a databank. Around 1700 the province had c. 17,000, now about 6 million people. The PRDH takes care of the period until 1800. Over 700,000 certificates from birth, death, and marital registers have been entered. Automatic record linkage is used to reconstruct the demographic history of persons. SOREP is responsible for the period after 1800. Currently, 75-100,000 records per year are being computerized. Since the start of the project in 1971, 1.6 million records have been entered.

In the Netherlands, a databank is being created with individual data on the basis of a 0.5 per cent sample of nineteenth century birth certificates from public archives. In a pilot project a sample of 3,650 persons in the period 1812-1922 was taken. The persons in the sample were traced by burial and marital certificates and in the population register. Currently, the databank is being expanded to the whole of the Netherlands (Mandemakers 1993). In France, another sampling strategy has been followed in order to make it simpler to find persons in different sources. Here, the members of 3,000 families from 1803 to the present have been followed, whose surname start with the three letters TRA (Dupâquier and Kessler 1992).

Apart from population and parish registers, historical censuses form an important source for retro-conversion projects, which is demonstrated by examples from Norway, Denmark, United Kingdom, Ireland, and the US.

Conclusion

As everywhere in the humanities, the buzzword for electronic archives in the 1990s is Internet, Internet, Internet. Although archives are gradually entering cyberspace, it should be noted that most services on the Internet that call themselves 'archives' are not archives at all: they 'may not be permanent, are not necessarily coordinated, and may not retain files' (Hedstrom 1995, 87, quoting a guide for Internet users). So be warned.

References and bibliography

ACCIS, *Management of electronic records: issues and guidelines* (New York, NY: United Nations, 1990).

ACCIS, *Strategic issues for electronic records management: towards open systems interconnection* (New York, NY: United Nations, 1992).

Anderson, S., and Winstanley, B., 'Review of documentation procedures at the ESRC Data Archive', *Historical Social Research*, 18.1 (1993), 113-121.

Bearman, D., and Hedstrom, M., 'Reinventing archives for electronic records: alternative service delivery options', in Hedstrom, M. (ed.), *Electronic records management program strategies* (Pittsburgh: Archives and Museum Informatics, 1993) Technical Report 18.

Bikson, T.K., and Frinking, E.J., *Het heden onthouden/Preserving the present: toward viable electronic records* (Den Haag: Sdu, 1993).

Chell, R., 'The impact of computers in British archives', *Archivi & Computer*, 2 (1992), 128-133.

Cook, T., and Frost, E., 'The electronic records archival programme at the national archives of Canada: evolution and critical factors of success', in Hedstrom, M. (ed.), *Archives and Museum Informatics Technical Report* 18 (1993).

Danish Data Archive, *Danish data guide 1993* (Odense: Odense University Press, 1993).

Davis, C., Deegan, M., and Lee, S. (eds.),*CTI Centre for Textual Studies: Resources Guide March 1992* (Oxford: CTI Centre for Textual Studies and Office for Humanities Communication, 1992).

Dollar, C., *Archival theory and information technologies: the impact of information technologies on archival principles and methods* (Ancona: University of Macerata, 1992).

Dupâquier, J., and Kessler, D. (eds.), *La société française au xixe siècle: tradition, transition, transformations* (Paris: Fayard, 1992).

Garskova, I.M., *Bazy i banki dannykh v istoricheskikh issledovaniyakh* (Moscow/Göttingen, 1994).

Gemeentelijke Archiefdienst Utrecht, *Het WIIS Archiefopslag- en raadpleegsysteem: projectrapport van het Utrechtse beeldplaatproject* (Utrecht, 1992).

Genet, J.-P. (ed.), *Standardisation et échange des bases de données historiques* (Paris, 1988).

Gonzalez, P., 'Computerisation project for the "Archivo General de Indias"', in Doorn, P., Kluts, C., and Leenarts, E. (eds.), *Data, computers and the past* (Hilversum, 1992), 52-67. Cahier VGI 5.

Haussmann, F., Härtel, R., Kropac, I.H., and Becker, P. (eds.), *Datennetze für die historischen Wissenschaften? Probleme und Möglichkeiten bei Standardisierung und Transfer maschinenlesbarer Daten* (Graz, 1987).

Hedstrom, M., 'Descriptive practices for electronic records: deciding what is essential and imagining what is possible', *Archivaria*, 36, Autumn (1993).

Hedstrom, M. (ed.), *Electronic records management program strategies* (Pittsburgh: Archives and Museum Informatics, 1993) Technical Report 18.

Hedstrom, M., 'Electronic archives: integrity and access in the network environment', in Kenna, S., and Ross, S. (eds.), *Networking in the humanities: proceedings of the second conference on scholarship and technology in the humanities held at Elvetham Hall, Hampshire, UK, 13-16 April 1994* (London: Bowker Saur, 1995), 77-95.

Higgs, E., 'Historians, archivists and electronic record keeping in UK government', in Ross, S., and Higgs, E. (eds.), *Electronic information resources and historians: European perspectives* (St. Katharinen: Halbgraue Reihe zur historischen Fachinformatik, A20, 1993; and as British Library R&D Report 6122).

Higgs, E., *Can one convey meaning via the Internet? Some thoughts on the differences between information, historical artefacts and context in electronic access to archives*, paper presented at the annual conference of the UK branch of the AHC, Cambridge, April 19-21, 1995.

Inter-university Consortium for Political and Social Research (ICPSR), *Guide to resources and services 1994-1995* (Ann Arbor, MI, 1995).

Jeub, U.N., *Parish records: 19th century ecclesiastical registers (information from the demographic data base)* (Umeå 1993).

Kenney, A.R., and Personius, L.K., *The Cornell/Xerox/CPA Joint Study in Digital Preservation, Phase 1*. Commission on Preservation and Access, September 1992.

Kiecolt, K.J., and Nathan, L.E., *Secondary analysis of survey data* (Beverly Hills: Sage, 1985) Sage University Paper 53 (Series: Quantitative Applications in the Social Sciences).

Mandemakers, K., *Eindrapport HSN-Proefproject Provincie Utrecht* (Amsterdam: IISG, 1993).

Marker, H-J., 'Data conservation at a traditional data archive', in Ross, S., and Higgs, E. (eds.), *Electronic information resources and historians: European perspectives* (St. Katharinen: Halbgraue Reihe zur historischen Fachinformatik, A20, 1993; and as British Library R&D Report 6122).

Oberwittler, D., and Ross-Strajhar G. (eds.), *Historische Sozialforschung: Forschungsdokumentation 1982-1990* (Bonn: Informationszentrum Sozialwissenschaften, 1991).

O'Shea, G., 'The medium is NOT the message: appraisal of electronic records by Australian archives', *Archives and Manuscripts,* The Journal of the Australian Society of Archivists, May (1994).

Parcer, J., Levermann, W., and Grotum, Th., 'Remembering the Holocaust: preservation and improved accessibility of the archives in the Memorial Oswiecim/Brzezinka

(Auschwitz/Birkenau)', in *Historical informatics: an essential tool for historians* (a panel convened by the AHC at the 19th annual meeting of the SSHA, Atlanta, Georgia, October 14th 1994), 44-51.

Parer, D., 'Australian archives: preserve your valuable electronic records', *Archives and Museum Informatics Technical Report* 18 (1993).

Parer, D., and Terry, R., *Managing electronic records: papers from a workshop on managing electronic records of archival value* (Sydney, April 1993).

Roberts, D., 'Defining electronic records, documents and data', *Archives and Manuscripts*, The Journal of the Australian Society of Archivists, 22.1 (1994).

Ross, S., and Higgs, E. (eds.), *Electronic information resources and historians: European perspectives* (St. Katharinen: Halbgraue Reihe zur historischen Fachinformatik, A20, 1993; and as British Library R&D Report 6122).

Rothenberg, J., 'Ensuring the longevity of digital documents', *Scientific American* (January, 1995), 42-47.

Rütimann, H., and Lynn, M.S., *Computerization project of the Archivo General de Indias: a report to the CPA*, Seville, Spain (CPA, March 1992).

Schröder, W.H., *Historische Sozialforschung* (Cologne: Zentrum für Historische Sozialforschung/Centre for Historical Social Research). Supplement *Historical Social Research*, 6 (1994).

Schürer, K., and Anderson, S.J. (comp.), *A guide to historical datafiles held in machine-readable form* (London: Association for History and Computing, 1992).

State Archives of Western Australia, 'Electronic records: an investigation into retention, storage and transfer options', *LISWA Research Series*, 4 (1993).

Swade, D., 'Collecting software: preserving information in an object-oriented culture', in Ross, S., and Higgs, E. (eds.), *Electronic information resources and historians: European perspectives* (St. Katharinen: Halbgraue Reihe zur historischen Fachinformatik, A20, 1993; and as British Library R&D Report 6122).

Waters, A., and Weaver, S., *The organizational phase of Project Open Book* (CPA, Washington DC, September 1992).

Zweig, R.W., 'Virtual records and real history', *History and Computing*, 4.3 (1992), 174-182.

Further reading

Archivi & Computer (Archivio Storico Comunale, San Miniato, Pisa, Italy). Journal dedicated to the application of computers in archives. Some articles in English.

Bearman, D., 'Diplomatics, Weberian bureaucracy, and the management of electronic records in Europe and America', *Electronic evidence: strategies for managing records in contemporary organizations* (Pittsburgh: Archives and Museums Informatics, 1994).

Cook, T., 'Easy to byte, harder to chew: the second generation of electronic records archives' *Archivaria* (Winter, 1991-1992).

Hedstrom, M., 'Understanding electronic incunabula: a framework for research on electronic records', *American Archivist,* 54.3 (Summer, 1991), 334-354.

History and Computing, 4.3 (1993), 174-210. Special issue devoted to the archiving of electronic records.

Michelson, A., and Rothenberg, J., 'Scholarly communication and information technology: the impact of changes in the research process on archives', *American Archivist,* 55.2 (Spring, 1992), 236-315.

Further information

1. International Federation of Data Organizations

Archivio Dati e Programmi per le Scienze Sociali, Italy (ADPSS)

Belgian Archives for the Social Sciences (BASS)

Centre d'Informatisation des Données Socio-Politiques/Banque de Données Socio-Politiques, France (CIDSP/BDSP)

Danish Data Archives, Odense (DDA)

Data and Program Library Service, University of Wisconsin, USA (DPLS)

ESRC Data Archive, University of Essex, UK (ESRC-DA)

Indian Council of Social Science Research—Data Archive (ICSSR—DA)

Institute for Research in Social Science (IRSS) and the Louis Harris Data Center, University of North Carolina, USA

Institute for Social Science Research, Social Science Data Archive, UCLA, USA (ISSR-UCLA)

Inter-university Consortium for Political and Social Research, Ann Arbor, MI, USA (ICPSR)

Jerusalem Social Sciences Data Archive, Israel (SSDA-IL)

Leisure Studies Data Bank (LSDB), University of Waterloo, Canada

National Archives of Canada (NAC)

National Opinion Research Centre (NORC), University of Chicago, IL, USA

Netherlands Historical Data Archive, Leiden, the Netherlands (NHDA)

New Zealand Social Research Data Archive (NZSRDA)

Norwegian Social Sciences Data Services (NSD)

Roper Center for Public Opinion Research, USA

Social Research Informatics Center, Hungary (TARKI)

Social Science Data Archives, Australian National University, Canberra (SSDA-AUS)

Social Science Data Library, Carleton University, Canada (SSDL-CU)

South African Data Archive (SADA)

Steinmetz Archive, Amsterdam, the Netherlands (STAR)

Swedish Social Science Data Service (SSD)

Swiss Information and Data Archive Service for the Social·Sciences (SIDOS)

University of British Columbia (UBC) Data Library, Canada

Wiener Institut für Sozialwissenschaftliche Dokumentation und Metodik, Austria (WISDOM)

Zentral Archiv für Empirische Sozialforschung, Cologne, Germany (ZA)

Zentrum für Historische Sozialforschung, Cologne, Germany (ZHSF)

2. A guide to historical datasets in US and European social science data archives, published in Historical Social Research (HSR).

1. Inter-university Consortium for Political and Social Research, Ann Arbor (MI), USA (*HSR* 14.2, 1989, 168-181; *HSR* 14.3, 1989, 123-134).

2. Economic and Social Science Data Archive, Colchester (Essex), UK (*HSR* 14.4, 1989, 143-155).

3. Danish Data Archives, Odense, Denmark (*HSR* 15.1, 1990, 82-93).

4. Norwegian Social Science Data Service (*HSR* 15.2, 1990, 83-88.

5. Swedish Social Science Data Archive (*HSR* 15.3, 1990, 199-202).

6. The Netherlands Historical Data Archive (*HSR* 15.4, 1990, 197-200; *HSR* 16.1, 1991, 83-88).

7. Central Archive for Empirical Social Research (Center for Historical Social Research), Cologne, Germany (*HSR* 16.2, 1991, 182-189; *HSR* 16.3, 1991, 152-158; *HSR* 16.4, 1991, 135-143).

8. Data and Program Library Service, Univ. of Wisconsin, Madison (WI), USA (*HSR* 17.1, 1992, 117-122).

9. The Roper Center for Public Opinion Research, Storrs (CO), USA (*HSR* 17.2, 1992, 95-120; *HSR* 17.3, 1992, 106-113).

10. Organization for Economic Co-operation and Development (OECD), Paris, France (*HSR* 18.2 1993, 196-204).

11. Steinmetz Archive Data Catalogue and Guide, Amsterdam, the Netherlands (*HSR* 18.2, 1993, 205).

12. World Bank Socio-economic Data 1960-1986 (*HSR* 18.3, 1993, 72-77).

13. Social Science Data Archive, Hebrew University (Mount Scopus Libraries), Jerusalem, Israel (*HSR* 18.4, 1993, 109-111).

14. Archivio Dati e Programmi per le Scienze Sociali (ADPSS), Instituto Superiore di Sociologia, Milano, Italy (*HSR* 18.4, 116-117).

3. The Center for Electronic Records of the NARA

'The Center for Electronic Records is the organization within the National Archives of the United States that appraises, collects, preserves, and provides access to US. Federal records in a format designed for computer processing. The Center maintains electronic records with continuing value created by the US. Congress, the courts, the Executive Office of the President, numerous Presidential commissions, and nearly 100 bureaux, departments, and other components of executive branch agencies and their contractors. Among the types of holdings or subject areas represented in the Center's holdings are the following:

a. Attitudinal Data (including surveys about equal opportunity, crime, violence, surveys sponsored by the US. Information Agency (USIA), and the "American Soldier" surveys of soldiers during World War II).

b. Demographic Data (including data from the Bureau of the Census, US. Department of Commerce).

c. Economic and Financial Statistics (including income, labor, securities, tax, trade, and transportation statistics).

d. Education Data (including data illustrating the variety of education programs of the US. Federal government).

e. Health and Social Services Data (including data incorporating both biomedical and sociological information and efforts to measure the effectiveness of a variety of social programs).

f. International Data (including import-export statistics and USIA-sponsored surveys).

g. Military Data (including "American Soldier" surveys, repatriated prisoners of war records from World War II and the Korean and Vietnam conflicts, casualty records for the Korean and Vietnam conflicts, and a large collection of data files resulting from the use of computers for military operations, management, and research dating from the 1960s, especially during combat in Southeast Asia).

h. Scientific and Technological Data (including registers and surveys of scientific and technical personnel, and data from the National Ocean Survey).'

Source: Based on NARA's Gopher-information

The Changing Face of Research Libraries

Robin. C. Alston

When I undertook to contribute a chapter on libraries to this book it assumed a certain shape in my mind. As I began to structure my thinking and address the issues presented by the widespread adoption of computers in libraries during the past five years, it soon became apparent that the shape I had thought appropriate needed quite drastic revision. It used to be the case that those responsible for libraries and the services they provide shared with their readers a common understanding of the nature of research and the way the curious mind accumulates and sifts evidence. In recent years that has changed, and the ubiquitous adoption of computers in all the activities which are necessary to the functioning of a library, largely driven by the supposed efficiencies thereby gained, has resulted in the belief that access to knowledge depends less on the traditional skills that used to be taught in schools of librarianship than on skills which are associated with what is called 'information management'. This is true; but implicit in this truth are far-reaching consequences for all who depend upon libraries for the successful execution of their chosen topic of enquiry, whether casual or exhaustive.

If those using libraries in the past experienced difficulties in finding what they wanted there was usually a helpful reference librarian who could get the reader on the right road; starting with a handful of relevant references, and equipped with a knowledge of the various reference tools at their disposal, the enquiry would gradually evolve to the point where many a researcher has felt overwhelmed by the sources available. The computer, however, is an environment radically different from books on a shelf, or cards in a drawer, and those who would discover the resources available electronically, whether in their home library or a library in a different continent, must now understand a great deal more than before about how information is stored and how it can be retrieved. What follows may seem to be more relevant to those who manage libraries than to those who use them: but I am convinced that both have a part to play in shaping the library of the future. The advancement of knowledge since the fifteenth century has depended upon the fruitful collaboration between the writers of books, those who publish and distribute them, those who collect and make them available for general use, and those who study them and create new syntheses, or suggest new understandings of history or reality. As technology develops it is imperative that all who play their part in the information cycle understand the issues and ensure that we gain more than we might lose.

In 1990 students and researchers in the humanities in British universities could not expect to find much of the material useful for their research available via JANET—the Joint Academic Network linking institutions of higher learning and research institutes throughout the British Isles. A few universities had, by then, made their catalogues available on the network, but for the most part what was available were records for modern works. The keyboarding of the British Library's *General Catalogue*, after two abortive attempts at conversion, had still only proceeded as far as the letter O. The pre-1920 catalogue of the Bodleian Library, though in machine-readable form according to a plan devised by John Jolliffe in the 1970s, was still not available online, though the cumbersome guard books which contained the original catalogue slips had been replaced by a computer printout. Libraries in Europe were accessible only if they used OCLC (Online Library Computer Center, based in Dublin, Ohio) as a shared cataloguing service, and the EPIC search software had only recently been made available in Europe on a trial basis. Libraries in North America had, by 1990, begun to make their online catalogues available on the Internet, but for the most part these were of marginal interest because they contained almost exclusively modern works appropriate to undergraduate studies. The only guides to the Internet available were Ed Krol's *The Hitchhiker's Guide to the Internet* (a slim volume of 23 leaves published by the University of Illinois), and a six page pamphlet by Marilee Birchfield, *Casting a New Net: Searching Library Catalogues via the Internet*. There have been over 500 books on, and guides to, the Internet published since 1990.[1]

When I started the Research Seminars for users of the Reading Room in the British Library in March 1990 the principal databases which I used to assist readers in their research were: (1) the incomplete file of the British Library's *General Catalogue*; (2) OCLC; and (3) RLIN, the

Research Libraries Information Network funded by the Research Libraries Group and maintained at Stanford University. Discounting duplicates (a phenomenon found in all collaborative databases not subject to editorial control) readers discovered quickly that computer access to some sixty million records could provide them with sources which would have taken years to discover. In the four years over which the Research Seminars extended the sources available for online searching had multiplied to the point where it had become difficult to adopt practicable search strategies. By January 1995 the number of online catalogues exceeded two thousand, covering libraries throughout the world. The countries still represented very patchily are those in Central and South America, Japan, China, India, Africa, Eastern Europe, and Russia. Even within Europe the number of catalogues available from France, Italy, and Spain is still very limited. The Bodleian catalogue of pre-1920 imprints became available on CD-ROM in 1994, but the Library of Congress retrospective database, completed by Carrollton Press in the late 1970s (formerly available on DIALOG) has only recently been made available on the Library of Congress Information System (LOCIS).

In spite of the fact that many libraries in the United States have received special funding to catalogue in machine-readable form particular collections of importance for historical research, most of the literature printed before 1900 is still unavailable remotely. For manuscripts and archives it is going to be a long time before we have access electronically to more than a fraction of what exists.

In the 1850s the Society of Arts tried to inaugurate a project to produce a universal catalogue: the Prince Consort was to be the patron and his numerous royal relations throughout Europe were supposed to play a part in convincing governments of the manifold benefits which would derive from such an imaginative project. It came to nothing, of course, and there were those who argued that if only the British Museum were to produce a printed catalogue most demands would be satisfied. A printed catalogue was produced between 1881 and 1905, but we now know that the total collections of printed materials in the British Library, though enormous and of the first importance for historical research in almost every discipline, nevertheless account for less than 20 per cent of all books, periodicals, newspapers, and ephemera printed before 1990.

Although research in the humanities depends upon access to historical materials (printed and manuscript) there is also a pressing need to have access to works published in the past twenty (or so) years and because research libraries have, during this period, suffered very real cuts in acquisition budgets, discovering what has been published on any given topic requires access to large collaborative databases such as OCLC or RLIN. The growth in academic publishing since 1970 has necessitated a much more rigorously applied selection policy for even the largest university libraries.

Edited databases

The Eighteenth-Century Short-Title Catalogue (ESTC), the first edited catalogue of historical materials in machine-readable form, was started at the British Library in 1976 following an international conference jointly sponsored by the National Endowment for the Humanities in Washington and the British Library, and held in London during June of that year. The record of printing in the English speaking world from 1701 to 1800 was generally regarded as a desideratum of the first importance in a survey carried out by the Society for Eighteenth Century Studies. Pollard and Redgrave's *Short-Title Catalogue (STC)* had been successfully revised since its first publication in 1926, and Donald Wing's catalogue which takes the record to 1700 was undergoing revision: to continue the record to 1800 seemed logical, if daunting. From the outset, ESTC was conceived as an Anglo-American project with the British Library's holdings (the largest in the world) properly judged to be the core of what would become a union catalogue.[2] During the first phase of the project the aim was to produce a definitive catalogue of the collections of the British Library. For a variety of reasons, this aim has still to be achieved after nearly twenty years of effort. As far as the total universe of individual titles printed in the British Isles, North America, India, and the Caribbean, and books in English printed anywhere, is concerned, the file is probably 80 per cent complete, though the record of editions and copies in the world's libraries still has a long way to go. The problem with any collaborative enterprise is ensuring uniform practices in cataloguing and accuracy. The imperative of good housekeeping routines can hardly be over-emphasized.

In 1992 it was decided that ESTC should be amalgamated with machine-readable records for the period covered by Pollard and Redgrave (1476-1640) and Wing (1641-1700). The amalgamated file, available to those with access to RLIN special databases on a fee-paying basis, contains almost 400,000 records. When completed, the file will contain probably 500,000 records with perhaps 2,000,000 locations worldwide. It was never part of ESTC's brief to provide subject access, though records incorporated in the amalgamated file created by University Microfilms do have subject headings. The new ESTC (where the E stands for 'English' not 'Eighteenth-Century') will, therefore, for the foreseeable future be a hybrid. It will never be quite like the bibliography in which every item or copy recorded has been examined by the same pair of eyes, but it is the best one can hope for in an imperfect world.

ESTC spawned a number of projects, amongst which retrospective catalogues undertaken for Dutch printing up to 1700 (based in Amsterdam) and the University of Göttingen deserve particular mention. The former is an online file available on the Royal Library's PICA system at The Hague (access difficult), while the latter appeared as a printed catalogue in eight volumes between 1980 and 1990. In the British Library, David Paisey's monumental short title catalogue of German books printed before 1700 was published in 1994 (Paisey 1994) and, though compiled in machine-readable form, is so far only available as a printed catalogue. A short title catalogue of Scandinavian books is in preparation.

Encouraged by the enthusiasm with which ESTC was greeted by librarians and scholars throughout the world it was not long before the post-1800 period engaged the attention of a small but dedicated team at Newcastle-upon-Tyne. Conceived in three stages (1801-1815, 1816-1871, 1872-1919) NSTC (Nineteenth-Century Short-Title Catalogue) has, since 1986, been publishing in printed form a union catalogue based on selected printed catalogues of major British research libraries. Although bibliographical detail is necessarily restricted to what is revealed in the catalogues on which NSTC is based it nevertheless does include subject access—via a three-figure Dewey Decimal Code (DDC). Given that these are applied on the basis of title information only and not examination of the books it follows that anomalies abound. Yet the project does, however imperfectly, make a substantial contribution to our knowledge of what was printed between 1801 and 1871.

On a smaller scale, and conceived as a finding-aid rather than a bibliographical catalogue, is the ISTC (Incunabula Short-Title Catalogue) begun shortly after ESTC. Given the attention devoted to the description of incunabula by libraries which own them it was sensible not to follow the *Gesamtkatalog* in describing books printed before 1501 but rather to adopt the principle of normalized entries. The normalization follows, essentially, the forms of names (personal and geographic) and titles adopted by Frederick Goff in his *Census* (Goff 1973). By adding to the record for each item abbreviated references to the works describing copies of it, the labour of duplicating information available elsewhere is obviated. If ISTC has a weakness it is that of generally omitting notes on the peculiarities or provenance of copies, thereby making it necessary to consult the appropriate reference if one is in search of, say, copies with manuscript annotations or interesting provenances.

Unedited databases

The 1980s witnessed the development of numerous cooperative schemes to rival the huge success of OCLC which started in the 1970s, under the leadership of Fred Kilgour, as a union catalogue resource for the State of Ohio, and then based in Columbus. The Research Libraries Group (RLG), which had its origin in a collaboration between Harvard, Yale, Columbia, and the New York Public Library, expanded in the 1980s to include about thirty major university research libraries. The network which links member institutions is RLIN, and is based in California. One of the recent additions to membership is the British Library. Although RLIN makes available a number of specialized databases (including ESTC), the principal database used by members of RLG is the collaborative monograph file which contains some 20,000,000+ records and is seen by the academic community as a rival to OCLC, with 32,000,000+ records. In the publicity war which is relentlessly waged by both parties statistics should not be taken at face value. Both databases suffer, as one might expect, from similar defects. Conspicuous amongst these is the high incidence of duplicate records. OCLC has, it should be noted, made some effort since 1993 to reduce these. It has also done something to reduce the number of variant headings for well known authors. There used to be no fewer than twenty-three for T.S. Eliot! There are now (as of writing) just thirteen.

The Research Libraries Group in North America provided Britain with a model, and the 1980s saw the creation of a comparable consortium in Britain: the Consortium of University Research Libraries (CURL). Starting as a group of seven it now numbers twelve libraries and plans to expand in the future to include most of the British university libraries. The CURL database will be located at the University of Manchester, and should, when completed, provide researchers with a remarkable resource.

More recently, a group of European research libraries (twelve of them British) are proposing to form a consortium (CERL) which holds the promise of making available electronically the important historical collections held in Europe's major national and university libraries. Often overlooked by those in search of English books printed before 1900, the research libraries in Europe have significant collections which deserve to be better known, so CERL will, if it succeeds, be of benefit to those concerned with the English as well as the European printed heritage.

In America, where the consortium principle has been extensively developed in recent years, there are now computer systems which enable researchers to interrogate collections as widely separated as the libraries within the University of California system. These networks are generally developed to serve a state (such as those for Colorado or Arizona), or a city (such as Boston or Washington, DC). These are described more fully below.

Conversion programmes

The last decade has seen a concerted effort by libraries in North America to convert their catalogues to machine-readable form. The process is an evolving one, of course, and there are still a large number of important research collections which await conversion, but there is every likelihood that by the beginning of the next century most will have been converted and the familiar card catalogue will be no more than a memory for those whose active research life extends back to the 1970s. Converted catalogues, while they undoubtedly save the space formerly allocated to 5 x 3 cards, are not always the blessing they are made out to be by library administrators. Much depends on the manner in which the conversion was done and the specification drawn up to guide the bureau undertaking the task. Converting a card catalogue into an accurately coded Machine Readable Cataloguing (MARC) structure is no trivial task, and it can be done in a variety of ways.

For a catalogue consisting for the most part in records for modern books (a college, branch campus of a state university, or town public library) the technique most often used is to match Library of Congress Card Numbers (LCCNs) or International Standard Book Numbers (ISBNs) against a large file such as the Library of Congress MARC database. These numbers can be entered on a personal computer (IBM or Apple) and sent to the bureau which will return MARC records for an agreed fee. It is then up to the library to add local data such as shelfmarks, copy notes, borrowing restrictions, etc. For books which have neither LCCN nor ISBN the library generally creates a MARC record *de novo*. There are now several programs which simplify the production of a

MARC record, notably MITINET, developed by Hank Epstein in Madison, Wisconsin. Many hundreds of college, school, and public libraries have been successfully converted in this way. OCLC has been undertaking the conversion of large library catalogues for some time now, and these include collections as large as Harvard and the Bodleian. The conversion of the Bodleian Library's post-1920 holdings by OCLC was announced in July 1994, and it is estimated that the project will take four years. At Harvard, the conversion of the Yenching Library (60,000+ Chinese and Korean titles) by OCLC will prove of immense value for students of East Asian cultures. Similar conversion projects for oriental collections are planned for research collections at the University of California, Los Angeles, the University of Washington, Seattle, and the San Francisco Public Library.

Large card catalogues, on the other hand, are sometimes entirely re-keyed or the cards are converted using an optical character recognition (OCR) system combined with automatic format recognition (AFR) which applies appropriate MARC tags based on the relative position of the data elements (author, title, imprint, pagination, shelfmark, etc.) on the card. The more consistent the layout of the cards the better the result. This was the procedure adopted for the conversion of the Library of Congress shelf-list in the 1980s. The British Library's *General Catalogue* was eventually re-keyed, after disappointing results with OCR in the 1970s using the Newcastle III computer used for converting Department of Health records. On the whole it has been the experience of libraries that OCR techniques produce inferior, if cheaper, results and need careful proofreading. Where cards in use by readers or staff have become dirty the likelihood of achieving acceptable results is reduced. However a catalogue is converted it is accepted that proofreading is essential, especially for data elements vital for retrieval: authors' names, dates, subject headings, and shelfmarks.

Derived records

Large cooperative systems, such as OCLC, provide participating libraries with the opportunity to derive records from those already on the database for an agreed fee. It frequently happens that a library bases its record on one which is manifestly incorrect; or, where bibliographical niceties regarding issue or edition are involved, attaching a new location to the wrong record. If this can happen in a relatively controlled database like ESTC it is hardly surprising that it happens with such frequency in one which does not benefit from strict editorial control. When using very large collaborative databases such as OCLC or RLIN it is essential that users whose needs depend on accurate bibliographical information are aware of the limitations inherent in them because of the manner in which they are created. The problems are, in general, similar to those which researchers have found in the *National Union Catalogue of pre-1956 Imprints*.

Online catalogues

Library catalogues available on the Internet now number over two thousand worldwide and new catalogues become available every week. Keeping track of these is virtually impossible, though Peter Scott's listserv (HYTEL-L) is a valiant and invaluable guide. Subscribers to this online list are informed via electronic mail of additions to his remarkable navigational aid, Hytelnet.

While many library catalogues have interfaces developed locally most libraries use one of the numerous commercially developed OPACs (Online Public Access Catalogues). These interfaces have been developed to simplify the process of searching a machine-readable MARC catalogue: instead of having to learn a search language users find what they want by using simple on-screen menus. Since researchers in the humanities generally find the larger systems most useful, a very simplified guide to what researchers will find if they intend to search them is provided at the end of this chapter.

CD-ROM databases

Although there are hundreds of CD-ROM products available (the TFPL annual list is an invaluable guide—see bibliography) there are still only a small number which are of self-evident usefulness for historical research in the humanities. The Saztec CD-ROM of the holdings of the British Library up to 1975 is one such. Others would certainly be the latest ESTC disc (1992) published by the British Library, and the Bodleian Library pre-1920 Catalogue (1994) published by Oxford University Press.[3] Of all the attempts to produce a machine-readable catalogue of the holdings of a great research library, the Bodleian CD-ROM deserves particular acclaim: it is about as good as anything one could hope for. It took many more years to produce than its architect, John Jolliffe, ever imagined, but the wait has been worth it and it represents a genuine example of what computers can do to assist research: it takes into account the needs of the user in ways that many a converted catalogue fails to do. A smaller corpus is available from Chadwyck-Healey Ltd. in Cambridge for the Nineteenth Century Microfiche Project which currently has some 16,000 very detailed records held on the British Library's Register of Preservation Microforms (RPM) file. The Chadwyck-Healey disc contains records for British Library holdings as well as records for books on art from the Victoria & Albert Museum, but the records provide a window on nineteenth-century publishing not found in most bibliographical databases, and there are few compromises as far as detail is concerned.

Surfing the Internet

The number and range of research library catalogues now available on the Internet present one overriding problem: while there are guides like Hytelnet which facilitate connection,[4] there is still no useful guide to what you will find if you choose to visit a particular library's catalogue. Libraries seem unwilling to indicate on their welcome screens exactly what proportion of their collections has been catalogued or even from which year of publication. Much of the available network resource is wasted by fruitless searches for material that has not yet been catalogued, and there appears to be no impetus to establish a mechanism for research libraries to inform the scholarly community of progress in converting research collections. Many of the libraries which use OCLC receive grants for converting special collections which researchers need to know about and there should be some easily accessible listserv (or online discussion group) developed for just this purpose. An even better solution would be to update Hytelnet files with this information so that before considering a connection a remote user can ascertain whether or not it will prove positively helpful. Such a scheme would certainly require resources to maintain, but the benefits for all who depend on the Internet would be incalculable. In the age of print we all came to depend on guides to the research collections held in the world's libraries: the need is now all the greater with so much electronic information readily available.

OPACs

The simplicity which most OPAC interfaces lend to the searching process is historically due to the fact that they have been designed with relatively simple objectives. In most university library systems they are designed to serve undergraduate needs. They are seldom useful as browsing tools. For the most part bibliographical records can be searched by author, title, and subject, and classification (Dewey or Universal). Some, like the one still being developed at the British Library, provide readers with access to date of publication (a recent improvement) and shelfmark. There is none I know of which can provide a researcher with the flexibility to search across fields, though CD-ROM search software typically makes this possible. Yet the whole point of having an electronic catalogue is to enable readers to ask questions which conventional manual systems render impossible. The huge investment in automation which libraries have made in the past ten years can only be justified if the tools available enable us to conduct enquiries never before possible, quickly and efficiently. Trying to second-guess the uses to which an intelligently constructed database served by imaginative software can be put is a pointless exercise, since no one can predict the sorts of questions in which researchers are interested. Suppose that I am curious to discover how many sermons published in cities other than London, Edinburgh, or Glasgow between 1750 and 1800 were printed in octavo format rather than quarto: there is only system I know of which will enable me to discover the answer—the ESTC file on BLAISE-LINE. In order to test the thesis that universities in the United States are purchasing fewer books in the major European languages I set about trying to establish statistics using the OPACs available on the Internet for holdings of books in German, French, Italian, and Spanish for every year since 1980. It cannot be done, since very few systems provide searching on language and date of publication. A good online system should be able to satisfy such an enquiry as a matter of routine; yet even RLIN failed to help since date of publication is not indexed.

Researchers have, in the past few years, begun to appreciate the very real advantages which automation can bring and it is ironic that some of the more imaginative approaches to novel ways of manipulating information are coming from academic departments rather than from libraries. This is an altogether healthy development, of course, but it serves to underscore the extent to which libraries and their users are drifting apart. In spite of all the protestations we have heard in the past decade about the manifold benefits which discarding the old card catalogues would bring, they have been replaced with tools unworthy of the effort and expense it has taken to bring about the transformation.

What remains?

In spite of the countless millions of bibliographic records maintained on the computer systems of the world's research libraries we have still succeeded in bringing under control only a small proportion of the world's manuscript and printed heritage. If your research is concerned principally with events since the death of Queen Victoria then the networks and the electronic databases can serve you quite well. If your interests lie in the history of Europe in the sixteenth century they will not be so well served. Even for those concerned with twentieth-century literature the vast manuscript collections at the Humanities Research Center in Austin are still inaccessible electronically. While university libraries have found the resources to convert their catalogues (in part), what of research libraries such as the Folger Shakespeare Library in Washington; or the Huntington in San Marino; or the Pierpont Morgan in New York? The nature of such libraries, and the way in which they are funded, means that we may have to wait some time before their catalogues are available on the Internet. And what of the vast collections of books printed before 1900 in the major university libraries in Europe and the Americas? What of the world's great collections of materials in non-roman scripts? Given their sheer bulk as well as the intrinsic difficulties presented by non-roman scripts I see little prospect of their being widely available in the near future.

The average IBM-compatible personal computer today has a line editor supplied as part of MSDOS (Microsoft Disc Operating System) which was formerly served by Edlin: a primitive piece of software which took twelve years to replace. For nearly as long we had to put up with a character set constrained by 128 codes: now we have 256, which just about copes with most European languages. There are, it is true, word processors which can handle just about any language; but when will we have the ability to compose a letter or a contribution to a debate in any language using a standard chip-set and send it anywhere by e-mail?

Libraries in the future

There can be only a few concerned with research libraries and their evolution who do not consider what they might be like in the next century. That they will contain a great deal of electronic gadgetry no one seriously doubts. But will they have changed out of all recognition from the institutions we now use? Given the enormous investment in automation during the past twenty years, to which much of what this chapter is about is witness, are we on the threshold of a new age in which acquiring knowledge will be easier than ever before, or have we merely substituted one form of access to that knowledge for another? Are we, indeed, about to substitute for the book (in all its varied manifestations) information exclusively in electronic form? Has civilization so burdened our librarians with the responsibilities of acquiring, accommodating, preserving, and making available print on paper that we must, of necessity, alter our habits? And even if we are persuaded that the future of information really is only possible electronically, what are we proposing to do with all that has been accumulated from the past? Even if we succeed in converting it all into digital form, are we going to throw away the originals when so much research still needs to be done that can only be done with originals? One of the lessons we are learning from enterprises like ESTC, global in its excavations of the printed record of the English-speaking eighteenth century, is how much we do not know. Sound enumerative bibliography always paves the way for new interpretations of the past and this is now becoming possible because of what ESTC has unearthed in the world's libraries. Like its antecedent, Pollard and Redgrave's *STC* and the many correlative works it spawned which nourished much historical research for half a century, it will surely take a long time for scholarship to take advantage of the riches uncovered by ESTC. And I have no doubt that many of its records will require adjustment as scholars probe more deeply into the history of particular texts. But they will only be able to do so if the books themselves are permitted to survive. Much useful investigation can be done with photographic/digital surrogates; but some questions can only be answered when the original is available.

It is a matter of fact that libraries are fashioned as much by those who use them as by those who govern them. The best developments in library management occur when there is a consensus between the two, but that happens rarely today because we no longer entrust our manuscript and printed heritage to those who understand how scholarship functions. In time, that may change; but it is certainly true that the 'managers' we have exchanged for 'librarians' are unable to tell us with any certainty what libraries are going to be like in ten years. They simply do not know.

One hears, occasionally, wild speculation about how the future will transform our entire world heritage on paper into more convenient, instantly available, digital form. Given that we have not as yet succeeded in cataloguing and describing that heritage in its inconvenient form, how long will it take for the transformation and the necessary means of locating it digitally? The medium in which a piece of information is stored is irrelevant: it must still be described and located before it can be used.

The statistics published by those organizations concerned with inter-library loans and document supply suggest that, at the moment, the demand for hard-copy information far outstrips that for electronic. Electronic mail is, of course, a fact of life, and, in spite of the primitive facilities provided on most mainframe computers for producing accurate, well considered prose, widely used in preference to conventional 'snail-mail'. Then there are the facilities for distributing electronic conversations (listservs using robot computers) to societies of persons interested in some aspect of knowledge. How much of this traffic is worth preserving I cannot say, but very likely only a tiny portion. The problem is, which portion? Should we contrive to keep it all, or jettison the lot? And if we decide to keep the huge quantity of electronic information that daily stretches the networks to their limits where shall we keep it? Who will index it? There are occasions when someone contributes a carefully argued and documented piece of prose to a listserv debate. Instinctively, I print it out, perhaps for the benefit of my students. But what if I wish to cite it at some later date? Where is it by then?

Survival

Those engaged in exercising their curiosity to know more about some aspect of the past or present have, historically, shown both tenacity and ingenuity in overcoming the obstacles presented by the dispersion of primary sources in the world's libraries and archives. There are some areas of research where it is perfectly possible to obtain access to everything one needs in one place, but for most kinds of historical investigation the sources are dispersed and must be identified before they can be evaluated. Identifying sources is what bibliographers and archivists have been doing for centuries. Their task is never complete, however, because books and documents are essentially fragile and vulnerable: they may simply deteriorate, or they may be destroyed, both by accident and by design. In the case of books (manuscript or printed) survival has, in large measure, been due to the existence of libraries, private and public. But bringing books together to form what we term a 'collection' is no guarantee of survival, for a single act of deliberate or accidental destruction can result in huge losses. For the entire output of printing in Europe between 1450 and the year 1700 fewer than five copies (on average) survive for every known edition. In many thousands of cases just one copy survives. It is probably true to say that every library in the world contains some unique items, and uniqueness extends beyond the artefact: marginalia and indications of provenance can be materially significant, which is why bibliographers go to such extraordinary lengths not simply to identify a work but to identify copies of it. They also understand the fact that very few books fail to benefit from what is observed by a different pair of eyes.

Computers have contributed nothing to the task of identifying the world's printed and manuscript heritage: that can only be achieved by people. What they have contributed to the process is the means of storing bibliographical information in a medium which permits infinite addition and correction. There is a price to pay, of course, for this benefit which a computer database has over a printed bibliography. The price is order.

Every bibliography or catalogue is constructed according to some pre-conceived order, which may be alphabetical, by subject (or topic), chronological, or (as is common for books printed before 1501) by country, subdivided by place of printing and printer. Other arrangements are possible but rarely found. A computer database, on the other hand, is constructed on no order other than time of entry. It follows, therefore, that unless each entry carries with it the information needed to enable the computer to output entries according to some coherent and meaningful sequence additional to that imposed by the author's name, the wording of the title, the place and date of printing, the format, and any of the other characteristics which bibliographers use to determine a sequence of editions, computer output will follow an invariable principle: last in, first out. Computers *can* sort entries in a database (OCLC permits a chronological or other sort, providing the number of selected records does not exceed 500), but there must be instructions (codes) which it can be programmed to follow. This is why bibliographical databases have automatically generated indexes: authors' names, titles, place of publication, printer or publisher (seldom both), date of publication, subject, etc. So it is possible to search the millions of records on OCLC and retrieve all books by, or about, T.S. Eliot—but *only* if every such book carries the identical form of his name; which is, in fact, not the case. Similarly, I can retrieve all the books printed in 1501—but *only* those where the cataloguer either entered the date correctly or guessed that 1501 was the correct date (i.e. the imprint has '1401' or no date at all). What cannot be done (and this applies to most large databases) is to request all the books by T.S. Eliot in chronological order. While it is possible to add filing fields in a database (such as ESTC) these have no significance online and have effect only when the file is output to hard-copy or microfiche. When dealing with computer databases it is an unpleasant fact that the responsibility for arranging a meaningful sequence falls to the user. The British Museum *General Catalogue* is ordered according to principles which were, broadly speaking, laid down in the nineteenth century. It is a simple matter to turn to the relevant pages and follow the printing history of *Dombey and Son*. This is impossible on the computer version of the catalogue. There are sound reasons why card and printed catalogues are governed by filing rules, and the sequences they adopt are generally those understood to be meaningful and helpful to those consulting them. There are, sadly, few such helpful principles at work when searching computerized catalogues. There are, however, stratagems which can assist the user facing an inchoate body of records displayed in no order other than reverse order of input. But these stratagems will make demands on users of libraries that they may well find disagreeable.

It has never been accepted that in order to carry out research in a library one must become a librarian and learn the intricate rules governing cataloguing, classification, or subject indexing. Most researchers assume, sometimes wrongly as it turns out, that the principles underlying a library catalogue must be so straightforward that a little experience will make all clear. They will have learned something about the arrangement of a card catalogue as undergraduates, and postgraduate studies, especially if conducted with some elementary training in research methodology, will certainly have contributed much to their understanding. In Europe, experience in dealing with the peculiarities of library catalogues is commoner than in North America where the 5 x 3 card catalogue has been the norm since the second half of the nineteenth century, and with Library of Congress cataloguing practice being standard since the development of the printed card service established in 1901.

I remember well the puzzlement expressed by fellow readers in the British Museum in the 1950s and 1960s at the peculiar rules governing the placement of anonymous titles and of publications which the rules dictated should be placed under large arrangements like ENGLAND, LONDON, FRANCE, etc. To this day readers experience difficulties with periodicals which are entered under place of publication rather than title. The same confusion existed for the publication of learned societies until the old heading ACADEMIES was abandoned—though the shelfmark Ac[ademies] testifies to its former existence. The rules for anonymous books has given rise since the publication of Donald Wing's *Short Title Catalogue* (1641–1700) to numerous problems for researchers: Wing entered, as most American libraries do, anonymous works under the first significant word other than the definite article (whatever the language), but since his titles are brief it frequently requires ingenuity to discover the item in the *General Catalogue*. That problem is one which automation has, mercifully, relieved since works can be discovered by searching on the title field.

But automation brings its own problems for users of catalogues, especially those which, like the British Library's *General Catalogue*, provide sequences which the computer is unable to follow. Further problems arise from the fact that when the *General Catalogue* was converted it was decided that sequences of editions under a heading distinguished from each other only by the statement in square brackets [Another edition] or [Another copy] or a note indicating that this particular item is a variant of the one adjacent to it should be keyed as one record with repeat values attached to the different entries. This mistake, which confounds so many apparently reasonable searches, was not made when the Bodleian catalogue of pre-1920 imprints was edited prior to release on CD-ROM. In this manifestation of the old guard book catalogues (which owed much to British Museum practice) the principle of the unit record—the only kind a computer database can successfully deal with—was adopted: at considerable expense, I have no doubt, but of significant benefit to users. The OPAC developed for use in the British Library's reading rooms has, quite recently, smoothed out some of the difficulties, but the online file, which permits quite sophisticated searches to be performed, still produces an unintelligible sequence for works frequently reprinted.

Given the nature of data which a computer is expected to process it follows that unless researchers take the trouble to acquaint themselves with the rules governing data entry their searches are likely to be frustrated. The detailed level for which this applies concerns almost every field in a MARC record—the standard universally accepted. MARC is a language, like Esperanto, developed to be a universal benefit for international communication. Unfortunately, it has already subdivided itself (as far as the rules for applying it are concerned) into numerous, rigorously defended dialects. Like systems of divinity, *rules* are subject to interpretation, and so it is not surprising that they are interpreted differently in different libraries by cataloguers with different perceptions and understanding. This can be demonstrated in any database containing records created by different libraries. Only when the basis for the rules is understood can a researcher perceive ways of working around inconsistencies and errors. A failure to understand this explains why so many researchers complain that automated library catalogues seldom reveal books the existence of which they do not already know. To find a book in a library the existence of which you know should now be trivially simple. To discover a book, the existence of which you never suspected, is what a good catalogue should make possible, and many scholars have testified to the fact that the British Museum *General Catalogue*, whatever its idiosyncrasies, makes this more likely than a merely alphabetical arrangement. It is also the reason why generations of scholars have found dictionary catalogues, such as that for the New York Public Library (now available in 800 printed volumes), so valuable and revealing. The subject catalogues found in German university and French public libraries are, likewise, a revelation to scan. The greatest subject catalogue I know is that started at the University of Göttingen in the eighteenth century and now housed in hundreds of volumes in the church which forms part of the Old Library. It is generally agreed that subject cataloguing represents the most expensive part of a modern machine-readable bibliographical record, whether in the form of verbal phrases (such as Library of Congress headings) or numbers (such as the Dewey or Universal Decimal Systems). The advantage of numbers over words in a computerized environment is obvious: numbers can be truncated in order to generate larger subsets whereas phrases cannot.

What should now be clear is that research using computer databases to lead our curiosity fruitfully in the direction of books which might otherwise escape our attention provides opportunities while at the same time presenting difficulties which traditional catalogues did not. Because the transformation of research libraries in recent years has been effected by the introduction of computers it seems clear that users of libraries must, if the promise of greater flexibility of access is to be realized, come to terms with the nature of that transformation and understand both the gains and the losses. They must also understand the processes involved in transforming a conventional catalogue from paper to electronic format. These processes are no longer the exclusive concern of librarians, as any scholar who has tried to compile a bibliography using one of the many available database systems developed for microcomputers will testify. The construction of a MARC record demands absolute accuracy and consistency in following established rules for coding and tagging:

data incorrectly entered are as good as lost. Users of libraries often show a touching faith in the integrity of the electronic catalogues at their disposal and conclude that if they cannot find a particular book it is simply not there. In a drawer of cards filed under the name of ELIOT, Thomas Stearns, mistakes in the spelling of his name may be non-significant: in an electronic file any variation in spelling will result in that record being indexed so that it does not appear in the correct place. The superiority of electronic catalogues over manual ones is obvious: but only if the catalogue data are correctly and consistently entered. The complexity of an electronic record is such that errors are both frequent and difficult to identify. For reasons which should now be obvious we have made gains, but there have been significant losses.

It is, for example, quite possible to scan a drawer of 1,000 5 x 3 cards in less than an hour; it is possible to read the entire ENGLAND heading in the printed *General Catalogue* of the British Library in three days: scanning the 143,000+ records on the OPAC would take weeks. It is a fact with which most scholars I know would concur, that scanning a printed catalogue does, with a little practice, yield results in far less time than retrieving records on a screen, especially if the former is following a meaningful arrangement and the latter not. This situation need not, however, have been so, but for a number of circumstances in the history of the British Museum catalogue since the end of the Second World War.

When the revision of the *General Catalogue*, undertaken in 1929, was abandoned in 1954 after publication of volume 50 which covers the alphabet from DEO to DEZ, the decision to embark on a printed version which would combine the revision (known as GK2) with the information in the laid-down duplicate set of the volumes in the Reading Room was begun in association with the firm of Balding and Mansell (Mansell was later to produce and market the Library of Congress *National Union Catalog* mentioned above). The result, known as GK3, became the familiar folio blue-bound volumes to be found in most of the research libraries of the world, but it suffered from a number of errors and omissions.[5] After the completion of GK3 in 1966 it became necessary for the British Museum to issue a series of printed *Supplements* (1956-65 = 50 volumes; 1966-70 = 26 volumes; 1971-5 = 13 volumes). In 1979 the firm of G.K. Saur undertook to publish an amalgamation of GK3 and its three supplements. This version of the catalogue became known, inevitably, as GK4, and was completed in 360 volumes in 1987: this was the exemplar used for the Saztec conversion. When the catalogue was keyed by Saztec it was part of the specification that each record should have a control number which would identify its place by volume, columns, and line number. If GK4 in 360 volumes had not, because of the haste with which it was produced, omitted many thousands of entries, and if Saztec had keyed the catalogue without omissions, then the control numbers would, at a stroke, have enabled meaningful output, since the entire database could have been inverted on this control number. But there had to be a series of six supplementary GK4 volumes (numbered 361–6) to make good some of the omissions; and these do not carry control numbers which would ensure their being filed in the proper place: records for the six supplementary volumes have control numbers starting with the three digits: 361xxxxxxxx through 366xxxxxxxx. Consequently, while most of the records for Andreas Aubert begin with 013, one of them (*Det nye Norges malerkunst*, 1904) begins with 361.

I suspect that most conversions of library catalogues have been frustrated by unforeseen problems, the errors to which all endeavours are subject, and sometimes by unseemly haste to follow the Moderns in favour of the Ancients. That was certainly the burden of Nicholson Baker's article in *The New Yorker*.[6]

Digital libraries

In the last two years libraries have begun to experiment with image databases based on digital scanning. It is argued that digital libraries represent the way ahead since a digitized image can be economically stored, electronically refreshed when required, and transmitted anywhere over the world's evolving telecommunication networks. The technology lends itself, theoretically at least, to many of the services currently offered by libraries: notably document supply and interlibrary loan. There are, as might be expected, a number of problems presented by remote access to the kinds of material most frequently used by researchers in the humanities. These problems are technical and legal.

One of the most difficult problems which the proponents of digital libraries must address concerns intellectual property. Copyright law is constantly undergoing revision, but the rapidity of technological developments far outruns the machinery of legislation and it is not easy to predict how the agencies which form part of the legal protection of intellectual property will adjust to electronic publishing. Historically, libraries have played a crucial role in controlling the distributive processes to which both manuscript and print can be put: micro-reproduction and photocopying. The laws governing these ubiquitous processes, found in libraries worldwide, is quite straightforward, and publishers have come to accept the principle that distributing a library's resources carries a fee element comparable to the royalties paid to an author. Agreements between libraries and publishers generally have clauses which restrict third-party exploitation of both microforms and photocopies derived from them. Such agreements are not difficult to monitor since microforms are principally acquired by libraries which are able to enforce adherence to them. But electronic data are less easy to monitor, so it is hardly surprising that publishers and libraries are understandably nervous at the prospect of their materials entering an environment which is effectively uncontrolled.

A huge quantity of electronic information is currently available to anyone with legitimate access to the Internet: some of it is subject to control, some not. A university may, for example, negotiate with *Encyclopedia Britannica* to make the electronic version available to faculty and students, but not to remote users, access being controlled by the user's logon identification. Remote access to files held on computers via anonymous ftp requires the user to enter a valid Internet e-mail address, a mechanism designed to control misuse of valuable information. A number of agreements are currently being negotiated between university libraries and publishers which grant site-licences for unlimited distribution of published texts on local university networks. How widespread this innovative approach will become remains to be seen. Certainly the notion of partnership between the parties which produce and acquire scholarly materials is preferable to the situation we have seen in recent years where diminishing funds for acquiring books has led librarians to regard publishers as the enemy. The spiralling costs of conventional publishing and the means of distribution have had serious consequences for all whose research demands access to scholarly monographs and journals and a solution must be found.

If the concept of the digital library has a future then it can only be achieved on the basis of cooperation and the creation of a universally available database of accurate bibliographical records for every digitized item: it would be an irresponsible waste of precious resources to create redundant electronic versions of the same item as we have, over the past fifty years, created redundant microform versions of identical items. Preservation microfilming has been a conspicuous activity in research libraries during the last decade, but there are few mechanisms in place to minimize redundancy. Given the shrinking budgets which most libraries face it is difficult to see how resources will be found to both digitize and catalogue accurately our printed and manuscript heritage. And we might consider the quite sensible proposition articulated in the 1970s that the advent of the electronic record of a book would reduce significantly the insupportable burden of redundant cataloguing: a promise which still awaits fulfilment!

As we approach the twenty-first century it is hardly surprising that librarians throughout the world are looking with interest (and perhaps not a little anxiety) at the two colossal libraries undergoing construction in London and Paris: they are, after all, the two most important research libraries in Europe, and it is fitting that two such institutions enjoying the benefits of vast resourcing should show the rest the way. Whether either will remains to be seen.

Notes

1. Of the many (over 500) books currently available on the Internet, researchers in the humanities will probably find the following collection of essays informative: *Libraries and the Internet/NREN* (London and Westport: Mecklermedia, 1994), edited by Charles R. McClure, William E. Moen, and Joe Ryan. 'The impacts of the evolving Internet/National Research and Education Network (NREN) on libraries are likely to be monumental in both scope and practice. As the Internet/NREN develops, as connectivity to the network becomes ubiquitous, and as individuals and organizations learn how to exploit the network, the very nature of the networked electronic information resources will uproot and redefine many of the previously held assumptions that librarians and information specialists have traditionally taken as gospel.' (Preface.)

2. For an account of the genesis of ESTC see Alston, R. C., and Janetta, M. J., *Bibliography machine readable cataloguing and the ESTC* (London: The British Library, 1978). Published on microfiche in 1983 and on CD-ROM in 1992. Available as an online catalogue on BLAISE-LINE (the British Library Automated Information Service) and RLIN (the Research Libraries Information Network) based in California. Since 1994 the file includes records for books listed in both *STC* and Wing and accordingly the acronym now stands for English Short-Title Catalogue.

3. For an appraisal of the Bodleian Pre-1920 CD-ROM see: Alston, R. C., *The Library*, xvi, no. 4, December, 1994, pp. 327–332. In a class of its own, this compact disc is as impressive an achievement in 1994 as Hyde's catalogue was in 1674.

4. Updated versions of Hytelnet (usually twice a year) are available at several sites, including the University of Oxford (rsl.ox.ac.uk) and the University of Arizona (sabio.arizona.edu). Hytelnet can be used offline as a memory resident hypertext program and invoked at will, or it can be used as an online navigational aid. Hytelnet for Unix was written by Earl Fogel and is available via ftp from the University of

Saskatchewan (ftp.usask.ca). An offline Macintosh version is available from Charles Burchill at the University of Manitoba (burchil@ccu.umanitoba.ca).

5. For an account of the history of the British Museum *General Catalogue* see: A.H. Chaplin, *GK: 150 years of the General Catalogue of Printed Books in the British Museum* (Aldershot: Scolar Press, 1987). Chaplin documents clearly the important role that those involved in the history of this great enterprise recognized of a library catalogue and the ways in which it can support research.

6. In the April 4 (1994) issue of *The New Yorker* Nicholson Baker contributed a substantial article on the 'trashing' of American library card catalogues. This produced, as might be expected, considerable comment on the Internet. Since I joined the debate, I received numerous communications of interest. One such was from Cornell where, I was told, not only has the card catalogue disappeared but so have all the finding aids to the Special Collections: indexes to provenance, binding, place of publication, date of publication, etc. In my experience, most major research libraries have created, over the years, important finding aids to their collections: to discard these is simply irresponsible. My *Handlist of unpublished finding aids to the London Collections of the British Library* (British Library, 1991) has 1,517 entries.

References and bibliography

Goff, F.R., *Incunabula in American libraries. A third census of fifteenth century books recorded in North American collections* (New York, 1973).

Kommission für den Gesamtkatalog der Weigendrucke, *Gesamtkatalog der Weigendrucke* (Leipzig [& Stuttgart]: 1925–1991). 9 vols. [A-Grassus]

Paisey, D., *Catalogue of books printed in the German-speaking countries and of German books printed in other countries from 1601 to 1700*, 5 vols. (London: The British Library, 1994).

Pollard, A.W., and Redgrave, G.R., *A short-title catalogue of books printed in England, Scotland, and Ireland and of English books printed abroad 1475–1640*, Second edition, 3 vols. (London: The Bibliographical Society, 1986–1991).

TFPL, *The CD-ROM directory* (London: TFPL Publishing, 1986-). Published annually.

Wing, D., *Short-title catalogue of books printed in England, Scotland, Ireland, Wales, and British America and of English books printed in other countries 1641–1700* (New York, 1982–1994). Revision in progress.

Further information

A selection of online catalogue systems

OCLC

When OCLC developed its EPIC software for a cataloguing resource that had originally been designed for use by cataloguers in American libraries, it made available what is, without doubt, the largest bibliographical resource anywhere. Although students and researchers have access to EPIC in many North American universities it is, understandably, an expensive tool—especially in the hands of someone who does not understand how the database is constructed and is unfamiliar with the search grammar. EPIC searches are typically carried out by skilled staff for library users. Like other large systems it is not a menu-driven interface and requires the user to formulate at the prompt an argument. A typical argument might take the following form:

> f ti (vegetable and system) and yr 1780

This parses: f[ind] ti[tle word] vegetable *and* system *and* y[ea]r [of publication] 1780.

Indexes are directly accessible using the s[can] command:

> s su=africa

This will place the user in the *subject-phrase* index (which is distinct from the *subject-word* index) beginning with *africa* and through all the subheadings.

EPIC provides a variety of indexes which can be searched, though some are of use mostly to cataloguers. Those which researchers will find most useful are: *author, title keyword, place of publication, publisher, language, subject heading, classification,* and *type of publication* (e.g. books, manuscripts, serials, musical scores, audiovisual, etc.). Oddly, *country of publication* is not indexed though records do contain the appropriate code in field 008. Access to EPIC is available only to institutions having an account. The most recent statistics available for the OCLC database (November 1994) include the following:

> Records: 32,000,000+
> Number of locations (copies): 525,000,000+
> Libraries represented: 18,000 +
> Languages: 370
> Membership: 6,700+
> Online system connect hours: 8,000,000+
> Records added: 2,200,000+
> Books and other materials catalogued online: 23,200,000+
> Online interlibrary loan transactions: 7,000,000+

In addition to the main database OCLC provides convenient access to a large number of commercial databases (formerly only available through DIALOG), all of which are searchable using EPIC grammar. New databases are being added regularly. Unless users are skilled at constructing efficient arguments, charges for using these commercial databases can easily become high. Fortunately, OCLC provides inexpensive access to 'practice' subsets of all the EPIC databases. For researchers in the humanities the most important of these are: ABI/INFORM, ArticleFirst, Art Index, Arts and Humanities SEARCH, Biography Index, Book Data, Book Review Digest, ContentsFirst, Dissertation Abstracts, Education Index, ERIC, Humanities Index, Library Literature, MLA Bibliography, Periodical Abstracts, Readers' Guide Abstracts, Readers' Guide to Periodical Literature, and Social Sciences Index. Soon to be added include: Cumulative Book Index, Essay and General Literature Index, PapersFirst, and ProceedingsFirst. The OCLC Annual Report for 1993/94—*Furthering Access to the World's Information*—provides full statistics on all aspects of the organization and the databases available.

RLIN

RLIN is the bibliographical network of the universities belonging (as full or associate members) to the Research Libraries Group. As with EPIC, RLIN uses an individual search grammar, quite easy to master. The search verb is fin[d], but the scan verb is bro[wse]. There is little difference between the two databases as far as searching data elements is concerned. Access to RLIN is available to member institutions, and others with an account. In addition to the main database (BKS), RLIN maintains a number of special databases of which the Archives & Manuscript Control (AMC) and ESTC are the most useful for researchers in the humanities.

LOCIS

LOCIS is the Library of Congress Information System and uses a unique, and to many users difficult, search grammar. It provides access to the following databases:

Library of Congress Catalog
Federal Legislation
Copyright Information
Braille and Audio
Organizations
Foreign Law
Searching Hours and Basics
Documentation and Classes
Library of Congress General Information

BLAISE-LINE

BLAISE-LINE is the British Library's automated information service and provides access to numerous databases maintained within the library's system. It is only available to institutions with accounts. The search grammar is unique and not easily learned. Users of the Library's many reading rooms have access to a few of the databases via the Online Catalogue, an Online Public Access Catalogue (OPAC) designed in-house. During 1994 academic and research libraries were being offered the software necessary to access the OPAC remotely over the Internet free of charge. None of the British Library's catalogues is openly available on the Internet, though there are CD-ROM versions of both the *General Catalogue* (books published before 1975) and ESTC. The principal databases and their abbreviated file names maintained by the British Library are:

Audiovisual Materials (AV)
Library Association Library (BLISS)
Maps (MAPS)
Conference Proceedings (CONF)
Document Supply Monographs (DSCM)
Eighteenth Century STC (ESTC)
HMSO Publications (HMSO)
Current Humanities and Social Sciences Catalogue from 1975 (HSS)
Incunabula Short Title Catalogue (1450–1500) (ISTC)
Printed Music (MUSIC)
Register of Preservation Microforms (RPM)
Grey Literature (SIGLE)
Science Reference and Information Service (SRIS)
Whitaker—Books in Print (WHIT)
British National Bibliography (BNB)
Library of Congress (LC)
University of London (UOL)
ISSN UK Centre (ISSN)
Department of the Environment (DOE)
Higher Education Learning Programmes Information Service (HELPIS)

MELVYL

MELVYL is the system serving the libraries of the University of California and provides access to the catalogues of the various campuses from San Francisco in the north to San Diego in the south as well as the California State Library. The system allows searching of the book catalogue, the periodical catalogue, journal article database, as well as Internet access to other library catalogues worldwide. Other specialized databases available include: HUM— Humanities Databases; GOV— Government/Legal Databases; SOC— Social Sciences Databases. The opening menu provides an option to look at the complete alphabetical list of available databases (ALPHA), or a typological list (DBTYPE). As of January 1995, the MELVYL Catalog contained 8,000,000+ titles representing 12,000,000+ holdings. The search verb f(ind) can be used with the following indexes: PA (personal author), CA (corporate author), TW (title words), UT (uniform title), SE (series), DA (date), LA (language), XT (exact title), SU (subject), and XS (exact subject). Help is always available. The verb EXPLAIN is used (as on many systems) to get help on commands, displays, and indexes. The Telnet address is: melvyl.ucop.edu.

CARL

The Colorado Alliance of Research Libraries (CARL) is a state-wide service that includes university, college, school, and public libraries. In addition to making the libraries within the state available CARL also provides access to large databases of articles in periodicals (UnCover and ERIC). Searching these is free but there is a charge if the article is delivered by fax, the amount depending on what fee has to be paid to the publisher. CARL permits searching by Name (N), and Word (W). The indexes are accessed by Browse (B) followed by the appropriate index. In order to leave the system it is sometimes necessary to enter //EXIT more than once. Of the many libraries in the CARL system the most important are: Colorado State University, Denver University, Northeastern University, the University of Colorado, Boulder, and the University of Wyoming.

Some of the facilities and databases available to users within the system are not available to remote users. CARL was responsible for building the Boston Library Consortium and provides connection to participating libraries. The Telnet address is: pac.carl.org.

BLC

The Boston Library Consortium is a cooperative association of academic and research libraries in the greater Boston area, including the following:

Boston College
Boston Public Library
Boston University
Brandeis University
Northeastern University
Massachusetts Institute of Technology
State Library of Massachusetts
Tufts University
University of Massachusetts—Amherst
University of Massachusetts—Boston
Wellesley College

The Telnet address is: blc.lrc.northeastern.edu.

C/W MARS

Another CARL system has been developed for central and western Massachusetts and provides access to a number of important research collections. Of the eighty participating libraries the following are probably the most important: Amherst College, Clark University, Northampton, Forbes Library, University of Massachusetts Medical Center, and Worcester Public Library. The Telnet address is: cwmars.mass.edu.

Other consortia which provide access to research library collections include:

Florida State University System (luis.nerdc.ufl.edu)
Illinet—Libraries in Illinois (illinet.aiss.uiuc.edu)
Olli—University System of Georgia (library.gsu.edu)
Tri-College Consortium (Haverford, Bryn Mawr, Swarthmore) (tripod.
   brynmawr.edu)
University of Maryland System (victor.umd.edu)
Washington (DC) Research Library Consortium (gmuibm.gmu.edu).

Electronic Publishing

Marilyn Deegan

Introduction: from print to CD-ROM

The publishing industry is one of the traditional bedrocks of scholarship in the humanities, producing in printed form many of the primary artefacts which are the subject of humanistic scholarship, as well as the secondary studies which are its products. Thus scholars rely on publishers to bring out novels, poems, plays, facsimiles, museum and gallery catalogues, and all the many works which we study, and to keep such materials in print for as long as possible. Publishers also make available the monographs, books of essays, editions, and journals which we write each year and which validate the world of scholarship and are so necessary for our career progress. If we want jobs, promotions, and peer approval, publication is how we obtain them, and partnership with publishers is a necessary corollary to this. I refer here to the tradition of paper publication, an established publishing industry, and the roots of scholarship. However, great changes are being wrought in publishing with the advent of electronic media; every corner of the publishing industry is being affected by this, not least academic publishing.

Publishers have long used computers in many of the stages leading up to publication in book form. Computer-typesetting, for instance, has replaced movable type or hot metal typesetting, and there are services available for typesetting in academic environments outside the publishing houses—the National Academic Typesetting Service at Oxford University, for instance. In the production of ephemeral, in-house publications—newsletters, course notes, conference announcements—desktop publishing (DTP) has replaced typesetting, and most modern word processing packages provide a host of DTP features which allow those wishing to do so to produce their own publications without even investing in extra software. The rise of DTP packages and typesetting services has encouraged the rather worrying practice of publishers asking academics to produce camera-ready copy of their own books. Books are designed and produced by those who have training in the necessary skills; it is not realistic to imagine that because academics can write books, they can also produce them.

But the production of books using electronic methods is not electronic publishing (with one notable exception, discussed below), and while this has undoubtedly caused changes in the practices and economics of publishing and printing houses, these are not sufficiently significant to constitute a revolution. There is a revolution occurring, however, but it is in the actual product, not the means by which the product is arrived at. In the last two or three years, there has been a huge increase in the number of publishers producing materials in electronic form; most of these are conventional academic and trade publishers, although there have also been some firms specifically established purely to create or to publish electronic media. A recent report on electronic publishing presented to the Sir Stanley Unwin Trust states:

> The market for electronic books may be in its infancy, but it is growing fast, and while in some sectors it may complement the book trade, it is encroaching and may threaten to supersede it in other areas, where the advantages of compressed storage, sophisticated retrieval and cross-reference, or multimedia display are particularly relevant (Dixon 1994, 1).

The report also quotes Peter Kindersley of the publishers Dorling-Kindersley as saying that the book has a future, but he is not sure that this will be in paper form (Dixon 1994,1).

One instance of a major change in book publishing in a more or less conventional form through electronic media is, however, relevant and deserves mention here. That is the publishing of on-demand, customized textbooks and course materials from electronic text databases. A good example of this is the McGraw-Hill Primis electronic database publishing system. This allows teachers to select course materials from a large database of articles and book chapters, and integrate them in whatever order and mix are best suited to the course. Teaching materials and course notes can also be added to the published materials, and the whole output as a printed textbook which is specific to that course alone. They are then produced in just the numbers which are needed, exactly when they are needed. The students pay only for the texts which are going to be recommended for the particular course, which means that they (theoretically) save money and do not end up with materials redundant to their needs. All material in the database is copyright managed, which means that authors receive revenue from their work, something which does not happen with the illegal copying of materials for courses which is sadly common practice in some institutions (Lynch 1994). While this seems a useful service, there are some disadvantages to it. When recommending course readings, for example, the teacher usually recommends (and hopes) that students will read more widely than the bare minimum to pass the course. When a particular article or book.chapter is suggested, the expectation is that the student will browse the whole journal or book for other references of interest or relevance. This is not possible with such customized anthologies, though to be realistic in today's educational climate, perhaps students are too busy to do more than the recommended core of the readings on any course.

One of the key questions which publishers are needing to ask themselves in the face of the new developments concerns the ontology of electronic publications. Most publishers are, at the moment, producing their electronic publications as CD-ROMs (though a few small ones are available on floppy disc). But what exactly is a CD-ROM? Is it a special case of a book, or a special case of a piece of software? Is it content which defines it, or is it form? Is, as McLuhan has taught us to ask, the medium the message? A CD-ROM may contain exactly the same *content* as a book, but presenting it in a different *form* has implications beyond the simple fact of whether you read from page or screen. For instance, the *Oxford English Dictionary* on CD-ROM or Chadwyck-Healey's *Patrologia Latina*, described elsewhere in this volume, are both based on multi-volume books. The CD-ROMs are of interest to the same scholars as the books; they may be accessible in the same areas in the library; but if they are made available across networks they will also be available in many other places at the same time. They also need other entities interposed between themselves and their readers such as hardware, software, interfaces, and operating systems in order that their arcane internal representations can be translated into symbols and structures which readers understand. This also brings considerations such as support, obsolescence, upgrades, maintenance—not generally factors with which publishers of books need concern themselves. Once a book is published and launched, apart from perhaps reprints and new editions, publishers need take little further action in relation to it. The maintenance of the object on the part of libraries or individual owners requires routine care, and perhaps rebinding of a popular book which has received rough handling, but little else. Neither publishers nor librarians ever expect to have to train users actually to *read* the books. So, even when an electronic publication has exactly the same content as a book, it is a very different object. How, then, are these new objects to be marketed? Which shelves do they occupy in bookshops and libraries? If we feel that, despite the differences, content is more important than form, then they would be found alongside books on the same topic. Most bookshops, however, have a special section with a machine close-by to allow the perusal of CD-ROMS: unlike with a book, taking a CD-ROM down from a shelf and looking at it gives no real sense to the reader/user of how useful it will be. It is interesting to look at the packaging of CD-ROMs which are found on the shelves of bookshops: they are generally book-sized and book-shaped, though when opened they often have only a single CD and a very small booklet or sheet of paper with installation instructions. Customers and booksellers feel comfortable with the current design of CD-ROM packaging, as they recognize the status of the object they have in front of them. This is a contrast to the marketing of audio CDs which are sold in just the small plastic slip case. As far as I know, there was never a phase in the production of CDs when they were sold in cases as large as the covers of vinyl long-playing records. Perhaps the fact that an audio CD is a disc, like a record, and is played on a very similar looking piece of equipment allowed a sense of familiarity which we have not yet acquired with the CD-ROM.

Another serious consideration in electronic publishing is the status accorded to the publication in the assessment of the research output of the individual academic. It has to be pointed out that publication on paper, in monographs published by reputable presses with rigorous review procedures or in prestigious refereed journals, is still preferred when considering someone for promotion or new posts, or when rating the output of a department or institution. This is changing, certainly in the UK, where, in the Higher Education Funding Councils' current Research Assessment Exercise, electronic publications are specifically mentioned as appropriate products to be considered. This situation will improve further as high quality publications appear in electronic form, validated by major presses or in electronic journals with prestigious editorial boards. It is incumbent upon the community to take responsibility for ensuring the quality of electronic publication. Academic peer review has always been the process by which research is judged: this should be no different when work appears in a different medium.

Although there are many questions which still need to be answered, electronic publishing has a number of advantages and disadvantages for the scholar, for the publisher, and for the custodians: those we charge with looking after, storing, and cataloguing our scholarly materials. One of the key advantages for the modern publishing industry is that CD-ROMs, the currently favoured medium of electronic delivery, are much cheaper to produce than weighty and complex reference works produced in book form; the objects themselves are small, and smaller production runs can be contemplated, meaning that there is less need for expensive warehouse storage. Indeed, some CD-ROMs could be produced by 'just-in-time' methods (i.e. they are produced to specific orders rather than in batches for sale), making production and storage even more efficient. Electronic publications allow easier retrieval of complex information structures and can permit better integration of different media, for instance an encyclopaedia can include video clips and sound, as well as text and still images. It is also useful that resources can be more easily shared—for example, CD-ROM-based teaching materials can be mounted on a network for access by a whole class of students simultaneously—and that information which changes rapidly can be updated more easily, quickly, and cheaply.

As with anything in life, there are always disadvantages which must be offset against advantages, particularly with something new. For example, the rapid pace of change of hardware and software brings the potential of rapid obsolescence; and the constituent materials need to be permanently 'managed' which has never been necessary in quite the same way with books. Also, the integration of large volumes of diverse media brings problems of copyright and intellectual property rights on an unprecedented scale. It has to be assumed, too, that all potential users will have access to the relevant hardware; and also that they will require a level of training which is not needed for them to use books. Cost of development can also be a significant disadvantage: producing electronic publications is not cheap. Some projects which are driven by scholars are fortunate enough to secure funding from grant bodies, some are funded by commercial publishers, some are carried out using traditional scholarly resources: the hard work and dedication of serious scholars who believe that electronic publication can be the best method of producing particularly complex works—the *Piers Plowman* project discussed below is one such. Sir Charles Chadwyck-Healey argues that:

It is essential for the future of electronic text publishing that the commercial publishing community invest in it ... Such an important new area of publishing, as important in its own way as the transfer of text from manuscript to print, cannot be dependent on the largess of the few foundations willing to fund such projects. (Letter to the *TLS*, January 1993, quoted in Dixon 1994, 20).

Some examples of electronic publications

A growing number of different kinds of electronic publications are now being produced for the humanities scholar; I will mention only a few. First, there are some scholarly editing projects which are adopting electronic publication as the most effective means of presenting the complex materials which push the printed book to the limits of its organizational possibilities. These include the *Canterbury Tales* project, discussed elsewhere in this volume (Deegan). The publishers of this, Cambridge University Press, are also planning electronic editions of other major authors including Shakespeare, Johnson, Hardy, and Yeats in their Cambridge Electronic Editions series. The *Piers Plowman* Archive, also discussed elsewhere, is to be the first publication of SEENET (Society for Early English and Norse Electronic Texts) which has been established recently by a group of scholars in North America and Europe. This is specifically for the publication of electronic scholarly editions of early texts and is analogous to the Early English Text Society which has existed for more than a hundred years to publish scholarly editions in book form. The SEENET texts are being published by University of Michigan Press.

In contrast to the detailed study of single works or single authors which the above projects are carrying out, some publishers are producing vast archives of whole genres of works or of existing massive scholarly resources. Chadwyck-Healey has produced the enormous work of Latin patristics known as the *Patrologia Latina* as a CD-ROM; the printed version of this occupies some 221 huge volumes, the electronic, four CD-ROMs. Chadwyck-Healey is also producing major resources for scholars and students of English Literature: for instance, the English Poetry Full Text Database which contains the work of over 1,000 poets from the earliest period of English writings up to 1900. This again is contained on four CD-ROMs and may seem expensive until one realizes the enormous cost of purchasing each of the works singly. Many libraries now find that it is an economy to purchase such a massive data resource just in order to have all these texts. Being able to make them available simultaneously throughout the university campus networks is a huge added bonus. Indeed, some licences for such large textbases are being purchased on a larger scale than just the university campus. In the USA, some are available on a state-wide basis, which means that smaller or perhaps less well-funded institutions can have access to resources they could never dream of if they had to fund them alone. The company has also produced a more popular version of the English Poetry Database, Poetry Plus, which contains major canonical authors and has more multimedia capability than the main full-text database. They have also published the full-text databases, English Verse Drama, and Editions and Adaptations of Shakespeare, and will soon release The Bible in English. The Shakespeare package is a full-text database of major historical editions and theatre adaptations of the works of William Shakespeare. It contains the complete text of eleven major editions of Shakespeare's works, twenty-five contemporary quarto and octavo editions, and over a hundred adaptations, sequels, and burlesques. The Bible package will include the complete text of fifteen editions of the Bible, ranging from the earliest Anglo-Saxon translations through the Middle Ages and the Renaissance to the modern period. The company is also embarking on the publication of electronic versions of literary works in other European languages, including the works of Voltaire and of Goethe. Resources produced on this scale, in particular in areas like English literature which are receiving such wide coverage, constitute a whole digital library which could be mounted on a network and accessed from anywhere.

Chadwyck-Healey produces large, complete corpora which are aimed at libraries and whole academic sites. Oxford University Press (OUP) is producing reference materials which can be used by the individual department, academic, or even, for some of their cheapest products, by the student. The *Oxford English Dictionary* on CD-ROM is their flagship publication, one which has already had great success, and the *Shorter Oxford English Dictionary* will soon be available. The Reference Shelf Series, a set of resources for writers in different subject areas—business, languages, science—is now also available. Each Reference Shelf contains dictionaries and guides for the writer to have easy access to a range of information which can be called up from within standard word processors. For instance, the Language Shelf has the *Oxford French, English, Italian,* and *German Minidictionaries* in one package. They also produce a range of literary texts for text analysis, including the works of Shakespeare, Chaucer, and Jane Austen. Soon to appear is a series of major bilingual dictionaries. OUP have also just launched the electronic *Dictionary of National Biography*, a massive resource for all scholars in the humanities. As well as the scholarly works being produced by major academic publishers there are a number of organizations producing works aimed at the more popular market. These include: *Romeo and Juliet* published by HarperCollins, Attica Cybernetics, and the BBC; and the numerous publications from Voyager Expanded Books, which include *The Annotated Alice,* Martin Gardner's annotated version of *Alice in Wonderland,* as well as a range of modern popular novels. There are also publications which offer complete sets of classic authors or works, such as the Classic Library advertised by the catalogue *Multimedia World.* This is marketed as '2,000 unabridged texts on a fully interactive CD-ROM' and invites the user to 'browse through great works of literature from the Code of Hammurabi to President J.F. Kennedy's inaugural speech'. While not intended for scholars, these works are of interest because of the assumption by those who produce them that they will substitute for printed books. They are also aimed at the general reader rather than the scholar: it is, for instance, not always easy to ascertain which printed edition of an author's work has been used to produce the electronic version, and the producers, when asked, sometimes do not understand why it might be important. There are of course some works of reference which are much better produced as interactive CD-ROMs than as books—the major dictionaries, encyclopaedias, or very large textual corpora, for instance—but for other texts assumptions are made which I think we could query: for a straightforward novel, and for a comfortable reading experience, most readers would agree that nothing beats a paperback.

Network publishing

At least a CD-ROM is an identifiable object, as is a book. Though it poses the extra problems discussed above, it inherits certain properties as a clear definable object: it can be delivered to bookshops or libraries; it can have a price; it cannot be altered, therefore it is possible to know that we have what the author and publisher intended us to have; it can be owned; it could be sold second-hand, and there are apparently shops opening in North America which offer second-hand CD-ROMs. The status of a networked publication is much less clear as it is a 'virtual' product. Of course, the information on a CD-ROM is virtual, in that it is not accessible other than through the machine's RAM and screen display, and once the machine is switched off the information disappears. But the information is contained on a solid object, so the virtuality does not seem such a problem for the user. But once the information is only available through networks, this is a different situation. Payment becomes problematic: how does one operate fair charges, and in the academic world, who pays them? Various schemes are being scrutinized: pay-per-view; pay for downloading; licensing by institutions; even national licensing. However, there needs to be more work in the areas of encryption and security to protect users who might be asked to pay by some method such as credit card. Publishers also need security measures to protect works from plagiarism, illegal access or downloading, or from unofficial changes. Watermarking is one fruitful line of research currently being pursued: an interesting example of watermarking which can protect an image without impairing the quality of the viewing experience has been developed by IBM for the Vatican Library images which are being made available online.

If there are further moves towards networked publication, these are certain to have an even more radical effect on the publishing industry than CD-ROMS. One of the key questions here is the status of the research library which, in the academic world, is one of the routes through which publications are made available to the end-user. The traditional role of the research library is the acquisition of publications, which it then catalogues, stores, protects, and makes available. There is a physical place to which readers go, and they are supplied with physical objects with which they then work. Very few scholars would ever use only one library, and typically might use more than twenty in different towns or even countries. The means of access to the holdings of other libraries are: travel (which is now becoming expensive at the same time as funds for travel are dwindling); inter-library loan; or document supply and offprint services. With electronic publications, there is a move in libraries from the acquisition of resources towards provision of the means of access to resources, which is a radical shift in the role of the library. The electronic library concept is one which is being hotly debated in academic circles around the world, and is discussed briefly elsewhere in this volume (Deegan). While many electronic library projects are concerned with the digitization of holdings in order to provide wider access or to conserve fragile originals, libraries are also the places where gateways to electronic publications will be provided. Many libraries now hold large numbers of CD-ROMs and make them available on stand-alone machines. They also provide some CD-ROMs on networks, and are increasingly offering access to databases of information. But with networked publication, the role of the library will change even further. If publishers make available their wares over the Internet, how will this affect the role of the library? Readers could interact with works directly instead of going via the library, but will have to pay as individuals. This could prove costly, and licensed access via the library could prove more cost-effective. As noted above, some publishers offer licences on a wider basis than a single institution, and this is another possible route to information provision and payment. A mixed model of information supply, access, control, and payment is probably going to be the most appropriate one for the academic world. Controls and methods which are too centralized and uniform are unlikely to map adequately onto existing practices.

Electronic journals

There has been a crisis in scholarly libraries in the UK over the last fifteen years because of serious cuts in public spending for higher education and public services. This has also been the case in North America and Europe, and probably in other parts of the world too. One of the consequences of this crisis has been a serious decline in the amount of money available for the purchase of scholarly journals. This starts a descending spiral of availability of these journals, accompanied by escalating costs, which further deepens the availability spiral. Libraries stop taking journals which are not widely read, publishers cannot then afford to keep producing the journals with lower demand, and the price inevitably goes up. During the 1980s in the UK, periodicals prices rose 50 per cent faster than the rate of general inflation (Jones 1993, 130). Production costs for journals, unlike other serial publications, are almost all reclaimed by sales, with very little revenue generated by advertising. Added to this is an increasing pressure upon academics to publish, which means that new journals start up in order to cope with the increasing volume of publications in new areas. Therefore we have a large volume of papers to be published, and large numbers of journals, but with low print runs and high costs. The increasing output of publications by scholars has also made journal publication a slow business, with publication times of six months to several years in many high quality humanities periodicals. All of these factors have resulted in a patchiness in the availability of journals in any one library, with some important journals not taken at all, and incomplete runs of others: a serious problem in a research library. Of course, journal articles can always be obtained from somewhere, but this means visits to other libraries, which can be costly and time-consuming, or the use of inter-library loan and document supply services. These are excellent facilities, but require a degree of exactness in knowing what you want in advance that is difficult if only the article title or a brief abstract is available. It is possible to wait several days or even weeks for an article to arrive, only to discover that it is not really relevant for the topic in hand.

Because of the above problems, the move towards the production and delivery of journals electronically is to be welcomed. Indeed, the wider scholarly community will probably accept journal publication by electronic means more readily than it will accept the electronic publication of other forms of scholarly output. Books, especially to those who have dedicated their professional lives to their study, raise many emotional as well as intellectual responses. Suggestions that we may soon witness the death of the book as we know it raise howls of protest, with questions such as 'How will one read an electronic book in the bath or in bed?' Books are often physically beautiful objects, and there is a sensual element to them—the feel of the paper, their smell, perhaps a leather binding, or illustrations—which add to their status as artefact rather than merely conveyor of information.

There are few such emotional responses to academic journals, which are regarded as tools of the trade and are almost never owned by individuals. They are generally used in a different way from books too. One scans the table of contents, notes articles of use, and then photocopies them, scribbling all over the copies in the process of extracting the information. The reading of them in bed or in the bath is not a common practice. The provision of journals electronically could easily result in the scholar obtaining much the same output; he or she would scan the table of contents, something which it is perhaps easier to do with electronic searching aids, note something worth reading, then print out the relevant article, which is then subject to the same process of use as the photocopy. Therefore, the electronic product is at least as much use, and could be utilized in a familiar way, posing no threat to a scholar's feelings of tactile attachment to the object of study which notions of the electronic book pose. But the electronic journal can be so much more use than this: it makes articles available much more quickly, and not being confined by schedules of paper publication, these articles can be mounted singly as soon as they are ready, rather than being batched, as they are at the moment. Costs can be kept down as articles are almost certainly submitted electronically so there is no typesetting and printing of electronic journals. One of the problems of paper journals is the high cost of adding illustrations to text, so subjects like film studies, art history, and archaeology can be better served by electronic delivery with the possibility of the addition of multimedia facilities. Indeed, one needs to consider where to use the advantages of new media and where to build on former traditions. It is of course natural to translate old methods to new media: for instance, many early printed books kept the fonts and layouts characteristic of handwritten manuscripts. But there are often better ways of doing things in the new media, and these need to be given careful consideration. Journal publishing in electronic form is moving forward rapidly in some disciplines: in the sciences, timeliness of publication is the crucial consideration and so the electronic periodical has little serious opposition. This has never been quite so vital an issue in the humanities, but is now becoming more so in our new 'publish or perish' era. One exciting possibility is that posited by Ann Okerson who suggests that the replacement of paper journals by electronic 'may lead to a new type of scholarly discourse' (Okerson 1991, 5). This, of course, only applies to new material being produced in electronic form; humanists still rely heavily on older materials, and their needs will only be served fully by retrospective conversion of key journals, something which is time consuming and expensive.

Some examples

There are now a number of electronic journals becoming available for humanists; I have chosen three very different examples to illustrate some of the possibilities offered by this new and exciting development. *Internet Archaeology: An International Journal for Archaeology* has recently received funding from the UK Higher Education Funding Councils through their Electronic Libraries Programme (eLib). One of the programme areas was electronic journals, where the Councils agreed to fund a number of initiatives to improve the status and acceptability of electronic journals, the promotion of new forms of electronic journals, and opportunities for parallel publishing. The team which put together the proposal for the archaeology journal explains:

The intention is that the production and dissemination of the journal will be network-based, ultimately available to all via the Internet. The journal will publish the results of archaeological research, including excavation reports (text, photographs, data, drawings, reconstructions, diagrams, interpretations), analyses of large data sets along with the data itself, visualisations, programs used to analyse data, and applications of information technology in archaeology: for example, geographical information systems and computer modelling. Conventional publication via the printed page cannot do justice to the rich diversity of archaeological information. Electronic publication, by contrast, offers opportunities to overcome these difficulties. The journal will be fully-refereed. It will set a high academic standard. Contributions will be provided by archaeologists throughout the world, and the journal will be aimed at an international audience (Heyworth, Ross, and Richards 1995).

(Re)Soundings: A World Wide Web Publication is originally the idea of two members of the English Department of Millersville University. It has been conceived as a community of readers who collaborate in creating and responding to a variety of multimedia texts. The publication is intended to provide an opportunity to explore theoretical and technological boundaries through collaboration via the World Wide Web. Each annual volume will develop a different topic; the focus of the first volume will be Early English (pre-1700) materials and a call for papers for that volume has just been sent out. Members of the Board of Directors have been chosen from among those who have interest and expertise in literature or textuality, the history of criticism, postmodern approaches to textuality, or arts and humanities applications of the World Wide Web and allied multimedia computing applications. The Board of Directors acts in an advisory capacity; members are encouraged to take as active a role in the publication as their time and circumstances allow. Articles are to be selected for the journal through editorial review, and once the reviewed materials are on the Web, responses are invited and only minimally screened by the editorial staff to ensure that the pieces meet announced size and technological constraints and show general relevance to the topic. Articles are available for public comment for a limited period of time, and some of the comments then become part of the

archived version of the article. An archived article therefore has both the original ideas of its author, and also a layer of responses and debate which it has engendered.

Postmodern Culture is a peer-reviewed electronic journal which provides an international, interdisciplinary forum for discussions of contemporary literature, theory, and culture. It accepts work from in its contributors in a variety of forms: finished essay, work in progress, reviews, etc. It started in 1990, and at that time was made available through e-mail and also on floppy discs, It is now accessed through the World Wide Web which allows for hypertext capabilities to be exploited; this, for a journal discussing all aspects of contemporary culture, is a great boon and full use is made of it by the contributors. In articles on film, movie clips are shown; in articles on music, sound files can be accessed. Writers on other forms of cultural media than text have always had problems 'quoting' from the subjects of their analysis, so a great deal of their critical comments include merely summarizing what happens in a scene from a film or play, or describing in words musical motifs. These summaries or descriptions are interpretative acts before the writer even begins to analyse or discuss ideas. For the reader to experience the primary art form, and not someone's description, is vital but is only now possible in the world of electronic media where all forms of cultural object can be digitized, linked, and accessed. One could raise the objection that digitizing is a secondary form of representation which offers a different experience of interaction, at one remove from the original cultural objects, but, while this is true, it is still closer than giving only verbal descriptions and is therefore vastly to be preferred.

Standards in electronic publication

One of the problems of electronic publication which needs to be addressed is that of standards. These operate in a number of different areas, and are of particular concern for libraries which have to deal with a plethora of products, adhering to a wide range of standards. Publishers, of course, offer products which have to be distinguished from those of their competitors, and therefore need to be given characteristic features. This has always been the case with books, and it is therefore very easy to tell a Penguin paperback from a scholarly monograph by an academic press, from a major dictionary or encyclopaedia. Electronic publishers and software houses therefore have different styles, designs, interfaces, and other features for their products, just as book publishers do. But when the product is a book, it does not take very long for an experienced reader to find out how to extract the desired information, even from books which appear different. We are trained to this from an early age, and there are not too many different ways in which a book can be used. With an electronic product, this is more problematic. The access software can vary from company to company, and even from product to product produced by the same company. The interfaces can be different and the design can greatly influence the ease of use of a product. The documentation or help facilities may not be uniform, and companies offer variable levels of support for users. Added to this are the different methods available to publishers for the encoding of information in electronic publications. This is particularly important if the information is to be interchanged, perhaps over networks, and if it is to survive beyond the generation of hardware and software available when it was created. Currently, the main text encoding and interchange formats are Standard Generalized Markup Language (SGML), TeX, and Acrobat. These all have advantages and disadvantages, each has champions who will argue forcefully for their particular choice being the most appropriate standard. These issues are discussed in more detail elsewhere in this volume (Popham).

Preservation of electronic publications

Perhaps the most serious question we need to be asking about electronic publications, is how are they to be read in ten, fifty, or a hundred years time? Given the rapid pace of change in hardware developments, this means that the life of an electronic publication is potentially very short, shorter even than that of a text printed on the most fragile acid-based paper. It is, of course, possible to transfer the materials between generations of hardware and software, but this means that materials have to be constantly managed and cared for if they are to survive; this costs significant amounts of money. Contrast this with a medieval manuscript written on parchment which will be readable after 1,500 years, even (or perhaps especially) if it is never opened during those years. Libraries, especially research libraries, are concerned with information for the long term, not the short term. A document may sit on library shelves for twenty years or even a hundred years between each use of it, but readers expect it to be available, easy to find, and in a good state of preservation when they need it. It needs care, but little routine maintenance to ensure that these requirements are met. Not so with electronic publications. One writer has suggested that there are three kinds of preservation which we need to consider in the digital research library (Graham 1994). These are: medium preservation; technology preservation; and intellectual preservation. Medium preservation is concerned with the survival of tapes, discs, CD-ROMs, etc. Technology preservation is perhaps more important than medium: if the technology is not available to access our information, what will it matter if we can preserve the medium or not? Intellectual preservation is preservation of the information as originally recorded and is perhaps the most serious concern of all. Electronic information can be changed, altered, added to, and unless the changes are specifically recorded, this process leaves no trace. This is very different from a printed book or manuscript, many of which bear witness to their reception and use over centuries, which is itself an important witness to changing cultural uses of information. In the USA, the Commission on Preservation and Access and the Research Libraries Group have commissioned a report (CPA and RLG 1995) from a task force on the Archiving of Digital Information; this is vital reading for anyone in the business of creating or using digital records. In the UK, the Higher Education Funding Councils through the eLib Programme, and the British Library Research and Development Department are also looking into these problems.

Conclusion

It may seem from some of the problems and issues discussed here that perhaps electronic publishing will not succeed. However, there are some resources which are so much more useful in electronic form than on paper that they will almost certainly never appear in paper form again. Dictionaries and encyclopaedias, for instance, are greatly enhanced by just the change of form, allowing retrieval of information under so many more headings than in printed form. To search for words in a dictionary derived from Arabic, for instance, is almost impossible and certainly very time consuming in paper form, involving just reading through all the entries. To perform such a search using the electronic version can be done in seconds. If we add to the search capabilities the enrichment by the addition of different media, then we have a resource which is so valuable and flexible that it is probably worth the present disadvantages. The access to integrated resources on a large scale through networks will also bring huge benefits to scholars, allowing them to compare and contrast unique works from the four corners of the earth on one computer screen. The problems must be solved when the benefits are so huge.

References and bibliography

Amiran, E., and Unsworth, J., *'Postmodern Culture:* publishing in the electronic medium', *The Public-Access Computer Systems Review*, 2.1 (1991), 67-76.

Commission on Preservation and Access and the Research Libraries Group, *Preserving digital information*. Draft Report of the Task Force on Archiving of Digital Information. Version 1.0, August 23, 1995.

Dixon, J., *Electronic publishing: American developments, British implications*. A Report for the Sir Stanley Unwin Foundation (1994).

Graham, P., 'Intellectual preservation: electronic preservation of the third kind', *Commission on Preservation and Access Report* (March 1994).

Heyworth, M., Ross, S., and Richards, J., *'Internet archaeology: an international electronic journal for archaeology'*, available at http://britac3.britac.ac.uk/cba/projects/ejournal.html

Jones, K., 'Network publishing: a librarian's perspective', in Smith, J.W. (ed), *Networking and the future of libraries* (Westport, CT: Meckler, 1993), 129-135.

Lynch, R., 'Electronic book publishing on demand—McGraw-Hill's Primis Electronic Database Publishing System', in Blunden, B. and Blunden, M., (eds.) *The electronic publishing business and its market* (Leatherhead, Surrey: IEPRC/PIRA, 1994), 119-136.

Meadows, J., 'Electronic publishing and the humanities', in Kenna, S., and Ross, S. (eds.), *Networking in the humanities* (London: Bowker Saur, 1995), 141-156.

Okerson, A., 'The electronic journal: what, whence, and when', *The Public-Access Computer Systems Review*, 2.1 (1991), 5-24.

Rosenheim, A., 'Selling the *OED on CD-ROM* to individuals and institutions: how to have your cake and eat it too', in Blunden, B. and Blunden, M., (eds.) *The electronic publishing business and its market* (Leatherhead, Surrey: IEPRC/PIRA, 1994), 111-118.

Ter Meer, L.P., and Zijlstra, J., 'Network publishing: the publisher's perspective', in Smith, J.W. (ed), *Networking and the future of libraries* (Westport, CT: Meckler, 1993), 136-143.

Further information

Attica
Unit Two, Kings Meadow, Ferry Hinksey Road, Oxford OX2 0DP.

Cambridge University Press, http://www.cam.ac.uk/

Chadwyck-Healey Ltd
The Quorum, Barnwell Road, Cambridge, CB5 8SW.
http://www.chadwyck.co.uk/

Internet Archaeology, http://britac3.britac.ac.uk/cba/projects/ejournal.html

Electronic Publishing
Oxford University Press, Walton Street, Oxford OX2 6DP, UK.

Postmodern Culture, http://jefferson.village.virginia.edu/pmc/

(Re)Soundings, http://www.millersv.edu/~english/resoundings/call.html

Society for Early English and Norse Electronic Texts (SEENET)
http://www.press.umich.edu/TitlesS95/seenet.html

Voyager Expanded Books, http://www.voyagerco.com/

The Internet and
the Humanities Scholar

Stuart Lee

Media hype and a series of elaborate claims about the way the 'Information Superhighway' will change our lives gives the impression that the Internet is only a recent development; in fact, the Internet has been around for almost thirty years. In the 1960s the US Advanced Research Projects Agency (ARPA) linked up four computers (three in California, one in Utah) to investigate the possibility of maintaining a communications network in the event of a nuclear war. The system developed by ARPA, called ARPAnet, was soon copied by other computer centres, and eventually these sites became connected to each other or internetworked. In 1973 the first international connections to ARPAnet appeared with links to England and Norway. Gradually networking became more and more popular and three major networks were formed. 1981 saw the appearance of BITnet (Because It's Time network) and CSnet (Computer Science network), and in 1986 came the NSFnet (National Science Foundation network). It was NSFnet that was to form the backbone of the Internet as we now know it and win through against its rivals. In the first days of NSFnet, connections could handle approximately 56 kilobytes per second (around 5,000 words of plain text), and in 1989 this was upgraded to 1.5 megabytes per second. Even more impressive is the rate of growth of the Internet. At the end of 1991 it was estimated that there were approximately 500,000 computers connected to the Internet. By the end of 1994 this figure had risen to 10 million (with some estimates claiming it is now as high as 30 million).

In many ways the Internet is the most promising resource available to the academic (and in the context of this chapter—the humanities scholar), yet at the same time can prove to be the most baffling. Confusion arises from the fact that: (a) it is, for the most part, free; and (b) the wealth of information that is available can be both daunting and overwhelming. This chapter will attempt to explain some of the technical jargon which surrounds the Internet, but, more importantly, will illustrate some of the major advantages of using the resources in humanities teaching and research.

What is the Internet?

It is perhaps appropriate at this point to explain some of the more common terms used when discussing Internet resources, particularly from a UK perspective. The term 'internet' itself is short for 'internet-working'. When two computers are linked together via some form of cable to allow for communication between the two, they can be said to be 'internetworked' or 'networked'. 'Networks' themselves can, of course, vary in size. Local Area Networks (LANs) are usually limited to a single department or campus (approximately 2km maximum radius). In the educational sector almost every higher education institution has its own LAN. Obviously it is beneficial to join all of these LANs together so there can be communication between institutions, and therefore LANs are joined or networked together by Wider Area Networks (WANs). The WAN in the UK educational sector is known as the Joint Academic Network or JANET, which is currently being superseded by Super-JANET. This is a high-speed backbone for the educational sector (only available to some sites at the moment) which allows for a much quicker rate of data transfer. Most countries have their equivalent of JANET (or something similar for commercial purposes) and internationally they are joined together by the largest network of all, the Internet. In essence then, the Internet is simply a large network joining together all the LANS and WANs in the world.

Communication

The Internet is used for two distinct purposes: communication and remote access. The first of these (and the most popular) is predominantly the use of electronic mail or e-mail: the means by which users send messages to each other electronically. The analogy of posting a letter using the Royal Mail is a useful one: here you would write out your message on paper, put it in an envelope, write the address on the front, and post it. With e-mail you type the message into the computer, use a piece of mailing software, type in the person's e-mail address, and send the message. The difference is that for academic purposes e-mail is free (even for commercial purposes it is very cheap), messages only take a matter of seconds to reach their destination (worldwide), and they do not just have to be a few lines of greeting but can be chapters, books, images, sounds, movies, and so on.

In the above process (once you are familiar with your own mailing system) the only confusing aspect can be the e-mail address. Thankfully these have now been standardized so that they generally consist of the following—userid@location (e.g. Stuart.Lee@oucs.ox.ac.uk). Here, the first part is the individual username, or 'id', which singles the owner out from other users; this is then followed by the @ sign or 'at', and then the site. So in the example above this tells you that Stuart Lee is at (@) Oxford University Computing Services (oucs) in Oxford (ox) within the academic community (ac) in the United Kingdom (uk). Other abbreviations one may encounter are 'edu' (educational—the US equivalent of 'ac'), 'gov' (government), and 'com' (commercial).

However, communication is not restricted to the direct exchange of information. For some time now there have been a variety of discussion lists in existence which academics can join free of charge, and which act as electronic forums focusing on specific subjects or topics. Upon subscription, any message sent to the list will be forwarded directly to all the other members, speeding up dissemination of the posting and allowing others to continue the debate (usually again via the central list address). Furthermore, in addition to facilitating discussion, these lists often hold archives of useful resources such as electronic texts, fonts, or other pieces of software which would be of interest for that particular subject. These lists have both advantages and disadvantages: they can yield valuable contacts and information, but are now so numerous that it can be difficult to select the right one. For example, in English literature a cursory survey of what was available revealed over twenty lists. All of these could be joined free of charge by sending the appropriate subscription message to the administrator's address and from then on (if desired) any posting to the list would automatically be forwarded to the subscriber's mailbox.

The most useful guide to the lists which academics in the humanities may wish to subscribe to can be found in Abbott (1994), Hughes and Lee (1994), and Strangelove and Kovacs (1993, 147–222). The UK also has an excellent service which houses and monitors a variety of existing lists and allows academics to create their own. This is the Mailbase service based at the University of Newcastle (e-mail: mailbase@mailbase. ac.uk). In addition, specific lists will often hold their own guides and introductory resources which academics can make use of. However, the largest, and the most widely used of all lists in the humanities is Humanist@brownvm.brown.edu, which caters for general discussion and news on humanities computing. HUMANIST is also a worthwhile starting place for people to request information on other lists.

Remote access

The other popular use of the Internet is to access data stored on a machine elsewhere (i.e. it is remote from the user's machine, hence 'remote access'). This is not hacking; hacking is when you access another person's machine illegally, usually with criminal intent. Information stored elsewhere may take many forms: library catalogues, databases, electronic texts, software archives, and so on. An extensive collection of these can be found at the NISS (National Information Services and Systems) Gateway under http://www.niss.ac.uk/reference/index.html. An excellent example of such a resource can be found in the Bath Information and Data Services or BIDS (particularly the Arts and Humanities Citations Index). Similarly, Online Computer Library Centre's (OCLC) FirstSearch facility allows users to find books, articles, theses, films, and computer software via their title, author, year of publication, and subject. Access is provided to nearly fifty databases through a system of authorization codes and passwords.[1] An example of this is given below. Looking at the 'Article1st' section under FirstSearch (an index of articles from over 12,500 journals) a student working on First World War poetry could initially search all the articles that contain 'first world war' in their title or abstract (over the past five years, for example, this revealed 189 'hits', or results) and then limit this to those which were also concerned with 'poetry' (reducing the total to 8 hits, as in Figure 1). It is possible to perform fast and accurate searches, and in addition, by allowing keyword searches through vast quantities of journals, the serendipity of browsing through shelves of books has not altogether been lost.

Similarly, the online catalogues of most of the world's libraries are now available for searching. Not only are these accessible to academics who may have restricted access due to geographical problems, these archives will also often contain more information than the usual card catalogues and will allow for Boolean searches (i.e. using such operators as AND, OR, NOT, etc.). Users wishing to access these online catalogues, or to keep in touch with the latest developments concerning

Figure 1: *A search under OCLC's FirstSearch*

```
═══════════════════════ wwwwH25.niss.ac.uk ═══════════════════════
+ * * * * * * * * * * * * * List of Records * * * * * * * * * * * * * * * * +
DATABASE: Article1st                   LIMITED TO:
SEARCH: su:first world war and su:poetry FOUND 8 Records

___NO.__AUTHOR_____TITLE_____YEAR
|
|   1   Bonaventura, Paul   Arts in Society.                       1994
|   2                       Trade Paperbacks.                      1993
|   3                       Hardcovers.                            1993
|   4   Springman, Luke     Elizabeth A. Marsland.  The Nation's  ..  1993
|   5                       Trade Paperbacks.                      1993
|   6                       Hardcovers.                            1993
|   7   Norgate, Paul       Dominic Hibberd, The First World War; ..  1992
|   8   Feldman, Gayle      Hardcovers.                            1992
|_____

HINTS:   View a record . . . . . . . . . . . . . . . . type record number.
         Decrease number of records . . . . type L (to limit) or A (to 'and').
         Do a new search . . . . . . . . . . . . . . . type S or SEARCH.

ACTIONS: Help  Search  And  Limit  Print  Database  BYE  Reset

RECORD NUMBER (or Action): ■
```

libraries and the implications of Internet access, should read the pages of Bulletin Board for Libraries (BUBL—http://www.bubl.bath.ac.uk/BUBL/home.html).

With the enormous increase in the number of Internet sites around the world it has become increasingly necessary to develop some easy means of finding and searching all of this information. Many systems have appeared such as WAIS (Wide Area Information Server), Gopher, and Hytelnet, but the most popular (at the moment) is the system developed at the CERN laboratories in Switzerland known as the World Wide Web (or the Web).

The World Wide Web

The World Wide Web is a system whereby machines around the world store their documents in a standard form. These documents consist of plain text but can be linked to graphics, sound files, movies, and to other documents, thereby constituting a hypertext environment. The revolutionary feature of the World Wide Web is that the linking of these documents can be international as long as the address of the document to be linked to is known.

Web documents are stored as plain text files (i.e. ASCII) and are marked-up using a system called the Hypertext Markup Language (HTML). These documents then reside on a machine that acts as a server. To access these documents (and make any sense of them) a Web browser is needed. The browser, when launched, awaits a command to go to a certain location and retrieve a file. Most of the time this will be a plain text document marked up in HTML which it will obtain and reformat according to the elements tagged in the document. Common browsers used at the moment are Netscape, Mosaic, and Lynx (for use as a plain text browser on a terminal); but there are many others already available or under development. A particularly promising piece of software is SoftQuad's new viewer, Panorama Pro, which permits the browsing and searching of documents marked up in SGML.

A browser must, of course, know the address of a particular document before it can retrieve it. Ford summarizes this as follows:

> The World Wide Web uses a universal naming scheme, the Uniform Resource Identifier (URI), to identify and address documents and other resources on the Net...Two new schemes, the Uniform Resource Name (URN) and the Uniform Resource Citation (URC), are under discussion, which together will allow copies of resources to be distributed across the Web and facilitate retrieval of the closest or cheapest copy. These make use of the current scheme used on the Web, the Uniform Resource Locator (URL), which expresses the address of a resource and the method by which it can be accessed. (Ford 1995, p. 34)

In short, at the moment when browsing a document on the Web you will need to know its Uniform Resource Locator or URL. Though daunting to look at, these simply record the scheme or protocol of the document and its pathname (i.e. the location of the document itself). One of the major advantages of the Web is that it can interface with several systems such as Gopher, ftp, or WAIS, thus allowing it to retrieve previous Internet resources with ease. Documents produced for the Web and marked up in HTML use the hypertext transfer protocol or http. For example, the URL for *The Times Higher Education Supplement* is: http://www.timeshigher.newsint.co.uk/. Here the prefix 'http' denotes that it is marked up in HTML for the Web, and 'www.timeshigher. newsint.co.uk' is the pathname or Internet address of the document. The problem with the URL system of addressing is that it enforces a rigid path structure, tied to a particular machine and location. One of the more annoying tasks that has to be performed by anyone maintaining a Web site is that of constantly checking if links still work (i.e. the URL might have changed without any form of notification). Solutions to these problems are being sought by 'naming authorities' who are proposing centrally managed address systems. Also under development are URCs (Uniform Resource Citations) which will contain metadata about a particular source (such as author, name, date created, last revision, version number, etc.).

Within Web documents themselves, links can be made to images (so that they appear as part of the file when reformatted by the browser), other documents (including remote access to sites elsewhere), sound files, and video files. Interactive graphics can be displayed with links attached to a number of elements; users need only click on the relevant section to activate them (e.g. see the interactive maps at Xerox— http://pubweb.parc.xerox.com/map). With the presence of links, graphics, sound, and video, the Web is clearly the first step towards providing hypermedia on an international basis (approaching Ted Nelson's visionary concept of the Xanadu project in the 1960s in which he envisaged a global network of knowledge accessible to all).

Needless to say, commercial and academic publishers are keen to explore the new potentials of the World Wide Web for disseminating their products. Electronic journals (or e-journals), which up to now have been posted out as simple, plain text e-mail messages to subscribers, can now be formatted to include appropriate multimedia elements and hypertext links. An example in the humanities is the recent appearance of the well-established philosophy journal *Analysis* which now has its own Web site (see Figure 2). The printed version of this has been running since 1933, but the electronic version has only appeared in recent months. Users who access the site (http://www.shef.ac.uk/uni/academic/N-Q/ phil/analysis/homepage.html) can find out information about the journal, explore lists of contents, download preprints of articles, and even go automatically to other international archives, such as the American Philosophical Association's site.

Similarly, popular newspapers such as *The Guardian*, *The Times*, *The Times Higher Education Supplement*, etc., are all creating and maintaining their own Web services. A comprehensive list of such newspapers

Figure 2: The e-journals Analysis *and* Analyst *as viewed through the* WWW

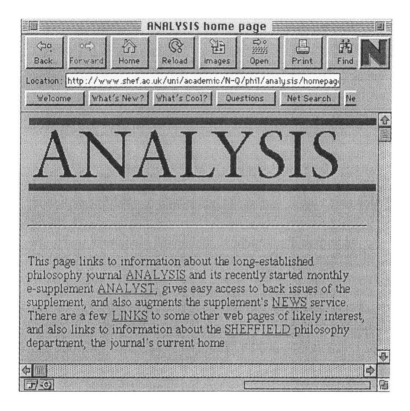

(both national and international) is available at MediaInfo Interactive's site (http://marketplace.com/e-papers.list.www/e-papers.home.page. html) but scholars interested in the whole area of electronic publishing should browse the Internet Bookshop (http://www.bookshop.co.uk/), or the Publisher's Catalogues Home Page (http://www.lights.com/publisher/) which includes thirty-eight UK-based publishers.

Another feature of the Internet which humanities scholars might find valuable is the downloading of whole files from a remote site onto a local machine. Although this is probably not feasible (or allowed) when it comes to a library catalogue, it can be useful to download other texts, such as plays, poems, novels, historical documents, etc., for a variety of purposes. An example of such a repository of available texts is the long-established Oxford Text Archive (OTA). Housed at Oxford University Computing Services, the OTA holds over 2,000 titles in a variety of languages. Many of these electronic texts are available for access via a system known as File Transfer Protocol (or ftp). As the World Wide Web interfaces with ftp sites this can be a simple matter of merely clicking on the desired title of the text and waiting for it to come across to the local machine. For example, Figure 3 illustrates the list of titles in English that the OTA has made available for retrieving (see ftp://ota.ox.ac.uk/pub/ota/public/ for the list of files available, or http://info.ox.ac.uk:80/~archive/ota.html for information about the OTA). Here, one could choose 'Dickens' and be taken to the list of texts available by the author; a complete version of *Great Expectations* could be downloaded which could then be analysed locally using a standard text analysis package.

Figure 3: Directory of publications in English available through the Oxford Text Archive's ftp archive

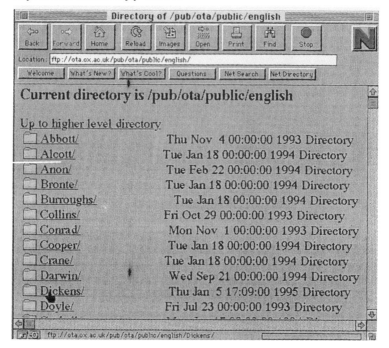

Because of the size of the Internet, and the ease with which people can 'publish' on it, one of the most pressing problems for the scholar is that of finding something that is genuinely useful in the myriad of information out there. The information overload that Vannevar Bush foresaw in 1945 is even more daunting now. Exacerbating this is the problem of 'chaining' whereby a browser will follow a link, which in turn simply leads to more links, and thence to more links, so that it can take several 'jumps' or connections to finally reach the end-resource. This can lead to extraordinary amounts of time wasting and frustration for the user.

To overcome this problem, this last year or so has seen the development of gateways or indexes which users can go directly to and have all the appropriate links listed for them. The WWW has a series of 'Virtual Libraries' which are subject specific and therefore permit quick and easy access to resources of relevance to the user's area of interest. A guide to all the various WWW virtual libraries is available at http://info.cern.ch/hypertext/DataSources/bySubject/Overiew.html. Similarly, the humanities has its own general gateway known as HUMBUL (http://www.ox.ac.uk/depts/humanities/international.html) which provides links for most of the categories of interest to academics in the related subjects: e.g. anthropology, archaeology, classics, electronic text archives (including literature), film and media studies, history, hypermedia, languages and linguistics, medieval studies, music, philosophy, religious studies, and visual arts (see Figure 4). HUMBUL (standing for the HUManities BULletin board) was originally designed as a bulletin board where news items about various projects, institutions, associations, etc. could be posted. However, with the proliferation of useful materials on the WWW, a bulletin board was deemed no longer necessary.

HUMBUL is a gateway to a plethora of resources, but gateways can be more defined and restricted in their scope. An example of this is Jack Lynch's list of Eighteenth-Century Resources at the University of Pennsylvania (http://www.english.upenn.edu/~jlynch/18th.html). These more focused collections, plus Internet searching tools such as the widely-used Lycos (http://lycos.cs.cmu.edu/), all help in allowing the user to locate a relevant resource as quickly and as easily as possible.

A teaching example

When discussing the Internet it is very tempting merely to list site addresses and archives without giving any feeling for how they could be

Figure 4: The HUMBUL Gateway

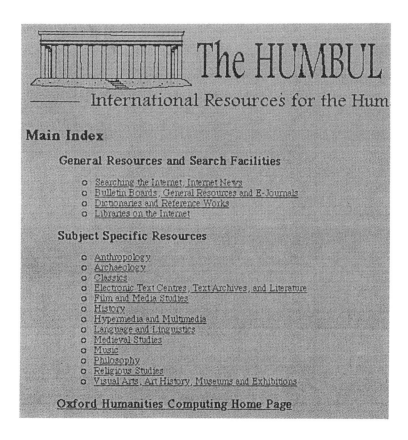

used. In relation to this a hypothetical example is given of how an academic (in this case teaching medieval literature), could draw on the resources already available.

One of the more difficult works of English literature which an undergraduate might encounter is the Anglo-Saxon epic *Beowulf*. Lecturers face the daunting task of not only having to teach the basics of the Old English language, but also to impart information on the historical and social context of the poem, the palaeographical and codicological points of interest of the *Beowulf* manuscript, as well as discussing the more literary aspects of the piece. Hindrances to this process are many. Time with the students will limit the number of tutorials or lectures which can be delivered; individual tuition dealing with problems of the language is more or less impossible nowadays with the decreasing staff/student ratios in universities; the cost of books can be prohibitive to many students as a result of decreases in student grants, and the libraries are also being forced to face severe cut-backs.

Hypothetically (i.e. assuming the hardware and software are available) the use of electronic communication and interaction with Internet resources can help to overcome some of these problems. First, by contacting local computing services a lecturer could set up a small (internal) discussion list accessible through the campus e-mail system which students could logon to at any time to post questions and comments about the poem (possibly prompted by initial questions posted by the lecturer).[2] This could then be expanded by allowing students to subscribe to ANSAX-L, the electronic discussion list for Anglo-Saxonists based at West Virginia University, thus opening up any of the more interesting debates to a wider audience. If access to the World Wide Web is possible, students could be directed to the wealth of medieval resources available such as Georgetown University's Labyrinth (http://www.georgetown.edu/labyrinth/labyrinth-home.html). Using this they could look at past discussions of the poem and analogous material. Next, the British Library's Electronic *Beowulf* project (http://portico.bl.uk/access/electronic-beowulf.html—see Figure 5) would allow the students to access facsimile images of some of the folios, study discussions on the preservation of the manuscript, and view later transcriptions of the text. As mentioned earlier, the Web can link to audio files with relative ease and thus the problems many students face with familiarizing themselves with Old English sounds can be tackled to some degree by accessing Catherine Ball's 'Hwæt! Old English in Context' project which includes sound files of correct pronunciation (http://www.georgetown.edu/cball/hwaet/hwaet06.html).

Although the above strategies are open to many problems (e.g. access to hardware and software, sporadic unavailability of some Internet sites, speed of access to some resources, level of computer literacy amongst students) it does give an example of how imaginative use, and knowledge of appropriate sites, can help a teacher surmount some of the common problems faced, whilst at the same time introducing a strong element of IT into teaching.

Figure 5: The British Library's Electronic Beowulf

The Netscape presentation was prepared by Professor Kevin S. Kiernan, University of Kentucky, and is reproduced by permission of the British Library Board.

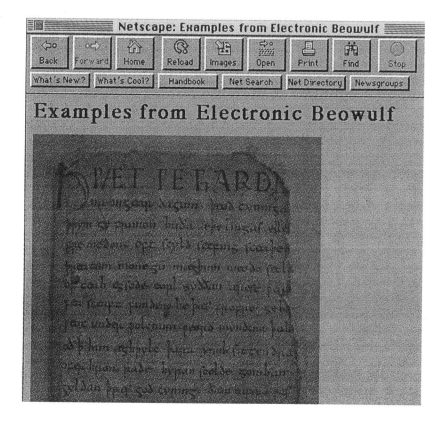

The future: problems and solutions

Even with many advances in navigation and information retrieval, there are still some major underlying problems with the Web which should be mentioned.

Already mentioned are the problems of disappearing URLs, and the information overload brought about by the incredible expansion of the Internet (and the Web in particular); and there are other issues which arise from this whole area. The ease of publishing on the Internet has meant that many sites are appearing which could be considered libellous and offensive. The Internet was deliberately established as a dispersed and decentralized organization for military reasons, and this has resulted in an anarchic maelstrom of individuals and sites which are impossible to police. There have, however, been prosecutions for misuse of the Internet for obscene or offensive purposes. Second, there is the issue of security. As discussed above, it is easy to access and to download information: that is the whole purpose of the Internet. Once obtained, however, material can easily be printed off or incorporated into a user's own documents. Encryption techniques and watermarking of files, though currently under development, are both still some way off preventing the breaching of copyright and plagiarism. Similarly, although commercial firms are continually experimenting with registration schemes and pay-as-you-view methods of delivery (thus allowing some financial recompense for the producers of the site) security of information is still at such an elementary stage that one would be reluctant to post out any confidential details (e.g. a credit card number).

Nevertheless, the future of the Internet is rich with possibilities. On the one hand there is the much-vaunted (though never seriously believed) view that it will replace all forms of communication ranging from the book to the telephone. Conversely, the liberal attitude of supplying access to the Internet to as many people as possible will come under increasing pressure as commercial companies buy up larger and larger sections of the market. The recent announcement of Microsoft's Internet-browser as a rival to Netscape is a good example of this. The almost naive attitude that you can say or type what you like and send it out will surely be discredited soon under pressure from copyright lawyers (and not to mention libel suits). The possibility of an increasing gap between rich and poor countries who may become divided into the Internet haves and have-nots is another potential problem. Yet, even with these uncertainties the advantages of tapping into these resources for the humanities scholar can be extensive, and as the archives and forums grow and become better organized for scholarly use, the usefulness of the Internet can only increase.

At the Second Elvetham Hall Conference on Scholarship and Technology in the Humanities (13th–16th April, 1994) the problems of harnessing the potential of these new resources were recognized. One speaker (Breaks 1995) noted 'the lack of a national electronic archive for the humanities' and the need for a 'national strategy...for the holding, maintenance, and provision of access to electronic material'. Michelson (1995) developed this idea and suggested that:

> Programs that are successful in addressing the information needs of humanists as the next millennium approaches will involve collaboration—the collaboration of librarians and archivists and other information providers with technologists...who in turn must work with content specialists.

It is pleasing, therefore, in the context of such comments, to report the recent announcement by the Joint Information Systems Committee to fund a national Arts and Humanities Data Service (see Burnard and Short, 1994). This will provide effective low-cost access to a wide range of digital resources for UK humanities academics, covering development of existing archives, training in the use of these datasets, identification of new areas which need targeting, and the creation of new resources. With such a national initiative starting, backed by substantial financial resources, the future possibilities for the humanities scholar wishing to use the Internet are extensive.

Notes

1. For more information contact: David Buckle, Managing Director, OCLC Europe, 7th Floor, Tricorn house, 51-53 Hagley Road, Edgbaston, Birmingham B16 8TP

2. For an example of this see Jim O'Donnell's successful experiments with electronic seminars based around modules on Boethius and Augustine (http://ccat.sas.upenn.edu:80/jod/). For studies of using electronic communication on a more internal basis see Beauvois (1994–5).

References and bibliography

Abbott, T., *On Internet 94* (London: Mecklermedia, 1994).

Beauvois, M.H., 'E-Talk: attitudes and motivation in computer-assisted classroom discussion', *Computers and the Humanities*, 28 (1994–5), 177–190.

Breaks, M., 'Information resources on the network or "the virtual library"', in Kenna, S., and Ross, S. (eds.), *Networking in the humanities: proceedings of the second conference on scholarship and technology in the humanities held at Elvetham Hall, Hampshire, 13–16 April, 1994*, (London: Bowker Saur, 1995), 45–61.

Burnard, L., and Short, H., *An Arts and Humanities Data Service: report of a feasibility study commissioned by the Information Services Sub-committee of the Joint Information Systems Committee of the Higher Education Funding Councils* (Oxford: Office for Humanities Communication, October 1994).

Bush, V., 'As we may think', *Atlantic Monthly*, 176.1 (1945), 101-108.

Ford, A., *Spinning the Web* (London: International Thomson Publishing, 1995).

Gaffin, A., 'Visiting museums on the Internet', *InternetWorld*, (March/April, 1994), 24-29.

Hughes, L.M., and Lee, S.D., *Resources guide* (Oxford: CTI Centre for Textual Studies, 1994).

Kessler, J., *Directory to fulltext online resources 1992* (Westport: Meckler, 1992).

Krol, E., *The whole Internet* (Sebastopol, CA: O'Reilly and Associates, 1992).

Michelson, A., 'Networking and the scholarly community', in Kenna, S., and Ross, S. (eds.), *Networking in the humanities: proceedings of the second conference on scholarship and technology in the humanities held at Elvetham Hall, Hampshire, 13–16 April, 1994*, (London: Bowker Saur, 1995), 201–223.

Strangelove, M., and Kovacs, D., *Directory of electronic journals, newsletters, and academic discussion lists* (Washington DC: Association of Research Libraries, 1993).

Tennant, R., Ober, J., and Lipow, A.G., *Crossing the Internet threshold: an instructional handbook* (Berkeley: Library Solutions Press, 1993).

APPENDICES

Appendix 1
The Technical Background

Peter Adman and Lorraine Warren

Computers first became available for academic usage in the 1960s, in the form of large mainframes. Although such machines were very powerful, they were initially perceived as being suitable only for the rapid processing of numerical data. Moreover, they were expensive, usually requiring a specially prepared site and a staff of computer professionals for their operation and management. It is not surprising, therefore, that usage in the humanities was mainly, though not totally, confined to specialist research projects of a largely statistical nature. Even relatively simple textual analysis required source data to be numerically coded for input. It was not until the end of the 1970s that the emergence of minicomputers with more user-friendly software enabled researchers to analyse humanities data without having to become computer experts. However, it was the widespread availability of cheap and powerful desktop microcomputers in the late 1980s, together with the realization that pictorial, as well as textual and numerical data could be processed, that led to computing becoming a mainstream activity in the humanities. That is not to say that mainframe computers can no longer be of any use; many services are only available on mainframe computers and will continue to be so. Yet in practice, it is the microcomputer which is used to provide access to such services.

In the 1990s, humanities computing has grown further, fuelled by the flexibility of the microcomputer, which can now provide desktop access to both worldwide communications networks and multimedia resources. Nowadays, microcomputers are used across the whole spectrum of academic activity in the humanities, for teaching and administrative purposes, as well as for research. As a result, humanities academics are frequently becoming involved in the purchase as well as the end-use of both hardware and software for microcomputers. However, purchasing the right equipment in a volatile and immature market requires extensive expertise in evaluating the potential and limitations of different components of computer systems. Acquiring such expertise can appear to be an almost impossible task to undertake in addition to the everyday demands of an academic career. Moreover, the rapid pace of technological change adds further complexity to the situation. Giving advice on purchase in a volume such as this is a task doomed to failure and readers are recommended to consult other sources of information which are likely to be much more up-to-date: the latest computer magazines, specialist shops, and computer centres. This appendix is aimed merely at introducing some of the main principles of the technology so that an informed choice of hardware and software, appropriate to the job in hand, might be made.

Some basic principles of microcomputer systems

Though all-in-one portable laptop and notebook computers are becoming more popular, as far as the workplace is concerned, it is the traditional desktop computer, where input and output are handled by the keyboard (or mouse) and the monitor (and often a printer) respectively, which still holds sway. The three main functional components of any microcomputer are: the microprocessor, which carries out the actual processing; the memory (Random Access Memory, or RAM), which holds both the application in use and the operating system during operation; and the secondary storage, usually a hard disc, for permanent storage of data. These components are located in the system unit. It is not intended to discuss the relative merits of basic input and output devices here. Firstly, such information is readily available from computing/IT services, computer magazines, and standard textbooks; secondly, the system unit itself is the most complex and expensive component of the system. For reasons explained below, the two key objectives when choosing a microcomputer are, firstly, to maximize processing speed, and secondly to maximize data storage capacity, within given budgetary constraints.

There is a continuing demand for increased processing speed due to:

- the growing size and increased number of features of applications software, particularly since the advent of graphical user interfaces;

- new application areas, such as multimedia, which require higher processing power;

- the increased use of networks, requiring computers to run network protocols in the background, whilst supporting applications software in the foreground;

- the demand for multitasking, enabling users to run more than one application at once.

The ever increasing size of applications software places heavy demands on storage capacity, as does the growth of multimedia: a large amount of data is required to store a high quality graphic, a sound, or a video clip. Compared with obtaining the fastest microcomputer within a given price range, maximizing storage capacity is a relatively simple task: purchase the largest hard disc possible. In the last eight to ten years, microcomputer permanent storage capacity has increased tenfold, and with the advent of multimedia increases of this order of magnitude in this timeframe look set to continue. There have also been a number of new developments in storage media technology, with magneto-optical discs, rewritable CD-ROMs, ZIP drives, and other devices becoming cheaper and more easily available. There is, however, a move away from storing large quantities of material on stand-alone machines, towards remote storage with local access through terminals (which might be personal computers) linked by networks. This is known as 'client-server architecture': the remote computer, which can be anything from a powerful personal computer with a large storage capacity to a supercomputer, holds the mixed-media information which the user needs to access. It also holds the programs which can be activated by the user to process the information. This is the server, to which can be attached a number of less powerful client machines which allow the user to access his or her data and programs. There are a number of advantages to this kind of arrangement: it can be cheaper to have one powerful server, with much less powerful machines acting as clients; data and programs can be updated regularly at one point rather than many; protection from attack by viruses is easier to ensure; licensing of software and copyright of data are easier to keep track of. There will, however, be many tasks which individuals will want to carry out in a stand-alone environment, but the advantages of the client-server architecture with a PC as client is that it can, when required, also be used in isolation.

In terms of microcomputers used in the humanities, two families have dominated the scene: the IBM PC-compatible family, based on the Intel series of microprocessors, and the Apple Macintosh family, based on the Motorola series. The two families each contain a number of members, reflecting advances in processing power. These are not described in detail as they change and advance rapidly. The IBM PC architecture quickly became accepted as a world standard for two main reasons. Firstly, Intel have always ensured 'backwards compatibility', which means that every member of the family can run most software originally written for the earliest model. Thus, it is possible to buy a more powerful computer to run existing software more efficiently. Secondly, IBM allowed other manufacturers to make copies, (IBM-compatibles, or clones) of the PC, often with a better specification and price. As a result, other third-party manufacturers have produced a myriad of competitively-priced hardware and software for the PC, making it a very versatile and flexible machine which can be configured to meet a wide range of specialist demands.

In contrast, Apple Macintosh computers have been criticized for their lack of flexibility, as compared with the PC. Apple exerted tight control over developers of both peripheral devices and application software; this regulation meant that there was no opportunity for competition amongst developers, leading to the maintenance of high prices and a lack of product choice. However, the difficulties of establishing the company in the market with its massive installed base of PC-compatibles has inevitably led to relaxation of controls, resulting in an increase in the range of application software and peripheral hardware now being available. Currently, IBM and Apple are working together to produce specifications for personal computers, and the Apple PowerPC can run software written for both the Macintosh and the IBM personal computer architectures, and conversely the latest version of MicroSoft Windows, Windows 95, allows the IBM PC to be used much more like a Macintosh. Given that most software and data are now produced in a form which can run on both types of hardware, reasons for choosing one rather than another now have more to do with cost or personal taste than with functionality.

Communications and multimedia

Communications

The 'communications revolution' is based on the convergence of traditional telecommunications and data communications. Computers can communicate not only with those to which they are directly cabled, but with any computer accessible by telephone lines (traditional analogue as well as new digital services), or by a range of cableless links including satellite transmissions.

Since advances have been rapid, pervasive, and complex, it is not possible to cover the whole range of communications technologies here. It might be useful, however, to introduce some of the better established standards which have passed into common parlance and need to be considered seriously when communications equipment and services are being purchased.

The two standards bodies of most importance are the International Organization for Standards (ISO) and the Comité Consultatif International Télégraphique and Téléphonique (CCITT). The ISO standard for communications is known as the Open Systems Interconnection (ISO-OSI) Reference Model. The OSI Model consists of a complex set of functional layers, each with its own set of standards attached. The most important sets of standards as far as everyday communication technology is concerned are the X series and the V series. The X series describe the use of digital networks and include:

- X.25 for connecting computers to public telephone networks;

- X.400 for handling electronic mail;

- X.500 for maintaining directories of electronic mail users.

The V series are concerned with analogue communication using modems, for example:

- V.32 bis operates at 14400 bits per second, full duplex.

It should be noted that although widely adhered to in Europe, the OSI model has yet to find widespread acceptance in the USA. One well established non-OSI standard is TCP/IP (Transmission Control Protocol/Internet Protocol). TCP/IP was originally developed by the US Department of Defense to support the ARPAnet network, the starting point for the Internet links which span the world today. TCP/IP has gained acceptance in the USA, not only for long distance links, but also for local area networks, and is becoming widely accepted in Europe.

Multimedia

Multimedia can be defined as the computer-coordinated combination of text, graphics, sound, photographic images, and video to form a single presentation. Interactive multimedia systems allow the user to pose questions, to browse at will, and to give and receive answers, and as such have excited a great deal of interest in the educational world. Multimedia has become strongly associated with commercially available CD-ROMs and also, recently, with the World Wide Web. Although multimedia CD-ROMs are available in higher education, for example Perseus, a database designed to facilitate the study of Archaic and Classical Greece (see Economou, this volume), they are only part of the story. This erroneous conception has arisen because the CD-ROM is currently the only cost-effective way of storing and distributing the amount of data involved. Certainly, anyone wishing to explore the potential of multimedia seriously will require a CD-ROM drive in their computer system. This does not necessarily require a new microcomputer: CD-ROM drives may be easily added to many existing machines.

However, it is possible for any enthusiastic individual to assemble his or her own multimedia presentation, linking individual components by means of 'authoring software'. The presentation may be stored either on a magnetic disc or a CD-ROM (the latter usually by means of a specialist external service, though CD-ROM writers are becoming cheaper and many university computer centres have invested in the hardware). It should be noted that this is an extremely demanding task, except for small, simple presentations, and is therefore not to be undertaken lightly and without expert advice. Eventually, educational multimedia software will be available via the 'Information Superhighway', the proposed high capacity international network of the future. Those wishing to develop their own presentations will have to convert their existing source media, that is documents, pictures, photographs, and videotapes, into digital form, so that they may be processed and stored on a computer.

Both PC and Apple Macintosh platforms support the production and display of multimedia material, provided the machine is of high enough specification (Cain 1995). An industry group known as the Multimedia Marketing Council has laid down a minimum specification for the 'Multimedia PC'; the current details of this specification should be available from standard sources of hardware information.

One of the most demanding processes in the production of multimedia is the digitization and display of video: producing full screen video of television quality demands that around 20Mb of data per second be delivered to the screen. This is clearly an enormous engineering task which has been achieved by using special CODECs, algorithms which COmpress the data contained in a video frame and DECompress them for playback. The compression is usually carried out by the application developer, with the end-user decompressing the video for playback, the CODEC being supplied with the application. The most commonly used CODECs are Indeo, developed by Intel for the PC (and more recently, the Macintosh), and SuperMac's Cinepak, developed for the Macintosh (amongst others). Compressing video still requires the installation of a dedicated hardware card, although software methods, notably fractal compression, are currently generating positive publicity. At one time, this limitation applied to decompression as well, which seriously curtailed the demand for computer-based video. Nowadays, software decompression is widely available, by means of Apple's Quicktime and Microsoft's Video for Windows, albeit at reduced quality. Early versions of both systems displayed a 1/16 screen size running at around 10 frames per second, about a third of television quality. Video of this quality could not be expected to add much in the way of educational content! Quality nowadays is much better, depending on machine specification, though still not as good as from a hardware-based system. Only a PowerMac (a Macintosh with a PowerPC microprocessor) can display full screen television quality video by means of software decompression.

Although the current media emphasis is on the conversion of source material from television or videotape into digital form for manipulation on the computer, the reverse process is also available and should not be overlooked. Computer-based material may be readily downloaded onto videotape; whilst interactivity is lost, the resultant medium is readily accessible by anyone in their own home.

Choosing hardware and software: general guidelines

The purchase of new hardware and/or software may result from the need to undertake a new research or teaching project which requires the processing power of a computer. Alternatively, the objective may be to perform an existing task (manual or computer-based) more efficiently. Whatever the circumstance, before committing any financial resource, it is necessary to carry out a detailed analysis of the task in question. The oft-cited key benefit of performing a task by computer, namely increased overall productivity, is frequently not realized; this is because computing has considerable overheads (in addition to the initial cost of the equipment) which are not always taken into account in the early stages of a project. These overheads include the costs of installation, maintenance, supervision, and, not least, the training of users of the new system. Nor are much-vaunted new computer-based services always taken up as enthusiastically as expected, due to a variety of reasons including apathy on the part of potential users, and poor user interfaces.

The initial analysis phase should identify the costs and benefits of the proposed project, and will help those concerned decide whether to proceed, modify, postpone, or abandon the project. Key questions which must be asked to establish the feasibility of any proposed new computer system include (Yeates *et al.* 1994, chapter 7):

- what are the costs: initial and ongoing?

- what are the functional requirements on the proposed system: what is it expected to provide, and for whom?

- how much usage is expected, including peaks and troughs?

- where will it be established—are there any security implications?

- where does managerial responsibility lie?

Given that the feasibility of the project has been established, the next phase may be undertaken: choosing the hardware and the software. The following list provides guidelines to ensure that some key considerations are taken into account.

Seek advice

The importance of seeking advice cannot be overemphasized. It is best to consult as many sources as possible: some people become attached to particular products, particularly if they were involved in developing or promoting them. This attachment, however well meaning, often results in a partisan attitude which may not serve the best interests of the enquirer. Good sources of advice include:

- Staff in institutional computing/IT services

- Other computer professionals on campus, such as staff in computer science departments, in the library, in computer workrooms, or in IT-based learning centres

- Computers in Teaching Initiative (CTI) Centres

- Conferences

- Special interest groups. These may be institutionally, regionally, nationally, or internationally based and often readily accessible by means of communications networks

- Computer exhibitions. Whilst exhibitions are inexpensive to visit and 'hands-on' experience is usually available, it is important to bear in mind that these are sales events

- Written information, including journals and computer magazines; however, anything over two years old is likely to be seriously out of date.

Hardware or software first?

A 'rule of thumb' exists that states that the software necessary to perform the task in question should be chosen first, then hardware of sufficient power to run that software efficiently should be selected. It is, of course, vital that the problem is well understood before any moves are made towards finding a computerized solution. Nowadays, it could be argued that this rule no longer holds true; certainly, there are many exceptions. First, the hardware may already be in place, with no funding available to supplement or replace it. Second, the cost of hardware has fallen so dramatically over the last few years that for all but the most demanding software, hardware power is not normally a limiting factor. Third, some of the newer functionality available on microcomputers, for example in the multimedia and communications areas, is very much hardware-based. Hardware components are added to the microcomputer system; these components usually come supplied with their own operational software.

Compare costs

Clearly, it is important to consider the initial cost of the equipment: the hardware, software, and any peripheral devices, such as printers. It can often pay to shop around, but not if this requires dealing with potentially unreliable sources: the computer industry has a high rate of business failure. Institutional computing services can usually provide up-to-date information on companies which have good track records, and may also be in a position to negotiate a better deal than an individual. The cost of any consumable items such as printer cartridges, or special papers should always be taken into account, as these can be significant if usage is heavy.

Guarantees and service contracts must be carefully evaluated. Not only is it important to establish where responsibilities lie right at the beginning if things go wrong, but also charges for attractive yet non-essential services may be applied. For example, it may be critical for a commercial organization to expect on-site maintenance or replacement of hardware within twenty-four hours. Yet it is unlikely that academic margins will be so tight as to require such an expensive service.

Allow for expansion

The needs of those involved in computing activity rarely remain static. Successful projects tend to spawn further schemes, so it is important to allow plenty of room for growth. To a certain extent, the computer industry has made a rod for its own back by shortening the time gap between technological advances and successive rounds of price cuts. There are many anecdotes about those who have purchased new computers or software packages at seemingly competitive prices, only to discover shortly after that higher specification products are already on sale at an even lower price. In this situation, it is understandable that it is sometimes preferable to sit on the fence, convinced that the next exciting advance is just around the corner. Nevertheless, it is reasonably straightforward to choose suitable equipment which not only fulfils the requirements of today, but has the built-in capacity to be viable for years to come.

Consider support

It is rare that expert help is not required at some stage in a computing project. This is particularly likely at the beginning, when teething problems may occur with the computer system itself, and later on when highly individual demands may be made on the system. It is unlikely that manuals will provide many of the answers! Support may be obtained from the dealer concerned, usually in the form of a telephone hotline. At one time, such support was often available free for an unlimited time period; today, this is less likely to be the case. Support may also be available within institutions, in the form of help desks or training courses. The longer a product has been on the market, and the larger the existing user base, the more likely it is that expertise has built up in its operation. Being able to access this expertise can save an enormous amount of time: pioneers may become famous, but this route has its costs!

References and bibliography

Blissmer, R.H., *Introducing computers: concepts, systems and applications 1993-94 edition* (New York: John Wiley and Sons Inc., 1993).

Cain, C., 'What is multimedia?', *Personal Computer World Multimedia Supplement* (January 1995), 8–10.

Deegan, M., Timbrell, N., and Warren, L., *Hypermedia in the humanities* (Universities of Oxford and Hull, 1992).

Hodson, P., *Local area networks* (London: DP Publications, 1992).

Lansdown, J., 'Selecting a package for graphics presentation', *Hitch-hiker's guide to graphics* (Advisory Group on Computer Graphics, c/o Dr A. Mumford, Loughborough University, 1992).

Robinson, P., *The digitization of primary textual sources* (Oxford: Office for Humanities Communication Publications Number 4, 1993).

Yeates, D., Shields, M., and Helmy, D., *Systems analysis and design* (London: Pitman Publishing, 1994).

Appendix 2
Glossary of Terms

A4
Standard European page size: 11.2 by 8.7 inches, or 29.5 by 21 cms.

Analogue (or analog)
The representation of data in the form of continuously variable physical quantities. Contrasts with *digital*.

Archives & Manuscript Control
The online database of records for archives and manuscripts available as a separate file on RLIN.

ARPAnet
A four-node network, established by ARPA, Advanced Research Projects Agency, in 1969.

ASCII
American Standard Code for Information Interchange. A standard character encoding scheme introduced in 1963 and used widely on many machines.

Authoring package
Software which allows the user to create a computer-based learning package from his or her own materials.

Authoring tools
Specialized software packages which allow the design of interactive *multimedia* applications.

Autocorrelation
The extent to which the values of a spatial variable in one location influence the values in adjacent locations. Commonly measured with Moran's I statistic.

Automatic Format Recognition
A system which applies tags to data depending upon their position on the card or page which has been scanned.

Backup
An identical copy of computerized material—used in the event of damage to the original.

Binary image
A computer image where each dot may have just two values, either black ('0', for absence of light) or white ('1', for presence of light). Suitable for printed text or line art.

Bit
The basic unit of computer information. A single bit is either '0' (absence, or 'off'), or '1' (presence, or 'on'). More complex values are represented by collecting single bits together: two bits may have four values ('00', off; '01', near-off; '10', near on; '11', on); eight bits 256 values, and so on.

BITnet
Because It's Time Network. An IBM-sponsored network that began in the early 1980s.

BLAISE-LINE
The British Library's online service for its many databases.

British Library Catalogue
Refers variously to the latest version of the printed catalogue and its online version.

Buffer
An area defined by its maximum distance from a geographic object or objects.

Bulletin Board
Free service often run on a dedicated computer which users can access via their own computer. The bulletin board allows users to read items of news and interest left by previous users and to make contributions of their own.

Button
A 'hot spot', an active area on screen which can be pressed to initiate an action.

Byte
A collection of *bits*. By convention, a byte is eight bits.

Case Law
Law as interpreted by judges, as opposed to that defined by Acts of Parliament (see *Statute Law*).

CD-ROM (Compact Disc-Read Only Memory)
An *optical disc* which can store up to 650 Mb of *digital* data. Once the information is pressed on the disc, it cannot be altered.

CD-ROM drive or player
A hardware device which is connected to a computer and enables the viewing of *CD-ROMs*.

CD-ROM-Extended Architecture (CD-XA)
An extension of the *CD-ROM* standard integrating audio, stills, text, and animation.

Choropleth
Refers to geographic data which takes the form of discrete areas of constant value, such as is found on geological maps, or county maps.

Colorado Alliance of Research Libraries
A corporation serving the libraries of the State of Colorado. CARL has been influential in creating other systems in the United States.

Compact Disc-Interactive (CD-I)
A compact disc which carries audio, stills, text, graphics, animation, and computer data. Its dedicated player can work with a computer or a television.

Consortium of University Research Libraries
Originally the university libraries of Oxford, Cambridge, London, Edinburgh, Glasgow, Manchester, and Leeds. Since 1994 expanding.

Copyright
The principle that a work of the intellect is the property of its creator—hence the term *intellectual property*.

Cost surface
A *theme* in which the values represent the cost expended in reaching each location from a given starting location or locations. See *friction surface*.

Coverage
Another term for *theme*.

Cumulative viewshed
The sum of a series of related *viewshed* maps.

DIALOG
Commercial online service providing access to a large number of specialized databases in the sciences, social sciences, and humanities.

Digital
The use of discrete numerical values to represent data in the form of numbers or characters, as opposed to a continuously fluctuating current or voltage.

Distance surface
A *theme* in which the values represent the linear distance of each location from a given starting location or locations.

Dithering
A technique for creating an image with apparent levels of grey by grouping black and white dots into cells. According to the number of black and white dots and their arrangement in the cell, the eye perceives the cell as a single grey, not as a group of black and white dots. Commonly used by laser printers to simulate grey images.

Document Type Definition
The definition of the markup rules for a given class of documents (written according to the rules of Standard Generalized Markup Language).

dpi
The number of *pixels* in the computer image measured per linear inch, horizontally or vertically, of the original image. Thus: 100 dpi means that each square inch of the object is represented by 100 pixels vertically by 100 pixels horizontally, hence 10,000 pixels in the computer image.

Eight-bit image
An image where each dot may have any one of either 256 possible grey values or 256 possible colour values.

Electronic mail
A system which allows computer users to send messages to each other; analogous to the traditional mail system.

EPIC
The software used to enable comprehensive searching of the *Online Library Computer Centre* (OCLC) database.

File Transfer Protocol
Software used to transfer files between host computers. Generally referred to as 'anonymous ftp' because the remote user logs on as 'anonymous' and must enter a valid *Internet* e-mail address before access is granted.

Flowchart
Diagram illustrating the general structure of a *multimedia* or other computer application, where concepts are represented as boxes linked by lines.

Friction surface
A *theme* in which the values represent the cost of traversing the landscape at each location (see *cost surface*).

Fundamental Mappable Object
A geometric entity (either a point, line, area or surface) used to represent some real-world object within a *spatial database*.

Georeferenced
Data are said to be georeferenced if all *themes* are recorded within and can be queried through reference to a common geographical reference system.

Gigabyte (Gb)
= about one thousand *Megabytes* = about one milliard *bytes*

GK1
The printed catalogue of the British Museum Library, 1880–1905.

GK2
The revision of the British Museum General catalogue, 1931–54. Abandoned after DEZ.

GK3
The printed catalogue issued between 1959 and 1966 and which incorporated GK2 and the Reading Room catalogue.

GK4
The latest printed catalogue of the British Library, incorporating the supplements published since the completion of GK3.

Gopher
A program to find material held for public access on machines at remote sites, and to transfer it to your home machine if required.

Graph theory
The mathematics of connected graphs of lines and nodes.

Graphical User Interface
A pictorial computer environment for communication between the user and the system.

Greyscale image
An image where each dot may have more than two values, representing levels of grey ranging between pure black and pure white. Typically, greyscale computer images are 'eight-bit', permitting a single dot to have any one of 256 possible grey values. Suitable for monochrome halftones and minimal quality reproduction of manuscript materials.

Hackers
Those who break into computer systems to obtain a sense of achievement in overcoming the host security systems.

Hypermedia
A *hypertext* system enhanced by graphics, audio and visual capabilities, with links between various media besides text.

Hypertext
A body of textual documents joined together with automated conceptual links, or the computer system used to create and read these types of documents.

Hypertext Markup Language
A set of commands for tagging, linking in a *hypertext* way, and viewing online documents on the *World Wide Web*.

Hypertext Transfer Protocol
Scheme used to denote a document that has been marked up in *Hypertext Markup Language* for publishing on the *World Wide Web*.

Incunabula Short-Title Catalogue
An online finding aid to books printed before 1501 based on collections worldwide. Available on *BLAISE-LINE*.

Intellectual property
See *Copyright*.

Interactive videodisc
A type of *optical disc* used for storing *analogue* video.

Internet
Abbreviation of 'internetworking', a wide area network spread over the world and connecting thousands of disparate computer networks in education, research, government, and industry.

Juke-box
Device that can hold multiple (magnetic or optical) discs to be inserted automatically in a disc drive.

Kilobyte (Kb)
A unit of a thousand *bytes*, or eight thousand *bits*, of computer information. Used to refer to computer file sizes and storage capacity.

Layer
Another term for *theme*.

Link
The electronic connection between different units, nodes of a *hypertext* system.

Machine-readable
Able to be processed by a computer and software.

Megabyte (Mb)
A unit of a thousand *kilobytes*, or a million *bytes*, or eight million *bits*, of computer information. Used to refer to computer file sizes and storage capacity.

Modem
The hardware device which is attached to a computer to allow the communication with networks over telephone lines.

Moral rights
This principle gives authors of a literary, dramatic, musical, or artistic works the right, firstly, to be identified whenever their work is used, and secondly, to object to derogatory treatment and false attribution of authorship.

MUD/MOO
A MUD is a text-based virtual reality environment, originally based on the early Dungeons and Dragons adventure games (hence the original name), but increasingly being used for virtual seminars and other academic purposes. The MUD software allows users to log onto a computer and meet other users in real time. Movement through a virtual building and conversations with other users take place through typing commands or sentences. MOO is a particular implementation of the MUD, standing for MUD, Object-Oriented, which reflects the nature of the software. Most academic uses of these virtual worlds tend to be MOOs.

Multimedia
The integration and delivery of various forms of information—text, images, graphics, sound, video—in a single medium, in most cases a computer enhanced by audiovisual resources.

Multiple viewshed
The boolean sum of a series of related *viewshed* maps.

National Science Foundation Network
The main backbone and support to the *Internet* (although this may not be the case in the near future).

Navigation
Movement of the users through a *multimedia* system.

Nearest-neighbour statistics
Statistics about point-patterns which are based on the distance of each point to the nearest other point in the distribution.

Network (Geographic Information Systems)
Line data which also contain the connections between lines, usually in the form of *nodes*, which can be analysed using *graph theory*.

Node (Geographic Information Systems)
A location at which two or more line entities are connected.

Node (multimedia)
The individual unit of textual or other information which forms part of a *hypertext* system.

One-bit image
See *binary image*.

Online Library Computer Center
The cooperative database at Dublin, Ohio, which started in the 1960s as the cataloguing centre for Ohio libraries. Now a worldwide facility.

Optical Character Recognition
OCR software attempts to convert the image of a character into a *machine-readable* character. OCR is sometimes also used to refer to the whole process of scanning and converting a printed text into machine-readable form.

Optical disc
A disc that requires a laser light beam to read the information encoded on its reflective surface.

OSIRIS
A software package for statistical analysis.

Overlay
Another term for *theme*.

Phase Alternation Line
Colour TV broadcasting system generally used in Europe.

Photo CD
A Kodak product which stores 35 mm photographic film digitally.

Pixel
A single 'picture element'. A computer image is built up from a sequence of pixels, each pixel representing an area (a 'dot') of the original object. The density of the image, and thus its detail, is measured in terms of 'dots per inch', or *dpi*. This is the number of pixels per linear inch, horizontally or vertically, of the original image. Thus, 100 dpi means that each square inch of the object is represented by 10,000 pixels in the computer image.

Platform (multimedia)
The system, disc, or device used to deliver *multimedia* programs.

Predictive Model
A statistical model which predicts some phenomenon for an entire geographical region. Frequently this involves predicting the presence or absence of a feature from correlated information.

Proximity surface
Another term for *distance surface*.

Quadrat statistics
Statistics of point distributions which are based on imposing a regular grid of square sample areas over the distribution.

Raster data
Data which are recorded as a regular matrix of values, as in digital image processing.

Scanning
The process of using a scanner and associated software to create an electronic image of a printed document. If the image is of text, *Optical Character Recognition* software can be used to convert the text into *machine-readable* form.

Scenario
Document presenting the details about each component of a *multimedia* application, including user-interface guidelines and general design principles.

Site Catchment Analysis
The analysis of the economic territories of one or more sites.

Spatial database
A database in which the entities are objects within a two-dimensional geographic coordinate system. A spatial database must therefore be *georeferenced* and will usually contain data about *topology*.

Stacks
The name used for HyperCard applications.

Standard Generalized Markup Language
Defined by the International Organization for Standards in ISO 8879. An abstract language for defining markup languages.

Statute law
Law passed by legislature; in the UK, this refers to Acts of Parliament (see *Case Law*).

Storyboard
Graphical representation (usually including a sequence of screen designs) of the way the user will perceive the content of a *multimedia* application.

Text Encoding Initiative
An international cooperative project to develop a set of guidelines for the encoding and interchange of electronic text.

Theme
A subdivision of a *spatial database*. For a given geographic region there may be many *themes* each of which represents closely related information. Thus a region may have one theme for rivers, one for roads, one for geology and one for settlement sites.

Topology
Data about the relationships between *fundamental mappable objects*, which indicate the logical relationships between them.

Twentyfour-bit image
A colour image where each dot may have any one of 16.7 million colour values. The 24 *bits* are typically made up of three eight-bit values, with each eight-bit value representing a separate colour (usually, red, green, and blue).

Unicode/Unicode Standard
A new standard for encoding characters that offers much better support for non-Latin character sets than is available using *ASCII*.

Uniform Resource Locator (URL)
The scheme and address of a document published on the *World Wide Web*.

Universal Decimal System
A numeric system for classifying books as well as non-book materials.

Vector data
Data which are composed of geometric descriptions of *fundamental mappable objects*, and their *topology*.

Videodisc
A 30cm/12" *optical disc* which can store 54,000 or 108,000 frames (on two sides) of *analogue* still images, or 30 minutes' to one hour's video.

Viewshed
A *theme* in which the values are either 1 or 0, where 1 indicates that a particular feature (or features) is visible, and 0 that it is not.

Virus
Self-replicating programs which can be designed to carry out destructive activity.

Wide Area Information Server
Allows users to search multiple collections of data.

World Wide Web
A collection of protocols for providing and retrieving hypermedia information over the *Internet*; now often thought of by many users as synonymous with the Internet itself. Originally developed at the CERN laboratories. WWW documents can be viewed with various shareware programs, called browsers, like Mosaic, Lynx, or Netscape.

WYSIWYG
What You See Is What You Get. A feature of most modern word processors such that the image of the document that the user sees on-screen is a close approximation to how it will look when printed.

Appendix 3
Abbreviations and Acronyms

AACR   Anglo-American Cataloguing Rules

ACCIS   Advisory Committee for the Coordination of Information Systems

ACH   Association for Computers and the Humanities

ACLL   Archive of Celtic-Latin Literature

ACM   Association for Computing Machinery

ADMYTE   *Archivo Digital de Manuscritos y Textos Españoles*

AFR   Automatic Format Recognition

AHC   Association for History and Computing

AHDS   Arts and Humanities Data Service

AI   Artificial Intelligence

AIIM   Association for Information and Image Management

AL   Artificial Life

ALLC   Association for Literary and Linguistic Computing

AMC   Archives [&] Manuscript Control

ARIADNE   Ashmolean Retrieval Index and Data Network

ARPA   Advanced Research Projects Agency

ARTFL   American and French Research on the Treasury of the French Language

ASCII   American Standard Code for Information Interchange

BCP   *Book of Common Prayer*

BIDS   Bath Information and Data Services

BIRON   Bibliographic Information Retrieval ONline

BITnet   Because It's Time Network

BL   British Library

BLAISE   British Library Automated Information Service

BLC   British Library Catalogue, *also* Boston Library Consortium

BM	British Museum
BNB	British National Bibliography
BNC	British National Corpus
BUBL	Bulletin Board for Libraries
BUFVC	British Universities Film and Video Council
CAD	Computer-Aided Design
CARL	Colorado Alliance of Research Libraries
CATH	Computers and Teaching in the Humanities
CBL	Computer-Based Learning
CCARH	Centre for Computer-Assisted Research in the Humanities
CCAT	Computer Centre for the Analysis of Texts
CCD	Charge-Coupled Device
CCITT	Comité Consultatif International Télégraphique et Téléphonique
CD	Compact Disc
CD-DA	Compact Disc-Digital Audio
CD-I	Compact Disc-Interactive
CD-ROM	Compact Disc Read-Only Memory
CD-XA	CD-ROM Extended Architecture
CEC	Commission of the European Communities
CECI	Center for Educational Computing Initiatives (MIT)
CERL	Consortium of European Research Libraries
CERN	Centre Européen de Recherche Nucléaire
CESSDA	Council of European Social Science Data Archives
CETEDOC	Centre de Traitement Electronique des Documents
CETH	Center for Electronic Texts in the Humanities
Charm	Common Hierarchical Abstract Representation for Music
CHEST	Combined Higher Education Software Team
CISC	Complex Instruction Set Computer
CITED	Copyright in Transmitted Electronic Documents
CLCLT	CETEDOC Library of Christian Latin Texts
CM	*Computing in Musicology*
CNR	Consiglio Nazionale delle Richerche

CNRS	Centre National de la Recherche Scientifique
COCOA	Word Count and Concordance Generation on Altos
CODEC	COmpression/DECompression
CPA	Commission on Preservation and Access
CPET	Catalogue of Projects in Electronic Text
CSnet	Computer Science Network
CTI	Computers in Teaching Initiative
CTISS	Computers in Teaching Initiative Support Service
CTT	Center for Text and Technology (Georgetown University)
CURL	Consortium of University Research Libraries
DARMS	Digital Alternate Representation for Music Scores
DBMS	Database Management System
DCRM	Directory of Computer-Assisted Research in Musicology
DDA	Danish Data Archive
DDC	Dewey Decimal Code
DENI	Department of Education, Northern Ireland
DFG	Deutsche Forschungsgemeinschaft
DOE	*Dictionary of Old English*
DOS	Disc Operating System
dpi	Dots per inch
DSP	Digital Signal Processing
DTD	Document Type Definition
DTP	Desktop Publishing
EDM	Electronic Distance Measurement
EFL	English as a Foreign Language
ELINOR	Electronic Library Information Online Retrieval
E-mail	Electronic Mail
ESAC	Essen Associative Code
ESRC	Economic and Social Research Council
ESTC	Eighteenth-Century Short-Title Catalogue. Re-named the English Short-Title Catalogue
FAST	Federation Against Software Theft
FDDI	Fibre Distributed Data Interface

FIGIT	The Follett Implementation Group on Information Technology
ftp	File Transfer Protocol
Gb	Gigabyte
GIS	Geographic Information System
GK	General Katalog
GUI	Graphical User Interface
HCU	Humanities Computing Unit
HDU	History Data Unit
HEFCs	Higher Education Funding Councils (UK)
HIRP	Humanities Information Review Panel
HSR	*Historical Social Research*
HTML	Hypertext Markup Language
http	Hypertext Transfer Protocol
HUMBUL	Humanities Bulletin Board
HyTime	Hypermedia/Time-based Structuring Language
Hz	Hertz
IASSIST	International Association for Social Science Information Service and Technology
ICMC	International Conferences on Computer Music
ICPSR	Inter-University Consortium for Social and Political Research
IETF	Internet Engineering Task Force
IFDO	International Federation of Data Organizations
IFLA	International Federation of Library Associations
ILS	Information Locator System
IRCAM	Institut de Recherche et Coordination Acoustique/Musique
IRIS	Institute for Research in Information and Scholarship (Brown University)
ISBN	International Standard Book Number
ISDN	Integrated Services Digital Network
ISI	Institute of Scientific Information
ISO	International Organization for Standards
ISSN	International Standard Serial Number
ISTC	Incunabula Short-Title Catalogue

IT	Information Technology
ITAG	Interactive Technologies Advisory Group
ITTI	Information Technology Training Initiative
JANET	Joint Academic Network
JISC	Joint Information Services Committee
JPEG	Joint Photographic Experts Group
Kb	Kilobyte
KNAW	Koninklijke Nederlandse Akademie van Wetenschappen (Royal Dutch Academy of Arts and Sciences)
ksh	KornShell
LAN	Local Area Network
LC	Library of Congress, Washington, DC
LCCN	Library of Congress Card Number
LCD	Liquid Crystal Display
LCSH	Library of Congress Subject Heading
LGPN	Lexicon of Greek Personal Names
LOB	Lancaster-Oslo-Bergen (corpus)
LOCIS	Library of Congress Information System
MALT	Machine-Assisted Logic Teaching
MARC	Machine Readable Cataloguing
Mb	Megabyte
Mhz	Megahertz
MIDI	Musical Instrument Digital Interface
MIT	Massachusetts Institute of Technology
MOO	MUD, Object-Oriented
MPC	Multimedia Personal Computer
MSDOS	Microsoft Disc Operating System
MUD	Multi-User Dimension, or Multi-User Domain, originally Multi-User Dungeon
NADB	National Archaeological Database
NARA	National Archives and Records Administration
NASA	National Aeronautics and Space Administration (USA)
NCET	National Council for Educational Technology

NEH	National Endowment for the Humanities
NHDA	Netherlands Historical Data Archive
NHDC	Norwegian Historical Data Centre
NIF	Notation Interchange Format
NISS	National Information Services and Systems
NREN	National Research and Education Network
NSA	National Sound Archive
NSF	National Science Foundation
NSTC	Nineteenth-Century Short-Title Catalogue
NTSC	National Television Standards Committee
OCLC	Online Computer Library Center
OCR	Optical Character Recognition
OED	*Oxford English Dictionary*
OHC	Office for Humanities Communication
OHCO	Ordered Hierarchy of Content Objects
OUCS	Oxford University Computing Services
OPAC	Online Public Access Catalogue
OSI	Open Systems Interconnection
OTA	Oxford Text Archive
OUP	Oxford University Press
PAL	Phase Alternation Line
PC	Personal Computer
PCI	Peripheral Component Interconnect
PDF	Portable Document Format
PDP	Parallel Distributed Processing
PLD	*Patrologia Latina* Database
PHI	Packard Humanities Institute
PRDH	Programme de Recherche en Démographie Historique
PRO	Public Records Office
PSTN	Public Service Telephone Network
RAM	Random Access Memory
RAMA	Remote Access to Museum Archives

RDBMS	Relational Database Management System
RGB	Red Green Blue
RILM	Répertoire International de la Littérature Musicale
RISC	Reduced Instruction Set Computer
RISM	Répertoire International des Sources Musicales
RLG	Research Libraries Group
RLIN	Research Libraries Information Network
RPM	Register of Preservation Microforms
RSP	Romanesque Sculpture Processor
SARA	SGML-Aware Retrieval Application (program)
SD	(Standard) Study Description (Scheme)
SEENET	Society for Early English and Norse Electronic Texts
SGML	Standard Generalized Markup Language
SIMM	Single Inline Memory Model
SMDL	Standard Music Description Language
SOREP	Société du Recherche sur la Population
SQL	Structured Query Language
STAR	Steinmetz Archives
STC	Short-Title Catalogue
STELLA	Software for the Teaching of English Language and Literature and its Assessment
SWIDOC	Sociaal-Wetenschappelijk Informatie en Documentatie Centrum
TCP/IP	Transmission Control Protocol/Internet Protocol
TEI	Text Encoding Initiative
TIFF	Tagged Image File Format
TLG	*Thesaurus Linguae Graecae*
TLS	*Times Literary Supplement*
TLTP	Teaching and Learning Technology Programme
UDC	Universal Decimal Code
URC	Uniform Resource Citation
URI	Uniform Resource Identifier
URL	Uniform Resource Locator

URN	Uniform Resource Name
VASARI	Visual Arts System for Archiving and Retrieving of Images
WAIS	Wide Area Information Server
WAN	Wider Area Network
WWW	World Wide Web
WYSIWYG	What You See Is What You Get
YCC	The proprietary file format used by Kodak's Photo CD process
ZA	Zentral Archiv für empirische Sozialforschung
ZHSF	Zentrum für historische Sozialforschung (Centre for Social Historical Research)

Appendix 4
List of Software and Trademarks

Advanced Imaging
PTN Publishing Co., 445 Broad Hollow Road, Melville, New York 11747, USA.

Advisory Group on Computer Graphics
Dr Anne Mumford, Computing Services, Loughborough University, Loughborough LE11 3TU. E-mail a.m.mumford@uk.ac.lut

AIIM, Association for Information and Image Management
1100 Wayne Avenue, Suite 1100, Silver Spring, MD 20910, USA.

Apple Media Kit and HyperCard
Apple Computer, Inc. Check your local Apple Authorized Dealer.

Arc/Info
A complex, comprehensive, vector-based GIS available for DOS and UNIX. Produced by ESRI (Environmental Systems Research Institute Inc, 380 New York St., Redlands CA, 92373 USA). Arc/Info is available to Universities through the CHEST agreement.

Asymetrix Multimedia Toolbook
Docklands Business Centre, 14 Tiller Road, Docklands, London E14 8PX.

British National Corpus/SARA
Lou Burnard, Oxford University Computing Services, 13 Banbury Road, Oxford OX2 6NN, UK.

Cardbox Plus
Business Simulations Ltd., 30 St James Street, London SW1A 1HB.

Canterbury Tales **Project**
Dr Peter Robinson, International Institute for Electronic Library Resources, De Montfort University, Hammerwood Gate, Kents Hill, Milton Keynes MK 6HP. E-mail peterr@uk.ac.ox.vax.

CD-ROM Professional
Pemberton Press Inc., 462 Danbury Road, Wilton, CT 06897-2126, USA.

Collection
Vernon Systems, P O Box 6909, Auckland, New Zealand.

Collate
International Institute for Electronic Library Research, De Montfort University, Hammerwood Gate, Kents Hill, Milton Keynes MK7 6HP.

Convert-It
Heizer Software, 1941 Oak Park Boulevard, Suite 30, PO. Box 232019, Pleasant Hill, CA 94523, USA.

Cornell/Xerox/Commission on Preservation and Access Joint Study in Digital Preservation
Cornell University Library, Department of Preservation and Conservation, 215 Olin Library, Ithaca, New York 14853, USA.

Corpus of Romanesque Sculpture in Britain and Ireland
Dr Seamus Ross, The British Academy, 20-21 Cornwall Terrace, London NW1 4QP.

Cimtech Ltd.
University of Hertfordshire, College Lane, Hatfield, Herts. AL10 9AB.

English Poetry Full Text Database
Chadwyck-Healey Ltd, The Quorum, Barnwell Road, Cambridge, CB5 8SW.

GRASS
A public-domain raster GIS for UNIX systems. Originally written by the US Corps of Engineers Construction Engineering Research Laboratories (USAC-ERL), but extensively developed by a variety of agencies. GRASS is available in source code form, or as binaries for SGI, SUN, HP or Linux by anonymous ftp from moon.cecer.army.mil.

Geo/Navigator
Large vector GIS with some raster capacities available for Apple Mac, Windows, Sun and HP 9000 workstations. PAX Technology, Hither Ascension House, Lambridge Wood Road, Henley-on-Thames, Oxon RG9 3BS.

Guide
OWL International Ltd., Rosebank House, 144 Broughton Road, Edinburgh EH7 4LE.

Finale
Coda Technologies, 6210 Bury Drive, Eden Prairie, MN 55346-1718 USA.

IDRISI
A low-cost raster GIS intended primarily for teaching and research IDRISI only runs on PCs with DOS, although a MS-Windows version is due for release in Summer 1995. Produced by Clark University Graduate School of Geography, Worcester, Massachussetts, 01610, USA.

Image Processing
Reed Business Publishing, Oakfield House, Perrymount Road, Haywards Heath, Sussex RH16 3DH.

Ingres
Computer Associates plc, Computer Associates House, 183/187 Bath Road, Slough, Berks SL1 4AA.

Kodak Limited
P.O. Box 66, Station Road, Hemel Hempstead, Herts. HP1 1JU.

Kontron Digital Camera
Imaging Associates Ltd., 8 Thame Park Business Centre, Wenman Road, Thame OX9 3XA.

Macromedia Director and Authorware Professional
Macromedia, 4 Wellington Business Park, Dukes Ride, Crowthorne, Berks RG11 6LS.

MapInfo
PC and Windows-based vector GIS with modelling language. MapInfo Corporation, One Global View, Troy, NY 12180-8399 USA (MapInfo UK: 28/32 Church St., Slough, Berkshire SL1 1PJ).

Mekel M400XL roll film digitizer
UK distributors: Plasmec Systems Ltd., Microphax Division, Farnham Business Park, Weydon Lane, Farnham, Surrey GU9 8QL.

Microcosm Project
For information contact: Dr Gerard Hutchings, Department of Electronics and Computer Science, University of Southampton, Highfield, Southampton SO9 5NH. E-mail: G.A.Hutchings@ecs.soton.ac.uk

The Oxford English Dictionary (Second Edition) on CD-ROM
Oxford University Press, Electronic Publishing, Walton Street, Oxford OX2 6DP.

ParaConc
Michael Barlow, Department of Linguistics, Rice University, Houston, TX 77251, USA. E-mail: barlow@ruf.rice.edu

PrimaGraphics Ltd
Melbourn Science Park, Melbourn, Royston, Herts. SG8 6EJ.

SAS
Originally the abbreviation stood for Statistical Analysis System. SAS is a registered trademark of SAS Institute Inc., SAS Circle, Box 8000, Cary, NC 27512-8000 USA.

SPIE, The International Society for Optical Engineering,
P.O. Box 10, Bellingham, WA 98227-0010, USA.

SPSS
Originally the abbreviation stood for Statistical Package for the Social Sciences. SPSS is a registered trademark of SPSS Inc., 444 North Michigan Avenue, Chicago, IL 60611, USA.

Sunrise Imaging Scanner DMS 50i
UK distributors: Headway Computer Products. Headway House, Christy Estate, Ivy Road, Aldershot, Hants. GU12 4TX.

SuperCard
Allegiant Technologies, San Diego

TACT
URL: http://www.cch.epas.utoronto.ca:8080/cch/tact.html

VASARI and MARC
Dr Kirk Martinez, Department of the History of Art, Birkbeck College, University of London, 43 Gordon Square, London WC1H 0PD.

WordCruncher
(Main distributors): Johnston & Company, Electronic Publishers, P.O. Box 446, American Fork, UT 84003, USA. (European distributors): INCOM GMBH, Herzogfreudenweg 16, 53125 Bonn, Germany.

Index

Note: References are to pages, with figures and tables indicated by *fig* or *tab* after the page number. This index was compiled by Elizabeth M. Moys, BA, FLA, Registered Indexer.